C For Electronics
and Computer
Engineering Technology

C for Electronics and Computer Engineering Technology

PETER J. HOLSBERG

Mercer County Community College

PRENTICE HALL, Englewood Cliffs, New Jersey 07632

Library of Congress Cataloging-in-Publication Data

Holsberg, Peter J.
    C for electronics and computer engineering technology / Peter J.
Holsberg.
        p. cm.
        ISBN 0-13-109703-2
        1. C (Computer program language)   I. Title.
QA76.73.C15C164   1990
005.13'3—dc20

Editorial/production supervision and
    interior design: Maria McColligan
Cover design: Wanda Lubelska
Manufacturing buyer: Gina Chirco-Brennan

For information about our audio products, write us at:
Newbridge Book Clubs, 3000 Cindel Drive, Delran, NJ   08370

Printed in the United States of America
10   9   8   7   6   5   4   3   2

ISBN   0-13-109703-2

Prentice-Hall International (UK) Limited, *London*
Prentice-Hall of Australia Pty. Limited, *Sydney*
Prentice-Hall Canada Inc., *Toronto*
Prentice-Hall Hispanoamericana, S.A., *Mexico*
Prentice-Hall of India Private Limited, *New Delhi*
Prentice-Hall of Japan, Inc., *Tokyo*
Simon & Schuster Asia Pte. Ltd., *Singapore*
Editora Prentice-Hall do Brasil, Ltda., *Rio de Janeiro*

Contents

Preface

Since their initial appearance in the late 1970s, microprocessors have revolutionized the field of electronics. Because they are general-purpose logic elements that can be programmed to do different tasks in different control systems, they have become the design tool of almost every electronics designer. For this reason, today's electronics engineering technology and computer engineering technology student studies microprocessor-based systems in detail.

While the microprocessor integrated-circuit chip has the advantage of being able to replace many individual, less capable chips, it has caused engineers, technologists, and technicians to need to know something about programming. Programability is the feature of the microprocessor that permits it to perform differently in different systems.

For ten years or more, engineers, technologists, and technicians wrote control programs in "assembly language," a microprocessor-specific language that permits control of the microprocessor hardware. However, as systems design became more complex and the number of different kinds of microprocessors grew rapidly, practitioners realized that assembly language programming had become very expensive on large complex systems. Further, maintenance of the programs for that system became more difficult if the original programmer-engineers had changed jobs. So they began to look for so-called "higher-level languages" that would give them the control over the microprocessor that they had with assembly language, but would allow programming to be easier to do and to maintain than assembly language programs. They found C.

C is a general-purpose programming language that has modern data structures and control flow, and also allows programming at the "bit level" so necessary for microprocessor-based control systems. It was developed in the 1970s and has become available on computers of every conceivable size in the last five years. This book is intended to teach you enough to make you familiar with the so-called "personal computer," the art of programming to solve problems, and some of the fundamental features of the C programming language. When you finish, you will know enough to be able to solve the kinds of technical problems you face in the first two years of your professional education. If you would like to become a truly proficient C programmer, you will need to take a traditional "Programming in C" course.

I would like to acknowledge the help I received from reviewers, both professional and amateur alike. I was flattered by their kind remarks and pleased with the detailed suggestions they made. I would especially like to thank a young programmer—Lisa Holsberg, my daughter—and my two EE135 classes of the fall 1988 semester. And I would be remiss in not mentioning the encouragement I received from my sons, Alan Holsberg and Bill Vandegrift, and my wife, Cathy Ann Vandegrift. It is to her I dedicate this book. To all, I say a sincere "Thanks!".

Peter J. Holsberg

*C For Electronics
and Computer
Engineering Technology*

1

Computers and Programming

1-1 INTRODUCTION AND OBJECTIVES

The purpose of this book is to help you learn enough about computers and programming so that you will be able to write simple programs that help you solve problems as you study electronics engineering technology (EET) or computer engineering technology (CET). The skills you learn will be valuable to you in your career, because most engineers and technologists are involved with computers in their jobs. One of the things they may be involved in is programming. Many people who started out with a strong interest in computer hardware and electronics circuits have become interested in writing programs because of the kinds of challenges and rewards that are associated with software.

Programs fall generally into two broad categories: *systems* and *applications*. Systems programs include things you have probably not heard of because they are the programs that make a computer system easier for us to use. They include text editors, operating systems, input/output schedulers, compilers, interpreters, assemblers, and more. Applications programs include most of the programs that you have heard of or have even used: games, word processors, banking systems, store credit card systems, income tax programs, inventory programs, and so on, and what engineers and technologists call *control programs*. Control programs are what engineers and technologists write to control systems—from relatively common things such as microwave ovens, TV sets, and VCRs to exotic items such as automotive antiskid brakes and aircraft navigation systems.

An Electronic System

As an example of a system that uses a control program, consider the microwave oven (see Fig. 1-1). The microwave oven contains an electronic circuit that controls both the temperature of the microwave heating element and the time that the heating element is on. The heart of the circuit is a *microprocessor*, a programmable electronic device. The fact that it is programmable means that the manufacturer

1

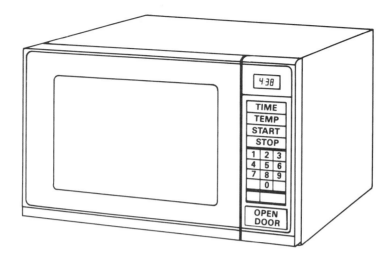

Figure 1-1 A microwave oven.

of the microwave oven can change how the oven works simply by changing the program that this microprocessor (MPU) runs. There is usually no need to develop an entirely new electronic circuit board for next year's model.

Although we do not know the details of the microwave oven program, we can determine what kinds of things it makes the MPU do. Since the oven has a keyboard, the program must contain instructions that tell the MPU how to get information from that keyboard. The oven also has a small display, so the program must contain instructions on what to display and how to display it. And the program must instruct the MPU how to keep track of the time that has elapsed since the user pushed the oven's "Start" button. In short, the program tells the MPU how to control the hardware—keyboard, display, timer, cooking element, and so on. Before you can write such a program, you will need to learn about MPU-based hardware and the instructions for a particular MPU.

Since so much of the electronics industry uses MPUs, you need to have some skills in writing programs to be successful after you are graduated. In this book, you will learn how to write general programs. In later courses, you will learn about MPU-based hardware devices, and then about writing programs to control them. In their last MPU course, the students at my college eventually design a traffic light system for a busy intersection; the system allows for every possible combination of "delayed green," turning lanes, day/night cycles, and so on. They use a microprocessor and MPU-based hardware connected to a variety of lights, switches, and timers, and write the program that controls the system.

We will begin by writing applications programs that will be useful in your "Circuits I" course. Later in your schooling, as you learn more and more about electronics, you will also learn more and more about control programming. This experience will not make you a professional programmer. If you wanted to be a professional programmer, you probably would have majored in computer science, not engineering technology. My goal is to provide you with the tools that let you write the programs that you will need to solve problems relating to CET/EET.

The C Language

I have chosen the programming language called C as the programming language for this book. My reasons were these:

1. Now that a standard has been published by the American National Standards Institute (ANSI), programs written in C can be used on any computer (i.e., they are portable.

2. C has many of the characteristics of a so-called higher-level language (HLL). These allow a programmer to write working programs without knowing a lot about computers.

3. C has many of the characteristics of a so-called lower-level language. These allow a programmer to use features of the computer hardware as they are needed. This feature will be important to us when we write control programs.

The particular C we use is published by Borland International and is called *Turbo C*, version 2.0. Although *any C that conforms to the 1989 ANSI standard for C may be used*, I chose Turbo C because I think that you will find the Turbo C "Integrated Development Environment" very easy to use. However, there is nothing in 99 percent of the programs in this book that depends on your using Turbo C. Turbo C runs on any computer that is compatible with the IBM PC.

Objectives

Upon successful completion of this chapter, you will be able to:

- State the name of the language we will use to solve problems on a PC in EET and CET
- Feel confident that you are not going to be forced to become a computer programmer
- State and explain that a PC has a CPU (also called an MPU), volatile main memory, nonvolatile secondary memory, a keyboard, and a screen
- Explain that information consists of programs or data values
- Explain that a program is a list of instructions for a computer
- State that Turbo C has an editor, a compiler, and a linker built in
- Use **#include** in a program
- Use comments (/*. . .*/) in a program
- Use **main**( ) in a program
- Use **puts**( ) in a program
- Know what a **string** is
- Know what a **newline** is

- Know what an **escape sequence** is
- Use braces in a program

Note: do not be concerned if some of the terms mentioned above are new to you. They are either part of the C language or technical terms, and will be explained in the text.

1-2 PROGRAMMING

Programming is the art of getting a computer to do what you want it to do. As an EET/CET, you will want a computer to do many things for you.

For example, in your first electronics circuits course, you will be required to solve a number of circuits problems. These will involve writing one or more equations, supplying values for some of the unknowns, and solving for others. Analyzing these circuits is the engineering technology aspect; plugging in the numbers and cranking out the answer is something that a junior high school student with a calculator can do. If you can program the computer to accept your equations and values, it will do the junior high school work for you. The advantage of having the computer do the tedious work of multiple calculations is that it can do them much more accurately and quickly than you can.

There are applications for computers in the EET/CET world that are even simpler than doing circuit calculations. For example, one of the first things that you will be asked to learn in your circuits course is a table of engineering prefixes and corresponding powers of 10 (e.g., "micro" means "10^{-6}"). If you write a program that will print the entire table, you will have a handy reference when you need it.

Figure 1-2 shows a very simple C program. You will see a detailed explanation of this program later in this chapter, but it will be easier to talk about C programs if you see one before we got too far along. Feel free to guess at what each line does; you may be surprised at how correct you are!

```
/* my first C program!  */

#include <stdio.h>

main()
{
        puts("\n\nhello, world!\n");
}
```

Figure 1-2 A simple C program.

1-3 COMPUTERS

Our focus is on the microcomputer or personal computer (PC). You may already have some experience using PCs, but in writing this book, I have assumed that you have no experience. I will tell you everything that I believe you need to know.

Here is a partial list of some of computers that are considered to be PCs:

1. The IBM PC, PC-XT, PC-AT, models of the PS/2, and so on.
2. Computers that behave just like these IBM computers; these include computers manufactured by Zenith, Epson, Compaq, Tandy, Toshiba, NEC, AT&T, Hewlett-Packard, AST Research, and others, as well as many "off-brands" manufactured in the United States and in the Far East. These are frequently called *compatibles* or *clones*, but I will call these PCs, too.
3. The Apple IIe, Macintosh, and other Apple computers.
4. The Commodore 64 and 128 and the Amiga.
5. The Atari family.

A PC usually has a microprocessor as its CPU (central processing unit—the "brains" of a computer); memory; a typewriter-like keyboard; a video display screen; some form of "mass storage," also called "secondary memory"—for example, one or more disk drives; and perhaps a printer. The CPU, memory, and disk drives are usually inside the case that houses the computer. The keyboard and screen are usually external to that case. If keyboard and screen are in one housing, it is called a *video display terminal* (VDT).

The CPU

The CPU's job is to execute a program's instructions. That is, if an instruction tells the CPU to take the number found in a specified place in memory (called the "location") and add it to the number found in another specified memory location, the CPU will examine the first location, copy the number stored there onto an electronic scratchpad, examine the second location, copy its number, add it to the first number, and write the result on the electronic scratchpad. The CPU has a built-in arithmetic-logical unit (ALU) that handles calculations.

All computers have CPUs. In some machines, the CPU is a microprocessor, so for those machines, we can refer to the "brains" as either the CPU or the MPU. The microprocessor is a miracle of electronics packaging techniques. It contains a vast number of simple electronic circuits interconnected to form a complex device, all on a chip of silicon.

The Memory

Memory is the place in the PC where **information** is stored. It is like the notebook you might use in a laboratory; the notebook contains the instructions for doing the lab experiment and has places for you to write the measurements you took during the experiment. Computer information is divided into two categories: **data** and **program**. Data are the pieces of information that are processed by the CPU. For example, the prefix "micro" and the number 10^{-6} are two pieces of information that would be part of a table of information for relating engineering prefixes and powers of 10. Processing these particular pieces of information might require nothing more than simply sending them to the screen for display. Other data may need calculations performed. For example, the number of hours you worked last weekend and the number representing your hourly pay rate can be considered as data items. For them, processing would include multiplying them together to determine your gross pay. A program, as I have said, is a list of instructions for the CPU to execute. But it is more than that. A program is a **complete** list of instructions that tell the CPU **exactly** how to perform a given task. Like the MPU, a PC's main memory is electronic and implemented on chips, usually called **RAM**. (*Note:* RAM was at one time a proper acronym, but today is simply the name given to main memory.)

Mass Storage

Mass storage is needed because main memory—the memory that is in the same box as the CPU—is **volatile**. That is, when we turn off the power to the computer, everything that was contained in RAM is lost. The next time we turn on the power, random values—called *garbage*—will be written into every memory location, so any programs or data we had in memory before are lost forever. Because of the volatility of main memory, we need to have some nonvolatile secondary memory (i.e., mass storage) to retain the results of our hard work. This almost always is some kind of magnetic disk. As you know from your experience with audiocassette recorders, magnetism is relatively permanent, so when a recorder magnetizes spots on a disk, they will stay magnetized until they are erased or remagnetized. Computer disks are relatively inexpensive and hold a lot of information, so we can safely store large amounts of data and/or many programs on a disk. For example, the computer I am using to write this book has drives for two "floppy" disks and two "hard" disks. A disk drive and a disk are related like a cassette deck and a cassette. The disk is the medium on which information is stored, while the drive is the device that reads and writes the information on the disk. Just as an LP record revolves past a nearly stationary pickup arm, a disk revolves past the drive's read/write heads. On PCs, disk drives are lettered starting at "A". Conventionally, "A" and "B" are floppy disk drives, while "C" is a hard disk. Your school's computers may differ.

One of my floppy disk drives can handle a disk that is 5.25 inches in diameter; such a disk can hold about 360,000 (360K—"K" means "1024") "characters" of information; a character is a letter or digit or punctuation mark. Figure 1-3 shows a 5.25-inch floppy disk. Just like an audiocassette, the floppy disk uses a very flexible plastic material (hence the name "floppy disk") embedded with magnetizable material. This material is the disk itself (sometimes called "the medium") and is permanently housed in a protective jacket, usually heavy black paper. NEVER attempt to remove the plastic disk from this jacket! The jacket has openings that give the read/write heads of the drive access to the disk as it rotates inside the jacket. NEVER touch the disk through any of these openings! Every disk you buy comes in a paper sleeve. Keep the disk in there when it is not in a drive. The sleeve will protect the medium from fingers, pencils, and so on.

The other disk drive is for a 3.5-inch disk; one of these can hold twice as much information as a 360K 5.25-inch disk. Figure 1-4 shows a 3.5-inch floppy disk. Its floppy medium is housed in a hard plastic jacket and has a sliding metal cover for read/write head access. The disk has no need for a separate sleeve.

In about the same physical space volume as a floppy disk drive, each of my

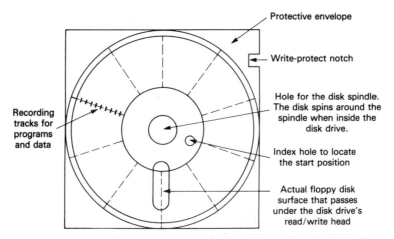

Figure 1-3 A 5.25-inch floppy disk. Dologite/Mockler, USING COMPUTERS, 2/e, © 1989, p. 59. Reprinted by permission of Prentice-Hall, Inc., Englewood Cliffs, N.J.

hard disks can store about 24,000,000 characters! Hard disks and their drives are usually integral; that is, the media cannot be removed from the drive. This permits the hard disk drive designer to design a system that not only holds much more information than a similar-sized floppy disk drive, but it can also be many, many times faster in reading and writing. However, this makes the hard drive system

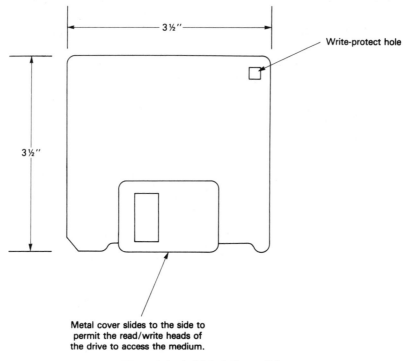

Figure 1-4 A 3.5-inch floppy disk.

more sensitive to vibration.   Don't bang on a computer or drop your books on the table.

To use a 5.25-inch floppy disk (sometimes called a "diskette"), remove it from its sleeve, place it into the floppy disk drive, and close the door.   (The 3.5-inch disk has no sleeve, and opening and closing the drive door is automatic.) Then you can either type commands that will transfer information from main memory to the disk, or vice versa, or you can use a program that will transfer information automatically.   When the transfer is completed, remove the floppy from the drive, put it back into its protective sleeve, and put it somewhere safe. That means away from coffee spills, cigarette smoke, magnetic fields, anything that would bend the disk, and so on.

Before a floppy disk can be put into service for the first time, it must be initialized, or "formatted."   Unlike an audio cassette or a VCR tape, you cannot just put a diskette into the drive and write information to it—you must format it first.   Formatting a diskette divides the surface into a fixed number of concentric "tracks" (like the rings on a dart board) and then slices each track into a fixed number of sectors (like the slices of a pie).   Next, the formatting program places location numbers (and some other information) on each sector; these permit the computer to find information written to the diskette.   When the computer needs to retrieve some information from disk, it looks in a table to find out where (i.e., the track number and the sector number) the information is stored.   Then it commands the drive to move the read/write heads to that track, and when the proper sector passes under the read/write heads, the drive reads the information from that sector.   Formatting also removes certain information from the disk, so for all practical purposes, anything you had stored on the disk will be lost, so be careful before you format any floppy—instead of it being the new one you just bought, it may be the one that has your lab projects on it!

Originally, floppy disks were 8 inches in diameter.   Advances in the production of magnetic media led to the 5.25-inch floppy diskette, and more recently, to the 3.5-inch floppy microdiskette.   Amazingly, as the floppy has grown physically smaller, its capacity has risen.   For example, the original 8-inch floppy disk could hold only 250,000 characters.   Table 1-1 shows the evolution of floppy disks.   "M" means "K^2" or 1,048,576.

Hard disk drives (also called "fixed disks") contain "platters" that can be as small as 3.5 inches or as large as 14 inches in diameter.   However, platters are generally not removable from their drives, so you will probably never see one.

TABLE 1-1   EVOLUTION OF FLOPPY DISKS

Diameter (in.)	Number of characters	
8	250,000	(250K)
5.25	360,000	(360K)
5.25	1,200,000	(1.2M)
3.5	720,000	(720K)
3.5	1,440,000	(1.44M)

The Keyboard

You will use the keyboard to enter information into the computer and to give commands to the operating system (see below). We call this *keying*, as in "key the 'A' ": this means "tap the key with the symbol 'A' on it." I say "tap" because most keyboards will automatically repeat the key you touch if you hold it down long enough—usually one-half to three-quarters of a second. You will use the "editor" program that is part of Turbo C to place into memory the information you key. The area of memory that holds your keystrokes is called the *edit buffer* or the *text buffer*. This information may be a C program (also called the *source code*) or it may be data needed by a program. When you have finished keying information into memory and have corrected all the errors, you then type a command that tells the editor to copy the contents of the edit buffer to a "file" on a disk. A file is nothing more or less than a collection of related information—the steps of a program, some data values, a list of your friends' names and addresses, and so on. Think of a paper file in a cardboard file folder in an office as being similar to a computer file on a computer disk.

You can key any of the keys you see, and some that are combinations of two keys. For example, when you key "A", you get "a". To get "A", you must press **Shift** and key "A" and release both. There are actually three "shift" keys: **Shift** itself, **Ctrl**, and **Alt**. "*A*" is shorthand for **Shift-A** (or **Sh-A**) and "^A" is shorthand for **Ctrl-A** (there is no shorthand for **Alt-A**).

The Screen

The display screen lets you see what is going on. For example, most commands you type will appear on the screen; this is called *echoing*. When a program produces results—for example, a table of prefixes and the corresponding powers of 10, or the results of a circuit calculation—they will appear on the screen if you have included instructions in your program that tell the CPU to send the results to the screen. If your computer system has a printer, you can get a "hard copy" of the table or calculation results, or even a copy of the source code (this is called a *listing*) by giving the commands that cause computer output to go to the printer instead of the screen. Our computer labs have one printer for every three computers, connected through a manually operated selector switch. To get hard copy, our students—after making sure that a neighbor is not using the printer—set the switch for their computer and then use the "TYPE" command to copy programs to the printer. Your lab may be similar, or it may have a printer for each computer. Your lab instructor will tell you how to get hard copy in your lab sessions.

The Operating System

A computer is just hardware—a collection of subsystems that includes electronics (e.g., CPU, memory), electromagnetic (e.g., disks), and electromechanical (e.g., disk drives, printer)—unless it has an essential program running. Without that program, the computer can do nothing. In the case of a PC (or any general-purpose computer), that piece of software is called the *operating system*. The operating system (OS) for IBM PCs is called *PC-DOS* and is a variation of MS-DOS ("MicroSoft Disk Operating System"). If you have an IBM PC, you will have PC-DOS for it; if you have a clone, you will have MS-DOS for it. For our purposes, consider PC-DOS and MS-DOS the same; I will refer to both as "DOS." The operating system controls the operations of all the subsystems of the computer.

When you turn the computer's power on, it goes through a self-initializing procedure called *booting* by reading special programs from the hard disk. Computers without hard disks will boot from a special floppy disk—called a systems disk—if it is placed in drive "A" before you turn the power on. Your lab instructor will have the details of the system you will use in your lab. The term *booting* comes from the phrase "pull yourself up by your own bootstraps," a seeming impossible task. It is called this because it looks like the computer is starting up without the help of a program! Actually, the *bootstrap* program is built into the electronics of the computer, in a device called the *boot ROM*. A *ROM* is a kind of electronic memory chip; thus it is **hardware**. The program is considered **software**. So the combination of a program built permanently into a chip is called **firmware**.

At the end of the bootstrapping process, the computer (actually, the OS) signals that it is ready to accept your commands by displaying what is called a *prompt*. The prompt will always include the letter of the *logged-in* disk drive—usually A on a floppy system, or C on a hard disk system. The logged-in disk drive is the one that contains the disk that holds the files that you can work with directly. The logged-in drive is also called the "current" drive and the "default" drive. A PC with two floppy drives usually labels them A and B, with A either above B or to the left of B. Your lab instructor will tell you about the computers in your lab.

Here are some sample prompts:

```
A:>
C:>
C:\TURBOC>
C:\TURBOC\INCLUDE>
```

The first says that you are logged in to drive A, while the second shows C as the *working* (i.e., logged in, current, default) drive. The last two show the names of *directories* and *subdirectories* separated by the "\". Think of directories and subdirectories the way you might think of the folders in a drawer in a file cabinet in an office. In each drawer, there will be one or more large folders that can contain other folders. The smaller folders might contain papers. Think of the file cabinet as a disk drive, a drawer as a directory, a large folder as a subdirectory, a small folder as a sub-subdirectory, and the papers in the smaller folder as files. For example, "C:\TURBOC" says that there is a folder called "TURBOC" in file cabinet "C:". "C:\TURBOC\INCLUDE" says that there is a folder marked "INCLUDE" in drawer "TURBOC" in cabinet "C:". As in an office, you would expect to find either files or more folders in the folder marked "TURBOC." In the computer, the files will be programs and data files. Figure 1-5 shows this kind of **hierarchical** ("*higher-ARK-ical*") scheme for the DOS file system.

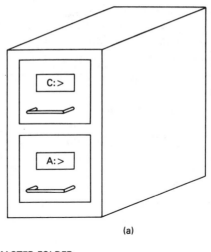

(a)

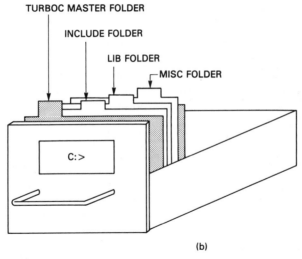

TURBOC MASTER FOLDER

INCLUDE FOLDER

LIB FOLDER

MISC FOLDER

C:>

(b)

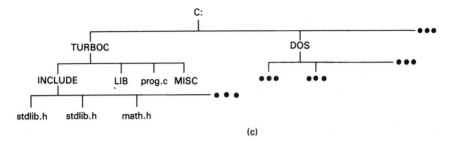

(c)

Figure 1-5 Disks, directories, subdirectories, files.

Some useful DOS commands. When you see an operating system prompt, you can type a command and DOS will execute it as soon as you tap the *Enter* key. There are a few such commands that are very useful, but remember—you *must* be at a DOS prompt in order to use them.

If you type **DIR** and tap *Enter*, DOS will list all the files that are stored in the current directory. If you type **DIR | SORT** and tape *Enter*, DOS will produce an alphabetized list of the files in the current directory. The "|" character usually lies on the same key as the "backslash" (\), usually near the right-hand end of the row that has the digit keys. (No one knows why the authors of DOS didn't write **DIR** so that it would alphabetize, but they didn't. Your instructor may have you use a different "directory lister," one that does alphabetize. I use one called "SuperDirectory," named SD.COM and found on many "bulletin boards" across the country.)

If you key **TYPE**, a space, and the name of a file (followed by a tap on the *Enter* key), DOS will display the contents of the file on the screen. If the file is longer than 25 lines, it will "scroll" off the screen before you get to read it. Try this instead.

```
A:\>TYPE PROG.C | MORE <enter>
```

DOS will display the first 25 lines and stop. Tap *Enter* to get the next 25, and so on. (Or, you could use LIST, to display a file on the screen, another very popular public domain utility program. Ask your instructor.)

At some point, your instructor will ask you to hand in a printed copy of your work (i.e., a "hard copy"). Log into the drive and directory that has a copy of the program (suppose that it is called P123-6.C), and key

```
COPY P123-6.C PRN: <enter>
```

PRN: (don't leave out the colon!) is the name of the printer.

Finally, if you find yourself logged into the correct drive but the wrong directory, use the **cd** command. For example, suppose you see a prompt like this:

```
C:\>
```

and you want to be in the \TURBOC\PROG subdirectory. Simply key

```
cd \turboc\prog <enter>
```

and the next thing you see will be

```
C:\TURBOC\PROG>
```

Isn't that neat? To change drives, just key the letter of the desired drive and a colon, and tap *Enter*, like this:

```
C:\TURBO\PROG>A: <enter>
A:\>
```

1-4 THE PROGRAMMING CYCLE

I mentioned before that you will use an editor to create a source code file. The editor accepts commands that (1) put keyed characters into the text buffer, (2) delete one or more characters from the text buffer, (3) move the cursor (the little box or underline that points to your position in the file you are editing), and (4) copy the contents of the text buffer to a disk file. You must give the file a "file name," which must be from one to eight characters long and must be followed by a period ("dot") and the letter "c." (This is a requirement of PC-DOS; other operating systems may have different requirements for valid file names.) Use only letters and digits in the program name. For example,

```
program1.c
ohmslaw.c
loops.c
```

but not

```
$stprog.c    (cannot use $)
ohm'slaw.c   (cannot use apostrophe)
```

Once you have a source file on a disk, you must tell the computer to translate it into a program that it can execute. Why is translation necessary? Because the source program is written in C, and the computer doesn't understand C. How can that be? The computer accepted everything you typed when you were keying in the source program; how can it be that it doesn't understand C? Let's answer that with a simple example. Say the following out loud:

EE PLOOR-uh-bus YOO-num

It is Latin ("*E pluribus unum*") for the motto of the United States of America and means "One out of many." Do you see the point? You could "speak" Latin without understanding it because I gave you the sounds of each Latin word. Similarly, the computer can accept the individual characters you key without understanding the program you are keying.

The translator for C source code is called a *compiler*. It will take a C source program file and create a new file from it. The new file is usually called the *object code* and is a version of the program that the computer can understand. If the program file name is "program1.c", Turbo C will produce an object code file on your disk, and it will be called "program1.obj". Turbo C's linker will then produce the executable code file automatically, and call it "program1.exe". When you tell the computer to run your program (see below), it actually loads the executable file (also known as the *binary file*) from the disk into main memory and starts executing the instructions it finds there. Figure 1-6 is a diagram of this process.

The ideas for the program come from you. You must first think out a solution to your problem and "sketch" it in computer terms. Then, you convert the solution to statements of the C language and create a source program on a disk using the editor. The compiler then takes the source program and produces an object code program. Finally, the linker takes the object code and any routines your program may need from a special library and produces the executable program. The object

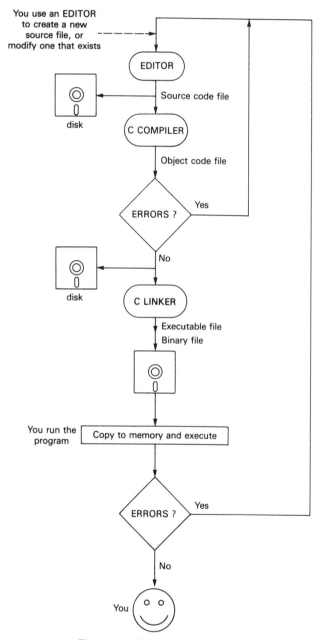

Figure 1-6 The programming cycle.

program and executable program are saved on the disk, just like the source program. (The linker is a program that is used automatically in the Turbo C Integrated Environment, so you do not have to concern yourself with what it does except in the most general terms.)

If you see the operating system prompt (e.g., A>), and you type

```
prog1<cr>
```

(or prog1<cr>—uppercase or lowercase doesn't matter here), the program "prog1.exe" will be loaded into memory and executed. Incidentally, "<cr>" means "tap the key marked either ENTER or RETURN. It does NOT mean "key <", "key c", "key r", "key >"!

The programming cycle then consists of the following steps:

1. Develop a procedure to solve the problem.
2. Write the procedure in computer-oriented terms.
3. Create the source code and save it, using the editor.
4. Compile the source code and link it.
5. Run (i.e., have the CPU execute) the program.
6. Note the errors.
7. Edit the source code to remove errors.
8. Repeat steps 4 through 8 until there are no more errors.

Turbo C provides an environment that makes this process easy to do. When you tell the operating system to load Turbo C, it places into memory a program that includes the editor, the compiler, the linker, and more. After you use the editor to create source code, you call on the compiler by tapping one of the function keys (a function key is one of the 10 or 12 special keys marked with the letter "F" and a number). If the compiler finds an error, Turbo C will stop compiling and, when you hit another function key, it will show you a split screen with the program in the top window and an error message window at the bottom. The error message window may contain a number of warnings and errors, with the current error highlighted. Turbo C tries to locate the line of source code that contains the error and highlights it. Frequently, the actual error will be on the line above the highlighted one, or—in some cases—the error will be many lines before the highlighted one! Once you locate the error, you then correct it with the editor, tap the "compile" function key to recompile the program, observe the next set of error messages, call up the editor again, correct the next error, call up the compiler again, and so on. When there are no more errors, there will be no more error messages and the compiler will report success. Then you can tap a function key to run the result. You don't have to leave the Turbo C environment until the lab period is over (or you have successfully completed your assignment, whichever comes first!). This is a substantial improvement over the traditional scheme in which you would have separate programs for editor, compiler, and linker, and would be required to know all the commands for each.

1-5 USING THE TURBO C EDITOR

Let's use the Turbo C editor to create a disk file of the program in Fig. 1-2. We'll call it PROG1.C. This is the *file specification* and is made up of three parts: the *file name*, a dot or period, and the *file type*. The file name must have from one to eight characters (I recommend letters or digits only); the file type will always be just the letter "C" in this course. (Incidentally, you can use either upper or lowercase letters interchangeably for the program file name, but in the source code file, uppercase and lowercase are treated differently.) Your instructor will give you specific instructions on how to call up Turbo C (it depends on whether your lab computers use a hard disk, a hard disk and a floppy, or just floppies), but in the examples, I will show what our students will do on a computer that has a hard disk drive and a floppy disk drive. I keep Turbo C in a subdirectory on the hard disk and ask our students to put their programs on a floppy disk in drive A. This lets them keep their source code and binary files private on their individual floppy disks. Here are the instructions given to our students:

1. Turn on the power to the computer and display. (Our systems have separate off switches for each.)

2. When you see

```
c:\ >
```

on the screen, put a formatted floppy disk in Drive A. Incidentally, if you make an error in typing, use the "backspace" key—it is marked "<--" and is probably colored gray. (The other key with similar marking "<-" is the "left-arrow" key, usually found on the "4" key of the numeric keypad.) It may move the cursor to the left one column, but it will not remove the character there.).

3. Now type

```
tc prog1.c<cr>
```

to invoke ("call up") the Turbo C Integrated Development Environment. (Our systems are set up to look for the student's disk in drive A:. Appendix C shows show to set this up, something that will be of interest to your instructor.) By including "prog1.c" on the line with the "tc" command, you are telling Turbo C the name of the file that you want to work with. If there is already a file called "prog1.c" on the disk in drive A, Turbo C will load it into the text buffer. Otherwise, it will create a brand new file on drive A, and you will start with an empty text buffer.

4. If PROG1.C is brand new, you will see a screen that looks like Fig. 1-7. Across the top is Turbo C's main menu. If you key the first letter of any of the words in the main menu, you will get either an immediate action or another menu, as explained below:

File brings up a menu of choices having to do with files and with exiting from the Turbo C environment.

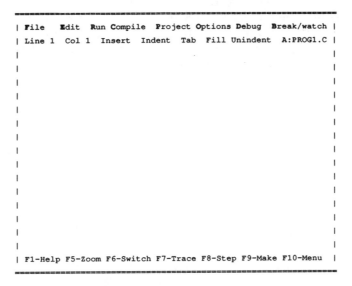

```
|==================================================================|
| File   Edit  Run Compile  Project Options Debug  Break/watch |
| Line 1  Col 1  Insert  Indent  Tab  Fill Unindent  A:PROG1.C |
|                                                              |
|                                                              |
|                                                              |
|                                                              |
|                                                              |
|                                                              |
|                                                              |
|                                                              |
|                                                              |
|                                                              |
|                                                              |
|                                                              |
|                                                              |
|                                                              |
|                                                              |
|                                                              |
|                                                              |
| F1-Help F5-Zoom F6-Switch F7-Trace F8-Step F9-Make F10-Menu |
|==================================================================|
```

Figure 1-7   Turbo C initial screen.

Edit puts you into the editor.

Run compiles, links, and runs your program.

Compile compiles and links your program and creates an executable file from it.

The other choices are more advanced and you can ignore them for now.

Line 1 Col 1 shows that the cursor is on line 1, at the left-hand margin (column 1).

Insert means that every character you type will be inserted into the text buffer for PROG1.C.

Indent means that automatic indenting is turned on.

Tab means that you can use the TAB key on your keyboard.

Fill can be ignored.

Unindent means that keying the *backspace* key will undo one level of indenting.

A:PROG1.C tells the disk drive letter (**A**) and the name of the file being edited (**PROG1.C**).

The line at the bottom of the screen shows which function keys will activate choices. For example, **F1** will give you a "help" screen, and **F10** will activate the main menu.

5. Now start typing the program. Don't worry about making mistakes. If you notice a mistake as you are keying, use the backspace key to rub out characters, going from right to left. If the mistake is too far away from the current position of the cursor, or if it is on a line above the cursor, ignore it for now. *Note:* The "\" ("backslash") key does not have a standard position on all keyboards (like the letters and digits). You will have to search for it on your keyboard. Do NOT type "/" if "\" is called for. "Slash" and "backslash" are treated quite differently by the C compiler. Figure 1-8 is another copy of Fig. 1-2, for your convenience.

```
/* my first C program!  */

#include <stdio.h>
main()
{
    puts("\n\nhello, world!\n");
}
```

Figure 1-8 A first C program.

To get the indenting I used, press the spacebar four times before typing

puts

After you type the semicolon (";") and hit <cr>, the cursor will jump to the next line, but instead of going all the way to the left-hand margin, it will jump to the column under the "p" in "puts." The is called *auto-indenting* and can be very useful in larger programs. However, in this case, we don't want to keep this level of indenting, so hit the "Home" key to put the cursor at the left-hand margin, and type "}" followed by <cr>.

1-6 EXAMINING THE PROGRAM

Now, we'll take the program apart, line by line.

The Comment

The first line of the program is a **comment**. A comment in C begins with the two characters /* and ends with the two characters */. The compiler will ignore comments (including the * and the /) when it compiles. So why have them? Comments exist for humans, not for computers. We use comments to help us understand what the program is supposed to do without having to read the source code; to give information about the author, the date of the program, the revision number; and so on. The form is not important. We could have written the comment on several lines, like this

```
/*    my
      first
      C
      program
      !
*/
```

or like this

```
/***************************
**   my first C program!  **
***************************/
```

depending on how fancy you want to be. That last one is rather nice, isn't it?
My students are required to have a heading at the beginning of each program,
something like this:

```
/******************************************************
 *  EE135 Computer Problem Solving   Prof. Holsberg *
 *                                                  *
 *  Iman A. Student              February 12, 1989  *
 *                                                  *
 *                   PROGRAM:  P2-6                 *
 *                                                  *
 *  This program displays all of the standard       *
 *  commercial resistor values.                     *
 *                                                  *
 ******************************************************/
```

Blank Lines

The second line of PROG1.C is blank, or, in C terms, "full of *whitespace*." Like
a comment, a blank line is for us. It makes the program easier for us to read.
The compiler usually ignores blank lines, indenting, and most spaces, and does not
require that they be included in a source file. For example, the compiler would
not have complained (i.e., sent out any error messages) if we had written the
program like this

```
/*myfirstCprogram!*/main(){puts("\n\nhello, world!\n");}
```

Of course, that's a little hard for us to read. If you get into the habit of leaving
out whitespace, you will have a more difficult time tracking down errors. The
mark of a sloppy programmer is the absence of spaces and blank lines. Like
comments, white space is for humans.

Preprocessor "include" Files

Getting back to our examination we see the third line,

```
#include <stdio.h>
```

The # signals the compiler that it should be alert for an instruction that is to be
executed by a special part of the system called the **preprocessor**. The preprocessor
interprets the **include** instruction as a request by the program to insert a file into
the program at this point. **stdio.h** is the name of the special file, and the angle
brackets (<>) tell the preprocessor where to look for it.

stdio.h is called a **header** file (the **.h** stands for "header"). A header file is one that contains certain definitions and declarations needed by certain elements of the program. Specifically, the line **#include** <**stdio.h**> tells the compiler that the program is going to do some input and/or output ("i/o" or "io") using the standard ("std") devices—the keyboard (called *stdin* in C) and the screen (called *stdout*). This particular statement will be needed in *every* program we write. Note that there is no semicolon at the end of a line that begins with a #. That is a rule of C, but you will probably break it a few times, like everyone else, as writing a semicolon at the end of each line is a common beginner's error. (Another common error is omitting a needed semicolon! Be on your toes, or you'll end up feeling that you can't win.) In Turbo C, the "help" system will tell you which header files you need. To get "help," put the cursor on any C keyword in your program and key ^**F1**, Ctrl-F1. For most keywords, a window of help will pop up on your screen. One of the lines in the window will say **Prototype in xxxxx.h**. That means "be sure that the line **#include xxxxx.h** appears before **main()** in your program." In fact, I recommend that before you compile a program, you put the cursor on each keyword in your program and key ^**F1** so that you can make a list of all the needed header files. Then type the **#include** lines into your program. Now you can try to compile it.

A Thing Called "main()"

The fourth line **main()**, is also present in *every* C program. It tells the compiler that the executable code begins with the statements that follow. The parentheses tell us (and the compiler that **main()** is something called a **function**, a piece of a program that performs a specific task. We will deal with functions in great detail later in the book, but for now, let me say just this: C has two kinds of functions. One is the built-in type whose names are the keywords I mentioned above. The other type is functions that you will write for your programs. Functions are also called **subprograms**.

The Opening Brace

The fifth line is the one character "{" (pronounced "left brace" or "open brace"). This signifies that the **body** or **definition** of **main()** follows.

The "puts" Function

The sixth line is the only executable code in the whole source file. It calls the function **puts()**, pronounced "*put ess.*" [How did I know that **puts()** is a function? Because of the parentheses.] Inside the parentheses, **puts()** has one *parameter*, the quoted **string**

```
"\n\nhello, world!\n"
```

The String

A **string** is a sequence of zero or more characters and is usually enclosed in quotation marks, sometimes called *double quotes* so as not to confuse them with *single quotes*, which are really apostrophes. The quotation marks are not part of the string; they show where the string begins and ends. (The computer science word for something that shows where an item begins and ends is *delimiter*.)

What does **puts**() do with the string it gets? Well, "puts" is short for "put string," and in C, "put" means "send to the standard device." So

```
puts("\n\nhello, world!\n");
```

will put the string

```
\n\nhello, world!\n
```

on the screen. Incidentally, **puts**() always sends an "extra" "\n" after putting the string. But what is a "\n"?

The "newline" Character

The pair of keystrokes "\n" is treated by C as a single character, called the **newline** character. "\n" is called the **escape sequence** for newline. "Escape" means that the character being "escaped" does not have its usual meaning. The usual meaning of "n" in a string is just the letter "n". "\n" means that **puts**() should treat the "n" as something special, not as the letter "n." When you send a **newline** to the screen, it moves the cursor to the beginning of the next line. In other words, you start a "new line." What we have done in our program is to cause two newline characters to be sent to the standard output device (usually the screen). Then the string

```
hello, world!
```

is "put," followed by another newline character. Finally, **puts**() puts its own final newline character. Here is what the actual screen will look like after you run (i.e., execute) the program:

```
A:\>prog1


hello, world!


A:\>
```

The first line of the "screen" **A:\>prog1** shows the operating system prompt and the name of the program that I wanted the operating system to load and execute. Keying <cr> at the end of that line sends the command to the OS *and* moves the cursor to the beginning of the next line. The first \n moves the cursor to the beginning of the third line, while the second \n moves it to the beginning of the fourth line. Then the string *hello, world!* is printed on the fourth line. There is another \n after the string and that moves the cursor to the beginning of the fifth line. Finally, **puts**( ) sends a newline that moves the cursor to the beginning of the sixth line.

The Closing Brace

The last line of the program, "}" ("right brace" or closing brace") indicates the end of **main**( ), that is, the end of the definition of **main**( ). The definition or body of a function is (1) always enclosed in braces, and (2) consists of the C code that must be executed to make the function perform the desired task. Now, back to our list.

6. Look at your program. If it does not match Fig. 1-8, move the cursor with the arrow keys (on the numeric keypad on the right of your keyboard—make sure that the NUM LOCK light is out!) until the cursor is over (or under) the incorrect character. Hit the delete key (marked "Del"—it's also in the numeric keypad). The incorrect character will disappear! Key the correct character. See how the rest of the line was pushed to the right to make room for the correct character? That's how "Insert" works. Continue until your code matches Fig. 1-8 exactly.

7. Now let's compile and run the program to see what it does. Just tap **F9**. It will instruct Turbo C to compile your program and create PROG1.OBJ on your disk. If there are not errors, Turbo C will automatically link PROG1.OBJ with the necessary library files and create PROG1.EXE. The library files are part of Turbo C; you don't have to do anything special to use them except for the **#include** <**stdio**>. (This is one of the reasons I chose Turbo C for you.) During compilation and linking, you will see a "window" that lets you keep track of the two processes—IF you are a fast reader. Watch the bottom of the window for the message "Success: Press any key" or the dreaded "Errors: Press any key." Figure 1-9 shows what that window looks like after successfully compiling *prog1.c*.

```
================ Linking ================
|                                        |
| EXE file : A:\PROG1.EXE                |
| Linking  : \TURBOC\LIB\CS.LIB          |
|                                        |
|                    Total      Link     |
|    Lines compiled: 220        PASS 2   |
|        Warnings:   0          0        |
|          Errors:   0          0        |
|                                        |
| Available Memory : 214K                |
| Success        :    Press any key      |
========================================
```

Figure 1-9 A successful compilation.

8. Since there were no errors, just tap any key to return to the editor. Then key **Ctrl-F9** (press the **Ctrl** key, tap the **F9** key, and release both) to run your program from inside the Turbo C environment. The screen will flash briefly and you will once again be returned to the editor. To see what the program did when it ran, key **Alt-F5**. Now, you will see on the screen

```
hello, world!
```

with some blank lines. Return to the editor by tapping any key.

9. Now we'll leave the Turbo C environment. Press **Alt-X** to exit. You will be given an opportunity to save PROG1.C. Do it.

1-7 PROGRAMMING ERRORS

Computers seem to delight in reminding us of how human we are. Every compiler has dozens of error messages and warnings to do just that! But it is important that you realize that there are just two kinds of errors we can make in C, and that the compiler can find only one kind of them! One type of error is exemplified by omitting a "{", or spelling **main** as **min**, or failing to close the quotation marks around the "\n\nhello, world!\n" string. This kind of error is a violation of the rules of the language, and is the kind that the compiler can find. It is called a **syntax error** and is of the same kind as spelling and grammar errors are in English.

However, if, in an English composition, we write, "My father was born seventeen years before his father," our English instructor will give us a funny look. While our sentence is perfectly good English (i.e., it is **syntactically** correct), it is quite nonsensical. The corresponding error in the computer world is called a **logical** error. Here's an example. Suppose we know that there are 16 ounces in a pound, and that someone asks us how many pounds there are in 22 ounces. We multiply 22 by 16 and get 352. The arithmetic is correct, but the answer is wrong. We should have *divided* 22 by 16 instead of multiplying. That's a logical error.

So the good news is that the compiler will notify us every time we make even the tiniest little syntax error. The bad news is that it will ignore all of our logical errors. This is a result of the fact that the computer will do only what we TELL it to do, not what we WANT it to do. Sorry.

If you have a syntax error in your program—such as leaving out the initial "(" in the **puts**( ) statement—the Turbo C compiler will stop and say "Errors: Press any key." When you press a key (perhaps the space bar), you will see a screen like Fig. 1-10.

You see two windows displayed. (*Note:* If you see only the *Message* screen, just tap **F5**.) The top one displays the source code and highlights the line that the compiler thinks contains the error. The bottom window displays error messages and warnings from the compiler, based on what it found when it tried to compile the source code (in this case, PROG1.C). The "6" in the error message means line 6 of the program. Note that there is a warning and three more error messages in this window. It is very likely that when you correct the error in line 6, all the rest of the warnings and errors will disappear.

```
    File   Edit   Run   Compile   Project   Options   Debug   Break/watch
=========================== Edit ============================
|      Line 6   Col 17   Insert  Indent        A:PROG1.C          |
|      /* my first C program!  */                                 |
|                                                                 |
|      #include <stdio.h>                                         |
|      main()                                                     |
|      {                                                          |
|              puts "\n\nhello, world!\n");                       |
|      }                                                          |
|                                                                 |
|                                                                 |
|                                                                 |
|                                                                 |
|                                                                 |
|                                                                 |
=========================== Message =========================
| Compiling A:\PROG1.C:                                           |
| Warning A:\PROG1.C 6: Code has no effect in function main       |
| Error A:\PROG1.C 6: Statement missing ; in function main        |
=============================================================
    F1-Help  F5-Zoom  F6-Switch  F7-Trace  F8-Step  F9-Make  F10-Menu
```

Figure 1-10   Turbo C error screen.

To correct the error, tap **F6**.   This puts the cursor into the top (i.e., edit)
window and calls up the Turbo C editor.   Insert a left parenthesis at the appropriate
place and tap F9 again.   The program will now compile without error.   If you try
to exit (Alt-X) at this time, Turbo C will ask if you want to save PROG1.C.

That error was an easy one for Turbo C to find.   It does not do quite as well

```
    File   Edit   Run   Compile   Project   Options   Debug   Break/watch
=========================== Edit ============================
|      Line 6         Col 17   Insert  Indent      A:PROG1.C         |
|      /* my first C program!  */                                   |
|                                                                   |
|      #include <stdio.h>                                           |
|      main(                                                        |
|      {                                                            |
|              puts ("\n\nhello, world!\n");                        |
|      }                                                            |
|                                                                   |
|                                                                   |
|                                                                   |
|                                                                   |
|                                                                   |
|                                                                   |
=========================== Message =========================
| Compiling A:\PROG1.C:                                             |
| Error A:\PROG1.C 5: Declaration syntax error                      |
=============================================================
    F1-Help  F5-Zoom  F6-Switch  F7-Trace  F8-Step  F9-Make  F10-Menu
```

Figure 1-11   More error messages.

if your error occurs at the end of a line. For example, I removed the ")" from 'main()' and tried to compile. Above, in Fig. 1-11, is the two-window display after responding to the "Errors: Press any key" message. Turbo C has highlighted the line **after** the error—the one with the opening brace—and has given an error message that has nothing to do with the actual error! (Don't blame Turbo C for this behavior; all compilers will do just about the same thing.) So if you see an error message that does not make sense to you and you cannot find the error on the line that is highlighted, look at the end of the line above it.

1-8 MODIFYING PROGRAMS

One of the things I ask you to do in the assignments is to modify an existing program. For example, at the end of this chapter, Problem 2 asks you to write a program in a certain way. Suppose that you start by typing **tc pl-2.c** and then write the program, debug it, and save it. Problem 3 asks that you modify the program you just wrote. My intention is that when you have finished, you will have BOTH programs on your disk.

One way to accomplish this, after typing **tc pl-3.c**, is simply to retype the entire program. However, there is an easier way. It uses the editor's ability to insert another file into the text buffer. To use this feature, type **tc pl-3.c** and enter the Editor (Alt-E). Now, key ^**KR**—that is, hold down *Ctrl*, tap **K** and release the *Ctrl* key. Then tap **R**. The editor will ask you for the name of the file; you type **pl-2.c<cr>** and it will copy that file into the text buffer. Now key ^**KH.** If you look at the top of the editor window, you will see that the file you are editing is still named **pl-3.c**. That means that, *right at this moment*, **pl-3.c** and **pl-2.c** are identical. Continue by modifying the code in the text buffer to meet the requirements of Problem 3. When you compile and save this program, it will be **pl-3.c**.

1-9 REVIEW

What have you learned so far? In general, you learned that:

- You will find out how to use the C language on a PC to solve problems in EET and CET.
- You are not going to become a programmer.
- A PC has a CPU, volatile main memory, nonvolatile secondary memory (usually a magnetic disk), a keyboard, and a screen.
- Information consists of programs or data values.
- A program is a list of instructions for a computer.
- Turbo C has an editor, a compiler, and a linker built in.

You also learned a few things about the C language:

- **#include**—causes the compiler to read a special file and make it part of your program.
- comment—lets the programmer describe the program and what it does.

- **main()**—is the primary function in C.
- **puts()**—sends a string to the screen.
- **string**—a sequence of characters delimited by double quotation marks.
- **newline**—a character that causes the cursor to jump to column one on the next line.
- **escape sequence**—a way to give a "normal" character a new meaning; **\n** is the escape sequence for **newline**.
- braces—are used to delimit the body of a function.

PROBLEMS AND QUESTIONS

1. Fill in the blanks for the computer system you will use in the lab for this course.
   (a) Manufacturer and model _Amiga 500; 286/AT Compatible._
   (b) How many floppy drives? _2_
   (c) Does it have a hard disk? _No; yes._
   (d) What does the prompt for the root directory of the hard drive (if any) look like? _C:\TC>_
   (e) What is the prompt for the floppy drive? _DF0:, DF1:; A:, B:_
   (f) Does every computer have a printer? _Yes_
   (g) Are the floppies 5.25-inch or 3.5-inch? _Both._
   (h) What is the capacity of the floppy? _400K; 360K, 1.2M._
   (i) What is the command that formats a floppy disk? _FORMAT <drive> <name>; FORMAT <drive>_

2. Take the program of Fig. 1-2 and modify it five times. Each time, select a step from the list below. Always go back to the program of Fig. 1-2 so that your program will have only one error in it. Record the error message each time you compile one of your programs, and comment on how useful it was in pinpointing the error. Here are the errors for you to introduce:
   (a) Spell **main** as **min**.
   (b) Omit the {.
   (c) Omit the first " in the string.
   (d) Omit the last " in the string.
   (e) Omit the }.

   Be sure to correct each error before introducing a new error, so that the program has just one error each time you compile it.

3. Write a program that will display your name on one line, your street address on another, and your city and state on a third. Enter the program and run it. Save it on your disk.

4. Modify the program you just wrote so that there is a blank line displayed between each of the printed lines.

5. Modify the program further so that there are two blank lines between each printed line.

2

Fundamentals of C

2-1 INTRODUCTION AND OBJECTIVES

In this chapter we will take a first look at some of the concepts and some of the actual commands of the C language. We'll restrict ourselves to those that are immediately useful and will cover more advanced aspects in later chapters.

Upon successful completion of this chapter, you will be able to:

- State the rules for writing **identifiers** and explain how they are used as the names of variables
- *Declare* an identifier and explain what the compiler does with the **declaration**
- Explain and use several *data types:* **int, long int, float, double,** and **char**; and explain and use **signed** and **unsigned** values
- Explain and use the basic arithmetic operations: + - * /
- Explain and use **assignment statements**: what they are and what they are not
- Explain and use **printf( )**
- Explain and use arguments to **printf( )**
- Explain and use *format strings* and *conversion characters*
- Make restricted use of **scanf( )**
- Explain and use the "**&**" character before the identifier in a **scanf( )**
- Define a constant using "**#define**"
- Set up a loop using **while**
- Explain and use the *relational operators* and *conditional expressions*
- Explain and use the shorthand operators + = and + +
- Explain choices, using "if. . . .," "if. . . else. . . .," and "if. . .else if. . .else. . ."
- Explain and use the AND and OR operators, **&&** and ‖
- Write a program to calculate the sum of two resistors in series

27

- Write a program to calculate the area of a circle of given radius
- Write a program to calculate the sum of several numbers
- Write a program to calculate current, charge, or time using $Q = I * t$.

Note: Some of the terms used above are part of the C language and are discussed in the chapter.

2-2 IDENTIFIERS, DATA VALUES, AND MEMORY

As an EET/CET, you are going to be doing many calculations during the course of your education and during your professional life. These calculations will usually involve solving one or more equations, so let's first learn how to solve an equation by computer in general, and then in C, specifically.

Earlier, I said that memory was used to hold information, and that information consisted of data values and programs. I now want to discuss the ideas behind data values in memory. Suppose you have a homework assignment that has five parts. Each part requires a lengthy calculation. The required result is the sum of the answers to the five parts. If you were doing this with paper and pencil and a calculator, you would calculate the result of part (a) and write it down. Then you would do the same thing for parts (b), (c), (d), and (e). If the results were -23.3456, 1.234, 99.765, 1.009, and 19.2833, your piece of paper might look like Fig. 2-1, or if you were better organized, it would look like Fig. 2-2.

Figure 2-1 is not acceptable in engineering technology; EETs and CETs must be able to report results so that others can understand them. Figure 2-2 shows the kind of organization that is needed. Each numeric result is associated with something that relates it back to the original assignment. If you wanted to know, for example, what you had calculated for part (c), it would be easy to look up the value 99.765 because it is labeled "(c)."

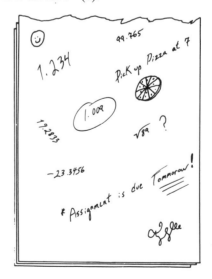

Figure 2-1   Scribbled results.

(a)	-23.3456
(b)	1.234
(c)	99.765
(d)	1.009
(e)	19.2833

Figure 2-2 Neat results.

Identifiers

In the computer, memory takes the place of the piece of paper, so the kind of organization exemplified by Fig. 2-2 is a must. Every data value that the computer places in its memory must have a name or **identifier** associated with it. C has some rules about identifiers:

1. An identifier may include letters, digits, and underscores (_).
2. An identifier starts with a letter.
3. A capital letter (uppercase) is different from a lowercase letter.

Here are some legal and some illegal identifiers in C:

resistor	(legal)
Resistor	(legal but different from "resistor")
R2D2	(legal)
V275	(legal)
r1	(legal)
r2	(legal)
r_total	(legal)
I-95	(illegal - dash not allowed)
1potato	(illegal - starts with a digit)

It is a very good idea to choose an identifier that has meaning in terms of the problem you are trying to solve. For example, choose *power* instead of *p*, *voltage* instead of *v*, and so on. Although this takes a bit more typing, it makes the program much easier to understand. And that is important for a very compelling reason. All but the most trivial programs contain logical errors, so you will be faced with rereading your programs to search for the "bugs." Having meaningful identifiers will make that work much easier.

When the C compiler notices an identifier in an executable statement of a program, it knows that the identifier refers to some value stored in memory. It knows that because it is a rule of C that every identifier must be **declared** before it can be used in an executable statement. A *declaration* tells the compiler to find some available memory to store a value in, and to associate that area of memory with the identifier specified in the declaration. A declaration also tells the compiler how much memory to set aside for the value. C has two kinds of numeric data:

integer numbers and real numbers; each takes a different amount of memory to hold a value. More on this below.

Data Values and Declarations

Integer values are numbers that have no decimal points. They can be positive, negative, or zero, but cannot be fractional. Integers are excellent for counting.

Real numbers are ordinary "decimal numbers," such as 1023.00087 or -10.6 or 11.7×10^{-3}. The last number has the same value as 0.0117, but is expressed in *scientific notation*. The *11.7* is called the *mantissa* and the -3 is called the *exponent*. [Notice that a "decimal number" is a "number with a decimal point." Both integers and reals are usually written in "decimal" (i.e., base 10).] Real numbers are the kinds of numbers used in almost every EET/CET calculation because they are the numbers of the world of measurements. Expect to use real numbers frequently in your C programs.

Here are some sample declarations:

```
float r_1;          /* float declares reals */
float r_2;
float r_total;
float v_1, v_2, v_3; /* declaring three identifiers */
int counter;        /* int declares an integer */
int i, j, k;
```

Note that we are permitted to declare several identifiers on one line by writing them as a list separated by commas; they will all be declared to be of the same type. Also, you see that the reserved word **int** is used to declare an identifier as an integer, while the reserved word **float** is the one used to declare an identifier as a real. (**Reserved** means that you cannot use it as an identifier name.) **Float** is short for **floating point**, a computer term for numbers that can be represented with a fractional part (i.e., mantissa) and an exponential part. The **point** in **floating point** refers to the **decimal point** [if we are talking about decimal (i.e., base 10) numbers].

The semicolon at the end of the line is an absolute necessity in C. It defines the end of a statement. C statements have many different forms, depending on the type of statement, but each—except for **preprocessor** statements—ends in a semicolon. Perhaps you noticed that three of the lines had "on-line' comments on them, just to explain what was occurring on each of those lines.

The Use of Memory by C

Understanding what goes on in a program requires that you have an idea of how things are laid out in memory. The memory of the IBM-type PC is organized as 1,048,576 (i.e., 1M or "1 meg") memory locations. Each location is like a box that can hold a number that has a certain maximum value. Also, each location is numbered, from 0 to 1,048,575.

A location in a PC is the electronic equivalent of eight on/off switches. We refer to the switch positions as "1" and "0" rather than "on" and "off," so we can interpret the switch settings as a number in base 2 (i.e., *binary*). Each switch position represents one binary digit (called a *bit*), and a group of eight bits is called a *byte*. The contents of a memory location (i.e., the switch settings) can be anything from 0000 0000 (eight zeros) to 1111 1111 (eight ones). We can consider these as binary numbers and can convert them to decimal numbers very easily. The digit farthest to the right, the least significant digit (LSD, "bit zero"), is worth either $2^0 = 1$, or 0. The one to its left, $2^1 = 2$, or 0. The next to its left, $2^2 = 4$, or 0, and so on. This is illustrated in Fig. 2-3. For example, take the binary number 0101 1100. Converting to decimal using Fig. 2-3 gives

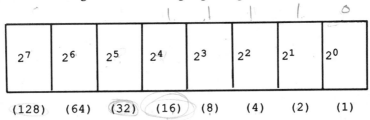

2^7	2^6	2^5	2^4	2^3	2^2	2^1	2^0
(128)	(64)	(32)	(16)	(8)	(4)	(2)	(1)

Figure 2-3 Binary-to-decimal conversion.

```
    0        1        0        1        1        1        0    0
=   0 * 2⁷ + 1 * 2⁶ + 0 * 2⁵ + 1 * 2⁴ + 1 * 2³ + 1 * 2² + 0 + 0
=   0 * 128 + 1 * 64 + 0 * 32 + 1 * 16 + 1 * 8  + 1 * 4  + 0 + 0
=   0        + 64     + 0      + 16     + 8      + 4      + 0 + 0
=   92, base 10.
```

The binary numbers 0000 0000 to 1111 1111 represent the decimal (i.e., *base 10*) numbers 0 to 255. This is called the "natural" or "unsigned" range for an eight-bit number.

There is a code prevalent in computers that allows us to treat the number stored in a memory location as a *signed* number. It is called the *two's-complement* code and is almost identical to unsigned binary. The only difference is that the most significant digit (MSD, farthest to the left, "bit 7") is interpreted as -2^7 (-128) rather than $+2^7$ ($+128$). For example, the binary number 0101 1100 is 92 decimal in both unsigned and signed, but binary 1000 1111 is treated differently depending on whether we want to treat it as signed or unsigned.

```
     1     0     0     0     1     1     1     1
   128 +  0  +  0  +  0  +  8  +  4  +  2  +  1  =   143  unsigned, but
  -128 +  0  +  0  +  0  +  8  +  4  +  2  +  1  =  -113  signed
```

The largest negative eight-bit number is -128; the largest positive is $+127$. So we write the range as -128 to $+127$ in decimal and as 1000 0000 to 0111 1111 in binary.

When we declare an identifier to be of type **int** in C, the computer treats it as a signed value. To declare something as unsigned, we must use the word *unsigned* in the declaration. For example,

```
unsigned int counter;
```

or simply

```
unsigned counter;
```

At this point, you may be wondering where you would use unsigned ints. I will point out potential applications as we go along. For now, just remember the differences between them.

Numbers that are represented by the contents of a single location are quite small (either 0 to 255 or -128 to $+127$), so computer languages usually combine the values stored in two or more adjacent (the computer science word is **contiguous**: *con-TIG-you-us*") memory locations to form larger numbers. For example, an **int** on a PC takes two locations or 16 bits. (This can be different for different CPUs!) The range is thus 0000 0000 0000 0000 to 1111 1111 1111 1111. In unsigned decimal, this is 0 to 65,535. In signed decimal, the range is $-32,768$ to $+32,767$; the most significant bit of the 16 is worth -32768 in two's complement. The most significant bit is called *bit 15* and the value comes from 2^{15}. C also has **long ints**; these are 32 bits (i.e., four bytes) long on a PC. The signed range for a **long int** is $-2,147,483,648$ to $2,147,483,647$, while the unsigned range is 0 to 4,294,967,295.

Floats take four bytes on a PC; one for the exponent and the rest for the mantissa. A **float** is always signed and has a value that is either 0, between -3.4×10^{38} and -3.4×10^{-38}, or between 3.4×10^{-38} and 3.4×10^{38}. See the number line in Fig. 2-4. There is a "long" version of **float** but it is called **double** rather than **long float**. It is eight bytes long on a PC and has a value that is either 0, between -1.7×10^{308} and -1.7×10^{-308}, or between 1.7×10^{-308} and 1.7×10^{308}. (The ranges for **float** and **double** are somewhat dependent on the compiler. These ranges are for Turbo C.)

Figure 2-5 shows some declarations that include all the data types mentioned so far.

If you were wondering about the unusual value for the number of memory locations in a PC—1,048,576—there is a perfectly sensible reason. Recall that each location has a number, called the **address** of the location. The number of addresses depends on the physical construction of the CPU. In the PC, the CPU chip has 20 pins used for addresses, so it can create $2^{20} = 1,048,576$ different address numbers. Since each address value refers to a byte of memory, 1,048,576

Figure 2-4 Number line for floats.

```
int i;
unsigned int j;
unsigned k;
long int l;
long m;
unsigned long n;   /* must include long */
float x;
double y;
```

Figure 2-5 Some representative declarations.

bytes is called "one megabyte" (1 MB), and 1024 bytes is called "one kilobyte" (1 KB). One megabyte is also 1024 KB.

2-3 FLOAT ARITHMETIC AND DISPLAY

C uses the following symbols for arithmetic calculations:

$+$ for addition: $x + y$

$-$ for subtraction: $a - b$

$*$ for multiplication: $m * n$, but NOT mn or $(m)(n)$

$/$ for division: z / w

Figure 2-6 is a simple program that uses **floats** and some simple calculations. The result of running this program is the display

10000.000000 + 20000.000000 = 30000.000000

```
#include <stdio.h>
main()
{
    /*  declarations first, ALWAYS!  */
    float r_1, r_2, r_total;

    /*  give them some values  */
    r_1 = 10.0E3; /* scientific notation!! */
    r_2 = 20.0E3;


    /* do a calculation */
    r_total = r_1 + r_2;

    /* show the results */
    printf("\n%f + %f = %f\n", r_1, r_2, r_total);
}
```

Figure 2-6 A simple program.

```
1:  #include <stdio.h>
2:  main()
3:  {
4:        float r_1, r_2, r_total;
5:
6:        r_1 = 10.0E3; /* scientific notation!! */
7:        r_2 = 20.0E3;
8:
9:        r_total = r_1 + r_2;
10:
11:       printf("\n%f + %f = %f\n", r_1, r_2, r_total);

12:  }
```

Figure 2-7

Explanation of the Program

First, let's list the program (without the comments this time) and number the lines (see Fig 2-7).

1:   #include <stdio.h>.

Line 1 is the usual beginning of a program.
Line 2 is the usual **main()**.
Line 3 is the opening brace and line 12 is the closing brace.

4:   float r_1, r_2, r_total;

Line 4 is the declaration of the three identifiers (another name for these is **variables**) r_1, r_2, and r_total as **floats**. This is absolutely necessary. The compiler will set aside a certain amount of memory of each variable and keep track of where each one is, so it can put values in those memory areas. "Where each one is" is another way of saying "its address." Humans rarely need to know what the address of a variable is, but the computer needs it all the time.

Lines 5, 8, and 10 are blank, to improve readability.

6:   r_1 = 10.0E3;   /* scientific notation!! */
7:   r_2 = 20.0E3;

Lines 6 and 7 are called **assignment statements**. They are used to give values to variables. When the compiler sees line 6, it checks that it has a declaration for r_1, and then puts the value 10.0E3 (the computer way of writing 10.0×10^3) into the memory area that is set aside for r_1. Line 6 is pronounced

"R 1 gets 10 point zero E 3"

Line 7 is pronounced

"R 2 gets 20 point zero E 3"

9:   r_total = r_1 + r_2;

Line 9 causes two things to happen. First, the computer evaluates the expression to the *right* of the **gets sign**, " = " (yes, it DOES look like an equals sign, doesn't it, but this sign has **nothing** to do with **equality**; it is C's **assignment operator**); the result of the evaluation will be a number. It works like this. The computer looks in memory for the value stored at r_1 (it finds 10.0E3) and the value stored at r_2 (it finds 20.0E3), and then it adds the two values. The result, in scientific notation, is the numeric value 30.0E3. Now, it can do the **gets** part: "r_total gets 30.0E3." The value 30.0E3 is stored in the memory area designated **r_total**.

I used the word "expression" in the preceding paragraph to describe **r_1 + r_2**. You know this word from algebra; it means a legal combination of variables and algebraic operators. C takes this idea a little further. In line 9 above, we have two expressions and a statement:

r_1 + r_2 is an expression.

r_total = r_1 + r_2 is an expression having the value *r_total.*

r_total = r_1 + r_2; is a statement (because of the semicolon).

11:   printf("\n%f + %f = %f\n", r_1, r_2, r_total);

Line 11 uses a new output function, **printf()**—pronounced "*print eff.*" The "f" stands for "formatted." **printf()**, like **puts()**, is part of the C library of functions. And, like puts(), it returns a value that we'll ignore.

Let's look at line 11 closely. Inside the parentheses, you will see several items separated by commas. Taken together, everything inside the parentheses is called the *argument list* for the function **printf()**. The four individual items in the argument list are

```
"\n%f + %f = %f\n"
r_1
r_2
r_total
```

Individually, each item in the argument list is called an *argument*. Every function has an argument list, although it may be empty [see **main()** as we have used it].

The first argument of **printf()** must be a string; it is called the *control string*, because it controls the format of the information that **printf()** displays. Our control string starts and ends with the newline character, an old friend. We also recognize the " + " and the " = " as the plus sign and the "gets" sign, respectively. In general, anything within the double quotes of a string is displayed "as is," with two exceptions: characters preceded by "\" and those preceded by "%". We know about

"\"; that is the "escape" character and is used most often in the grouping "\n". The form

"% followed by a letter"

is called a *format* or *conversion specification*. The letter is known as a *conversion character*. So "**%f**" is a format specification using the "**f**" conversion character. I'll tell you what that means in a moment.

Did you notice that there are three format specifications in the control string and three variables in the argument list? That correspondence is not coincidental. The format or conversion specification dictates how the value of a variable will look when it is displayed. So, for every variable whose value is to be displayed, we must have a format specification!

If you noticed the "three format/conversion specifications, three variables" match, you probably have also noticed that the conversion character "**f**" is the first letter of the word **float**. Again, that's no coincidence. "**%f**" says "display the value of the corresponding variable as a **float** number." A **float** number displayed with **%f** can have as many digits to the left of the decimal point as it needs, but has exactly six digits to the right of it. That's why the solution display looked like this:

$$10000.000000 + 20000.000000 = 30000.000000$$

Each of the three **floats** is displayed to six decimal places. Did you see what happened to the " + " and the " = "? They, along with any spaces in the control string, were just copied to the display—no conversions, no changes.

Suppose we wanted the outputs to be displayed in scientific or "E" notation. What would we have to change? Just change the conversion characters in line 11—change each "f" to an "e" (for "E" notation). Here's how to do that easily with the TC editor, assuming that our program is called **addup.c**:

1. Type: tc addup.c<cr>.
2. Press the "Control" key, tap "Q" then tap 'A' (^QA).
3. In response to "Find:", type **%f** and tap <cr>.
4. In response to "Replace with:", type **%e** and tap <cr>.
5. In response to "Options:", type **gn** and tap <cr>. Each **%f** will be changed to a **%e** automatically.
6. Tap F9, and then run the program. Here's the result:

$$1.000000e+004 + 2.000000e+004 = 3.000000e+004$$

Each mantissa is displayed with one digit to the left of the decimal point and six to the right. Note that each exponent is shown as a signed, three-digit value.

7. Tap Alt-X and save the file.

You have just used the editor's "find and replace" capability—the command is ^QA. The options I gave you were "g" for "global" (which means "search through the entire file") and "n" for "no questions" ("change every one the editor finds without asking 'YES or NO?' "). If you do not use these options, the editor will begin the search from wherever the cursor is right now (i.e., when you tapped ^QA), skipping everything from the beginning of the file to this point. Also, it will stop at every "%f" and ask if you want to change it. You must press either "y" or "n." If you want the editor to do another identical "find and replace," just press ^L (i.e., press and hold Ctrl, tap L, release both).

More Conversion Characters

If you want to display a value as an integer, use the format "**%d**" in **printf**(). The "**d**" conversion character stands for "decimal integer." C is also capable of displaying integers in base 8 (octal integer, "**o**") and base 16 (hexadecimal integer, "**x**" or "**X**"). An *unsigned* integer needs the conversion character "**u**." If any of the values are *long*, you must preface the conversion character with the letter "**l**" ("ell"). For example,

```
printf("%ld", long_identifier);
```

printf( ) will take the value stored in the identifier, convert it, and display the result!

Don't be discouraged if you find yourself making many errors in typing *printf( )* statements. These are probably the most common kinds of errors that students make, and are easily corrected.

Integer Arithmetic

Before we leave our discussion on arithmetic calculations, I want to point out several important differences when integers are involved.

1. The result of any arithmetic operation involving *only* integers is an integer. [If the expression is "mixed" (i.e., at least one real and at least one integer), the result is always real.] The true significance of this statement is the revelation that your elementary school math teachers did not tell you the whole truth! They told you that 9/6 = 1.5. They did this, not because they were mean or malicious or ignorant, but because they were not categorizing numbers as *either* real or integer—they were "just numbers." However, when computers came along and when people wrote programming languages that used data types, the picture changed. If an integer is stored in memory in a very different way from a real number, there *must* be a difference between arithmetic with just integers and arithmetic with mixed types—and there is.

2. Integer arithmetic uses the same four operators as does real arithmetic. However, as I just said, division is different. Here are some examples of what I mean.

$$9.0/6.0 = 1.5$$

$$9.0/6 = 1.5$$

$$9/6.0 = 1.5$$

$$9/6 = 1$$

The last example is *integer/integer*, so the result is an *integer*. Specifically, it is the **truncated result of the equivalent real division**. That is, to calculate 9/6, think of the computer calculating 9.0/6.0 = 1.5 and throw away the decimal point and everything to its right (i.e., .5). This leaves *1* ("one") as the answer.

3. Just so that the discarded part is not lost forever, there is an additional integer division operation. It is called **mod**, its symbol is % (don't confuse this with the % that's used with conversion characters!), and it gives the *remainder* of the integer division. Taking our old example 9/6, let's change that to **9%6**. If you do this by long division, you will remember these words: "6 goes into 9 one time (9 − 6 = 3), *with a remainder of 3*. Aha! **9%6 = 3.**

   The *mod* operator is very useful in problems in which you must determine if one number is "evenly divisible" by another. If it is, the remainder of such a division will be zero.

Initializing Variables

In Fig. 2-7, we wrote

```
float r_1, r_2, r_total;
r_1 = 10.0E3;
r_2 = 20.0E3;
```

This declared three identifiers and then assigned initial values to two of them. C has a shortcut that allows us to combine the declaration of a variable with an assignment statement that provides the first or *initial* value to that variable. We are permitted to write

```
float r_1 = 10.0E3; /* declare and initialize */
float r_2 = 20.0E3; /* declare and initialize */
float r_total;      /* declare ONLY          */
```

We can also write it as a single declaration, like this:

```
float r_1 = 10.0E3, r_2 = 20.0E3, r_total;
```

This is called *initializing the variables*. Choose the style that makes it easiest for you to understand what you are doing.

Please note that we are NOT allowed to do this:

```
        float r_1 = 10.0E3;
        float r_2 = 20.0E3;
====>>>>> float r_total = r_1 + r_2; <<<<<==== NO, NO!
```

Initializing can be done only with *constant* values on the right-hand side of the "=", not with expressions (such as *r_1 + r_2*).

Getting Values from the User

It would indeed be silly to think of the program in Fig. 2.7 as a real program, because it gives the same result every time we run it. After we have run it 20 or 30 times, we will get the idea that 10.0E3 + 20.0E3 always sums to 30.0E3, and we won't need the program in Fig. 2-7 any more. A real program would let the person using it specify the two numbers to be added, instead of always using 10.0E3 and 20.0E3.

C has a function, **scanf()**, that lets a user enter values from the computer keyboard. We use **scanf()** like this:

```
scanf("control string", &variable);
```

That is, we will use **scanf()** to get one value at a time from the user. Even though **scanf()** is capable of doing more, it gets "nasty" if we are not *very* careful. Better safe than sorry.

Conversion Characters

"Ah," you say, "**scanf()** has a control string just like **printf()**!" Yes, it does, so we can use "**%f**" to accept **float** numbers, or "**%e**" if we want the user to type values in scientific format (you wouldn't do that, would you?), or "**%d**" if the input will be a decimal integer. In Table 2-1, I show you many of the conversion characters for both *scanf()* and *printf()* so that you will see the similarities and differences.

TABLE 2-1

Data type	Conversion character	
	printf()	scanf()
int	d	d
long	ld	ld
octal	o	o
long octal	lo	lo
hex	x	x
hex	X	—
long hex	lx	lx
long hex	lX	—
unsigned	u	u
long unsigned	lu	lu
float	f	f
float	e	e
float	E	—
double	lf	lf
double	le	le
double	lE	—

Memory and Addresses

The second argument is the one that causes a little confusion among beginning C programmers. Do you see the "**&**" (pronounced "AMP er sand") at the beginning of "**&variable**"? Well, take a good look, because **omitting it will be the one of the most common errors you will make**! If you omit the &, **scanf**( ) will not put the user's value where the program can find it, and the program will give strange results. Omitting the ampersand is so common that many lab instructors place an "ampersand box" in their labs. If you make an ampersand error, you put a quarter in the box. At the end of the semester, there will usually be enough money there for pizza and whatever for the entire class.

Here's a typical use of **scanf**( ):

```
scanf("%f", &radius);
```

Here is what it does. When the computer executes this particular **scanf**( ), it simply waits for the user to type something and tap <cr>. When this occurs, it will try to convert what was typed to a **float** value and store it in memory in the area reserved for the variable "radius." (We are assuming that "radius" was properly declared as a **float** earlier in the program.) The ampersand is C shorthand for "the area reserved for" or "the **address** of." [*Note:* There is a certain category of variable for which the ampersand is not required in a scanf( ) statement. I will point it out when we come to it.]

The **address** of a variable is a number known to the computer and represents the location of the first of one or more bytes of memory allocated to that variable. This is how it works: When we declare a variable, the compiler sets aside the correct number of bytes of memory to hold a value of that data type (so far, either **int, long, unsigned, double,** or **float**) and will remember the address of the first byte. It is a little like your house number. The number serves to locate the front door (the "first byte"), but says nothing about how many rooms ("bytes") there are in your house. You may tell a friend who is coming to your home for the first time that you live at 123 Main Street, or in apartment 27 at 2825 Elm Road, so that he can navigate by the numbers to your front door. However, your neighbors probably know your home as "the Jones' house" (if your name happens to be Jones) or "the Washingtons' apartment." So your home has both a numerical address and a name (i.e., an *identifier*).

In a similar way, we tell the compiler the names of variables, and it keeps a table of memory addresses and names. Each name we use has an address associated with it. For example, when we declared r_1 above as

```
float r_1;
```

the compiler assigned an address to r_1. Suppose that the address was 1000. On a PC, it takes four locations to store one **float** value. Therefore, when the compiler assigned 1000 as the address of r_1, it also reserved 1001, 1002, and 1003 for the r_1. When we next declared r_2 as

```
float r_2;
```

the compiler assigned an address to r_2. The address could have been 1004 or

1005 or 2187 or 655345, but it could not have been 1000 or 1001 or 1002 or 1003 because they were no longer available. The computer would rather work with the address numbers, but we would rather work with the names. So, in order to get **scanf( )** to work properly with r_2 as an variable, we have to force it to look up the address of r_2. You might think that **scanf( )** would be smart enough to know that, but it isn't.

2-4 AN EXAMPLE PROGRAM

Figure 2-8 illustrates **scanf( )** (and a few other things as well).

```
#define   PI  3.14159
#include <stdio.h>
main()
{
        float radius;

        printf("\n%s\n\n%s",
              "This program calculates the area of a circle.",
              "Input the radius:  ");
        scanf("%f", &radius);

        printf("\n%s\n%s%.2f%s%.2f%s%.2f\n%s%.5f\n\n",
              "Area = PI * radius * radius",
              "     = ", PI, " * ", radius, " * ", radius,
              "     = ", PI * radius * radius);

}
```

Figure 2-8   Using **scanf( )**.

If we type this in without error and run it, we get the following:

```
This program calculates the area of a circle.

Input the radius:  3

Area = PI * radius * radius
     = 3.14 * 3.00 * 3.00
     = 28.27431
```

The "3" was the number we typed in response to

```
                Input the radius:
```

That's why it is underlined above.

Preprocessor Constants

The very first line of our program is something quite new and very useful.

```
        #define    PI     3.14159
```

This line is called a *preprocessor definition*, and defines the string **PI** to be the same as the string **3.14159**. (*Note:* As far as the preprocessor is concerned, strings do not need quotes.) We can now write our program using **PI** and not worry about the value. The *preprocessor* is the part of the C system that examines the program just before the compiler gets it, and what it does with **#define** (pronounced "pound define") is very much like the editor's "find and replace." The preprocessor scans the program and every time it sees **PI**, it replaces it with **3.14159**. It simply replaces one string (*PI*) with another (*3.14159*). There is, however, one exception: If **PI** is enclosed in quotation marks anywhere in the program itself, no replacement will occur. It is pretty easy to appreciate why we would want to be able to *#define PI* as **3.14159**; it saves lots of typing in the rest of the program. There are other good reasons, too. See if you can think of one or two. Incidentally, it is a C convention to write all preprocessor constants in *uppercase* letters.

More Preprocessor Activities

We have the usual lines with **#include** <**stdio.h**>, **main**(), "{", and "}" on them, and we declared "radius" as a **float** but did not initialize it. Incidentally, if you recognized that **#include** is handled by the preprocessor, give yourself a pat on the back! The # character appearing in the first column of a line alerts the preprocessor and calls it into action.

A Multiline *printf( )*

The next statement is spread out over three lines but is just a single statement:

```
printf("\n%s\n\n%s",
    "This program calculates the area of a circle.",
    "Input the radius:  ");
```

You can tell it's a single statement because it has just one ";", at the very end. It's a **printf**() with three arguments, all strings! The first string is, of course, a control string. The last two arguments are the "constant strings,"

```
    "This program calculates the area of a circle.",
```

and

```
        "Input the radius:  "
```

Each requires the format specification **%s** ("s" for "string").
    The control string

```
        "\n%s\n\n%s"
```

tells **printf**() to output a newline, display a string, output two newlines, and output another string. So the result of executing just this one command is

```
    This program calculates the area of a circle.
    Input the radius:  _
```

where the "_" represents the position of the cursor after this **printf**() has been executed. This last line is called a *prompt*; it tells the user what to do.
    Incidentally, an equivalent **printf**() statement is

```
printf("\nThis program calculates the area of a circle.\n\nInput the radius:  ");
```

but it is too long to fit on one line of the screen. This will cause an extra newline to be printed as the string "wraps" around the screen. The original form gives us much more control over what gets placed where on the screen.

Getting Input

The next line,

```
scanf("%f", &radius);
```

tells the computer to accept what the user types, convert it to a **float**, and put it in memory at the address of "radius." Note the ampersand!

Another Output Statement

Finally, another multiline **printf**():

```
printf("\n%s\n%s%.2f%s%.2f%s%.2f\n%s%.5f\n\n",
    "Area = PI * radius * radius",
    "     = ", PI, " * ", radius, " * ", radius,
    "     = ", PI * radius * radius);
```

If you count commas carefully, you will see that there are nine (NINE!) arguments to this **printf**(). They are shown in Fig. 2-9. With nine arguments, there must be nine formats in the control string. There are, and they are shown in Fig. 2-10. You recognize the "%s" as the format for a string. Recall that a string is zero or more characters enclosed in quotation marks. So that would include "*" as well as "Area". But what is the meaning of **%.2f** and of **%.5f**? They seem to be format specifications with fractional values placed between the % and the conversion character! They are format specifications indeed! The fractions (i.e., .2 and .5) specify the number of decimal digits in the display of the **float** number. That is, "%.2f" tells **printf**() to display the **float** value of the corresponding **float** variable (or constant—we used this with PI) with two digits to the right of the decimal point (i.e., to two decimal places). And "%.5f" means "display to five decimal places." This is how we change from the six-digit display that **%f** gives us. The result then has three displays with two digits to the right of the decimal point and one with five:

	Argument	Type
	"Area = PI * radius * radius"	STRING
	" = "	STRING
	PI	NUMBER
	" * "	STRING
	radius	FLOAT
	" * "	STRING
	radius	FLOAT
	" = "	STRING
and	PI * radius * radius	FLOAT

Figure 2-9 The nine arguments.

%s	STRING
%s	STRING
%.2f	FLOAT
%s	STRING
%.2f	FLOAT
%s	STRING
%.2f	FLOAT
%s	STRING
%.5f	FLOAT

Figure 2-10 The nine formats.

```
Area = PI * radius * radius
     = 3.14 * 3.00 * 3.00
     = 28.27431
```

A Special Preprocessor Action

In the output shown above, the string *PI* is shown one time, even though it appeared THREE times in the *printf( )* statement. The first time it appeared was between quotes as part of a string, so the preprocessor did not make the substitution (*3.14159* for *PI*). It did make the substitutions the other two times because *PI* was not "protected" by quotation marks during the rest of its appearances in the *printf( )* statement.

A Simpler Output Statement

It is not really necessary to have such complicated **printf**( ) statements. The version of this program in Fig. 2-11 will produce the same results and may be easier to

```c
#define  PI  3.14159
#include <stdio.h>
main()
{
    float radius;
    printf("\nThis program calculates the area of a circle.\n\n");
    printf("Input the radius:  ");
    scanf("%f", &radius);
    printf("\nArea = PI * radius * radius\n");
    printf("     = ");
    printf("%.2f", PI);
    printf(" * ");
    printf("%.2f", radius);
    printf(" * ");
    printf("%.2f\n", radius);
    printf("     = ");
    printf("%.5f\n\n", PI * radius * radius);
}
```

Figure 2-11 A simpler set of printf( )s.

read. You choose the one you prefer. This one requires much extra typing and it is difficult to line up the display lines properly. But it is easier to read!

Summary

So, now you know how to declare variables, how to get them values (by assignment, calculation, or input), and how to display results. Pretty good!

2-5 REPETITION

If we have a lot of things to do and they are all similar, it is better to write them in a **loop** than to write out each one explicitly. For example, suppose that I own a supermarket on the side (in case this book doesn't sell a zillion copies!) and that I've hired you to work part-time while you are going to school. Further suppose that I have given you the job of putting the contents of a box of apples—say there are 100 apples in the box—into an empty display case. I could give you the following detailed instructions:

1. Pick up an apple from the box.
2. Put it in the display case.
3. Pick up an apple from the box.
4. Put it in the display case.
5. Pick up an apple from the box.
6. Put it in the display case.
7. Pick up an apple from the box.
8. Put it in the display case.
9. Pick up an apple from the box.
10. Put it in the display case.

.
.
.

199. Pick up an apple from the box.
200. Put it in the display case.

But that would be rather silly, wouldn't it? After all, you are just repeating 100 times the pair of instructions:

1. Pick up an apple from the box.
2. Put it in the display case.

There is a much better way to instruct you to do exactly the same actions, better because the list of instructions is much shorter. I could have said this:

Do the following pair of instructions 100 times:
    1. Pickup an apple from the box.
    2. Put it in the display case.

That is simpler to write and it doesn't insult your intelligence: You know what each instruction means and you know how to count up to 100. So there's no need to write each pair of instructions 100 times. What I have illustrated here is the idea of "repetition"—a group of instructions is stated once along with a "rule" on how many times to repeat them.

But even this method has a pitfall—suppose that I didn't know exactly how many apples there were in the box to start with! I would not be able to say "do the following pair of instructions 100 times." Instead of using a loop based on counting, we need a loop based on an *event*.

> *Do the following until there are no more apples in the box:*
> *1. Pick up an apple from the box.*
> *2. Put it in the display case.*

Or

> *While there's at least one apple in the box, repeat the following:*
> *1. Pick up an apple from the box.*
> *2. Put it in the display case.*

Note: We use the word "while" to mean "as long as."

This approach requires that you can tell the difference between a box that contains one or more apples and a box that is empty. The **event** is an empty box. Here, "repetition" consists of a set of instructions and a rule that tells you when you can stop executing them.

To put this into terms that are more computer-like, let us think about the "emptiness" of the box. There are only two possibilities that interest us:

a. The box is empty (i.e., contains no apples).

b. The box is not empty (i.e., contains one or more apples).

Notice that each statement—"the box is [is]/[is not] empty"—is either TRUE or FALSE. Since I know what I mean by "empty" and "not empty" and have told you what those definitions are (just to be sure!), I am confident that you will successfully transfer apples until there are no more in the box. So I can rewrite the last form as:

> *While the box is not empty,*
> *1. Pick up an apple from the box.*
> *2. Put it in the display case.*

The repetition is implied by the word "while."

TRUE and FALSE

In C, we normally test the condition of a variable or expression against a special value. In our example above, we could test the variable

```
#include <stdio.h>
main()
{
    int i = 0;

    /* a simple loop */
    while (i <= 10)
    {
        puts("This is fun...");
        puts("Isn't it????");
        i = i + 1;
    }
    puts("All done!");
}
```

Figure 2-12 A loop in C.

number_of_apples_in_the_box against the value zero by making the assertion

"the **number_of_apples_in_the_box** is zero"

That will be either TRUE or FALSE. If it is FALSE, we know that there are more apples to be moved. If it is TRUE, we are finished. The assertions we test are usually called *conditional expressions* and involve *relational operators* such as

$<$ less than

$<=$ less than or equal to

$>$ greater than

$>=$ greater than or equal to

$==$ equal to   (*Note well!*)

$!=$ not equal to

as in

```
        (i <= 10)        /* a conditional expression */
```
or
```
        (r_1 == r_2)            /* another one   */
```

The quantity in parentheses, the **conditional expression**, is either TRUE or FALSE, and the computer can tell which it is. So, in C, we could have a loop like the one in Fig. 2-12.

A common fatal error   A very common error and definitely the hardest one to find is writing

```
        ( r_1 = r_2 )
```

instead of

```
        ( r_1 == r_2 )
```

(Did you spot the difference? Look at it again!) In most computer languages, the compiler would see the first as a syntax error and notify you, but not C. Because C is so flexible and powerful, it permits you to write the "wrong" thing here. Clearly,

$$\text{while (r\_1 = r\_2)}$$

does **not** test to see if the value of **r_1** is the same as the value of **r_2**, because

$$\text{r\_1 = r\_2}$$

is an **assignment** expression: It assigns the value of **r_2** to **r_1**. But how does C treat the result that is, after all, sitting inside an **while** statement in place of a conditional expression? Simple. C "understands" that an expression has a value, and it uses that value in place of TRUE and FALSE for the **while**. The rule is that an assignment expression has the same value as the identifier on the left-hand side. If that value is **zero**, C treats it the same as it treats **FALSE**. Any other value is treated the same as **TRUE**. So if your program seems to have trouble making decisions, look at the **while** statements; you may have written an assignment instead of a test!

An Example Program

The opening and closing braces under "while" are used to show that all statements between them are to be repeated; these statements are the **body** of the loop. The form of the *while*—writing the braces lined up under the "w" and the statements to be repeated indented one level in from the braces—is one I require my students to follow. Naturally, you will use the one your instructor requires.

Since the initial value of "i" is 0, the first test for (**i** <= **10**) will be TRUE, and the body will be executed, producing

```
This is fun...
Isn't it????
```

and adding 1 to "i". Now the new value of "i" (it is now 1) is tested in (**i** <= **10**) and if this value is less than or equal to 10 (it is), the expression is TRUE and the computer will display

```
This is fun...
Isn't it????
```

again, and then add 1 to "i" again. This process will continue until the conditional expression (**i** <= **10**) is FALSE (in this case, when "i" becomes 11), at which time the statements inside the braces will not be executed any more. Now, the final statement is executed, producing the message

```
All done!
```

How does

```
i = i + 1;
```

add 1 to "i"? Initially, we had 0 stored in the memory location allocated to "i". In executing

$$i = i + 1;$$

an assignment statement, the computer first evaluates the right-hand side:

$$0 + 1 \; \text{-->} \; 1$$

The right-hand side has a value of 1. Now the rest of the assignment is executed; it is "i gets 1," so the old value of "i" is lost and the new value, **1**, is placed into the memory area associated with "i." The next time this statement is executed, "i" has the value of 1, so the right-hand side is

$$1 + 1 \; \text{-->} \; 2$$

So "i gets 2" occurs. And so on. Now, you may begin to understand why we said "r_1 gets 10.0E3" at the beginning of the chapter instead of "r_1 equals 10.0E3." An assignment statement is NOT an equation! The value on the right-hand side is placed into the memory area reserved for the variable on the left-hand side.

Another Example Program

Let's look at a program that adds up 10 floats and reports the sum. It appears in Fig. 2-13. Figure 2-14 shows the results of executing the program. There are some interesting aspects to this program. First, notice that some of the values that were typed at the keyboard were real numbers, but others were integers. **scanf**() will *promote* an integer from the keyboard into the **float** that it is looking for: The **%f** tells it to do just that. But it will be very unhappy if anything except a digit, a decimal point, a sign, or an "e" is keyed. **scanf**() will convert everything

```
#include <stdio.h>
main()
{
      float num, sum = 0.0;
      int count = 0;

      printf("\nThis program adds ten numbers and ");
      printf("displays the sum.\n");

      while (count < 10)
      {
            printf("    Input a number:  ");
            scanf("%f", &num);

            sum = sum + num;
            count = count + 1;
      }
      printf("The sum of the 10 numbers is %f.", sum);
}
```

Figure 2-13 Adding some floats.

```
This program adds ten numbers and displays the sum.
    Input a number:  11.234
    Input a number:  -.098
    Input a number:  22
    Input a number:  33
    Input a number:  44
    Input a number:  -99
    Input a number:  1234.1
    Input a number:  1
    Input a number:  1
    Input a number:  1
```

Figure 2-14 Results of adding some floats.

```
The sum of the 10 numbers is 1248.235962.
```

up to the "bad" character and then quit. This will usually give the user some unexpected results.

Note that *count* started at 0 and the while-loop was executed whenever *count* was less than 10. That meant that when *count* had the values 0, 1, 2, 3, 4, 5, 6, 7, 8, and 9, the statements in the braces would be executed, but, as soon as *count* became 10, looping ended. While starting at 0 may seem strange to you, it makes excellent sense to a computer's electronic circuits. Remember that the contents of a memory location can be from 0000 0000 to 1111 1111? Binary 0000 0000 is 0 in decimal. So it is conventional to let all integers start at 0.

Accumulators. The statement

$$sum = sum + num;$$

in a loop is called an *accumulator* because at any point in the loop, "sum" is the total of all the values that have been input so far. That is, "sum" has **accumulated** a subtotal. Accumulating is such a common operation in C that there is special, shorthand notation for it. Instead of writing

$$sum = sum + num;$$

we can write

$$sum += num;$$

They have exactly the same meaning!

And there is another shorthand notation that deals with counting, such as

$$count = count + 1;$$

It is not

$$count += 1;$$

as you may think—although that is perfectly legal. The shorthand version is even shorter. Instead of

$$count = count + 1;$$

or even

$$count += 1;$$

we write

```
count++;     /* post-increment */
```

or

```
++count;     /* pre-increment */
```

We will use pre-increment and post-increment interchangeably until we run into a situation where there is a difference in the effect they have on the program.

There is a difference between

```
count = count + 1;
```

and

```
count += 1;
```

on the one hand, and the pre- and post-increment statements, on the other. The statement

```
++count;
```

is NOT an assignment statement. It is a special statement that changes the value of a variable. Changing the value of a variable without using an assignment statement is called a *side effect*. The form you see above, that uses **+ +count**; as a statement, is without any danger, whatsoever. Here are two statements that use incrementing in expressions:

```
i = ++count;
j = count++;
```

The first takes the current value of **count**, adds 1, and gives the result to **i**. In the second, the current value of **count** is assigned to **j** and THEN **count** is incremented. In both cases, **count** will have the same value after the statements as executed, but **i** will be 1 higher than **j**. You must be VERY careful when you use incrementing in an assignment statement.

Figure 2-15 shows a new version of the program from Fig. 2- 13.

```
#include <stdio.h>
main()
{
      float num, sum = 0.0;
      int count = 0;

      printf("\nThis program adds ten numbers and ");
      printf("displays the sum.\n");

      while (count < 10)
      {
            printf("    Input a number:  ");
            scanf("%f", &num);

            sum +=  num;
            ++count;
      }
      printf("The sum of the 10 numbers is %f.", sum);
}
```

Figure 2-15 Another way to add floats.

2-6 SOLVING EQUATIONS

Since an assignment statement is not the same as an equation, we cannot use circuit equations directly in a program. We must manipulate them algebraically into assignment statements. For example, suppose that we were given the equation

$$I = Q/t$$

which relates the amount of electric charge, Q in columns, passing a point during a certain interval of time, t in seconds, to the current, I in amperes. (C uses "/" for division and "*" for multiplication.) If we know the values for Q and t, and are supposed to calculate the value for I, we could use the equation as an assignment statement in the same form as it was given. But if we know the values for I and Q, and are supposed to calculate t, we will have to **rewrite** the equation, solving it for t:

$$t = Q/I$$

Now, this can be used as an assignment statement in a C program.

2-7 MAKING DECISIONS

Suppose that we want to write a single program based on the equation

$$I = Q/t$$

that would calculate the value of any unknown, given the values of the other two. To write a program to do this actually requires that we write THREE "subprograms," one for each distinct case! That is, we would need to write the equation as three assignment statements and use the one that has the unknown on the left-hand side. The three assignment statements would be

$$I = Q/t$$

$$Q = I*t$$

and

$$t = Q/I$$

Each of these would be in a different section of the program, and the program would have to ask the user which unknown to solve for. The program would then examine the answer, and choose the correct section. The code asking for the unknown and getting the answer might look like that in Fig. 2-16.

```
printf("What do you want to solve for?\n");
printf("Enter\n");
printf("\tI if you want to solve for current\n");
printf("\tQ if you want to solve for charge\n");
printf("or \tt if you want to solve for time.\n");
printf("\nWhat is your choice?  ");
scanf("%c", &choice);
```

Figure 2-16 Calculations and decisions.

The resulting display would look like this:

```
What do you want to solve for?
Enter
        I if you want to solve for current
        Q if you want to solve for charge
or      t if you want to solve for time.
What is your choice?
```

Notice that "\t" is the escape sequence for the TAB. It moves the cursor over to the next "tab stop." Tab stops are usually eight columns apart, and occur in columns 8, 16, 24, 32, and so on.

Character Data

Also, notice that there is a new format in

```
scanf("%c", &choice)
```

"%c". This is the *character* format. It lets **scanf**() accept one keystroke and saves it in a memory location allocated to a character variable. The data type for a character is called **char** and is used in the declaration for "choice" like this:

```
char choice;
```

A character is a little like a string, but it has two very important differences: (1) **single** quotation marks are used for character values, and (2) no more than **one** keystroke is permitted within those single quotation marks (with a few exceptions). For example, here are some legal character values:

```
'a'
'B'
'9'
'+'
'\n'
```

\n is considered to be a single character

Here are some illegal character constants:

"a"   (no double quotes permitted)
'this'   (too many characters between single quotes)

Characters in C include all the uppercase and lowercase letters, all the digits, all the punctuation marks, math symbols, parentheses, braces, brackets, and so on, that you see on the keyboard, plus some that you cannot see but which we'll ignore for now. Figure 2-17 shows a list of all of C's visible characters. Each **char** requires a single byte in memory. The **form feed** and **vertical tab** characters do nothing when sent to the screen, but watch the paper fly if you send one to the printer!

Incidentally, some of the characters in the fourth line of Fig. 2-17 have names

```
abcdefghijklmnopqrstuvwxyz
ABCDEFGHIJKLMNOPQRSTUVWXYZ
01234567890
!#%^&*()_+|-=\~{}[]:";'<>?,./
the blank character (key the space bar, ' ')
the newline character ('\n')
the backspace character ('\b')
the tab character ('\t')
the carriage return ('\r')
the form feed character ('\f')
the vertical tab character (\v')
```

Not included are @ $ `

Figure 2-17 Visible characters in C.

that you may not know, or which are peculiar to C.   They are

!	"bang"
^	"hat"
|	"stick"
\	"backslash"
~	"tilde" (TIL - duh)
/	"slash"

Most computers define the relationship between the characters they use and the numeric values representing those characters by selecting the American Standard Code for Information Interchange (ASCII).   Appendix A has a table of all 128 ASCII characters and their corresponding numeric codes (in base 10, base 8, and base 16).

C has a special function for reading a character from the keyboard; it is called **getchar**().   You could use it in place of **scanf(''%c'',&identifier)** if you like.   For example, in Fig. 2-16, in place of

```
scanf("%c", &choice);
```

write

```
choice = getchar();
```

Use whichever you prefer.

You can output a character value using either

```
printf("%c", choice);
```

or

```
putchar(choice);
```

The two statements are entirely equivalent.

The IF . . . ELSE Statement

After the user has entered a character in response to the prompt, the program tests to see which one it is: *I, Q,* or *t.* We will use the **if** test, as in

if the character stored in choice is an *I,*
    use the statement $I = Q/t$;

otherwise, if the character stored in choice is a *Q,*
    use the statement $Q = I*t$;

otherwise, if choice is a *t,*
    use $t = Q/I$;

otherwise
    tell the user he made an error entering his choice.

Did you see how we started to simplify the description above by saying "if choice is a *t*" in the third "if" instead of "if the value stored in choice is a *t*"? It is important that you recognize that they mean the same thing, because the second form leads directly to the C language form:

```
if (choice == 't')
```

This means "if the value stored in **choice** is the character *'t'.* " The parentheses are needed in an **if** statement for the same reason they are needed in a **while** statement: to delimit the conditional expression, **choice**=='**t**'. Notice how the test is made: We used the equality operator == and the character '**t**'.

Now, how do we handle the rest of the possibilities? Instead of the word "otherwise," C uses the word "else." So we can write the test like this:

```
if (choice == 'I')
{
        I = Q / t;
}
else if (choice == 'Q')
{
        Q = I * t;
}
else if (choice == 't')
{
        t = Q / I;
}
else
{
        printf("\nYou goofed!!");
}
```

Isn't that neat? The "logic" is the same as the statements in English. C goes through each **if** until it finds one that's TRUE. When it does, it executes the statements in the set of braces that immediately follow. You see that if none of the **ifs** is TRUE, the **printf( )** will be executed. The form of the **if** is the same as the **while**: The statements are indented and closed in a pair of braces that line up under the first letter of the keyword **if** or **else**.

Actually, what I have here is not complete. The statements between braces must include all of the steps needed to get the values of the knowns, calculate the value of the unknown, and report the results. I will do this very shortly, but first I want to tell you more about **if**.

The simplest form if the **if** statement is

```
if (<conditional expression>)
{
        <one or more statements>
}
```

If "conditional expression" is TRUE, then the statements inside the braces will be executed. But if "conditional expression" is FALSE, the statements within the braces will be ignored. This is an "all or nothing" situation. Figure 2-18 shows a diagram or *flowchart* of this idea.

The next situation is the "either/or" one. For example,

```
if (<conditional expression>)
{
        <statement set A>
}
else
{
        <statement set B>
}
```

If "conditional expression" is TRUE, the statements designated <**statement set A**> will be executed and the others ignored. If "conditional expression" is FALSE, <**statement set A**> will be ignored and <**statement set B**> will be executed. Figure 2-19 shows a flowchart for this construction.

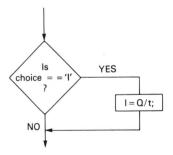

Figure 2-18 Flowchart for if.

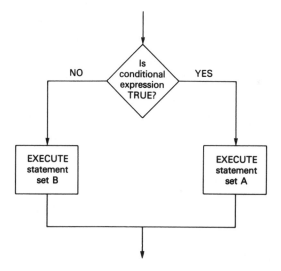

Figure 2-19 Flowchart for if . . . else . . . .

The IF . . . ELSE IF . . . ELSE Statement

Following this is the "either this or that or the other or. . . .,":

```
if (<conditional expression number 1>)
{
      <statement set A>
}
else if (<conditional expression number 2>)
{
      <statement set B>
}
else
{
      <statement set C>
}
```

Statement set C will be executed if "none of the above" conditional statements is TRUE.   Figure 2-20 has the flowchart for this situation.

Some Example Programs

Let's go back to our three-way program and finish it.   If we were going to do only $I = Q/t$, we could write the program that appears in Fig. 2-21.   Figure 2-22 shows two sample executions.   In the second example, the charge was given as 4 milli-coulombs or 4×10^{-3} coulombs and entered as 4e-3.   Also, the time was given as 80 microseconds or 80×10^{-6}, and entered as 80e-6.   Even though **scanf( )** had a **%f** conversion string, it accepted the scientific notation numbers without difficulty or error.   Nice.

The program to calculate Q, given I and t, is shown in Fig. 2-23.   And the

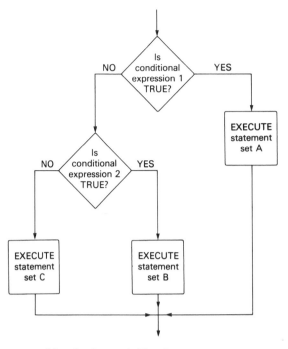

Figure 2-20 Flowchart for if . . . else if . . . else . . .

```
#include <stdio.h>
main()
{
    /* declare all variables */
    float Q, I, t;

    /* tell what's going to happen */
    printf("\nThis program calculates the current I,");
    printf("\ngiven Q, the charge in coulombs");
    printf("\nand t, the time in seconds.");

    /* prompt for input */
    printf("\n\nPlease enter the value of Q:  ");
    scanf("%f", &Q);
    printf("and the time:  ");
    scanf("%f", &t);
    printf("\nThank you.\n");

    /* do the calculation */
    I = Q / t;

    /* show the result */
    printf("The current is %.2f amperes.", I);
}
```

Figure 2-21 I = *Q/t* program.

(1)

    This program calculates the current I,
    given Q, the charge in coulombs
    and t, the time in seconds.

    Please enter the value of Q: 75
    and the time: 30

    Thank you.
    The current is 2.50 amperes.

(2)

    This program calculates the current I,
    given Q, the charge in coulombs
    and t, the time in seconds.

    Please enter the value of Q: 4e-3
    and the time: 80e-6

    Thank you.
    The current is 50.00 amperes.

Figure 2-22 Output from $I = Q/t$ program.


```
#include <stdio.h>
main()
{
    float I, Q, t;

    printf("\nThis program calculates the charge Q,");
    printf("\ngiven I, the current in amperes");
    printf("\nand t, the time in seconds.");

    printf("\n\nPlease enter the value of I:   ");
    scanf("%f", &I);
    printf("and the time:   ");
    scanf("%f", &t);
    printf("\nThank you.\n");

    Q = I * t;
    printf("The charge is %.2e coulombs.", Q);
}
```

Figure 2-23 $Q = I*t$ program.

```
#include <stdio.h>
main()
{
    float I, Q, t;

    printf("\nThis program calculates the time t,");
    printf("\ngiven Q, the charge in coulombs");
    printf("\nand I, the current in amperes.");
    printf("\n\nPlease enter the value of Q:   ");
    scanf("%f", &Q);
    printf("and the value of I:   ");
    scanf("%f", &I);
    printf("\nThank you.\n");

    t = Q / I;
    printf("The time is %.2e seconds.", t);
}
```

Figure 2-24 $t = Q/I$ program.

```
#include <stdio.h>
main()
{
    float I, Q, t;
    char choice;

    printf("\n\tEnter Q to calculate the charge Q,");
    printf("\n\tgiven I, the current in amperes");
    printf("\n\tand t, the time in seconds,");
    printf("\nor");
    printf("\n\tEnter I to calculate the current I,");
    printf("\n\tgiven Q, the charge in coulombs");
    printf("\n\tand t, the time in seconds.");
    printf("\nor");
    printf("\n\tEnter t to calculate the time t,");
    printf("\n\tgiven Q, the charge in coulombs");
    printf("\n\tand I, the current in amperes.");

    printf("\n\nPlease enter your choice:   ");
    scanf("%c", &choice);

    /* determine which calculation to do and then do it */
    if (choice == 'Q')
    {
        printf("\nEnter the current I:   ");
        scanf("%f", &I);
        printf("and the time t:   ");
        scanf("%f", &t);
```

Figure 2-25   All in one.

```
              Q = I * t;
              printf("\nThe charge is %.2e coulombs.", Q);
       }
       else if (choice == 'I')
       {
              printf("\nEnter the charge Q:  ");
              scanf("%f", &Q);
              printf("and the time t:  ");
              scanf("%f", &t);
              I = Q / t;
              printf("\nThe current is %.2f amperes.", I);
       }
       else if (choice == 't')
       {
              printf("\nEnter the charge Q:  ");
              scanf("%f", &Q);
              printf("and the value of I:  ");
              scanf("%f", &I);
              t = Q / I;
              printf("\nThe time is %.2e seconds.", t);
       }
       else
       {
              printf("\n\nYou goofed!!");
       }
}
```

Figure 2-25 (Continued)

program to calculate *t*, given *Q* and *I*, is shown in Fig. 2-24. Now, let's put them all together. The result is shown in Fig. 2-25. Four sample runs are shown in Fig. 2-26.

Take the time to go over the entire program to see how the pieces fit together. You should have no trouble understanding the whole thing if you understand the individual parts.

Complex Decisions—AND and OR

If you have tried this program during one of your lab sessions, you might have gotten the "You goofed!!" message when you typed "q" or "i" in response to the prompt. The program test for 'Q' and 'I' and, because C is a "case-sensitive" language, the test of

$$(choice == 'I')$$

fails (i.e., is FALSE) when **choice** has the value "**i**." It would make sense to let the user enter either "I" or "i"; "Q" or "q"; "T" or "t", and have the program accept either. For example, we would like the test to be TRUE if **choice** is either "Q" or "q." To do so, we must modify our conditional expressions. In place of

$$if\ (choice == 'Q')$$

(1)
```
      Enter Q to calculate the charge Q,
      given I, the current in amperes
      and t, the time in seconds,
or
      Enter I to calculate the current I,
      given Q, the charge in coulombs
      and t, the time in seconds,
or
      Enter t to calculate the time t,
      given Q, the charge in coulombs
      and I, the current in amperes.

      Please enter your choice: Q

      Enter the current I:  50
      and the time t:  80e-6

      The charge is 4.00e-003 coulombs.
```

(2)
```
      Enter Q to calculate the charge Q,
      given I, the current in amperes
      and t, the time in seconds,
or
      Enter I to calculate the current I,
      given Q, the charge in coulombs
      and t, the time in seconds,
or
      Enter t to calculate the time t,
      given Q, the charge in coulombs
      and I, the current in amperes.

      Please enter your choice:  I

      Enter the charge Q:  4e-3
      and the time t:  80e-6

      The current is 50.00 amperes.
```

(3)
```
      Enter Q to calculate the charge Q,
      given I, the current in amperes
      and t, the time in seconds,
or
      Enter I to calculate the current I,
      given Q, the charge in coulombs
      and t, the time in seconds,
or
      Enter t to calculate the time t,
      given Q, the charge in coulombs
      and I, the current in amperes.
```

Figure 2-26 Some sample runs.

```
Please enter your choice:  t

Enter the charge Q:  4e-3
and the value of I:  50

The time is 8.00e-005 seconds.
```

(4)
```
    Enter Q to calculate the charge Q,
    given I, the current in amperes
    and t, the time in seconds,
or
    Enter I to calculate the current I,
    given Q, the charge in coulombs
    and t, the time in seconds,
or
    Enter t to calculate the time t,
    given Q, the charge in coulombs
    and I, the current in amperes.

    Please enter your choice:  z

    You goofed!!
```

Figure 2-26   (Continued)

we will write

$$\text{if (choice == 'Q' || choice == 'q')}$$

Notice that the identifier **choice** has been written **twice**. This is absolutely *mandatory* because you are really combining two **if** statements: **if (choice == 'Q')** and **if (choice == 'q')**. You are not permitted to write **if (choice == 'Q'||'q')**, even though that is the way we would say that in English.

The conditional expressions have become more complicated. The symbol || represents logical **OR** and uses a pair of "stick" characters (usually found on the same key that produces the "\"). That is, if EITHER "choice" is 'Q' OR "choice" is 'q', execute the TRUE statements. Only one of them has to be TRUE to make the entire **if** TRUE when we use **OR**.

If we have a situation that requires that two conditional expressions both be TRUE at the same time—that is, two conditions must be met—use **AND**. In C, **AND** is represented by **&&**. For example,

```
        if (count >= 7 && count <= 10)
        {
                <statements>
        }
```

means that the statements will be executed if and only if the present value of count is either 7, 8, 9, or 10 (assuming that 'count' was declared as an **int**). That is, both **count>=7** AND **count <=10** are simultaneously TRUE.

Relational operators are "more important" (i.e., have a higher *precedence*) than AND and OR, so each subexpression (e.g., "count $>= 7$" is a subexpression) is evaluated to either TRUE or FALSE before the AND or OR is used. If we want to make that more clear to the person who reads our code, we can add more parentheses, like this:

```
if ( (count >= 7) && (count <= 10) )
{
        <"TRUE" statements>
}
```

These parentheses force C to evaluate **count $>=7$** and **count $<= 10$** before it tries to use the **&&** operator.

REVIEW

In this chapter you learned:

- The rules for writing identifiers and how they are used as the names of variables
- How to declare an identifier and what the compiler does with the declaration
- About several data types: **int, long int, float, double,** and **char**; and about **signed** and **unsigned** values
- The basic arithmetic operations: $+ - * /$
- About **assignment statements**: what they are and what they are not
- About **printf( )**
- About arguments
- About format strings and conversion characters
- About a restricted use of **scanf( )**
- That you must use the "**&**" character before the identifier in a **scanf( )**
- How to define a constant using "**#define**"
- How to set up a loop using **while**
- About the relational operators and what a conditional expression is
- The shorthand operators $+ =$ and $+ +$
- About choices, using "if . . . ," "if . . . else.," and "if . . . else if . . . else . . . "
- The AND and OR operators, **&&** and ‖

PROBLEMS AND QUESTIONS

1. What is the difference between an address and an identifier? How are they related?
2. Which of the following are illegal identifiers?
   (a) apple
   (b) peach1
   (c) R-2
   (d) VALUE

(e) float_number

(f) INT

(g) c

(h) 26.5

3. In C, the real numbers are stored in variables of type _____ or _____ .

4. In C, "decimal" means

(a) Any base 10 number

(b) A base 10 float number

(c) A base 10 integer

(d) Any number with a decimal point in it

5. What is the base 10 value of the following eight-bit signed numbers?

(a) 0000 1111   (b) 1000 1111

(c) 1111 1111   (d) 1000 0000

6. How many different addresses could a CPU with 16 address lines create?

7. Why does C insist that variables be declared before they can be used?

8. What is the purpose of **#include<stdio.h>**?

9. What does an assignment statement do?

10. What is the difference between an assignment statement and an equation? Give examples of each.

11. What does the "f" in **printf()** stand for?

12. What is the minimum number of arguments for **printf()**? Explain.

13. Write the conversion character for each of the following:

(a) float

(b) int

(c) string

(d) scientific notation

(e) character

14. What part of the C system is called on by the "#" (as in "#include" or "#define")?

15. Suppose you want to input the values of three resistors. Write a C program that does just that. The display should look like this:

```
Enter the value of the first resistor: 1000
Enter the value of the second resistor: 1500
Enter the value of the third resistor: 3200
```

The underline quantities are sample values as might be entered by a user.

16. Write a C program that displays the following:

```
                     X
                     X
                     X
                     X
                     X
```

The X's are all in column 6. You MUST use a loop!

17. Write a C program that displays integers from 1 to 16, eight per line. The display should look like this:

```
1   2   3   4   5   6   7   8
9  10  11  12  13  14  15  16
```

18. Modify the program you wrote for Problem 17 so that the user can specify the last integer (instead of 16). The display might look like this:

```
Enter the last number:  10

1   2   3   4   5   6   7   8
9  10
```

19. Modify the program you wrote for problem 18 so that the user can specify both the first and last integers. Thus, the program will print ANY number of ANY set of consecutive integers, and display them eight to a line. The display might look like this:

```
Enter the first number:  10
Enter the last number:   20

10  11  12  13  14  15  16  17
18  19  20
```

20. Modify the program you wrote for problem 19 so that the user can specify both the first and last integers, AND the number of integers on each line of the display. The display might look like this:

```
Enter the first number:  10
Enter the last number:   20
How many numbers do you want displayed on each line?  4

10  11  12  13
14  15  16  17
18  19  20
```

21. Write a program that adds up any number of values and calculates the average of all the values entered. *Hint:* Ask the user how many values will be entered. What happens when you divide a **float** value by an **int** value?

22. Write a program that will add up any number of positive values and calculate the average of all the values entered. *Hint:* Ask the user to enter a negative value after all the positive values have been entered. You will have to keep track of the number of values entered.

23. Write a program that asks the user for a character, and then reports whether it was (a) an uppercase letter, (b) a lowercase letter, (c) a digit, or (d) none of these.

3

Applying C to Simple Problems

3-1 INTRODUCTION AND OBJECTIVES

In this chapter we will see some C programs that solve problems having to do with powers of 10, resistance, and Ohm's law.

Upon successful completion of this chapter, you will be able to:

- Use the **for** statement
- Use the function **puts()**
- Use the escape character for the quotation mark
- Use the **switch** statement
- Use **case** and **default** in a switch statement
- Use **break** in a switch statement
- Implement user control of looping using the answer to the question "Any more?"
- Use the value returned by **scanf()**
- Set up a menu of choices for the user
- Use array variables
- Use the function **gets()**
- Use the function **strcmp()** and the header file **string.h**
- Initialize an array of characters
- Use an array of strings
- Use the /= operator
- Use the % operator
- Use the functions **rand()**, **srand()**, and **time()**
- Write a program to print a table of powers of 10 and scientific prefixes
- Write a program to calculate the resistance of a wire

- Write a program to make calculations based on the resistor color code
- Write a program to test someone's knowledge of the resistor color code

3-2 PREFIXES AND SCIENTIFIC NOTATION

Producing a Table of Values

As I mentioned in Chapter 2, you need to know how to use scientific notation and the prefixes for certain powers of 10. Figure 3-1 presents a C program that displays a table of the powers of 10 and the prefixes. I will discuss other approaches to answering the questions "What is the power of 10 for the prefix x?" and "What is the prefix for the x power of 10?"

The first thing you should notice is that when it is compiled and executed, this program simply displays a table of all of the powers of 10 and the corresponding prefixes. It handles our two questions by saying, in effect, "Here's the whole table; look up your own answers." This is an easy program to write.

You should also notice that I used only the **puts( )** and **printf( )** functions. It is true that I could have used only **printf( )** and not used **puts( )** at all. Using **puts( )** saves a few keystrokes because it automatically outputs a newline at the end of each string.

Did you spot the new escape sequence? Is is \"; it causes C to display the quotation mark character in the output. (It first appears just before "TEH.") Why do we need to escape the quotation mark? In C, the normal meaning for the quotation mark is "mark one end of a string." However, here, I wanted to display a quotation mark in certain places as just a plain old quotation mark, so had to escape it from its meaning as a delimiter. If I didn't escape it, C would have thought that I wanted to end the string

$$" \quad 12 \qquad Tera \ ("$$

after the left parenthesis. That would have produced an error message for certain.

```
#include <stdio.h>
main()
{
    printf("\nThis is a table of powers of 10 and ");
    puts("engineering prefixes");
    printf("-----------------------------------");
    puts("--------------------");
    puts("Power of 10        Prefix            Abbreviation");
    printf("-----------------------------------");
    puts("--------------------");
    puts("     12          Tera (\"TEH-rah\")      T");
    puts("      9          Giga (\"GHIG-ah\")      G");
    puts("      6          Mega (\"MEG-ah\")       M");
    puts("      3          Kilo (\"KILL-ow\")      k");
    puts("     -3          Milli (\"MILL-ee\")     m");
    puts("     -6          Micro (\"MIKE-row\")    u");
    puts("     -9          Nano (\"NAN-no\")       n");
    puts("    -12          Pico (\"PEE-co\")       p");
}
```

Figure 3-1

```
A:\>prog0301
```

```
This is a table of powers of 10 and engineering prefixes


---------------------------------------------------------

Power of 10               Prefix              Abbreviation
---------------------------------------------------------

      12            Tera ("TEH-rah")              T
       9            Giga ("GHIG-ah")              G
       6            Mega ("MEG-ah")               M
       3            Kilo ("KILL-ow")              k
      -3            Milli ("MILL-ee")             m
      -6            Micro ("MIKE-row")            u
      -9            Nano ("NAN-no")               n
     -12            Pico ("PEE-co")               p
A:\>
```

Figure 3-2

Figure 3-2 shows what the table looks like when the program (I named the source code "PROG0301.C," and Turbo C named the executable file "PROG0301.EXE") is executed from the A: disk (outside the Turbo C Integrated Environment).

Suppose we want a "smarter" program—one that won't just display everything it knows, but will reply only with the specific prefix that corresponds to the power the user enters. It would have to prompt the user with something like this:

```
This program will give you the engineering prefix
for any power of ten you enter.
What power do you want (e.g., -3)?
```

If the user entered -6, it would output

```
The prefix for -6 is Micro.
```

We could use the "if . . . else if . . . else if . . . else" construct, but C has a command that is a bit more applicable to this kind of situation. It is called the **switch** statement. It accepts a value for one variable and then tries to match it with a set of values that you write into the program. If it matches, it executes the code statements you write for that matched value. The switch statement looks like this:

```
switch (<identifier>)
{
    <statements>
}
```

The <**identifier**> is just the name of the variable we are trying to match up against; in our case, we might call it "user_power." The <**statements**> are a group of

```
switch(user_power)
{
case 3:
    puts("\n3 is the power for Kilo.");
    break;
case 6:
    puts("\n6 is the power for Mega.");
    break;
case 9:
    puts("\n9 is the power for Giga.");
    break;
case 12:
    puts("\n12 is the power for Tera.");
    break;
default:
    printf("\nThere is no prefix for %d.\n", user_power);
}   /* closing brace */
```
Figure 3-3

different **cases** to match against. For example, if one possible value for the identifier is 29, one of the switch statements might look like this:

```
case 29:
    puts("You matched 29!!);
    break;
```

In our situation, we would have a **case** for each of -12, -9, -6, -3, 3, 6, 9, and 12. The switch (for just the positive powers) might look like Fig. 3-3.

The word **case** means that the computer should compare the value of the switch identifier with the value to the right to the word **case**. If they are *exactly* equal, the statements that follow **case** shall be executed. Because of the requirement that the two values must be exactly equal, C does not allow us to use **floats** in **case** statements.

break is a special statement which, when used as part of a **case**, causes the computer to ignore all the statements following **break** until it sees the closing brace of the entire **switch** statement. (We will meet **break** again, in **while**, and **for** loops.) Then the program will continue executing at the first statement after the closing brace, skipping all the statements between **break** and }.

default means that "if there are no case matches, execute the following statement(s)." Thus, if user_power is, say, 2, for example, the computer will display "There is no prefix for 2." If user_power is 9, the computer will display "9 is the power for Giga."

Figure 3-4 shows a program to display a prefix, given a power. Figure 3-5 shows two sample executions.

We could have done the same thing with a series of **if . . . else if . . . else** statements to replace the **switch** statement, as shown in Fig. 3-6. Most C programmers prefer the **switch** statement, but it is certainly acceptable to use the **if . . . else if . . . else** if you prefer.

```
#include <stdio.h>
main()
{
    int user_power;

    /* Input section: prompt for values */
    printf("\nThis program will tell you the ");
    printf("prefix \nfor any power");
    puts(" of ten you input.");
    printf("\nWhat is your power of 10 (e.g., -3)?  ");
    scanf("%d", &user_power);

    /* Processing and output section */
    switch(user_power)
    {
        case -12:
            puts("\n-12 is the power for Pico.");
            break;
        case -9:
            puts("\n-9 is the power for Nano.");
            break;
        case -6:
            puts("\n-6 is the power for Micro.");
            break;
        case -3:
            puts("\n-3 is the power for Milli.");
            break;
        case 3:
            puts("\n3 is the power for Kilo.");
            break;

        case 6:
            puts("\n6 is the power for Mega.");
            break;
        case 9:
            puts("\n9 is the power for Giga.");
            break;
        case 12:
            puts("\n12 is the power for Tera.");
            break;
        default:
            printf("\nThere is no prefix for %d.\n",
                    user_power);
    }
    puts("\nThank you!");
}
```

Figure 3-4

User-Controlled Repetition

The only problem with this new, smarter approach is that it is not smart enough. It will do one and only one power of 10 and then return the user to the operating system (i.e., she would see the "A>" or "C>" prompt next). Most users would

```
A:\>prog302
This program will tell you the prefix
for any power of ten you input.
What is your power of 10 (e.g., -3)? -2
There is no prefix for -2.
Thank you!


A:\>prog302
This program will tell you the prefix
for any power of ten you input.
What is your power of 10 (e.g., -3)? -6
-6 is the power for Micro.
Thank you!
A:\>
```
Figure 3-5

probably prefer a program that handles a power of 10 and then asks to do another. To implement this smarter program, we need a loop, controlled by the answer to the prompt "Any more? (1 for YES, 0 for NO)." The program will accept an integer number for the answer and test to see if it's a 1. If it is, we will reexecute the statements in the loop. If it isn't 1, we'll skip the statements in the loop and go on to the statements after the loop. The loop might look like this:

```
while (ans == 1)
{
    [statements from the previous program]

    printf("\nAny more? (1 for YES, 0 for NO): ");
    scanf("%d", &ans);
}
```

Of course, we must declare **ans** as an **int**, and initialize it to 1. Why initialize it? Because if we don't, the value that is in the memory location for **ans** will be some random value, called "garbage." If **ans** is not 1 initially, the loop will never be executed! We need

```
int ans = 1;
```

to ensure that the loop will be executed at least one time.

There is one more problem with this approach. We're asking the user to enter either a 1 or a 0, an **int**. But what will the program do if the user is curious or playful or disruptive, and enters something other than an **int** value—a **char**, or a **float**, or just hits the <Enter> key? That depends on what **scanf("%d", &ans)** does when it is looking for an **int** and gets something else. If **scanf("%d", &ans)** doesn't get an **int**, it refuses to put anything at all into **ans** (i.e., ans will be left unchanged), and returns the value 0 [**scanf()** is a function, after all!]. So we can try **scanf()** and if it returns 0, we know that the user has not entered a legal integer value! (Incidentally, this is the first time that we will have used the value returned by a function, but it won't be the last.) Every time **scanf("%d", &ans)** is called to accept a value from the keyboard and store it, **scanf("%d", &ans)** will return

```
if (user_power == -12)
  {
        puts("\n-12 is the power for Pico.");
  }
 else if (user_power == -9)
  {
        puts("\n-9 is the power for Nano.");
  }
 else if (user_power == -6)
  {
        puts("\n-6 is the power for Micro.");
  }
 else if (user_power == -3)
  {
        puts("\n-3 is the power for Milli.");
  }

 else if (user_power == 3)
  {
        puts("\n3 is the power for Kilo.");
  }
 else if (user_power == 6)
  {
        puts("\n6 is the power for Mega.");
  }
 else if (user_power == 9)
  {
        puts("\n9 is the power for Giga.");
  }
 else if (user_power == 12)
  {
        puts("\n12 is the power for Tera.");
  }
 else
  {
        printf("\nThere is no prefix for %d.\n",
            user_power);
  }

 puts("\nThank you!");
```

Figure 3-6

a value.   The returned value will be 1 if the conversion is successful, and 0 if it is not.   Whenever **scanf("%d", &ans)** is successful, **ans** will get the value entered by the user.   But whenever **scanf("%d", &ans)** fails (i.e., whenever the user inputs something that is not an **int** value), we want **ans** to get 0.   Here are a couple of lines of code to do that:

```
test = scanf("%d", &ans);
if (test == 0)
{
        ans = 0;
}
```

where **test** is previously declared an **int**.   C allows us to combine the two statements and eliminate the extra variable **test**:

```
if ( scanf("%d", &ans) == 0 )
{
     ans = 0;
}
```

Both mean "if the value returned by **scanf("%d", &ans)** is 0, then **ans** gets 0."
So the loop will become

```
while (ans == 1)
{

     [statements from the previous program]

     printf("\nAny more? (1 for YES, 0 for NO): ");

     if ( scanf("%d", &ans) == 0 )
     {
          ans = 0;
     }
}
```

This technique of protecting the program from the user is called "bulletproofing" and is a very common and desirable practice.

Let's look at the entire new program, in Fig. 3-7.

```
#include <stdio.h>
main()
{
     /* declare ans = 1 so that the while loop starts properly */
     int user_power, ans = 1;

     while (ans == 1)
     {
          printf("\nThis program will tell you the prefix");
          printf("\nfor any power");
          puts(" of ten you input.");
          printf("What is your power of 10 (e.g., -3)?  ");
          scanf("%d", &user_power);

          switch(user_power)
          {
               case -12:
                    puts("\n-12 is the power for Pico.");
                    break;
               case -9:
                    puts("\n-9 is the power for Nano.");
                    break;
               case -6:
                    puts("\n-6 is the power for Micro.");
                    break;
               case -3:
                    puts("\n-3 is the power for Milli.");
                    break;
```

Figure 3-7

```
        case 3:
                puts("\n3 is the power for Kilo.");
                break;
        case 6:
                puts("\n6 is the power for Mega.");
                break;
        case 9:
                puts("\n9 is the power for Giga.");
                break;
        case 12:
                puts("\n12 is the power for Tera.");
                break;
        default:
                printf("\nThere is no prefix for %d.\n",
                        user_power);
        }
    puts("\nAny more?  1 for YES, 0 for NO: ");

    /* get the value and test it */
    if(scanf("%d", &ans) == 0)
    {
        ans = 0;
    }
    }
    printf("\nThank you!");
}
```

And here is a sample run:

```
A:\>p3-7

This program will tell you the prefix
for any power of ten you input.
What is your power of 10 (e.g., -3)?  -6

-6 is the power for Micro.

Any more?  1 for YES, 0 for NO:
1

This program will tell you the prefix
for any power of ten you input.
What is your power of 10 (e.g., -3)?  -8

There is no prefix for -8.

Any more?  1 for YES, 0 for NO:
1

This program will tell you the prefix
for any power of ten you input.
What is your power of 10 (e.g., -3)?  0

There is no prefix for 0.

Any more?  1 for YES, 0 for NO:
0

Thank you!
A:\>
```

Figure 3-7 (Continued)

3-3 RESISTANCE OF A WIRE

A piece of wire has a property that is fundamental to electronic circuits—the property is called "resistance." We can calculate the resistance of any piece of wire if we know (1) the material the wire is made from, (2) the length of the wire, and (3) the cross-sectional area of the wire. All of these quantities must be in a consistent set of units. For example, the property of the wire material that lets us calculate the resistance is called the "resistivity" and is usually listed in wire tables using the unit "ohm-circular mil/ft." That dictates that the length must be given in feet and the cross-sectional area in circular mils if we want to calculate resistance in ohms. The symbol for resistivity that is commonly used in formulas is the Greek lowercase letter ρ (rho, pronounced "row").

The circular mil (CM) is an invented unit that makes calculation of the cross-sectional area of a round wire easier. A mil is 0.001 inch, so a square mil is the area of a square that is 1 mil on a side. Figure 3-8 shows a square mil while Fig. 3-9 shows what a circular mil is: the cross-sectional area of a circle 1 mil in diameter. Notice that a CM is a little smaller than a square mil—smaller by the amount of area that is shaded in Fig. 3-9. For a circle having a diameter of 1 mil,

$$A = \pi\, r^2 = \pi(\tfrac{1}{2})^2 = \pi/4 \text{ square mil}$$

Another way of stating this relationship is

$$1 \text{ square mil} = 4/\pi \text{CM}$$

Consider a wire having a diameter of k mils. Its area in square mils is $\pi(k/2)^2 = \pi(k^2/4)$. To find the area in CM, multiply by the number of CMs in 1 square mil, $4/\pi$. The result is that the area is simply k^2 CM. Thus early engineers did not have to include π in their calculations of resistance; it was built in to the value of ρ. With calculators and computers available, we no longer need the CM, but because values of ρ in ohm-CM/foot have been the traditional ones published, we maintain that tradition.

The $\rho l/A$ Approach

The formula for this calculation is

$$R = \rho l/A$$

where ρ is the resistivity
l is the length,
A is the cross-sectional area

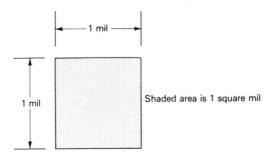

|← 1 mil →|

1 mil

Shaded area is 1 square mil

Figure 3-8 Cross-sectional area of a square.

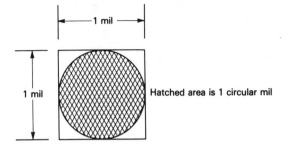

Hatched area is 1 circular mil

Figure 3-9 Cross-sectional area of a circle.

Let's set up a sample session. We'll have the program prompt the user with this:

Let's set up a sample session. We'll have the program prompt the user with this:

```
This program calculates the resistance of a copper wire.

What is the length in feet?
What is the diameter in inches?

The resistance is ___ ohms.
```

We're restricting ourselves to copper wire at this point to make the program a little less involved.

Here are the steps needed in the solution:

1. Prompt for length in feet. Store result in **length**.
2. Prompt for diameter in inches. Store in **diam**. Convert to circular mils, calculate the area, and store in **A**.
3. Calculate the resistance **R**.
4. Display the results.

Figure 3-10 shows a program that will do the job.

The "for" Loop

Before we leave the **R = rho * l/A** formula, let's write a program to print a table for the resistance of a copper wire of different lengths, say, every 10 feet from 10 feet to 100 feet long. All we need to do is enclose the basic **R = rho * l/A** program inside a loop like this one:

```
length = 10.0;
while (length <= 100.0)
{

    [R = rho * l / A program]

    length += 10.0;

}
```

```
/******************************************************************
        R = (rho)L/A calculation for copper wire
******************************************************************/

#define rho 10.37
#include <stdio.h>

main()
{
    float R, length, diam, mils, A;

    /* Prompts and input */
    printf("\nThis program calculates the resistance of a");
    printf(" copper wire.\n");
    printf("\nWhat is the length in feet?  ");
    scanf("%f", &length);
    printf("What is the diameter in inches?  ");
    scanf("%f", &diam);

    /* Some calculations */
    mils = diam * 1000.0;
    A = mils * mils;

    R = rho * length / A;

    /* The result is displayed */
    printf("The resistance is %.2f ohms.", R);
}
```

Figure 3-10

Notice that **length** is mentioned in three statements, on three different lines of code. This kind of looping is done better with a **for** loop, because the **for** loop places all three references to **length** in one statement. The equivalent **for** loop would be

```
for (length = 10.0; length <= 100.0; length += 10.0)
{
    [R = rho *l / A program]
}
```

Inside the parentheses, we see not one but three expressions, separated by semicolons, not commas. (*Note:* This is a new use for the semicolon.) We can call them "initialization," "loop condition," and "adjustment," respectively. The first and third expressions are frequently assignment statements (e.g., $i = 0$, or **length = 10.0**) or increment expressions (e.g., $++i$); the middle one is usually a conditional expression (e.g., $i < num$, or **length <= 100.0**). Here's how **for** works. First, the first expression, the initialization, is evaluated: **length = 10.0** means, as usual, "length gets 10.0". Then expression 2, the loop condition, is evaluated: **length <= 100.0** is either TRUE or FALSE, depending on the value of **length**. If this expression is TRUE, the statements inside the braces are executed. After that, expression 3, the adjustment, is evaluated, followed by another evaluation

```
/*************************************************************
        Produces a table of resistance values
*************************************************************/
#define rho 10.37
#include <stdio.h>
main()
{
        float R, length, diam, mils, A;

        /* Prompts and inputs  */
        printf("\nThis program produces a table of the resistances");
        printf(" of a copper wire \nof different lengths.\n\n");
        printf("What is the diameter in inches?  ");
        scanf("%f", &diam);

        /* Calculation of area */
        mils = diam * 1000.0;
        A = mils * mils;

        /* display the heading for the table */
        printf("\n\n\t\t%s\t\t%s\n\t\t%s\t\t%s\n\t\t%s\n",
          "length", "resistance", "(feet)", "(ohms)",
          "-----------------------");

        /* The for loop controls the calculations and output */

        for (length = 10.0; length <= 100.0; length += 10.0)
        {
                R = rho * length / A;
                printf("\t\t%6.2f\t\t%6.4f\n", length, R);
        }
}
```

Figure 3-11

of the condition.   If the value of the condition is TRUE, the statements inside the
braces are again executed.   The adjustment is evaluated again, and then the condition.   This continues until the condition evaluates to FALSE.   At that point,
the first statement after the closing brace will be executed and we will have exited
from the loop.

The **for** loop is used somewhat more frequently in C programming than the
while loop because it is more flexible and thus more powerful, so mark it well.
We'll see examples of this flexibility later in the book.

Our table of resistance values is produced by the program in Fig. 3-11, with
results shown in Fig. 3-12.

Formatting Decimal Numbers

Notice how nicely formatted our tabular values are.   The lengths all have two
decimal places and the decimal points are all lined up.   The resistances have four
decimal places and also have an aligned column of decimal points.   The "secret"

```
This program produces a table of the resistances of a copper wire
of different lengths.

What is the diameter in inches?  .020
```

length	resistance
(feet)	(ohms)

10.00	0.2592
20.00	0.5185
30.00	0.7778
40.00	1.0370
50.00	1.2962
60.00	1.5555
70.00	1.8147
80.00	2.0740
90.00	2.3333
100.00	2.5925

Figure 3-12

to the alignment lies in an extension of the **printf**( ) format. In the program, we used

```
printf("\t\t%6.2f\t\t%6.4f\n", length, R);
```

The first format is "**%6.2f**". This means "display a float number in 6 columns with two digits to the right of the decimal point." Graphically, this is shown as

xxx.xx

Note that the decimal point occupies a column. The second format is "**%6.4f**" or

x.xxxx

C is generally not a very forgiving language, but here it makes an exception. If the number we want to output is too large to fit the format, C will ignore the format. If the number is too small, C will put blanks in the leftmost columns that have no digits.

3-4 TEMPERATURE EFFECTS IN A WIRE

Suppose that we change our **rho * l/A** program to include the effects of temperature on the value of resistance, as given by the formula

$$R_2 = R[1 + \alpha_{20}(T_2 - 20)]$$

where R_2 is the resistance at temperature T_2
R is the resistance at 20°C
α_{20} is the temperature coefficient of resistance at 20°C (for copper, the value is 0.00393)

All we need to do is add a prompt for the temperature and a calculation for R_2. The new program appears in Fig. 3-13.

```
/************************************************************
  Determine the value of resistance at a different temperature
 *************************************************************/
#define rho 10.37
#define alpha 0.00393
#include <stdio.h>
main()
{
    float R, length_inch, length, diam, mils, A, temp, R2;

    /* prompts and inputs */
    printf("\nThis program calculates the resistance of a");
    printf(" copper wire.\n");

    printf("\nWhat is the length in feet?  ");
    scanf("%f", &length_inch);

    printf("What is the diameter in inches?  ");
    scanf("%f", &diam);

    printf("What is the temperature in degrees C?  ");
    scanf("%f", &temp);

    /* calculations */
    mils = diam * 1000.0;
    A = mils * mils;

    R = rho * length / A;
    R2 = R * ( 1 + alpha * ( temp - 20) ); /* calculation */

    /* display results */
    printf("The resistance is %.2f ohms at %.1f degrees C.",
                R2, temp);
}
```

Some sample results:

```
A:\>p306

This program calculates the resistance of a copper wire.

What is the length in feet?  .5
What is the diameter in inches?  .02
What is the temperature in degrees C?  25
The resistance is 0.01 ohms at 25.0 degrees C.


A:\>p306

This program calculates the resistance of a copper wire.

What is the length in feet?  1
What is the diameter in inches?  .01
What is the temperature in degrees C?  30
The resistance is 0.11 ohms at 30.0 degrees C.


A:\>p306

This program calculates the resistance of a copper wire.

What is the length in ?  8.33
What is the diameter in inches?  .005
What is the temperature in degrees C?  40
The resistance is 3.73 ohms at 40.0 degrees C.


A:\>
```

Figure 3-13

Sec. 3-4   Temperature Effects in a Wire

Note that we used two sets of parentheses and no brackets in the calculation, even though the original equation had one set of parentheses inside a set of brackets. While algebra treats ( ) and [ ] and {} as equivalent symbols, C (and most other languages) treat them completely differently. We must use *only* parentheses in algebraic expressions.

Specifying the Type of Wire

There's a more general form of the temperature effect formula, one that works between any two temperatures. It is

$$\frac{(-T + T_1)}{R_1} = \frac{(-T + T_2)}{R_2}$$

where T is the inferred absolute temperature of a particular material ($-234.5°C$ for copper)

T_1 and T_2 are the two temperatures
R_1 and R_2 are the two resistances

For example, suppose that the resistance of a copper wire is 50 ohms at 20°C. What will it be at 100°C?
Solution:

$$(234.5 + 20)/50 = (234.5 + 100)/R_2$$

or

$$R_2 = 334.5 * 50/254.5 = 65.72 \text{ ohms}$$

I used the formula in assignment statement form:

$$R_2 = (-T + T_2) * R_1/(-T + T_1)$$

We want to write a program that handles this calculation, but if it asks the user to input the inferred absolute temperature of the material, we might be expecting too much of him. After all, how many people know what the inferred absolute temperature of a given material is? Instead of that, we could build the values for a small list of materials into the program and prompt the user to select from the list of materials. The program would select the correct value from a list of values. The screen might look like Fig. 3-14.

The Array

Whenever we are confronted with a collection or set of values, we often find it convenient to store them in a special variable called an **array** variable. Think of an array variable as a box divided into several compartments. For example, the array variable for this program could be called **iat[ ]** (for *inferred absolute temperature*); the "[]" tells C that this is an array variable. Array variables are used in a somewhat different way from simpler variables, so please pay careful attention to this example. Our **iat[ ]** box will have four compartments, one each for aluminum, copper, gold, and nickel. The value stored in a compartment will be the inferred absolute temperature for that material (see Fig. 3-15).

```
This program will calculate the resistance at a given
temperature of a wire made from a given material.
You must also give the wire's resistance at a known temperature.

What is the known resistance (ohms) ?
At what temperature (degrees C)?
What is the new temperature (degrees C)?

Is the wire made from:
     1.  Aluminum
     2.  Copper
     3.  Gold
     4.  Nickel
Enter the number (1, 2, 3, or 4):

A wire which has a resistance of ___ ohms at ___ degrees C
will have a resistance of ___ ohms at ___ degrees C.
```

Figure 3-14

C insists on knowing how many compartments an array variable has (four, in this case). Thus the declaration for this array variable will be

```
float iat[4];
```

The [] tells C that **iat** is an array variable and the 4 specifies the number of compartments **iat** has (i.e., the number of **elements** in **iat**, or the **size** of **iat**); you **must** have both brackets and an integer number inside them. Since **iat** contains values, it must be declared with the data type it contains, in this case, **float**. *Note:* Every value contained in an element of **iat**[] must be the same data type.

Figure 3-16 contains a suggested program for us to examine.

First, we see the declarations

```
float iat[4];
float r1, r2, t1, t2;
```

which could have been written as

```
float iat[4], r1, r2, t1, t2;
```

along with

```
int wire;
```

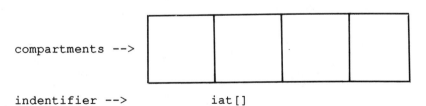

Figure 3-15 A prototype for "iat[4]".

```
/**********************************************************
    Inferred absolute temperature resistance calculation
**********************************************************/
#include <stdio.h>
main()
{
    /* declaring the array */
    float iat[4];

    /* declaring the simple variables */
    float r1, r2, t1, t2;
    int wire, i;

    /* give each element of the
       array its own value */
    iat[0] = 236.0;    /* aluminum */
    iat[1] = 234.5;    /* copper   */
    iat[2] = 274.0;    /* gold     */
    iat[3] = 147.0;    /* nickel   */

    /* prompts and inputs */
    printf("\nThis program will calculate the resistance at a ");
    printf("given\ntemperature of a wire made from a given ");
    printf("material.\nYou must also give the wire's resistance");
    printf("\n at a known temperature.\n");

    printf("\nWhat is the known resistance (ohms) ?   ");
    scanf("%f", &r1);

    printf("At what temperature (degrees C)?  ");
    scanf("%f", &t1);

    printf("\nWhat is the new temperature (degrees C)?  ");
    scanf("%f", &t2);

    printf("\n\nIs the wire made from:\n");
    printf("        1.  Aluminum\n");
    printf("        2.  Copper\n");
    printf("        3.  Gold\n");
    printf("        4.  Nickel\n");
    printf("Enter the number (1, 2, 3, or 4):  ");
    scanf("%d", &wire);

    /* calculations */
    r2 = r1 * (iat[wire - 1] + t2) / (iat[wire - 1] + t1);

    /* display results */
    printf("\n\nA wire which has a resistance of %.2f ohms
            at %.2f degrees C", r1, t1);
    printf("\nwill have a resistance of %.2f ohms at %.2f
            degrees C.", r2, t2);
}
```

Figure 3-16

Here, I have declared the array variable **iat**, the four **floats**, and a new **int** variable, **wire**. **wire** is the user's response—1, 2, 3, or 4—to the question that asks him to specify the material the wire is made from. I used the following values:

```
iat[0] = 236.0;    /* aluminum */
iat[1] = 234.5;    /* copper   */
iat[2] = 274.0;    /* gold     */
iat[3] = 147.0;    /* nickel   */
```

Notice that I have initialized each element in **iat** as if it were a separate variable. This is permissible because **iat[4]** is an "aggregate" variable (i.e., it is made up of four individual variables). You can treat each of the elements the same way that you would treat a simple variable such as **r1** or **r2**. The result of initialization is shown in Fig. 3-17. There are four elements, but the values in the brackets are numbered 0, 1, 2, and 3. That's the way C counts, starting at ZERO rather than ONE. Incidentally, the bracketed values are called **subscripts** or **indexes** (or **indices**—pronounced "*IN-dih-seas*," if you want to be strictly correct!) and must be **ints**.

Here is the beginning of the program.

```
printf("\nThis program will calculate the resistance at a given");
printf("\ntemperature of a wire made from a given material.");
printf("\nYou must also give the wire's resistance at a known");
printf("\ntemperature.\n");
printf("\nWhat is the known resistance (ohms) ?    ");
scanf("%f", &r1);

printf("At what temperature (degrees C)? ");
scanf("%f", &t1);

printf("\nWhat is the new temperature (degrees C)? ");
scanf("%f", &t2);

printf("\n\nIs the wire made from:\n");
printf("      1.  Aluminum\n");
printf("      2.  Copper\n");
printf("      3.  Gold\n");
printf("      4.  Nickel\n");
printf("Enter the number (1, 2, 3, or 4):  ");
scanf("%d", &wire);
```

These are the usual kinds of prompts and inputs. Nothing new here.

```
r2 = r1 * (iat[wire - 1] + t2) / (iat[wire - 1] + t1);
```

```
index or subscript -->    0     1     2     3


   contents -->        | 236.0 | 234.5 | 274.0 | 147.0 |


   indentifier -->         iat[]                        Figure 3-17
```

This is the heart of the program. It contains the strange-looking variable

`iat[wire - 1]`

which has the expression

`wire - 1`

as its subscript. Whenever the compiler sees an expression, it will evaluate it. In this case it will subtract one from the value stored in **wire**. Subtracting one adjusts the user's input value (1, 2, 3, or 4) to one of the subscripts (0, 1, 2, or 3, respectively). For example, if the user had entered "4" to select nickel as the material, we would want the program to use the value assigned to **iat[3]** because it is the value for nickel. Suppose that in response to the prompts, the user had entered

50

20

100

2

After substituting, the computer would evaluate

$$50 * (234.5 + 100)/(234.5 + 20)$$

and assign that value to r1. 234.5 is **iat[2-1]**.

```
printf("\n\nA wire which has a resistance of %.2f ohms at
        %.2f degrees C", r1, t1);
printf("\nwill have a resistance of %.2f ohms at %.2f
        degrees C.", r2, t2);
```

The final two statements provide the output, and are similar to **printf()** statements for output that we have used in the past.

Initializing an array. In the problem above, I did not initialize the array in the declaration, but used four assignment statements in the program to give a value to each element of the array. C does permit us to initialize an array. A suitable initialization for the program above is

```
float iat[4] = { 236.0, 234.5, 274.0, 147.0 };
```

The braces are mandatory. That is, initialize an array of numeric values by listing the values separated with commas, between a pair of braces.

Arrays and Loops

Because an array subscript is always an integer and because the control variable of a loop is often an integer, the combination of arrays and loops occurs quite frequently. For example, Fig. 3-18 shows a program that accepts values for the elements of an array and then displays each value.

```
#include <stdio.h>
main()
{
     /* declare the array but don't initialize it */
     float array[5];
     int i;

     printf("\nPlease enter five numbers as I ask for them.\n");

     /* a loop for getting five values from the user
        and putting them into the array   */
     for (i = 0; i < 5; ++i)
     {
          printf("\nEnter number %d:  ", i + 1);
          scanf("%f", &array[i]);
     }

     /*  humorous remark follows.... */
     printf("\nThank you.\n\nWait a second; I'm thinking.....\n");
     printf("\nYou entered the following numbers:\n\n");

     /* a loop for displaying the contents of each
        array element */
     for (i = 0; i < 5; ++i)
     {
          printf("%8d  %f\n", i + 1, array[i]);
     }

     printf("\nBye now.\n\n");
}
```

A:\>p317

Please enter five numbers as I ask for them.

Enter number 1: 1.23456

Enter number 2: -9

Enter number 3: 22.4

Enter number 4: 3.14158

Enter number 5: 0

Thank you.

Wait a second; I'm thinking.....

You entered the following numbers:

```
     1   1.234560
     2  -9.000000
     3   22.400000
     4   3.141580
     5   0.000000
```

Bye now.

A:\>   **Figure 3-18**

The loop

```
for (i = 0; i < 5; ++i)
{
        printf("\nEnter number %d:   ", i + 1);
        scanf("%f", &array[i]);
}
```

expands into the following code as **i** takes on each of the values 0 through 4:

```
printf("\nEnter number 1:   ");
scanf("%f", &array[0]);

printf("\nEnter number 2:   ");
scanf("%f", &array[1]);

printf("\nEnter number 3:   ");
scanf("%f", &array[2]);

printf("\nEnter number 4:   ");
scanf("%f", &array[3]);

printf("\nEnter number 5:   ");
scanf("%f", &array[4]);
```

As before, we number the array elements starting at zero. But notice that I prompted the user with 1, 2, 3, 4, 5 rather than 0, 1, 2, 3, 4 just to make life a little easier for people who want to start counting at 1 rather than at 0.

The second loop expands in much the same way.

3-5 OHM'S LAW AND SIMILAR RELATIONSHIPS

Ohm's law is stated as

$$V = I * R$$

where V is the voltage across the resistor, in volts
I is the current in the resistor, in amperes
R is the resistance of the resistor, in ohms.

Notice the striking similarity between $V = I * R$ and the formula we used to relate charge, current, and time, $Q = I * t$. Because of this, we should be able to use the same programs we wrote for the $Q = I * t$ equation. All we have to do is change Q to V and t to R (and of course we'll have to change the prompts, too). But there is no new programming to be done.

This is an important principle of programming, mathematics, and engineering: "Don't reinvent the wheel!" In other words, if you have solved a problem that is similar or—as you have here—mathematically identical to another, use what you did on the previous solution (program).

With that in mind, we can consider that we have solved not only $V = I * R$, but also $W = P * t$ (work = power × time), $P = V * I$ (power = voltage × current), and the efficiency equation: power_out = efficiency × power_in.

3-6 USING *YES* AND *NO* IN LOOPS

In a previous program, we asked the user to enter 1 if she wanted the program to execute again and 0 if she didn't. Although there is nothing wrong with that approach, you might have wondered why we didn't use good old "YES" and "NO." To do so requires that we work with a string instead of a simple integer. The problem is that C does not have a string variable. However, it uses an array of characters as a kind of string variable.

Strings of Characters

An array of characters (named **ans**) is declared like this:

```
char ans[4];
```

Recall that each keystroke is a character—'Y', 'E', 'S', 'N', 'O', and so on. To save a single character, we use a **char** variable. To save a group (or string) of characters, we use a **char** array.

We have two ways of getting a string from the keyboard and placing it into our character array:

```
scanf("%s", ans);
```

and

```
gets(ans).
```

[Compare these with the two ways to get a **single** character from the keyboard: *scanf("%c",&choice)* and *choice = getchar()*.] The two string functions behave almost identically to each other when used as shown: They put each character, in the order typed, into the array **ans,** and put a '\0' character (called "the null character") after the last character keyed. For example, suppose that we had the following in a program:

```
char ans[5];
        .
        .
        .
printf("Enter YES or NO:  ");
scanf("%s", ans);
        .
        .
```

And suppose that the user typed "y" "e" "s" and then hit the enter key. If we then inspected the elements of **ans**, we would see what is displayed in Fig. 3-19. Notice that <cr>, the character that corresponds to the enter key, is not stored in the array! **scanf()** treats the <cr> as a delimiter; that is, when the user taps the enter key, **scanf()** knows that there is no more input coming.

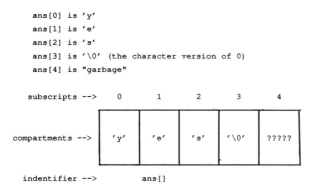

```
ans[0] is 'y'
ans[1] is 'e'
ans[2] is 's'
ans[3] is '\0'  (the character version of 0)
ans[4] is "garbage"


 subscripts -->     0      1      2      3      4



compartments -->   'y'    'e'    's'   '\0'   ?????



  indentifier -->        ans[]
```

Figure 3-19

A '**\0**' at the end of a bunch of characters in a character array is a C requirement; it tells the functions that manipulate strings where a string ends. If the '**\0**' is missing, these functions will return strange results. Certain C functions—**gets( )** and **scanf( )** in particular—put the '**\0**' there automatically. Others do not. If you use a function that doesn't put '**\0**' at the end of a string, **you** are responsible for placing the '**\0**' into the proper compartment. Also, you must declare the array with enough elements so that **gets( )** or **scanf( )** has a place to put the '**\0**'. Since I declared

`char ans[5];`

ans[ ] has enough room for four characters and a null.

Did you notice that the arrangement to **scanf( )** and **gets( )** was the name of the array, **ans,** and not something with an **&**? This is **not** an error! As I mentioned earlier, array variables are somewhat different from simple variables, and this is one of those differences. You recall that *scanf( )* needs to know the address of the variable it is getting a value for. In C, the **name** of an array is the address that *scanf( )* needs; it is the address of the first element of the array. That is, **ans** is a synonym for **&ans[0]**. So when we use the name of an array in a **scanf( )** or **gets( )**, we don't need to use the ampersand. Once *scanf( )* knows where the array starts, it can calculate where the individual elements are stored.

We will use **scanf( )** for our string inputs simply because we have more experience with it at this time. Later, we will use **gets( )** because it is a simpler function. C programmers tend to avoid using **scanf( )** whenever they can because it has some "tricky" behaviors. We have avoided tricky behaviors so far by using **scanf( )** with just two arguments—the format string and the variable—and will continue to do so.

The %s conversion character. The ability to use **%s** in **scanf("%s", ans)** is a big bonus. Without it, we would be forced to write code like this:

```
for (i = 0; i < 5; ++i)
{
     scanf("%c", &ans[i]);
}
ans[i]='\0';   /* must do this ourselves! */
```

in its place. That would input to the array, one character at a time. There would be no difference in what the user sees, but we would be forced to type many extra keystrokes. And we might have forgotten to tack on the '\0'.

Testing String Variables

How can we get the program to look at the array **ans** and see what the user entered? [Yes, we could use **printf**() but that would show *us*, not the program, what she entered.] We would like to be able to say something like

```
if ( ans == "yes" )
```

or

```
while (ans == "yes")
```

but we cannot. Since C doesn't have string variables, it cannot make simple relational tests on strings. Too bad. Instead, C provides a **string comparison** function from the library. It looks like this

```
strcmp ( string1, string2 )
```

The two string arguments can be the names of character arrays or they can be constant strings or they can be one of each. For example, "yes" is a constant (i.e., "literal") string. **strcmp**() returns 0 when the two strings are identical, and some other integer when they are not. So instead of

```
if ( ans == "yes" )
```

or

```
while ( ans == "yes" )
```

we can say

```
int test;
   . . .
test = strcmp(ans, "yes");
if (test == 0)
{
   . . . .
}
```

or the more compact

```
if ( strcmp(ans, "yes") == 0 )
{
   . . . .
}
```

My choice for a while loop is

```
while ( strcmp(ans, "yes") == 0 )
{
   . . . .
}
```

That is, "as long as the value returned by *strcmp()* is **0**, execute the statements between the braces." Notice that I have again used the *name* of the array **ans** as an argument of a function. Here's how **strcmp**() works. **strcmp(ans, "yes")** will cause the MPU to look into memory at the value of **ans[0]**, and compare it with the 'y', the first character of the string "**yes**". If they are different, **strcmp**() stops and returns a nonzero value. If they are the same, **strcmp**() will not return anything but will revisit memory to look at **ans[1]**, the second element of **ans**, and compare it to 'e', the second character of "**yes**". It will continue until there is either (a) a difference in the two characters, (b) one of the characters is '**\0**', or (c) both are '**\0**'. If (c) happens, it means that the strings are the same. If (b) happens, it means that one string is shorter than the other, so they are different for that reason. That is, the strings are identical as far as they go. For example, the strings "art" and "artist" would produce a (b) result. And if (a) occurs, it means that the

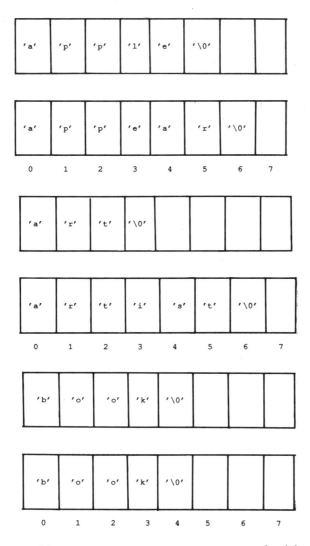

Figure 3-20

Applying C to Simple Problems   Chap. 3

strings are just different and we know nothing about their lengths. Figure 3-20 shows three pairs of strings, corresponding to (a), (b), and (c) as discussed.

Note: "Empty" cells may contain garbage!

In Fig. 3-20(a), the strings are identical at subscripts 0, 1, and 2, but at 3, one has the character 'l' while the other has 'e'. **strcmp**() will stop comparing at subscript 3 and report that there is a difference. In Fig. 3-20(b), the first character of difference occurs at subscript 3: One string has a null while the other has 'i'. For our purposes, there is no real difference between (a) and (b); we are interested only in whether or not the strings are identical. In Fig. 3-20(c), you see that the two strings are identical.

Since we are using a string function, **strcmp**(), we must have the line

```
#include <string.h>
```

before

```
main ()
```

This will import some definitions and declarations (contained in the header file **string.h**) that the compiler needs in order to use **strcmp**() properly.

Initializing a string array In our original program, we initialized the **int** variable **ans** to 1, and in a recent example, we initialized **iat[4]** to **iat[4] = { 236.0, 234.5, 274.0, 147.0 }**. Now, we must initialize the **char** array **ans** to "**yes**". You would expect to see something like

```
char ans[4] = { 'y', 'e', 's', '\0' };
```

That is, the string **yes** consists of four characters: **y, e, s,** and the null. C has a special declaration for initializing character arrays:

```
char ans[4] = "yes";
```

Incidentally, it is not always necessary to include the "4" when you initialize an array. That is, we could have written

```
char ans[] = "yes";
```

The compiler would then count up the number of characters in the initialization string and set aside an element for each, *plus* an element for the '**\0**'. So the effect is the same as if we had written

```
char ans[4] = "yes";
```

Note: This initialization is new to C, having been written in as part of the 1989 standard. If you are using a C compiler that does not support the 1989 standard, you will need to read its manual on initializing arrays. Since Turbo C does support the standard, I will say no more.

An Example Program

Figure 3-21 displays the program.

Note that the first line of the program is

```
#include <string.h>
```

```
#include <string.h>
#include <stdio.h>
main()
{
      int user_power;

      /* initialize the array so that the loop begins properly  */
      char ans[] = "yes";

      while (strcmp (ans, "yes") == 0)
      {
            printf("\nThis program will tell you the prefix for");
            puts("\nfor any power of ten you input.");
            printf("What is your power of 10 (e.g., -3)?  ");
            scanf("%d", &user_power);

            switch(user_power)
            {
            case -12:
                  puts("\n-12 is the power for Pico.");
                  break;
            case -9:
                  puts("\n-9 is the power for Nano.");
                  break;
            case -6:
                  puts("\n-6 is the power for Micro.");
                  break;

            case -3:
                  puts("\n-3 is the power for Milli.");
                  break;
            case 3:
                  puts("\n3 is the power for Kilo.");
                  break;
            case 6:
                  puts("\n6 is the power for Mega.");
                  break;
            case 9:
                  puts("\n9 is the power for Giga.");
                  break;
            case 12:
                  puts("\n12 is the power for Tera.");
                  break;
            default:
                  printf("\nThere is no prefix for %d.\n",
                  user_power);
            }

            /* get an answer from the user and
               put it in the array  */
            printf("\nAny more?  Enter yes or no: ");
            scanf("%s", ans);
      }
      printf("\nThank you!");
}
```

Figure 3-21

It tells the compiler to look for a header file called **string.h**. This file contains information that insures that the compiler will understand what we mean by **strcmp( )**. We will leave as an exercise the questions of what to do if the user enters **YES** (instead of **yes**), and if she enters neither **yes/YES** nor **no/NO**.

3-7 RESISTOR COLOR CODES

As you know, fixed carbon resistors have colored bands printed at one end. The colored bands correspond to numbers in a way that let us determine the resistance of that resistor. For example, a resistor with gray, red, and orange bands would be an 82-kilohm resistor. Using the table in Fig. 3-22, let us write a program that will accept a resistor value and report the colors that would be on the three bands.

Value	Color	Value	Color	
0	Black	5	Green	
1	Brown	6	Blue	
2	Red	7	Violet	
3	Orange	8	Gray	
4	Yellow	9	White	**Figure 3-22**

An Array of Strings

Since we have a set of 10 "colors," we would like to use an array variable to hold the names of the colors. From our earlier discussion, you will recall that "black" is a string, an array of characters. So we could declare (and initialize) 10 arrays, one for each color. But what we want is ONE array that has 10 character arrays as its elements, a kind of "super-array"! In other words, we want an array of strings. Its declaration might look like this:

```
        string colors[10] =
        {
                "black",
                "brown",
                "red",
                "orange",
                "yellow",
                "green",
                "blue",
                "violet",
                "gray",
                "white"
        } ;
```

That is pretty close to legal C, but not quite: C does not have a data type called "string"! Before we look at the correct C for this, review to be sure that you understand that we are trying to declare an array of 10 elements, each of which is a string (i.e., an array of characters).

Since each element is itself an array, we really have an array containing 10 *arrays of char*, or

```
char colors[10][??]
```

The "10" means that there are 10 elements; the "??" represents the number of characters in each element. Since there are a different number of characters in color name (e.g., "red" has two, "orange" has six), we choose the worst case, 7. (Why not 6?) Thus our legal C declaration is

```
char colors[10][7] =
{
    "black", "brown", "red", "orange", "yellow",
    "green",  "blue", "violet", "gray", "white"
};
```

A diagram of memory would show

	0	1	2	3	4	5	6
0	b	l	a	c	k	0	
1	b	r	o	w	n	0	
2	r	e	d	0			
3	o	r	a	n	g	e	0
4	y	e	l	l	o	w	0
5	g	r	e	e	n	0	
6	b	l	u	e	0		
7	v	i	o	l	e	t	0
8	g	r	a	y	0		
9	w	h	i	t	e	0	

It is important for you to understand that each element of the super-array **colors** is a character. Figure 3-23 shows a program that will help us understand this array of arrays (also called a "two-dimensional array") a bit better.

Displaying the contents of an array of strings. Look at the **printf** statement. It treats **colors[i][j]** as if it were **colors[i]**. That's just what we wanted: **colors[i]** is a one-dimensional array where each element is a string! The **for** loop translates into the 10 statements

```
printf("%d   %s\n", 0, colors[0]);
printf("%d   %s\n", 1, colors[1]);
printf("%d   %s\n", 2, colors[2]);
```

```
#include <stdio.h>
main()
{
        char colors[10][7] =
        {
                "black",
                "brown",
                "red",
                "orange",
                "yellow",
                "green",
                "blue",
                "violet",
                "gray",
                "white"
        };

        int i;
        for (i = 0; i < 10; ++i)
        {
                printf("%d    %s\n", i, colors[i]);
        }
}
```

Figure 3-23

```
printf("%d    %s\n", 3, colors[3]);
printf("%d    %s\n", 4, colors[4]);
printf("%d    %s\n", 5, colors[5]);
printf("%d    %s\n", 6, colors[6]);
printf("%d    %s\n", 7, colors[7]);
printf("%d    %s\n", 8, colors[8]);
printf("%d    %s\n", 9, colors[9]);
```

What we have done is use the subscript, i, of the array variable, colors[i], to "visit" each member of the array, colors[0] through colors[9], and print its value. The %s argument of **printf**() takes an entire string of data, so we can refer to a string in the array of strings simply by thinking of the array as if C actually had a string data type!

Here's the output:

```
0    black
1    brown
2    red
3    orange
4    yellow
5    green
6    blue
7    violet
8    gray
9    white
```

This approach lets us think of the array in memory as if it were

0	black0
1	brown0
2	red0
3	orange0
4	yellow0
5	green0
6	blue0
7	violet0
8	gray0
9	white0

Did you notice that the subscript of each color in this array is the number that corresponds to the color in the color code chart? We'll use that in the program.

Determining the Color Code

Let's get back to our problem. The user is going to enter a resistance value in ohms, and the program will output the color code. We'll need a variable, say R, to hold the resistance value input by the user. We'll then calculate three values— one for each color band—and then look up the colors. For example, suppose that the user enters 27000 as the resistance value. The three color band numbers would be 2, 7, and 3 (the number of zeros). How can we isolate the "2", then the "7", and then count the number of zeros? One way is to divide by 10 repeatedly until a two-digit number remains.

$$27000/10 = 2700$$

$$2700/10 = 270$$

$$270/10 = 27$$

For 27000, we had to divide three times to get a two-digit number, and there are three zeros. That is not a coincidence; let's try it with 4500000 to illustrate further.

$$4500000/10 = 450000$$

$$450000/10 = 45000$$

$$45000/10 = 4500$$

$$4500/10 = 450$$

$$450/10 = 45$$

4500000 has five zeros and required five divisions. We conclude that we must divide our original resistance value by 10 over and over until the result is a two-digit number. How can we tell when we get a two-digit number? Easy. A two-digit number MUST be less than 100. (It also must be bigger than 9.999999, but we won't need to use that piece of information.)

OK, we now have a two-digit number, and we also have the third value, the number of times the program divided the original resistance to get a two-digit value; it corresponds to the third color. The first two values are the two digits in our two-digit number. How can we isolate each of the two digits? If we divide by 10 again, we get 2.7, and if we could throw away the 0.7, we'd have our first value, 2. (The process of dropping the digits to the right of the decimal point is called "truncation.") Then we could multiply the 2 by 10 to get 20, and subtract 20 from our original two-digit number (27) to get the second value, 7. Let's write that out:

```
fraction = two_digit_number / 10
value_1 = truncated fraction
value_2 = two_digit_number - 10 * value_1
```

Casting One Data Value to Another Type.   But how to do the truncation? It looks like we have a mixture of reals and integers, and the results of doing arithmetic with such a mixture is always real.   C has an interesting property called **cast**.   "Casting" temporarily changes the data type of a value from what it is to what we want.   In this case, if we change the **float** value 2.7 to an **int**, we will get 2.   Then we can assign the 2 to an **int** variable.   To cast a value to an **int**, just write **(int)** in front of the name of the variable—the parentheses tell C that this is a cast.   This will truncate the value stored in the variable.   For example, if *fraction* has the value 2.7, then *(int) fraction* has the value 2 (not 2.0, but 2).

Figure 3-24 shows our program.

Now let's inspect the pieces of the code.

```
temp = R;


while ( temp >= 100.0 )
{
    temp = temp / 10.0;
    ++val_3;
}
```

In this section of code, we set up a temporary variable, **temp**, to hold the results of successive divisions by 10.0 (it is always a good idea to avoid mixing data types in a calculation, so I decided to divide the float variable **temp** by a float constant, 10.0).   The **while** loop is set up to terminate as soon as temp is less than 100.0, i.e., when **temp** is a two-digit number (we'll ignore digits to the right of the decimal point; we're going to truncate them, anyway).   Inside the loop, we divided temp by 10.0, stored the result in **temp**, and incremented **val_3**.   There is a shorter form of the division assignment statement:

```
temp /= 10.0;
```

```
#include <stdio.h>
main()
{
      int val_1, val_2, val_3 = 0;
      float R, temp;

      /* initialize the array of strings */
      char colors[][7] =
      {
            "black",
            "brown",
            "red",
            "orange",
            "yellow",
            "green",
            "blue",
            "violet",
            "gray",
            "white"
      };

      /* prompt for an input */
      printf("Enter a resistance value in ohms:  ");
      scanf("%f", &R);

      /* process the resistance value entered */
      temp = R;          /* it's good practice to keep
                            the original value */

      while ( temp >= 100.0 )
      {
            temp = temp / 10.0;
            ++val_3;
      }
      /* temp is now < 100; a two-digit number */

      val_1 = (int) (temp / 10.0); /* the "cast" */
      val_2 = (int) (temp - 10.0 * val_1); /* another one */

      /* look up the colors and display them */
      printf("The color code is: %s - %s - %s.",
            colors[val_1], colors[val_2], colors[val_3]);
}
```

Figure 3-24

(Remember + = from an earlier discussion?   C has lots of these!) As the comment says, the loop will terminate as soon as temp is a two-digit number.

```
      val_1 = (int) (temp / 10.0); /* the "cast" */
      val_2 = (int) (temp - 10.0 * val_1);
```

In the first assignment statement, we divide **temp**, a two-digit **float** number, by 10.0 and cast the result to an **int**.   For example, had **temp** been 39.0, then

```
Enter a resistance value in ohms:  220
The color code is: red - red - brown.

Enter a resistance value in ohms:  3.3e3
The color code is: orange - orange - red.

Enter a resistance value in ohms:  5.6e6
The color code is: green - blue - green.       Figure 3-25
```

temp/10.0 would have been 3.9 and the casting would have changed the value to
3. The cast value is then assigned to **val_1**.

Next we multiply **val_1** by 10.0 and subtract from **temp**. Using the same
numbers,

$$39.0 - 10.0 * 3 = 39.0 - 30.0 = 9.0$$

This result is cast to an **int** and assigned to **val_2**. Whenever we assign a **float**
value to an integer, it is a good idea to cast it to an **int** first. This will show
whoever reads our program that we had intended to do that, and that assigning a
real number to an integer variable wasn't an error.

```
printf("The color code is: %s - %s - %s.",
       colors[val_1], colors[val_2], colors[val_3]);
```

This outputs three strings. Each comes from the colors array, and each is
determined by the subscript: **val_1** for the first, **val_2** for the second, and **val_3**
for the third. Figure 3-25 shows some results.

3-8 TESTING YOUR KNOWLEDGE

Let's write a "drill" program on the color code. The program will present a
resistance value to the user, who will input three colors. Then the program will
tell him if he's right or wrong.

Random Numbers

The first thing we need is a routine to generate three integer digits, each in the
range 0 to 9. C has a function, **rand()**, which returns a random integer value in
the range from 0 to 32767. The declaration information for **rand()** is in the header
file **stdlib.h**.

Recall that C has two kinds of integer division: one gives the quotient and
the other, the remainder. Quotient division uses the / symbol; remainder or
"modulus" division uses the % symbol. For example, 9/6 → 1 (i.e., the quotient
is 1), but 9 % 6 → 3 (i.e., the remainder is 3). If we divide **rand()** by 10 and
keep the remainder, we should get integers in the range 0 to 9. When C divides
an **int** by another **int**, the result is also an **int**. That is, 9/6 → 1, not 1.5.

Figure 3-26 shows a program to produce some random numbers with values
that lie between 0 and 9, and its output.

Output of the program:

```
#include <stdlib.h>
#include <stdio.h>

main()
{
    int i;

    for (i = 1; i <= 200; ++i)
    {
        printf("%4d", rand() % 10);
        if (i % 8 == 0)
        {
            printf("\n");
        }
    }
}
```

8	6	4	8	1	9	2	0
2	1	3	7	9	1	0	5
4	9	2	1	9	6	1	1
5	3	4	0	9	5	1	2
9	8	6	4	2	3	6	4
9	1	7	0	5	2	8	6
7	2	4	9	9	3	6	1
0	8	5	9	0	3	3	9
5	2	3	7	6	8	0	8
6	0	2	2	7	5	6	8
6	9	8	9	1	7	5	1
5	0	0	1	7	5	3	7
2	1	3	3	4	3	6	8
6	0	4	4	1	9	6	0
4	1	2	5	3	6	4	0
8	4	9	8	5	6	5	0
3	0	8	6	7	4	8	0
3	5	9	3	0	2	5	1
9	2	4	1	0	0	1	6
3	5	2	2	3	8	2	1
1	1	2	2	2	4	8	5
9	3	2	6	5	5	9	3
2	6	9	3	9	7	0	6
3	2	8	7	3	6	5	7

Figure 3-26

To get three integers, we'll call **rand()** and do the indicated arithmetic three times. From the three numbers, we'll calculate the resistance value by forming a two-digit number from the first two digits, and then multiplying that by 10 n times, where n is the third digit. For example, suppose that the digits were 1, 7, and 4. Then we'd have

```
two_digit = first * 10 + second
two_digit = 1 * 10 + 7
two_digit = 17
```

```
r = two_digit;
for (i = 1; i < n; ++i)
{
        r = r * 10;
}
```

```
17 * 10 = 170
170 * 10 = 1700
1700 * 10 = 17000
17000 * 10 = 170000
```

So the resistance is 170000 ohms. We have to be a bit careful because of the limitations of the **int** data type. Recall that an **int** can be only as large as 32,767, and a **long int**, as large as 2,147,483,647. The color code is good for resistors up to 99,000,000,000, a value larger than the largest integer in C (on a PC)! Even an **unsigned long int** is not large enough. So we must either use a **float** when we calculate the resistance, or limit the third digit.

The program will accept three strings from the user and compare them with what the program has found for the three colors. I hope our users can spell!

The Example Program

Here's the layout of our program:

1. Initialize the **colors[10][7]** array.
2. Generate the three digits.
3. Find the colors corresponding to them.
4. Calculate the resistance.
5. Tell the user.
6. Accept three colors.
7. Compare to correct colors.
8. Say "Yay!" or "Boo!".

Figure 3-27 shows the program. Notice the format, **%.1e**, in the **printf()** that displays the resistance value. This will display the value in scientific form with one digit on either side of the decimal point. This makes it easy for the user to identify the first two digits. The exponent is actually one greater than the third digit.

Additional Randomness

If we run this program, we will find that it produces exactly the same resistance value every time. Our random number generator does not seem to be so random. Actually, random number generators need a new starting point if we want a new sequence of numbers each time we use one. The starting value is called the "seed" and is provided in C by using the function, **srand()**, with a nonnegative integer parameter value, for example, **srand(27)**. Let's get a number from the computer's

```
#include <string.h>
#include <stdlib.h>
#include <stdio.h>

main()
{
    int val_1, val_2, val_3, i, two_digit;
    float R;  /* I decided to use float rather than limit R */

    char band1[7], band2[7], band3[7];

    char colors[][7] =
    {
        "black",
        "brown",
        "red",
        "orange",
        "yellow",
        "green",
        "blue",
        "violet",
        "gray",
        "white"
    };

    /* generate three random numbers */
    val_1 = rand() % 10;
    val_2 = rand() % 10;
    val_3 = rand() % 10;

    /* calculate the resistance */
    two_digit = val_1 * 10 + val_2;
    R = (float) two_digit;

    for ( i = 1; i < val_3; ++i)
    {
        R *= 10.0;
    }

    /* prompt for input */
    printf("What's the color code for a %.1e ohm resistor?\n", R);
    printf("Enter band 1: ");
    scanf("%s", band1);
    printf("Enter band 2: ");
    scanf("%s", band2);
    printf("Enter band 3: ");
    scanf("%s", band3);

    /* test the user's answer */
    if ( (strcmp(colors[val_1], band1) == 0) &&
         (strcmp(colors[val_2], band2) == 0) &&
         (strcmp(colors[val_3], band3) == 0) )
```

Figure 3-27

```
{
        printf("\nCorrect!!\n\n");
}
else
{
        printf("\n Nope!  The correct answer is %s %s %s\n",
            colors[val_1], colors[val_2], colors[val_3]);
}
}
```

Figure 3-27   (Continued)

internal clock by using the **time(0)** function, and use it as the seed value.   **time()**
is an ANSI standard function.   It returns a **long** integer value equal to the number
of seconds since midnight, Greenwich Mean Time, on January 1, 1970, a "traditional" watermark.

```
#include <time.h>  /* needed by time()  */
srand(time(0));
```

Put the **srand()** anywhere in the program before the first call to **rand()**.   Figure
3-28 shows some results.

The response the program gives when the user is wrong could use a little
work because the answers are given in lowercase letters and may not stand out.
Turbo C has a function that converts all of the lowercase characters in a string to
uppercase characters.   It is called **strupr()** and it is not part of ANSI Standard C,
but we'll use it anyway.   Let's use it so that the output line will be

```
Nope!  The correct answer is VIOLET GREEN RED
```

The last **printf()** will change from

```
printf("\n Nope!  The correct answer is %s %s %s\n",
color[val_1], color[val_2], color[val_3]);
```

to

```
printf("\n Nope!  The correct answer is %s %s %s\n",
        strupr(color[val_1]),
        strupr(color[val_2]),
        strupr(color[val_3]));
```

Figure 3-29 shows the enhanced program.   Try it!   It works beautifully!!

Adjusting the Case of the Input

As long as I've presented a program that includes a nonstandard function, I might
as well go a bit further and improve it with another nonstandard function, *strlwr()*,
the opposite of *strupr()*.   We'll use it on each string the user inputs to insure that
we compare the lowercase version of what the user inputs to the lowercase strings
in the **color** array.   Figure 3-30 shows the final version of this program.

```
A:>prog0312

What's the color code for a 2.8e+006 ohm resistor?
Enter band 1: red
Enter band 2: gray
Enter band 3: blue


Correct!!


A:>prog0312

What's the color code for a 7.5e+002 ohm resistor?

Enter band 1: violet
Enter band 2: green
Enter band 3: orange


Nope!  The correct answer is violet green red

A:>prog0312

What's the color code for a 6.3e+004 ohm resistor?

Enter band 1: blue
Enter band 2: orange
Enter band 3: yellow


Correct!!
```

Figure 3-28

```
#include <time.h>     /* needed by time()   */
#include <string.h>
#include <stdlib.h>  /* needed by rand() and srand() */
#include <stdio.h>

main()
{
      int val_1, val_2, val_3, i, two_digit, seed;
      float R;
      char band1[7], band2[7], band3[7];
```

Figure 3-29

```
            char color[][7] =
    {
        "black",
        "brown",
        "red",
        "orange",
        "yellow",
        "green",
        "blue",
        "violet",
        "gray",
        "white"
    };

    /* set the seed */
    srand(time(0));

    val_1 = rand() % 10;
    val_2 = rand() % 10;
    val_3 = rand() % 10;

    two_digit = val_1 * 10 + val_2;
    R = (float) two_digit;

    for ( i = 1; i < val_3; ++i)
    {
        R *= 10.0;
    }

    printf("What's the color code for a %.1e ohm resistor?\n", R);
    printf("Enter band 1: ");
    scanf("%s", band1);
    printf("Enter band 2: ");
    scanf("%s", band2);
    printf("Enter band 3: ");
    scanf("%s", band3);

    if (  (strcmp(colors[val_1], band1) == 0) &&
          (strcmp(colors[val_2], band2) == 0) &&
          (strcmp(colors[val_3], band3) == 0) )
    {
        printf("\nCorrect!!\n\n");
    }

    else
    {
        printf("\n Nope!  The correct answer is %s %s %s\n",
            strupr(colors[val_1]),
            strupr(colors[val_2]),
            strupr(colors[val_3]));
    }
}
```

Figure 3-29   (Continued)

```
#include <time.h>      /* needed by time()   */
#include <string.h>
#include <stdlib.h>  /* needed by rand() and srand() */
#include <stdio.h>

main()
{
    int val_1, val_2, val_3, i, two_digit;
    float R;
    char band1[7], band2[7], band3[7];
    char color[][7] =
    {
            "black",
            "brown",
            "red",
            "orange",
            "yellow",
            "green",
            "blue",
            "violet",
            "gray",
            "white"
    };

    srand(time(0));

    val_1 = rand() % 10;
    val_2 = rand() % 10;
    val_3 = rand() % 10;

    two_digit = val_1 * 10 + val_2;
    R = (float) two_digit;

    for ( i = 0; i < val_3; ++i)
    {
        R *= 10.0;
    }

    printf("What's the color code for a %.1e ohm resistor?\n", R);
    printf("Enter band 1: ");
    scanf("%s", band1);

    /* now convert the input string to all UPPER CASE LETTERS  */
    strlwr(band1);

    printf("Enter band 2: ");
    scanf("%s", band2);

    /*  same here  */
    strlwr(band2);

    printf("Enter band 3: ");
    scanf("%s", band3);
```

Figure 3-30

```
/*  and here  */
strlwr(band3);

if ( (strcmp(colors[val_1], band1) == 0) &&
     (strcmp(colors[val_2], band2) == 0) &&
     (strcmp(colors[val_3], band3) == 0) )
{
    printf("\nCorrect!!\n\n");
}
else
{
    printf("\n Nope!  The correct answer is %s %s %s\n",
        strupr(colors[val_1]),
        strupr(colors[val_2]),
        strupr(colors[val_3]));
}
}
```

Figure 3-30 (Continued)

3-9 REVIEW

In this chapter you learned about:

- The escape character for the quotation mark
- **switch**
- **case** and **default**
- **break**
- User control of looping: "any more?"
- **scanf**() returning a value
- Setting up a menu of choices for the user
- Array variables
- How to use "yes/no" with "any more?"
- **gets**()
- **strcmp**() and **string.h**
- Initializing an array of characters
- Using an array of strings
- The /= operator
- The **for** statement
- The % operator
- **rand**(), **srand**(), and **time**()

PROBLEMS AND QUESTIONS

1. Write the **escape** characters for newline, tab, and quotation mark.
2. Rewrite the program in Fig. 3-4 using **if . . . else if . . .** instead of **switch**.
3. Write a program that will do Ohm's law calculations, based on the $Q = I \times t$ program.

4. Write a program to do work calculations (word = power × time), based on the $Q = I \times t$ program.

5. Write a program to do power calculations ($P = V \times I$), based on the $Q = I \times t$ program.

6. Write a program that will calculate the current and the power dissipated in a 500-ohm resistor fed by a voltage source that has an initial value of 9.0 volts (V) and falls to 5.0 V in steps of 0.5 V. Print the output in a table.

7. Write a program based on Problem 6 that will accept from the user values for the resistance, the "starting" voltage, the "ending" voltage, and the step size, and produce a table of voltage, current, and power values.

8. Rewrite the program of Fig. 3-10 so that the user is prompted for wire length in *inches*, and the program converts *inches* to *feet*.

9. Rewrite the program of Fig. 3-21 so that the user could enter either **yes** or **YES** to get a repetition.

10. C has a function **toupper(char)** that converts a lowercase character to its uppercase equivalent. The statement

$$\texttt{ch = toupper(ch)}$$

converts **ch** to uppercase if it is a lowercase letter, and does nothing to **ch** if it is anything else. Write a program that accepts a word of up to 24 characters from the user (where will you put the word?) and converts each lowercase letter to uppercase. The program should display both the original word and the new word. *Note:* This program is related to the Turbo C function **strupr()**.

11. The cost for operating an electrical device can be calculated from the formula

$$C = k \times P \times t$$

where C is the total cost in dollars (e.g., 16.34)
$\quad$ k is the cost in dollars per kilowatthour (e.g., .02)
$\quad$ P is the power dissipated in kilowatts
$\quad$ t is the time the device is "on"

Write a program that requests the *watts* dissipated by the device and the cost per kilowatthour in *cents per kWh*. The program is to convert data values as needed, and print a table showing the accumulated cost to operate the device each hour over a 24-hour period.

4

Applying C to DC Circuits

4-1 INTRODUCTION AND OBJECTIVES

We progress in this chapter to reading and writing programs that involve electronic circuits consisting of two or more resistors connected either in series or parallel, or in a "random" fashion. Also, we will learn more about the C language.

Upon successful completion of this chapter, you will be able to:

- Write a program to calculate the equivalent resistance of any number of resistors connected in series
- Write a program to calculate the equivalent resistance of any number of resistors connected in parallel
- Explain why **1e38** is appropriate to use as the value of a missing parallel resistor
- Write a program to calculate the equivalent resistance of any number of resistors connected in a ladder configuration.
- Write a program to calculate the current, voltage, and power dissipated in any part of an electronic circuit consisting of resistors and one voltage source
- Write programs that use the current- and voltage-divider rules
- Write simple functions in C

4-2 EQUIVALENT RESISTANCE

A string of resistors connected all in series or all in parallel can easily be reduced to a single equivalent resistance. If they are all in series, the equivalent resistance is simply the sum of each resistance. That is, $R_T = R_1 + R_2 + R_3 + \cdots$. If they are all in parallel, we need to calculate the conductance of each resistor (recall that conductance is the reciprocal of the resistance), add all the conductances, and take the reciprocal of the sum. You probably know a short cut when there are just two parallel resistors: The equivalent resistance is the product over the sum,

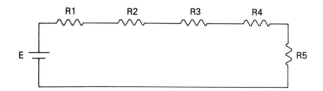

Figure 4-1 A series circuit.

but in general, you need to calculate conductances. To illustrate, we'll write a program to accept the values of up to five resistors and the answer to the question "series or parallel?", and then display the equivalent resistance. Figure 4-1 shows a series circuit with five resistors, while Fig. 4-2 shows a parallel circuit with four resistors. Here's a scheme to solve the problem:

get the number of resistors (from the user)
get the individual resistance values
get the answer to "series or parallel?"
if "series"
     add all values
else
     calculate each conductance
     add all conductances
     take the reciprocal
display result

The program is shown in Fig. 4-3, along with some sample results. Once again, we'll look closely at sections of the code.

```
printf("How many resistors (no more than 5)?  ");
scanf("%d", &num);

if (num > 5)
{
    printf("\n\n\nSorry, wrong number!!\n\n");
    exit(1);    /* bye-bye! */
}
```

If the user enters a value that is greater than 5, he gets an error message from the program, and **exit(1)** is executed. This is a special C function that causes an immediate termination of the program. The number *1* in parentheses is the value that **exit(1)** returns. It is traditional to return a nonzero value if the program

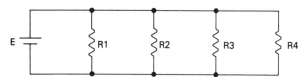

Figure 4-2 A parallel circuit.

```
#include <stdlib.h>   /* for exit() */
#include <stdio.h>
main()
{
        /* the array will hold the values
           of the resistors in the circuit  *
        float R[5], RE = 0, GE = 0;
        int num, conn, i;

        /* prompts and inputs */
        printf("Enter 1 for series or 2 for parallel:  ");
        scanf("%d", &conn);

        printf("How many resistors (no more than 5)?  ");
        scanf("%d", &num);

        /* test for valid input */
        if (num > 5)
        {
                printf("\n\n\nSorry, wrong number!!\n\n");
                exit(1);     /* bye-bye! */
        }

        /* get the values of the resistors */
        printf("Enter their values...\n");
        for (i = 0; i < num; ++i)
        {
                printf("R(%d): ", i + 1);
                scanf("%f", &R[i]);
        }

        /* calculate equivalent, based on
           the circuit connection */
        if (conn == 1)
        {
                for (i = 0; i < num; ++i)
                {
                        RE += R[i];
                }
        }
        else
        {
                for (i = 0; i < num; ++i)
                {
                        GE += (1/R[i]);
                }
                RE = 1/GE;
        }

        printf("The equivalent resistance is %.2f ohms.", RE);
}
```

Figure 4-3 Program for either series or parallel resistors.

```
A:\>p401

Enter 1 for series or 2 for parallel:  1
How many resistors (no more than 5)?  3

Enter their values...
R(1)  100
R(2) : 200.
R(3) : 300

The equivalent resistance is 600.00 ohms.

A:\>p401

Enter 1 for series or 2 for parallel:  2
How many resistors (no more than 5)?  2

Enter their values...
R(1) : 500
R(2) : 500

The equivalent resistance is 250.00 ohms.

A:\>p401

Enter 1 for series or 2 for parallel:  1
How many resistors (no more than 5)?  6

Sorry, wrong number!!

A:\>p401

Enter 1 for series or 2 for parallel:  1
How many resistors (no more than 5)?  5

Enter their values...
R(1): 100
R(2): 10
R(3): 1
R(4): 200
R(5): 300

The equivalent resistance is 611.00 ohms.

A:\>
```

Figure 4-3 (Continued)

is aborted.   However, we will not use the value.   The maximum number of resistors is 5 because of the way we have declared the array *R*.

```
printf("Enter their values...\n");
for (i = 0; i < num; ++i)
{
    printf("R(%d): ", i + 1);
    scanf("%f", &R[i]);
}
```

This piece of code uses the **for** statement for looping. I did a sneaky thing here. You and I are used to numbering things starting at 1, but the computer— especially C—likes to start numbering at 0. So I caused the display to show **R(1)** as the output the first time that **printf("R(%d):", i + 1)** is executed. The value of i is 0, so the first value the user keys will be stored in **R[0]**. **R(1)** is for the user; **R[0]** is for the computer.

```
if (conn == 1)
{
        for (i = 0; i < num; ++i)
        {
                RE += R[i];
        }
}
```

This code fragment shows what happens if the user specifies series connection (i.e., the value of **conn** is **1**). A **for** loop accumulates the sum of the individual resistances. This is the standard method for adding things with a loop: Accumulate a sum by adding the newest value to the total of all previous values. Note the shorthand notation (+ =), and that **RE** *MUST* be initialized to **0** if we want accurate results. That is, the first execution of

```
RE += R[i];
```

will be as if I had coded it like this:

```
RE = RE + R[0];
```

R[0] is the value obtained from the user, but what would the value of **RE** on the right-hand side of the assignment statement be? Whatever it was initialized to. If it is not initialized, the computer will use a garbage value! So the sum will not be correct.

```
else
{
        for (i = 0; i < num; ++i)
        {
                GE += (1/R[i]);
        }
        RE = 1/GE;
}
```

This fragment shows what is executed if the user specifies anything except a 1 for series connection. A third **for** loop sums the reciprocals of the individual resistances. **GE** must be initialized to **0** to insure proper calculations for the reason stated in the preceding paragraph. Outside the loop, a single calculation gets the equivalent resistance from the equivalent conductance.

4-3 SERIES AND PARALLEL CIRCUITS

Consider the circuits shown in Figs. 4-4 and 4-5. The first figure shows three resistors in series with a voltage source; the second, three resistors in parallel with a voltage source. We would like to write a program to calculate the current, voltage, and power dissipation for each resistor and for the entire circuit—for each circuit. We base our calculations on Kirchhoff's voltage law and Ohm's law. In the series circuit,

```
I1 = I2 = I3 = IT = E / (R1 + R2 + R3).
V1 = I1 * R1
V2 = I2 * R2
V3 = I3 * R3
VT = E
P1 = I1 * V1
P2 = I2 * V2
P3 = I3 * V3
PT = IT * VT
```

In the parallel circuit,

```
V1 = V2 = V3 = VT = E
I1 = V1 / R1
I2 = V2 / R2
I3 = V3 / R3
IT = I1 + I2 + I3
P1 = I1 * V1
P2 = I2 * V2
P3 = I3 * V3
PT = IT * VT
```

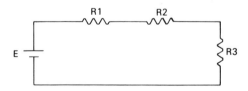

Figure 4-4 A series circuit.

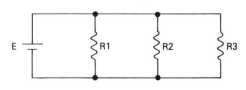

Figure 4-5 A parallel circuit.

Here's the scheme:

get the answer to "series or parallel?"
get the supply voltage
get R1, R2, and R3 values
if "series"
    calculate I1 = I2 = I3 = IT
    calculate V1, V2, V3, VT
else
    calculate V1 = V2 = V3 = VT
    calculate I1, I2, I3, IT
calculate P1, P2, P3, PT
display results

Because the power calculations use the same equations regardless of the circuit connections, I placed them after finding the individual currents and voltages.

When we write a program to do this set of calculations, we would like it to handle both the cases shown and the cases of two series or two parallel resistors. The question is this: If we have a program written for three resistors and our circuit has only two, what value shall we give to the program for the missing resistor? In a series circuit, the missing resistor can be thought of as one that has been replaced by a short circuit, a piece of wire with zero ohms resistance. In the parallel circuit, the missing resistor must be an open circuit or infinite resistance. The problem here is that there is no infinity possible on a computer! So we'll have to instruct the user to enter a very large **float** or **double** number for a missing resistor. Can you think of a good value? How about **1e38**? (Where did that come from?)

The program is in Fig. 4-6. Notice that I didn't use arrays this time. Do you see how much extra typing I had to do?

```
#include <stdio.h>
main()
{
    float R1, R2, R3;
    float I1, I2, I3;
    float V1, V2, V3;
    float E, P1, P2, P3;
    float IT, VT, PT;
    int ans;

    printf("Enter 1 for series or 2 for parallel:  ");
    scanf("%d", &ans);
    printf("What is the supply voltage E?  ");
    scanf("%f", &E);
```

Figure 4-6 Another program for series or parallel resistors.

(Continued)

```
printf("Enter the resistor values...\n");
printf("NOTE: if there is a missing resistor, and you ");
printf("have chosen \"series\"");
printf("\nenter a 0 for its value.  ");
printf("If you have chosen \"parallel\", enter 1e38.\n");
printf("R1 = ");
scanf("%f", &R1);
printf("R2 = ");
scanf("%f", &R2);
printf("R3 = ");
scanf("%f", &R3);

if (ans == 1)  /*  series circuit  */
{
     I1 = I2 = I3 = IT = E / (R1 + R2 + R3);
     V1 = I1 * R1;
     V2 = I2 * R2;
     V3 = I3 * R3;
     VT = E;
}
else  /*  parallel circuit  */
{
     V1 = V2 = V3 = VT = E;
     I1 = V1 / R1;
     I2 = V2 / R2;
     I3 = V3 / R3;
     IT = I1 + I2 + I3;
}

/* independent of connection */
P1 = V1 * I1;
P2 = V2 * I2;
P3 = V3 * I3;
PT = VT * IT;

printf("The results are:\n");
printf("\n\t%s%5.2f\n\t%s%5.2f\n\t%s%5.2f\n\t%s%5.2f\n",
   "V1 = ", V1, "V2 = ", V2, "V3 = ", V3, "VT = ", VT);
printf("\n\t%s%5.2f\n\t%s%5.2f\n\t%s%5.2f\n\t%s%5.2f\n",
   "I1 = ", I1, "I2 = ", I2, "I3 = ", I3, "IT = ", IT);
printf("\n\t%s%5.2f\n\t%s%5.2f\n\t%s%5.2f\n\t%s%5.2f\n",
   "P1 = ", P1, "P2 = ", P2, "P3 = ", P3, "PT = ", PT);
}
```

Figure 4-6   (Continued)

4-4 VOLTAGE- AND CURRENT-DIVIDER RULES

Figure 4-4 showed a series circuit with three resistors. Although we used Ohm's and Kirchhoff's laws to solve for the voltage across each resistor, we could have used a shortcut called the voltage-divider rule. It states that the voltage across any resistor equals the product of its resistance and the total voltage, divided by the total resistance. In a formula,

$$V_x = R_x(V_T/R_T)$$

This is very similar to the $V = IR$ formula, and thus the program we write to deal with the voltage divider will be quite similar to the Ohm's law program.

The current-divider rule occurs in parallel circuits. It states that the current in a resistor is the product of the total current and the total resistance, divided by the resistance of the parallel branch having the unknown current in it.

$$I_x = R_T(I_T/R_x)$$

Again this is quite similar to the Ohm's law formula.

4-5 LADDER NETWORKS

Most electronic circuits are neither exclusively series nor exclusively parallel. They fall into the general category called "series–parallel." A special case of series–parallel is the "ladder network." Figure 4-7 shows one such circuit. The source E is in series with R1 and the rest of the circuit to the right of R1. R2 is in parallel with the circuit to its right. R3 is in series with the circuit to its right. R4 is in parallel with the circuit to its right. R5 is in series with R6. To extend this network, we could add a "horizontal" resistor, R7, to the junction of R5 and R6, and then another resistor from the right end of R7 to the negative voltage source lead. And so on. Adding R7 and R8 will change the relationship between R5 and R6; they will no longer be in series. Only the "last two" resistors are in series. Generally, we want to know two things about this circuit: (1) the equivalent resistance (called the "driving-point resistance") of the ladder as seen by the voltage source, and (2) the current drawn from the source.

To solve this, we must start at the end furthest from the voltage source. The last two resistors, R7 and R8, are in series, as Fig. 4-7 plainly shows. The equivalent resistance, R78, is simply the sum, R7 + R8. R78 is in parallel with R6, and that equivalent resistance, R678, is R6 × R78/(R6 + R78). Now, R678 is in series with R5, so the equivalent resistance, R5678, is R5 + R678. And so on. Here is the process, written in a more general way.

> Get the last resistance value, RV (V because the resistor is drawn vertically)
> Get the next one, RH (H because of its horizontal orientation)
> Calculate the equivalent resistance, RE = RH + RV
>
> If there are any more resistors, get the next (working
>   right-to-left) vertical one, RV
>   Calculate the new RE = RV × RE/(RV + RE)
>   Get the next (still right-to-left) horizontal one, RH
> Calculate the new RE = RE + RH
>
> If there are any more resistors, get the next pair, RV and RH
>
> Calculate the new RE = RH + RV × RE/(RV + RE)
>
> And so on

It looks like there's a pattern here: a vertical resistor, RV, is combined in

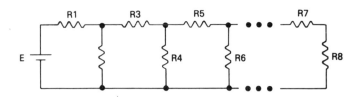

Figure 4-7 A ladder network.

parallel with the previous equivalent resistance, RE. It is followed by a horizontal one, RH, to be combined in series, yielding a new equivalent resistance, RE. Each pair is called a section of the ladder, so we can set up a loop that accepts data for one section, and then repeat that loop for as many sections as there are.

The program is shown in Fig. 4-8. Let's dissect it.

```
#include <string.h>
#include <stdio.h>
main()
{
        char ans[4];
        float rv, rh, re, e;

        printf("What is the supply voltage, E?  ");
        scanf("%f", &e);


        printf("\n\n");


        /* prompt by drawing the circuit */
        printf("\t\t----R1 ----- R3 ----- R5 ----- R7 ---\n");
        printf("\t\t          |       |       |       |\n");
        printf("\t\t          R2      R4      R6      R8\n");
        printf("\t\t          |       |       |       | \n");
        printf("\t\t------------------------------------\n\n");
        printf("First, enter the value of the resistor that's ");
        printf("furthest from the voltage source \n");
        printf("(R8, in the figure), and work your way toward ");
        printf("the source, a section at a time.\n");
        printf("If an R with an even subscript is missing, enter ");
        printf("1e38 as its\nvalue.  If one with an odd subscript");
        printf(" is missing, enter 0.\n");
        printf("NOTE: a section is a pair of resistors.\n\n");

        printf("Vertical resistor value is:  ");
        scanf("%f", &rv);


        printf("Horizontal resistor value is:  ");
        scanf("%f", &rh);


        re = rv + rh;
```

Figure 4-8 Program for a ladder network.

```
        printf("Any more resistors (yes or no)?  ");
        scanf("%s", ans);

        while (strcmp(ans, "yes") == 0)
        {
                printf("Vertical resistor value is:  ");
                scanf("%f", &rv);

                printf("Horizontal resistor value is:  ");
                scanf("%f", &rh);

                re = rh + (re * rv )/( re + rv );

                printf("Any more resistors (yes or no)?  ");
                scanf("%s", ans);
        }

        printf("\nThe driving point resistance is %.4f ohms,", re);
        printf("\nand the supply current is %.4f amps.\n\n", e/re);
}
```

Figure 4-8   (Continued)

The first two lines are preprocessor "#include" lines. We have seen these
before. We need **string.h** because we are using **strcmp()**. The header files are
followed by **main()**, the declarations, and some information for the user (including
a circuit diagram!). Next comes a prompt,

```
        printf("Vertical resistor value is:  ");
        scanf("%f", &rv);
```

that asks for the value of the vertically connected resistor. This is followed by
another prompt,

```
        printf("Horizontal resistor value is:  ");
        scanf("%f", &rh);
```

that asks for a value for the horizontally connected resistor. Next, the program
calculates the equivalent of the rightmost two resistors, and asks if there are any
more.

  If there are more resistors, the program enters a **while** loop and asks for the
next horizontally and vertically connected resistors and calculates the new equivalent resistance. When the user keys **no** in response to the **Any more resistors
(yes or no)?**, the program makes the final calculation and the results are reported.

4-6 SOLVING SPECIFIC CIRCUITS

At this point, we are ready to tackle almost any series–parallel circuit that has one
voltage source. For example, consider Fig. 4-9.

  We see that R1 and R2 are in parallel, and that R4 and R5 are in parallel,
and that R6 and R7 are in series. The R4–R5 combination is in series with R3,

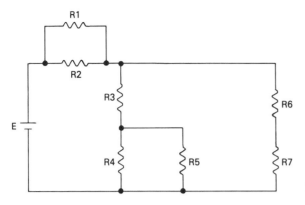

Figure 4-9 A series–parallel circuit.

and the R3–R4–R5 combination is in parallel with the series combination of R6 and R7. R34567 is in series with R12. The most straightforward way to solve this circuit with a computer is to find the equivalent resistance as seen by the voltage source (i.e., the driving-point resistance) and apply Ohm's and Kirchhoff's laws. Before we do, let's point out that we are not building a general method here. You will have to analyze each different circuit with Ohm's and Kirchhoff's laws, and write the needed equations. There are general-purpose electrical circuit programs, but writing one is beyond the scope of this book. Besides, if a good one already exists, why write another? You may be thinking, "If a good program for making calculations for electric circuits exists, why don't we use it instead if writing our own program?" The answer is that we want you to learn something about programming. In industry, you will undoubtedly need to write some programs, but you will also probably have access to one of the good electric circuit programs, too.

Back to our circuit and its program. Let's call the current in the source I, so that

$$I = I1 + I2$$

Also, it is true that

$$I3 = I4 + I5$$

$$I6 = I7$$

and

$$I = I3 + I6$$

If we can find the driving-point resistance, we can find I. Then we can use the current-divider rule to find I1, I3, I4, and I6. Kirchhoff's current law will give us I2, I5, and I7. With all the currents and resistances known, we can calculate each voltage drop and each power dissipation. Figure 4-10 shows the program that does the job.

```
#include <stdio.h>
main()
{
    /* arrays for the resistors and
       calculated values  */
    float R[8], I[8], V[8], P[8];
    float R67, R45, R345, R34567, R12, RT;
    int i;

    printf("This program solves the following circuit:\n\n");
    printf("\n                       -- R1 ---");
    printf("\n                       |       |");
    printf("\n              -------o- R2 --o-o------------------");
    printf("\n              |            |                 |");
    printf("\n              |            |                 |");
    printf("\n              ---          R3               R6");
    printf("\n         E    =            |                 |");
    printf("\n              |            o-----            |");
    printf("\n              |            |   |            |");
    printf("\n              |            R4  R5           R7");
    printf("\n              |            |   |            |");
    printf("\n              -------------------o-----o-----------\n\n");

    printf("Enter the resistance values.   ");
    printf("Use 0 for no series resistor, \n");
    printf("and 1e38 for no parallel resistor:\n\n");

    for (i=1; i<=7; ++i)
    {
        printf("R[%d] = ", i);
        scanf("%f", &R[i]);
    }

    printf("\nEnter the voltage of the source:  ");
    scanf("%f", &V[0]);

    /* calculations specific to this circuit */
    R12     = R[1] * R[2] / (R[1] + R[2]);       /* R1 || R2 */
    R45     = R[4] * R[5] / (R[4] + R[5]);       /* R4 || R5 */
    R345    = R[3] + R45 ;           /* R3 series (R4 || R5) */
    R67     = R[6] + R[7];                   /* R6 series R7 */
    R34567  = R345 * R67 / (R345 + R67); /*     R345 || R67 */
    RT      = R12 + R34567;          /*    driving point R */

    I[0] = V[0] / RT;               /* driving point current */
    I[1] = R[2] * I[0] / (R[1] + R[2]);
    I[2] = I[0] - I[1];
    I[3] = R67 * I[0] / (R345 + R67);
```

Figure 4-10 Program for a specific series–parallel circuit.

```
I[4] = R[5] * I[3] / (R[4] + R[5]);
I[5] = I[3] - I[4];
I[6] = I[0] - I[3];
I[7] = I[6];

for (i=1; i<=7; ++i)
{
    V[i] = I[i] * R[i];
    P[i] = V[i] * I[i];
}

printf("\nThe results are:  \n\n");
for (i=1; i<=7; ++i)
{
    printf("I[%d] = %f, V[%d] = %f, P[%d] = %f\n",
        i, I[i], i, V[i], i, P[i]);
}

printf("\nThe driving point current is %f\n\n", I[0]);
}
```

Figure 4-10 (Continued)

Shall we take this program apart?   The declarations

$$\text{float R[8], I[8], V[8], P[8];}$$

contain arrays for the resistor values and for the calculated values.   You'll see from the code fragments

```
for (i=1; i<=7; ++i)
{
    printf("R[%d] = ", i);
    scanf("%f", &R[i]);
}
```

and

```
for (i=1; i<=7; ++i)
{
    V[i] = I[i] * R[i];
    P[i] = V[i] * I[i];
}
printf("\nThe results are:  \n\n");
for (i=1; i<=7; ++i)
{
    printf("I[%d] = %f, V[%d] = %f, P[%d] = %f\n",
        i, I[i], i, V[i], i, P[i]);
}
```

that using arrays often cuts down on the amount of code we must type, by allowing us to use a loop based on the array subscript instead of having to declare a separate variable for each unknown in the circuit.

The declarations

$$\text{float R67, R45, R345, R34567, R12, RT;}$$

are simply the names of the equivalent resistances of the various sections of the circuit, while the fragment

```
R12      = R[1] * R[2] / (R[1] + R[2]);        /* R1 || R2 */
R45      = R[4] * R[5] / (R[4] + R[5]);        /* R4 || R5 */
R345     = R[3] + R45 ;              /* R3 series (R4 || R5) */
R67      = R[6] + R[7];                   /* R6 series R7 */
R34567   = R345 * R67 / (R345 + R67);      /* R345 || R67 */
RT       = R12 + R34567;                /* driving point R */
```

indicates how each is calculated from the resistor values and from other resistance combinations.   Quite straightforward.

The set of current assignments

```
I[0] = V[0] / RT;          /* driving point current */
I[1] = R[2] * I[0] / (R[1] + R[2]);
I[2] = I[0] - I[1];
I[3] = R67 * I[0] / (R345 + R67);
I[4] = R[5] * I[3] / (R[4] + R[5]);
I[5] = I[3] - I[4];
I[6] = I[0] - I[3];
I[7] = I[6];
```

is the application of Ohm's law, Kirchhoff's current law, and the current-divider rule.   Some sample runs are shown in Fig. 4-11.

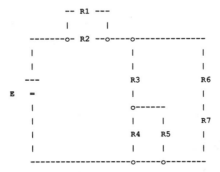

```
A:>p410

This program solves the following circuit:

           -- R1 ---
            |      |
      -------o- R2 --o----o---------------
      |               |               |
      |               |               |
     ---              R3              R6
   E  =              |               |
      |         o------          |
      |         |     |           R7
      |        R4    R5          |
      |         |     |           |
      ---------------------o-----o--------

Enter the resistance values.  Use 0 for no series resistor,
and 1e38 for no parallel resistor:

R[1] = 9
R[2] = 6
```

Figure 4-11   Some sample runs from the program in Fig. 4-10.

```
R[3] = 4
R[4] = 6
R[5] = 3
R[6] = 3
R[7] = 0
```

Enter the voltage of the source: 16.8

The results are:

```
I[1] = 1.200000, V[1] = 10.800000, P[1] = 12.960001
I[2] = 1.800000, V[2] = 10.799999, P[2] = 19.439999
I[3] = 1.000000, V[3] = 4.000000, P[3] = 4.000000
I[4] = 0.333333, V[4] = 2.000000, P[4] = 0.666667
I[5] = 0.666667, V[5] = 2.000000, P[5] = 1.333333
I[6] = 2.000000, V[6] = 6.000000, P[6] = 12.000000
I[7] = 2.000000, V[7] = 0.000000, P[7] = 0.000000
```

The driving point current is 3.000000

A:>p410

This program solves the following circuit:

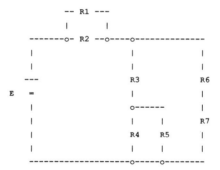

Enter the resistance values. Use 0 for no series resistor,
and 1e38 for no parallel resistor:

```
R[1] = 4
R[2] = 1e38
R[3] = 0
R[4] = 4
R[5] = 4
R[6] = .5
R[7] = 1.5
```

Enter the voltage of the source: 10

Figure 4-11

The results are:

```
I[1] = 2.000000, V[1] = 8.000000, P[1] = 16.000000
I[2] = 0.000000, V[2] = 0.000000, P[2] = 0.000000
I[3] = 1.000000, V[3] = 0.000000, P[3] = 0.000000
I[4] = 0.500000, V[4] = 2.000000, P[4] = 1.000000
I[5] = 0.500000, V[5] = 2.000000, P[5] = 1.000000
I[6] = 1.000000, V[6] = 0.500000, P[6] = 0.500000
I[7] = 1.000000, V[7] = 1.500000, P[7] = 1.500000
```

The driving point current is 2.000000

Figure 4-11 (Continued)

At this point, you may be wondering why we would want to go through this complicated procedure just to produce a few calculated values when you could have done it more easily using your trusty calculator. You know the argument that says that the computer approach saves doing the work of cranking out the numerical answers, but you are not convinced that the added work of entering the source code, correcting your typing errors (we are assuming that you have no logical errors—if you do, it won't matter whether you use a calculator, a computer, or the dean of the college: you won't get the correct answers!), compiling, executing, entering data, and so on. In fact, I agree with you! Solving this kind of problem on the computer is not a really wonderful idea. We do it to illustrate how to use the computer and as an introduction to real problems. For example, a real problem might be stated like this: "Given the circuit of Fig. 4-9 and the resistor values of sample run 2, determine how the power dissipation in R7 changes as the value of R7 changes from 0.5 to 2.5 in steps of 0.1 ohms." Now, we have a real problem involving 20 SETS of calculations! Each set requires about 10 to 15 calculations each. The computer program will do these flawlessly and rapidly. Can you say the same about you and your calculator?

How do we modify the given program to do a repetitive task like the one I just mentioned? One thing we must do is to put most of that program into a loop that is controlled by

```
for (R[7] = 0.5; R[7] < 2.6; R[7] += 0.1)
{
    . . . .
}
```

See how the **for** loop implements the statement "as the value of R7 changes from 0.5 to 2.5 in steps of 0.1 ohm"? Note that I used **R[7] < 2.6** rather than **R[7] <= 2.5**, a more "natural" expression, because of something I know about **floats** and **doubles.** It's this: **floats** and **doubles** stored in memory are always approximations to the actual values that we want to store. For example, because the computer uses binary values in its memory locations, the value 2.5 may be stored as 2.499999999999999999 or 2.50000000000000001—there's no way for us to know which. So, when comparing **float** or **double** values, you must avoid using

```
#include <stdio.h>
main()
{
        float R[8], I[8], V[8], P[8];
        float R67, R45, R345, R34567, R12, RT;
        int i;

        printf("Enter the resistance values.  ");

        for (i=1; i<=6; ++i)   /* 6 instead of 7 */
        {
                printf("R[%d] = ", i);
                scanf("%f", &R[i]);
        }

        printf("\nEnter the voltage of the source:  ");
        scanf("%f", &V[0]);

        /* looping through all the possible
           values of R7   */
        for (R[7] = 0.5; R[7] < 2.6; R[7] += 0.1)
        {
                R12      = R[1] * R[2] / (R[1] + R[2]);  /* R1 || R2 */
                R45      = R[4] * R[5] / (R[4] + R[5]);  /* R4 || R5 */
                R345     = R[3] + R45 ;         /* R3 series (R4 || R5) */
                R67      = R[6] + R[7];          /* R6 series R7 */
                R34567   = R345 * R67 / (R345 + R67); /* R345 || R67 */
                RT       = R12 + R34567;        /* driving point R  */

                I[0] = V[0] / RT;              /* driving point current */

                /* don't need I1 or I2 */

                I[3] = R67 * I[0] / (R345 + R67);
                I[6] = I[0] - I[3];
                I[7] = I[6];

                P[7] = I[7] * I[7] * R[7];

                printf("R[7] = %f, P[7] = %f\n", R[7], P[7]);
        }
}
```

Figure 4-12 Skeleton of a program to vary the value of a resistor and perform a set of calculations for each value.

$==$, $<=$, and $>=$. The chances of two floating-point numbers being absolutely equal to each other is pretty close to 0! Back to the program.

In the loop, we want to calculate the driving-point resistance and whatever currents we need to get the value of I7. Then we can calculate P7. Figure 4-12 shows a skeleton of the program. Figure 4-13 shows the full program. Figure 4-

```c
#include <stdio.h>
main()
{
    float R[8], I[8], V[8], P[8];
    float R67, R45, R345, R34567, R12, RT;
    int i;

    printf("This program solves the following circuit:\n\n");
    printf("\n                    -- R1 ---");
    printf("\n                     |        |");
    printf("\n            -------o- R2 --o--o-----------------");
    printf("\n            |                 |                |");
    printf("\n            |                 |                |");
    printf("\n            ---              R3               R6");
    printf("\n       E    =                 |                |");
    printf("\n            |               o-----             |");
    printf("\n            |               |   |             |");
    printf("\n            |              R4   R5            R7");
    printf("\n            |               |   |             |");
    printf("\n            --------------------o-----o-----------\n\n");

    printf("\nR7 will be varied from 0.5 to 2.5 in steps of 0.1 ohms\n");
    printf("and the power dissipated will be calculated.\n\n");

    printf("Enter the resistance values for the first six resistors.\n  ");
    printf("Use 0 for no series resistor, ");
    printf("and 1e38 for no parallel resistor:\n\n");

    for (i=1; i<=6; ++i)
    {
        printf("R[%d] = ", i);
        scanf("%f", &R[i]);
    }

    printf("\nEnter the voltage of the source:  ");
    scanf("%f", &V[0]);

    /* looping through all the possible values of R7  */
    for (R[7] = 0.5; R[7] < 2.6; R[7] += 0.1)
    {
        R12    = R[1] * R[2] / (R[1] + R[2]);   /* R1 || R2 */
        R45    = R[4] * R[5] / (R[4] + R[5]);   /* R4 || R5 */
        R345   = R[3] + R45 ;                    /* R3 series (R4 || R5) */
        R67    = R[6] + R[7];                     /* R6 series R7 */
        R34567 = R345 * R67 / (R345 + R67);      /* R345 || R67 */
        RT     = R12 + R34567;                    /* driving point R  */
        I[0]   = V[0] / RT;                       /* driving point current */
        I[3]   = R67 * I[0] / (R345 + R67);
        I[6]   = I[0] - I[3];
        I[7]   = I[6];

        P[7]   = I[7] * I[7] * R[7];

        printf("\nR[7] = %.1f ohms, P[7] = %.3f watts", R[7], P[7]);
    }
}
```

Figure 4-13

This program solves the following circuit:

```
                -- R1 ---
                |        |
        -------o- R2 --o---o--------------
        |               |               |
        |               |               |
        ---            R3              R6
    E   =               |               |
        |               o------         |
        |               |     |        R7
        |               |     |         |
        |              R4    R5         |
        |               |     |         |
        --------------------o-----o--------
```

R7 will be varied from 0.5 to 2.5 in steps of 0.1 ohms
and the power dissipated will be calculated.

Enter the resistance values for the first six resistors.
Use 0 for no series resistor, and 1e38 for no parallel resistor:

R[1] = 4
R[2] = 1e38
R[3] = 0
R[4] = 4
R[5] = 4
R[6] = .5

Enter the voltage of the source: 10

R[7] = 0.5 ohms, P[7] = 1.020 watts
R[7] = 0.6 ohms, P[7] = 1.126 watts
R[7] = 0.7 ohms, P[7] = 1.212 watts
R[7] = 0.8 ohms, P[7] = 1.282 watts
R[7] = 0.9 ohms, P[7] = 1.338 watts
R[7] = 1.0 ohms, P[7] = 1.384 watts
R[7] = 1.1 ohms, P[7] = 1.420 watts
R[7] = 1.2 ohms, P[7] = 1.449 watts
R[7] = 1.3 ohms, P[7] = 1.471 watts
R[7] = 1.4 ohms, P[7] = 1.488 watts
R[7] = 1.5 ohms, P[7] = 1.500 watts
R[7] = 1.6 ohms, P[7] = 1.508 watts
R[7] = 1.7 ohms, P[7] = 1.513 watts
R[7] = 1.8 ohms, P[7] = 1.515 watts
R[7] = 1.9 ohms, P[7] = 1.515 watts
R[7] = 2.0 ohms, P[7] = 1.512 watts
R[7] = 2.1 ohms, P[7] = 1.508 watts
R[7] = 2.2 ohms, P[7] = 1.503 watts
R[7] = 2.3 ohms, P[7] = 1.496 watts
R[7] = 2.4 ohms, P[7] = 1.488 watts
R[7] = 2.5 ohms, P[7] = 1.479 watts

Figure 4-14   Output of the program in Fig. 4-13.

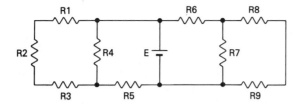

Figure 4-15 A series–parallel circuit.

14 shows a sample run (the computer produced the table in a couple of seconds!). That table at the bottom of Fig. 4-14 is the result of over 200 calculations!

Let's do one more specific circuit (Fig. 4-15). Problem statement: If the source voltage is 72 V, and the resistors are

R1 = 4 kilohms   R2 = 8 kilohms

R3 = 12 kilohms   R4 = 24 kilohms

R5 = 12 kilohms   R6 = 12 kilohms

R7 = 9 kilohms   R8 = 3 kilohms

R9 = 6 kilohms

find I5, I, and V7.

The solution involves Ohm's law and the voltage-divider rule.

$$R123 = R1 + R2 + R3$$

$$R1234 = R123 \parallel R4$$

$$R12345 = R5 + R1234$$

$$R89 = R8 + R9$$

$$R789 = R7 \parallel R89$$

$$R6789 = R6 + R789$$

$$RT = R12345 \parallel R6789$$

$$I5 = E/R12345$$

$$IT = E/RT$$

$$V7 = E * R789/(R789 + R6)$$

Our program is given in Fig. 4-16. The results are shown in Fig. 4-17.

The important thing that you should have noticed by now is that the computer does not analyze the circuit for you. It doesn't know Ohm's law or Kirchhoff's laws or any of those things. But *you* do. *You* write the circuit equations. *You* rewrite them in assignment statement form. *You* write the program. Then, the computer does the work of plugging in the numbers and cranking out the solutions.

```
#include <stdio.h>
main()
{
    float R[10], E, I5, V7, IT;
    float R123, R1234, R12345, R89, R789, R6789, RT;
    int i;

    printf("This program solves the following circuit:\n\n");
    printf("     --- R1 ---|----------|--- R6 ---|--- R8 ---|\n");
    printf("     |          |          |          |         |\n");
    printf("     R2         R4        ---        R7         |\n");
    printf("     |          |     E =            |         |\n");
    printf("     |          |          |          |         |\n");
    printf("     --- R3 ---|--- R5 ---|----------|--- R9 ---|\n");
    printf("\n\n\n");

    printf("Enter the resistance values.  ");
    printf("Use 0 for no series resistor, \n");
    printf("and 1e38 for no parallel resistor:\n\n");

    for (i=1; i<=9; ++i)
    {
        printf("R[%d] = ", i);
        scanf("%f", &R[i]);
    }

    printf("\nEnter the voltage of the source:  ");
    scanf("%f", &E);

    R123    = R[1] + R[2] + R[3];
    R1234   = R123 * R[4] / (R[4] + R123);
    R12345  = R[5] + R1234;
    R89     = R[8] + R[9];
    R789    = R[7] * R89 / (R[7] + R89);
    R6789   = R[6] + R789;
    RT      = R12345 * R6789 / (R12345 + R6789);

    I5 = E / R12345;
    IT = E / RT;
    V7 = E * R789 / (R789 + R[6]);

    printf("\nThe results are:  \n\n");
    printf("I5 = %f, IT = %f, V7 = %f\n\n", I5, IT, V7);
}
```

Figure 4-16 Program for another specific series–parallel circuit.

This program solves the following circuit:

```
--- R1 ---|----------|--- R6 ---|--- R8 ---|
 |         |          |          |          |
R2        R4         ---        R7          |
 |         |     E =  |          |          |
 |         |          |          |          |
--- R3 ---|--- R5 ---|----------|--- R9 ---|
```

Enter the resistance values. Use 0 for no series resistor,
and 1e38 for no parallel resistor:

R[1] = 4e3
R[2] = 8e3
R[3] = 12e3
R[4] = 24e3
R[5] = 12e3
R[6] = 12e3
R[7] = 9e3
R[8] = 3e3
R[9] = 6e3

Enter the voltage of the source: 72

The results are:

I5 = 0.003000, IT = 0.007364, V7 = 19.636364

Figure 4-17   Results from the program of Fig. 4-16.

4-7 WRITING YOUR OWN FUNCTIONS

One of the things that experience has taught computer scientists is that there is a
limit to the size program that a person can grasp all at once. A program that has
code that covers pages and pages of paper will contain so much that very few people
will understand it. So we try to simplify our programming by breaking the program
up into pieces (called **modules**). Each module will do just one job, one that is
both useful as far as the program is concerned, yet small enough to be easily
understood by the programmer. Then, **main**() will do little more than call each
module as needed. These modules are called **functions** in C. You have already
used several C functions—functions that are supplied as part of the standard C
library, but now it is time to learn how to write your own. For example, in the
last few programs, we included line drawings of the circuits. Those drawings,
implemented with a bunch of **printf()s**, were of great help to the user, but they

```
void ladder_picture(void)
{
        printf("\n\n");
        printf("\t\t----R1 ----- R3 ----- R5 ----- R7 ---\n");
        printf("\t\t          |        |        |       |\n");
        printf("\t\t          R2       R4       R6      R8\n");
        printf("\t\t          |        |        |       | \n");
        printf("\t\t-------------------------------------\n\n");
}
```

Figure 4-18 A simple function.

took up a lot of room in the source program. Wouldn't it be nice if we could take up all those lines of code and tuck them away somewhere under a name of our choice and just call them when we want them? It sure would be, and what's more, it's easy to do. We could test that group of statements, correcting them until they produced the circuit diagram we want, and then put them aside. To do this just write a function that draws the circuit picture and call the function from **main**().

A Simple Function

The definition of the function for the picture of the ladder network would look like Fig. 4-18. This is the definition for a function that neither returns a value nor receives one. The **void** before the function name indicates that **ladder_picture**() does not return a value, while the one inside the parentheses indicates that it does not receive one. Please take careful note that there is *no* semicolon (;) on the line with the function's name (this line is called the "function header" line). The absence of the semicolon tells the compiler that this is a *definition*, not a request to use the function and not its declaration. When the function is declared, that line will end in a semicolon. When the function is used (i.e., when it is "called" or when it is "invoked"), each calling statement will end in a semicolon. But the header line takes *no* semicolon!

Everything between the braces is the definition of the function. Before we can use this function, we must change **main**(). First we replace all the lines of code that previously produced the picture with the one line

ladder_picture();

This is a request to use the function (a **function call** or **invocation**).

And we must declare the function, too. The declaration will appear in the declaration section of the function that calls it [remember that **main**() is a function] and may be the same as the first line of the definition (the header) with a semicolon appended:

void ladder_picture(void);

This is known as a **prototype** declaration, and tells the compiler to display an error message if anyone tries to use the value the function does not return or if anyone tries to pass a value to the function. With these changes, our ladder network program becomes Fig. 4-19.

```
#include <string.h>
#include <stdio.h>
main()
{
      void ladder_picture(void);
      char ans[4], input[10];
      float rv, rh, re, e, i;

      printf("What is the supply voltage, E?  ");
      scanf("%f", &e);

      /* now call the function to draw the circuit */
      ladder_picture();

      printf("First, enter the value of the resistor ");
      printf("that's furthest ");
      printf("from the voltage source \n");
      printf("(R8, in the figure), and work your way ");
      printf("toward the source, ");
      printf("a section at a time.\n");

      printf("If an R with an even subscript is missing, ");
      printf("enter 1e38 as its ");
      printf("\nvalue.  If one with an odd subscript is ");
      printf("missing, enter 0.\n");
      printf("NOTE: a section is a pair of resistors.\n\n");
      printf("Vertical resistor value is:  ");
      scanf("%f", &rv);

      printf("Horizontal resistor value is:  ");
      scanf("%f", &rh);
      re = rv + rh;

      printf("Any more resistors (yes or no)?  ");
      scanf("%s", ans);

      while (strcmp(ans, "yes") == 0)
      {
            printf("Vertical resistor value is:  ");
            scanf("%f", &rv);

            printf("Horizontal resistor value is:  ");
            scanf("%f", &rh);

            re = rh + (re * rv )/( re + rv );

            printf("Any more resistors (yes or no)?  ");
            scanf("%s", ans);
      }
      printf("\nThe driving point resistance is %.4f ohms,", re);
      printf("\nand the supply current is %.4f amps.\n\n", e/re);
}
```

Figure 4-19 Ladder network program with a user-defined function.

Sec. 4-7   Writing Your Own Functions

```
/* This function draws a circuit diagram on the screen. */

void ladder_picture(void)
{
      printf("\n\n");
      printf("\t\t----R1 ----- R3 ----- R5 ----- R7 ---\n");
      printf("\t\t         |         |         |         |\n");
      printf("\t\t         R2        R4        R6        R8\n");
      printf("\t\t         |         |         |         | \n");
      printf("\t\t---------------------------------\n\n");
}
```

Figure 4-19 (Continued)

```
#include <string.h>
#include <stdio.h>
main()
{
      void ladder_picture(void), prompts(void);

      char ans[4], input[10];
      float rv, rh, re, e, i;

      printf("What is the supply voltage, E?  ");
      scanf("%f", &e);

      ladder_picture();

      prompts();

      printf("Vertical resistor value is:  ");
      scanf("%f", &rv);

      printf("Horizontal resistor value is:  ");
      scanf("%f", &rh);

      re = rv + rh;

      printf("Any more resistors (yes or no)?  ");
      scanf("%s", ans);

      while (strcmp(ans, "yes") == 0)
      {
            printf("Vertical resistor value is:  ");
            scanf("%f", &rv);

            printf("Horizontal resistor value is:  ");
            scanf("%f", &rh);

            re = rh + (re * rv )/( re + rv );
```

Figure 4-20 Ladder network program with two user-defined functions.

```
                    printf("Any more resistors (yes or no)?   ");
                    scanf("%s", ans);
        }

            printf("\nThe driving point resistance is %.4f ohms,", re);
            printf("\nand the supply current is %.4f amps.\n\n", e/re);
    }


    /*  Draws a circuit diagram on the screen */

    void ladder_picture(void)
    {
            printf("\n\n");
            printf("\t\t---- R1 ----- R3 ----- R5 ----- R7 ---\n");
            printf("\t\t          |        |        |        |\n");
            printf("\t\t          R2       R4       R6       R8\n");
            printf("\t\t          |        |        |        | \n");
            printf("\t\t--------------------------------------\n\n");
    }


    /* Displays all prompts for the program */

    void prompts(void)
    {
            printf("First, enter the value of the resistor that's");
            printf(" furthest ");
            printf("from the voltage source \n");
            printf("(R8, in the figure), and work your way toward ");
            printf("the source, ");
            printf("a section at a time.\n");

            printf("If an R with an even subscript is missing, ");
            printf("enter 1e38 as its ");
            printf("\nvalue.  If one with an odd subscript is ");
            printf("missing, enter 0.\n");
            printf("NOTE: a section is a pair of resistors.\n\n");
    }
```

Figure 4-20   (Continued)

Another Simple Function

Let's do the same thing with the instructions under the drawing; that is, replace them in **main**() with a function call. This function will also consist of a bunch of **printf**() statements and will neither return a value nor accept one. The definition of this function and, indeed, the new version of the program, are shown in Fig. 4-20.

A Function That Calculates

The function that neither receives a value nor returns one is the easiest to write and use. The next more involved type of function is one that accepts one or more values from the **calling function** and returns one value to it. [The **calling function** is nothing more than the function that calls the one we have written. So far, we have called them from **main( )**, but any function can call another function. For example, in the function *prompts( )*, we called *printf( )* several times.]

Incidentally, the limit for the number of values returned from a function in C is **one**. (There's an excellent way around this limit, and we'll examine it in a subsequent chapter.) The assignment statement

```
re = rh + (re * rv )/( re + rv );
```

is simple enough to use as the basis of a function definition. (Actually, it is too simple to be a practical function, but it will illustrate the ideas behind functions that accept values and return a result.)

Note that the statement calculates **re**, given values for **re**, **rv**, and **rh**. We will arrange to have the function accept values for **re**, **rv**, and **rh**. Then, when **main( )** (or whatever the calling function is named) calls the function, it will "pass" three values to the function. The function will calculate the new equivalent resistance and return it to **main( )**. We say that the calling function passes values to the called function, and the called function returns a value to the calling function. Here, in Fig. 4-21, is the definition of the required function.

```
float r_equiv(float r1, float r2, float r3)
{
        float temp;
        temp = r1 + (r2 * r3) / (r2 + r3);
        return (temp);
}
```

Figure 4-21 A function that accepts and returns values.

Consider the header line

```
float r_equiv(float r1, float r2, float r3)
```

The declaration **float** appears four times in the header. The first **float** says that **r_equiv( )** will return a **float** value. The prototypes inside the parentheses declare three variables, each of type **float**. *Note:* You are not allowed to write

```
float r_equiv(float r1, r2, r3)
```

You must specify a data type for each parameter. The calling function [**main( )**, in this example] will pass three **float** values to r_equiv( ). The call (in the calling function) might be

```
r_equiv(22.6, -1.0, 1e3);
```

or

```
r_equiv(Rh, Re, Rv);
```

or any combination of **float** constants and variables. Where does the calling function get the values for **Rh**, **Re**, and **Rv**? That's not our problem! When we write the function that processes these values, we must assume that the calling function will have them. Our job is to accept them into our function and see that our function does the right thing with the values.

What happens to the value **r_equiv()** returns? It is returned to the calling function, and then it's up to the programmer. Usually he will assign it as the value of some variable. In our example, the original assignment statement

```
re = rh + (re * rv )/( re + rv );
```

would be replaced in the calling function by the assignment statement

```
re = r_equiv(rh, re, rv);
```

The values that **rh, re,** and **rv** have at the moment that **r_equiv()** is called will be passed to the function **r_equiv()**. The function will do the calculation indicated in its definition, and return a value which is then assigned to **re.** That is, "**re** gets the value returned by **r_equiv().**"

The variable **temp** is "local" to **r_equiv().** That is, **main()** cannot use it. In fact, **main()** doesn't even know that **temp** exists. Only **r_equiv()** knows that. This is true of all local variables: Only the function in which they are declared knows about them. What makes temp **local** is that it is declared between the braces in the definition of the function that uses it.

return is used to signal the value that is to be returned by the function. Incidentally, **return** can take an expression, so that we could have written the function definition like this:

```
float r_equiv(float r1, float r2, float r3)
{
        return ( r1 + (r2 * r3) / (r2 + r3) );
}
```

but that is a little harder to read than the original definition.

Students are frequently puzzled by function definitions and ask "Where do the values for **r1, r2,** and **r3** come from? Don't I have to prompt the user for them? Where does the calculated value go? Don't I have to **printf()** it?" The answers are (1) "the calling function," (2) "no," (3) "the calling function," and (4) "no." As I pointed out above, the calling function is responsible for providing the values, and for taking care of the value our function returns. Normally, we do not use *scanf()* or *printf()* in the functions we write to do calculations. We accept values from the calling function and return a value to it.

The declaration in **main()** (i.e., the calling function) will be a prototype:

```
float r_equiv(float, float, float);
```

There is no need to list variable names in the declaration (but it is permissible), just the types. We are telling the compiler that each actual parameter is supposed to be a **float,** so it can tell us if we make an error by trying to pass an **int** or **char.**

Here's what the program will look like (see Fig. 4-22).

Notice that we have changed the names of the arguments in the function definition from **rh, rv,** and **re** to **r1, r2,** and **r3,** respectively. The arguments are

```
#include <string.h>
#include <stdio.h>
main()
{
    /* declare the functions with prototypes */
    void ladder_picture(void), prompts(void);
    float r_equiv(float, float, float);

    char ans[4];
    float rv, rh, re, e;

    printf("What is the supply voltage, E?  ");
    scanf("%f", &e);

    ladder_picture(); /*  draw the circuit diagram  */
    prompts();  /* ask for the resistor and voltage values */

    printf("Vertical resistor value is:  ");
    scanf("%f", &rv);

    printf("Horizontal resistor value is:  ");
    scanf("%f", &rh);

    re = rv + rh;

    printf("Any more resistors (yes or no)?  ");
    scanf("%s", ans);

    while (strcmp(ans, "yes") == 0)
    {
        printf("Vertical resistor value is:  ");
        scanf("%f", &rv);

        printf("Horizontal resistor value is:  ");
        scanf("%f", &rh);

        /* function will combine re and rv in
        parallel and then add rh in series to
        give a new equivalent resistance  */

        re = r_equiv(rh, rv, re);

        printf("Any more resistors (yes or no)?  ");
        scanf("%s", ans);
    }
    printf("\nThe driving point resistance is %.4f ohms,", re);
    printf("\nand the supply current is %.4f amps.\n\n", e/re);

}
```

Figure 4-22 Ladder network program with several functions.

```
/* draws the circuit diagram */

void ladder_picture(void)
{
        printf("\n\n");
        printf("\t\t----R1 ----- R3 ----- R5 ----- R7 ----\n");
        printf("\t\t    |         |         |          |\n");
        printf("\t\t    R2        R4        R6         R8\n");
        printf("\t\t    |         |         |          | \n");
        printf("\t\t-------------------------------------\n\n");
}


/* displays the prompts */

void prompts(void)
{
        printf("First, enter the value of the resistor that's");
        printf(" furthest ");
        printf("from the voltage source \n");
        printf("(R8, in the figure), and work your way toward ");
        printf("the source, ");
        printf("a section at a time.\n");

        printf("If an R with an even subscript is missing, ");
        printf("enter 1e38 as its ");
        printf("\nvalue.  If one with an odd subscript is ");
        printf("missing, enter 0.\n");
        printf("NOTE: a section is a pair of resistors.\n\n");
}


/* series-parallel resistance calculation:
combines the second and third arguments in parallel,
and adds result to the series argument   */

float r_equiv(float r1, float r2, float r3)
{
        float temp;

        temp = r1 + (r2 * r3 )/( r2 + r3 );

        return (temp);
}
```

Figure 4-22   (Continued)

"dummy" variables (computer scientists call them **formal parameters**); they exist only to carry the values of the actual variables used in the call by the calling function. The definition of the function is written in terms of the dummy variables. This means that you do not have to know the names of the variables that are used in the call by the calling function! For example,

```
float r_equiv(float r1, float r2, float r3)
{
    float temp;
    temp = r1 + (r2 * r3 )/( r2 + r3 );
    return (temp);
}
```

but the call is made with the actual variables,

$$re = r\_equiv(rh, \ rv, \ re);$$

When it sees the call, the computer will copy the float value of **rh** into **r1**, the float value of **rv** into **r2**, and the float value of **re** into **r3**. When the calculation is completed, the resulting float value is transferred back to the calling function through the function name. For example, suppose that **rh** = 10.0, **rv** = 20.0, and **re** = 30.0. Then the call

$$re = r\_equiv(rh, \ rv, \ re);$$

is evaluated as

$$re = r\_equiv(10.0, \ 20.0, \ 30.0);$$

The function then sees

$$temp = 10.0 + 20.0 * 30.0 \ / \ (20.0 + 30);$$
$$= 22.0;$$

Thus the value **22.0** will be returned. On return to the calling function, the original assignment statement evaluates to

$$re = 22.0;$$

The most complex type of function is the kind that returns more than one value. We'll learn about that in a later chapter.

4-8 REVIEW

In this chapter you learned how to:

- Write a program to calculate the equivalent resistance of any number of resistors connected in series
- Write a program to calculate the equivalent resistance of any number of resistors connected in parallel
- Justify using le38 as the value of a missing parallel resistor
- Write a program to calculate the equivalent resistance of any number of resistors connected in a ladder configuration

- Write a program to calculate the current, voltage, and power dissipated in any part of an electronic circuit consisting of resistors and one voltage source
- Write programs that use the current- and voltage-divider rules
- Write simple functions in C

PROBLEMS AND QUESTIONS

1. Rewrite the program of Fig. 4-3 so that there is just one **for** loop for calculating equivalent resistance. *Hint:* Calculate both RE and GE in the loop, and then decide which to print.

2. Rewrite the program of Fig. 4-6 using arrays for resistance, current, voltage, and power. Use loops. *Hint:* Ask the user how many resistors there are in the circuit.

3. Rewrite the program of Fig. 4-6 to use the current-divider rule for the parallel circuit and the voltage-divider rule for the series circuit.

4. Rewrite the program of Fig. 4-10 using a function for the circuit diagram.

5. Rewrite the program of Fig. 4-13 using functions for the circuit diagram and the prompts.

6. For the circuit in Fig. 4-23, write a program that will print a table of the voltage across R3 and the power in R3 for E from 5 to 50V in steps of 5V.

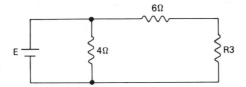

Figure 4-23

7. Suppose that you have four electrical devices and want to calculate the cost of operating them for a day (you did this for one device in Chapter 3). Write a program that will request the wattage for each device and the cost of electricity, and print a table of the accumulated cost for each device for each hour for 24 hours. Use **arrays**.

5

Creating C Functions

5-1 INTRODUCTION AND OBJECTIVES

In Chapter 4, we began our study of C functions. We continue that study in this chapter, for the purpose of giving you tools that will eventually make your C programming easier and more bug-free.

Upon successful completion of this chapter, you will be able to:

- Use **return()** appropriately in C functions
- Declare functions correctly
- Write your own simple function definitions
- State the differences between "pass by value" and "pass by reference"
- State the differences between a formal parameter and an actual parameter
- State the properties of local variables
- Explain how a function can change the values stored in an array that is an actual parameter in the call to that function
- Use the "address of" operator with function parameters
- Use pointer variables correctly
- Use the "indirection operator" with pointers
- Convert programs without functions into programs with appropriate functions
- Use **atof()** appropriately
- Use **gets()** appropriately

5-2 RETURNING VALUES FROM FUNCTIONS

A C function can return at most one value. In that respect it is like most of the functions on a typical scientific calculator. For example, the x^2 calculator function returns one value, the square of the number you key just before you press the x^2

button. The value returned appears in the display window of the calculator. You can write it down, copy it into the calculator's memory, multiply it by 6.12345, or do any one of a number of things. We might say that "the x^2 key returns one value."

Returning No Values from the Function—The void Type

Some C functions return no values. For example, if I write a function to clear the screen on the computer, it will simply clear the screen and return nothing. Such a function should be declared **void**, as in

```
void clear_screen(whatever);
```

void is not an actual data type; it is just a notation to remind the compiler (and us) that a function declared **void** doesn't return anything. In an earlier chapter, you wrote some functions that drew circuit diagrams; they did not return any values.

Returning One Value from the Function

A C function is able to return a value of any data type: any integer type, *char*, or any real type. C requires that we specify our choice (1) when we write the definition and (2) when we declare it in the function that calls the one we wrote. For example, a function that returns a **long int** should be declared like this:

```
long int sample_function(whatever);
```

and defined with a header like this:

```
long int sample_function(whatever)
```

You'll recall that C permits us to omit the word **int** when you use a **long**, so I might have correctly written

```
long sample_function(whatever);
```

and

```
long sample_function(whatever)
```

Here's an example of a silly function that returns the value −2 every time it's called:

```
int silly(void)
{
        return(-2);
}
```

The **void** in the parentheses of the definition header means that nothing is passed *to* the function. It might be used like this, in **main**():

```
int r;
r = silly();
```

Every time this program is executed, **r** will get −2.

Returning one value is then the simplest concept attached to C functions.

5-3 PASSING TO THE FUNCTION BY VALUE

The header of a function that has a value passed to it will have a data type in parentheses. For example, the header:

```
int square(float foo)
```

tells the compiler that **square**() is a function that accepts a **float** value (called **foo** here) and returns an **int** value. This definition is a "prototype" and alerts the compiler to check to see if in fact the programmer used **square**() correctly. For example, the program fragment in Fig. 5-1 shows the square function called properly. The declaration

```
int square(float);
```

tells **main**() that the call must pass a **float** value to the function which will then return an **int** value. The call occurs in the statement

```
j = square(x);
```

main(), the calling function, passes the value of 'x' to the function **square**(). It returns an **int** value which **main**() immediately assigns to 'j'. The, **main**() causes the value of 'j' to be printed. (If you had tried to call **square**() with an **int** argument, the Turbo C compiler would have complained!)

A function call works like your calculator. Suppose that you had an assignment to calculate the reciprocals of several numbers. Your calculator has a key, '1/x', which takes the reciprocal of a number. Why did the calculator manufacturer use the notation '1/x' to depict the reciprocal? Because 'x' is shorthand for "any value": If you key in any value and press '1/x', the calculator will calculate the reciprocal of that value. 'x' is what the computer scientists call an "actual parameter." The only thing the calculator can understand is the value, not the letter 'x'.

In C, a function also wants only the value. However, it will do something for you that the calculator will not. If you write the name of a variable in the calling statement—and if the variable (1) has been declared, and (2) is of the correct type according to the prototype declaration—C will look up the value of the variable and pass that value along to the function. This is pretty nice, isn't it? It allows you to use the same function may times, but with a different variable

```
main()
{
    float x;
    ...
    int j, square(float);    /* declaration */
    ...
    scanf("%f", &x);
    ...
    j = square(x);           /* the call */
    printf("%d", j);
    ...
}
```

Figure 5-1   Calling a simple function.

```
main()
{
        float x, y, z;
        ...
        int j, square(float);   /* declaration */
        ...
        scanf("%f", &x);
        ...
        j = square(x);       /* call number 1, actual parameter is x  */
        printf("%d", j);
        ...
        scanf("%f", &y);
        ...
        j = square(y);       /* call number 2, actual parameter is y  */
        printf("%d", j);
        ...
        scanf("%f", &z);
        ...
        j = square(z);       /* call number 3, actual parameter is z  */
        printf("%d", j);
        ...
        j = square(11.234); /* call number 4, actual parameter is 11.234  */
        printf("%d", j);
        ...

}
```

Figure 5-2   Calling a simple function frequently.

or value each time. For example, Fig. 5-2 shows a program fragment where **square()** is called several times.

Call number 1 in Fig. 5-2 is the same as the call in Fig. 5-1. Calls 2 and 3 are quite similar to call 1; they simply use different variables. C will look up the value of 'y' for call 2 and pass it to the function, and will look up the value of 'z' for call 3 and pass it to **square()**. Call 4 shows a constant (or "literal") value being passed to the function. For call 4, C has less work to do, but this form isn't very useful because there is no way to change the value 11.234.

I want to show you my definition for **square()**, a function that calculates the square of a **float** value and truncates the result to an **int**. It is shown in Fig. 5-3.

The *header* line shows that we have declared **square()** as a function that returns an **int** and has a **float** passed to it (i.e., "accepts a **float** value"). In addition, I

```
int square(float foo)      /* header */
{
        int dummy;
        float squared;

        squared = foo * foo;
        dummy = (int) squared;  /* a cast! */
        return(dummy);

}
```

Figure 5-3   A simple function definition.

placed an identifier (**foo** is for some unknown reason a popular name in the C world for a variable that has no physical significance) after the word **float** inside the parentheses. This identifier is called a "formal parameter" or "dummy variable" and is the key part of the mechanism of passing a value from the calling function to the called function. When the calling function calls **square()** as in

$$j = square(x);$$

for example, the computer looks up the value of 'x' and passes it to the function **square()**, which puts the value into **foo**, the dummy variable. Now that **foo** has a value, the business of calculating the square of that value and then truncating it can proceed.

The variables inside the braces, **squared** and **dummy**, are "local" to the function **square()**. Nothing outside of **square()** knows they exist. This is OK, because they exist in **square()** for just one reason: to permit the calculation of the returned value. Once it has been calculated and returned, they are no longer needed. Of course, if **square()** is called again with a different value passed to **foo**, both **squared** and **dummy** will be created again and will have different values in the calculation.

To summarize, a function must be declared as to the type of value it will return, and it will usually have at least one formal parameter (i.e., dummy variable).

```
#include <stdio.h>
main()
{
     /* this is the "stub" for
     testing the function square() */

     int i, square(float);
     float x;

     printf("Enter a value: ");
     scanf("%f", &x);

     i = square(x);
     printf("The value squared and truncated is %d\n", i);
}

/* squares the value passed and returns the truncated
   integer equivalent value  */

int square(float foo)     /* header */
{
     int dummy;
     float squared;

     squared = foo * foo;
     dummy = (int) squared;
     return(dummy);
}
```

Figure 5-4 Simple function and program.

In addition, it may have local variables to use in calculations within the function itself.

Figure 5-4 shows our function and a "stub"—a small program to "drive" or exercise the function we wrote.

To illustrate the meaning of "local" variable, let's try to print the values of **foo**, **squared**, and **dummy** from inside **main()**. I'll add the line

```
printf("%f  %f  %d", foo, squared, dummy);
```

as the last statement. Figure 5-5 shows what happened when we compiled. As you see, **main()** believes that **foo**, **squared**, and **dummy** do not exist!

Let's see if **square()** knows about **x**. I'll add a statement to the function just before the **return**:

```
printf("%f", x);
```

and press F9 again. The result is in Fig. 5-6.

So the function **square()** doesn't know about the variables in **main()**! Not only are **square()**'s local variables hidden from **main()**, but the variables in **main()** are hidden from **square()**! That calling functions can hide variables from called functions, and vice versa, is a very powerful scheme that lets us write programs with fewer bugs in them. That may be hard to believe but it is true. As you gain experience in writing C programs, you will realize the truth of this statement. Hiding variables limits communication between called functions and calling functions to (1) the value(s) of the formal parameter(s) and (2) the returned value.

A function may have more than one formal parameter. If it does, you must

```
=============================== Edit ===============================
|        Line 21    Col 29   Insert Indent      A:SQ2.C          |
|                                                                |
|main()                                                          |
|{                                                               |
|     int i, square(float);                                      |
|     float x;                                                   |
|                                                                |
|     printf("Enter a value: ");                                 |
|     scanf("%f", &x);                                           |
|                                                                |
|     i = square(x);                                             |
|     printf("The value squared and truncated is %d\n", i);      |
|     printf("%f  %f  %d", foo, squared, dummy);                 |
|}                                                               |
============================== Message =============================
| Compiling A:SQ2.C:                                             |
| Error A:SQ2.C 21: Undefined symbol 'foo' in func main          |
| Error A:SQ2.C 21: Undefined symbol 'squared' in func main      |
| Error A:SQ2.C 21: Undefined symbol 'dummy' in func main        |
|                                                                |
|                                                                |
===================================================================
```

Figure 5-5 A function's variables are hidden.

```
=========================== Edit ===============================
|      Line 6        Col 19  Insert Indent      A:SQ2.C      |
|{                                                          |
|    int dummy;                                             |
|    float squared;                                         |
|                                                          |
|    printf("%f", x);                                       |
|                                                          |
|    squared = value * value;                               |
|    dummy = (int) squared;                                 |
|    return(dummy);                                         |
|}                                                          |
|                                                          |
|main()                                                     |
|{                                                          |
=========================== Message ============================
| Compiling A:SQ2.C:                                        |
| Error A:SQ2.C 6: Undefined symbol 'x' in function square  |
|                                                          |
================================================================
```

Figure 5-6 Hiding variables in the calling function.

declare each in the prototype. For example, I've written a function that calculates the voltage across a resistor when the current and resistance are passed to it. Figure 5-7 shows its definition. And a stub in shown in Fig. 5-8. Figure 5-9 displays a typical run.

```
float calc_volts(float current, float resistance)
{
        return( current * resistance );
}
```

Figure 5-7 A function with two formal parameters.

```
#include <stdio.h>
main()
{
     float i, r, calc_volts(float, float); /* declaration */

     printf("Enter the current:  ");
     scanf("%f", &i);
     printf("and the resistance:  ");
     scanf("%f", &r);
     printf("The voltage is %f volts.", calc_volts(i, r));
}                              /* call --------/\    */

/* calculates product of two parameters */
float calc_volts(float current, float resistance) /* header */
{
     return( current * resistance );
}
```

Figure 5-8 A test program.

150   Creating C Functions   Chap. 5

```
Enter the current:  3e-3
and the resistance:  10e3
The voltage is 30.000000 volts.
```
Figure 5-9 Output of Fig. 5-8.

Compare the three lines: definition header, declaration, and call.

```
header:         float calc_volts(float current, float resistance)
declaration:    float calc_volts(float, float);
call:           printf("The voltage is %f volts.", calc_volts(i, r));
```

The header spells it all out by giving the return type, the formal parameter types and the identifiers for the formal parameters that are used in the function definition. The declaration doesn't specify the names of the identifiers; we are free to pass the values of any variables we like. The call shows the names of the actual parameters whose values we want to pass to **calc_volts( )**. *Note:* It is absolutely necessary to remember to keep the parameters in the proper order! That makes it very important that you examine a function's header before you write a call for it. In this case, my function multiplied two values, so the order didn't matter. But it will in almost every other case!

5-4 FUNCTIONS AND ARRAYS

An array variable is not a simple variable; it is a combination of several simple variables, all under one identifier. However, passing the value of one array element to a function is exactly the same as passing the value of a simple variable. Figure 5-10 shows a simple case.

Passing the Value of an Array Element

As you can see, the definition of **square( )** hasn't changed a bit. **main( )** will pass one **float** value every time it calls the function. The **floats** are x[0], x[1], x[2], x[3], and x[4]. Each is a simple **float** variable.

Passing an Entire Array

If you want to pass the entire array at one time, you will need to change the function. Figure 5-11 shows the new function and the new **main( )**.

Let's examine this one in some detail.

The header. The header line

```
void square(float foo[], int how_many)
```

shows how you tell C that the first formal parameter is an array of **floats**: Use the usual declaration for an array, **foo[ ]**, but do NOT put a number inside the brackets. C does not require that the formal parameter for an array include a specific size. However, the function needs to know how many array elements it will work with, so I included a second formal parameter (**how_many**) to tell the function just how many array elements I want it to process. The value passed to **how_many** should *not* be larger than the number of elements in the original array, but it may be smaller. Finally, since we do the display of the calculations right in the function

```
#include <stdio.h>
main()
{
        /* stub to demonstrate passing an
        element of an array to our
        previously-defined function square() */

        int i, j, square(float);

        float x[5];  /*  array declaration */

        for (j = 0; j < 5; ++j)
        {
                printf("Enter a value: ");
                scanf("%f", &x[j]);  /* one at a time */
        }

        for (j = 0; j < 5; ++j)
        {
                i = square(x[j]);  /* pass one element at a time */

                printf("The value squared and truncated is %d\n", i);
        }
}

/* this is the same function definition as in Figure 5-4 */

int square(float value) /* header */
{
        int dummy;
        float squared;

        squared = value * value;
        dummy = (int) squared;
        return(dummy);
}
```

Figure 5-10 Passing an array element to a function.

(an abnormal situation, but one that is justified on the grounds of making the function easier for you to understand), we do not ask the function to return a value. So I declared it **void**.

The definition.   The rest of the function definition is straightforward. Take each element of the array, one at a time, square it, truncate it, and output the result. Notice the loop that uses **how_many**.

The declaration.   The prototype declaration of **square()**

```
void square(float [], int);
```

has an interesting aspect. There is no need to use identifiers to prototype declarations, so in order to tell **main()** that the first actual parameter is an array, we use just the brackets [], no identifier!

```
#include <stdio.h>
main()
{
        /* stub to demonstrate the new function */

        void square(float [], int);  /* declaration of new function */
        int i;
        float x[5];

        for (i = 0; i < 5; ++i)
        {
                printf("Enter a value: ");
                scanf("%f", &x[i]);    /* one at a time */
        }

        square(x, 5);   /* the call - handles all
                              values at one time! */
}

/* accepts an array of a given size and squares
   each value in the array */

void square(float foo[], int how_many)    /* header */
{
        int i, dummy;
        float squared;

        for (i = 0; i < how_many; ++i)
        {
                squared = foo[i] * foo[i];  /* one at a time */
                dummy = (int) squared;
                printf("%f squared and truncated is %d\n", foo[i], dummy);
        }
}
```

Figure 5-11 Passing an entire array.

The call.   Finally, the call

$$square(x, 5);$$

also has an interesting aspect: To pass the entire array, use just the identifier name. That is, we passed the array *x[5]* just by using its name, *x*.   We have done this before, in **scanf**().   Remember

$$scanf("%s", ans);$$

Arrays, functions, and brackets.   Some of this may be quite confusing. Sometimes we use brackets ([ ]) and sometimes we don't.   Sometimes [ ] must have a value between the brackets and sometimes it does not need one.   And sometimes an array needs an identifier and sometimes it doesn't!   Let me try to clarify the situation for you.   First of all, the only time you don't need the [ ] when dealing with an array is when you are passing the array to a function.   Second, the only time you can use just the [ ] and not the array name is in a prototype declaration.

Finally, there are two unrelated places where [] can be "empty." The first is during an array declaration in which you are also initializing the array elements. The second occurs in a function header when a parameter is an array.

Hidden names. Did you notice that I used 'i' as a variable in both **main**( ) and **square**( )? Because variables in **main**( ) are hidden from **square**( ), and variables in **square**( ) are hidden from **main**( ), this is perfectly legal. We can write the function definition using any names we like for the formal parameter and for the local variables, knowing that these names will not be noticed by the calling function.

Changing the Values Stored in an Array

There's an interesting thing you can do with array variables that you cannot do with simple variables. C will not let us change the values of simple variables we pass to it, but it will let a function change the values of the elements of an array that we pass! Figure 5-12 shows the attempt to modify a simple variable, and Fig. 5-13 shows changing an array.

And a sample run:

The line **return(foo)** is an attempt to use the formal parameter, **foo**, to carry a value back to the calling function **and** give it to 'x'. However, **square**( ) refuses to do it, and the value of 'x' is the same as it was before the function was called. What happened to the newest value of **foo**? It is lost forever.

In Fig. 5-13, the statement

```
foo[i] = foo[i] * foo[i];
```

is an attempt to change the value of the array element **x[i]**. C approves of this and will make the change, as can be seen from the sample run.

```
#include <stdio.h>
main()
{
     float x, square(float);

     printf("Enter a value: ");
     scanf("%f", &x);

     square(x);
     printf("The squared value is %f\n", x);
}


float square(float foo)     /* header */
{
     foo = foo * foo; /* using foo as both "input" */
     return( foo );   /* and "output"!!            */
}
```

And a sample run:

```
Enter a value: 1.2
The squared value is 1.200000
```

Figure 5-12 Cannot change 'x'.

```
#include <stdio.h>
main()
{
      void square(float [], int);  /* declaration */
      int i;
      float x[5];

      for (i=0; i < 5; ++i)
      {
            printf("Enter a value: ");
            scanf("%f", &x[i]);     /* one at a time */
      }

      square(x, 5);   /* the call */

      for (i = 0; i < 5; ++i)
      {
            printf("The squared value is %f\n", x[i]);
      }
}

void square(float foo[], int how_many)    /* header */
{
      int i;

      for  (i=0; i < how_many; ++i)
      {
            foo[i] = foo[i] * foo[i];
      }
}
```

And a sample run:

```
Enter a value: 1
Enter a value: 2
Enter a value: 3
Enter a value: 4
Enter a value: 5

The squared value is 1.000000
The squared value is 4.000000
The squared value is 9.000000
The squared value is 16.000000
The squared value is 25.000000
```

Figure 5-13 Changing the elements of an array.

Keep in mind these facts about the actual parameters in a C function call: The function cannot change a simple variable or a single array element, but it can change an entire array.

5-5 PASSING TO THE FUNCTION BY REFERENCE

By now, you may have gotten a hint as to why using the name of an array as an actual parameter in a function call is different from using the name of a simple variable. That hint requires that we recall the other situation where we used the name of an array in a slightly different manner from the way we used the name of a simple variable. That situation occurred in using **scanf**(). For a simple variable, we wrote

```
scanf("%d", &number);
scanf("%f", &current);
scanf("%c", &choice);
```

but for an array, we wrote

```
scanf("%s", ans);
```

The difference lies in when the **&** is needed: It is necessary for simple variables, but we found that it was not needed with arrays.

I said previously that **&** was the "address of" operator, and that **scanf**() uses it to find out where in memory it should put the value that the user entered at the keyboard. C does not need the **&** prepended to the name of an array because the *name of an array is the address of the first element of the array*. That is,

```
ans == &ans[0]
```

This means, whether you realized it or not at the time, that when I defined the function with

```
void square(float foo[], int how_many)
```

and declared it with

```
void square(float [], int);
```

I was setting up the function to receive the **address** of the first element of an array. When I called it with

```
square(x, 5);
```

I was telling the function *where* the array **x[]** is stored in memory. Since the function knows the address, it can find the array and change the values of its elements! Giving a function the *address* of a variable (instead of its value) is called "passing by reference." By the call

```
square(x, 5);
```

we have passed the address of the array variable **x[0]** to the function **square**(), and thus **square**() is able to change the values of **x[0]**, **x[1]**, **x[2]**, **x[3]**, and **x[4]**, as can be seen from Fig. 5-13.

The Address of a Simple Variable

Perhaps you are thinking "Is it possible to use the 'address of' operator to pass the address of a simple variable to a function?" Yes, it is. Using the **&** to pass addresses of variables to functions makes C functions much more useful then they seemed when we returned only one value from a function. If a function can change the values of any variables (and it can if it knows the addresses of those variables), it can "return" as many values as you want it to!

A good example of a function that uses "pass by reference" is one that interchanges the values of two variables. That is, if **a** is 12 and **b** is 5 before, then after the interchange, **a** is 5 and **b** is 12. The function call can look like this:

```
swap( &a, &b );
```

&a means "the address of 'a' " and **&b** means "the address of 'b'. " This call will tell the function where 'a' is stored and where 'b' is stored, so it can change their values.

The Pointer Variable

What does the function do with the address passed to it? It does what it does with any value passed to it: It stores it in a formal parameter. What kind of variable (or formal parameter) can store an address? Not an **int** or **float** or **char** or any of the other data types. Even though the address is indeed an integer number, it is NOT an **int** or a **long** or even an **unsigned long**! You are about to discover a new kind of variable in C. It is a variable whose value is *the address of another variable* and is called a **pointer**. That is a pretty good name; a variable, having a value equal to the address of another, is said to "point to" the second variable.

Let me repeat this. An address is just an integer number—on a PC, it can be anything from 0 to 1,048,575. On a PC, an **unsigned int** can only be as large as 65,535, while a **long** can be 2,147,483,647. An **int** is too small to hold an address; a **long** is too large.

A pointer variable is a variable whose value is an address. Compare that with these statements: **An *int* variable is a variable whose value is an *int***; a *char* **variable is one whose value is a *char***; and so on. We know what **ints** and **chars** are; we have an idea what an **address** is—on a PC, it is a number between 0 and 1,048,575. The major difference between a pointer variable (usually shortened to just "pointer") and another variable is that we almost always want to know the value that the other variable has, but we **never** need to know the value stored in a pointer! I know that this is confusing, but try to remember this and keep going. It will begin to make more sense when we see some examples of pointer usage.

A pointer variable must be declared so that the compiler knows how to allocate memory for it. That makes it just like every other kind of variable. However, it is not declared to be a "pointer data type" because there is no "pointer data type." That is, it is *not* declared like this:

```
pointer p;
```

Instead, it is declared using the data type of the variable it points to! The reason for that is certainly less than obvious. It's simpler to write the declaration than to talk about it, so here goes. Figure 5-14 shows the declarations for several pointers.

Declaring pointers. The "*" between the data type and the identifier is what tells the compiler that **q**, **zzz**, **r_ptr**, and **this_is_a_pointer** are pointer variables. **q** will point to a variable of type **int**; **zzz** will point to a variable of type **int**; **r_ptr** will point to a variable of type **float**; **this_is_a_pointer** will point to a

```
int * q, * zzz;
float * r_ptr;
char * this_is_a_pointer;    Figure 5-14   Pointer declarations.
```

variable of type **char**. Specifically which variables will they point to? We don't know—yet. All we know at this time is that four identifiers have been declared as pointer variables. [Incidentally, most C programmers omit the space between the "*" and the identifier, but I keep that space because I believe that the space makes the notation a little easier to understand if you pronounce the "*" as "*is a pointer to an.*" This makes

```
                        int * q;
```

read (right to left) as

q is a pointer to an int

The "*" is used with pointers in a second, different manner, and the "*" is also the multiplication operator!]

```
        int *q, *zzz;
        float *r_ptr;
        char *this_is_a_pointer;
```
Figure 5-15   Alternative pointer declarations.

The declarations—without that space—could have been written like Fig. 5-15, and that is perfectly acceptable to the compiler. However, I pronounce

```
                        int *q;
```

as

"what q points to (i.e., *q) is an int

so I prefer to leave the space.

Pointing a pointer to a variable.   After being declared, a pointer cannot be used until it points to something. That means that after declaring an identifier to be a pointer variable, we must then assign the address of a simple variable to it. We do that with the "address of" operator **&**. Consider Fig. 5-16.

```
int number, count;      /* declare some simple variables */
float resistance;
char choice;

int * q, * zzz;         /* declare some pointers  */
float * r_ptr;
char * this_is_a_pointer;

/* make some assignments */

q = &number;            /* "q gets the address of 'number'" or
                           "q points to 'number'"  */
zzz = &count;           /* "zzz points to 'count'" */
r_ptr = &resistance;    /*      and so on      */
this_is_a_pointer = &choice;
```
Figure 5-16   Pointer assignments.

```
ADDRESS     IDENTIFIER    CONTENTS
------------------------------------
  1000        number        ???
  1002        count         ???
  1004        resistance    ???
  1008        choice        ???
```

Figure 5-17 Assumed memory map for declarations.

The four assignment statements give address values to the four pointers. Let's peek into memory and see if we can find out what's going on. We have eight variables: two **ints**, a **float**, a **char**, and four pointers. Suppose as a result of the first four declarations in Fig. 5-16 that memory looked as shown in Fig. 5-17. The addresses are just arbitrary guesses on my part. Don't put any stock in their actual values.

After the declarations for the pointers were made, memory might look as shown in Fig. 5-18. Again, the address values are just arbitrary guesses.

```
ADDRESS    IDENTIFIER    CONTENTS
------------------------------------
  1000      number          ???
  1002      count           ???
  1004      resistance      ???
  1008      choice          ???
  1100      q               ???
  1200      zzz             ???
  1300      r_ptr           ???
  1400      this_is_a_pointer ???
```

Figure 5-18 Assumed memory map for pointer declarations.

Now let's examine memory after the four assignments are executed (see Fig. 5-19). The new numbers are *not* guesses.

The assignment statements have given the addresses of the four simple variables to the four pointer variables. This makes sense because of the way we have pronounced assignment statements.

```
                    q = &number;
```

```
ADDRESS    IDENTIFIER    CONTENTS
------------------------------------
  1000      number          ???
  1002      count           ???
  1004      resistance      ???
  1008      choice          ???
  1100      q              1000
  1200      zzz            1002
  1300      r_ptr          1004
  1400      this_is_a_pointer 1008
```

Figure 5-19 Memory map for pointer assignments.

is pronounced "*q gets the address of number.*"   The value of **q** is 1000, the address of **number**.

All we need are some assignments to the simple variables to fill out the memory map.   Suppose that the following statements followed those of Fig. 5-16:

```
number = 1;
count = -99;
resistance = 1.2;
choice = 'y';
```

The memory map would become as shown in Fig. 5-20.

Indirection.   Let's concentrate on **count** and **zzz** for a moment.   **count** is a simple variable having the value − 99, and **zzz** points to **count**.   That means that we should be able to have access to the value of **count** in two ways: one using the identifier **count** and the other involving **zzz**.   For example,

```
printf("%d", count);
```

and

```
printf("%d", <what_zzz_points_to>);
```

should both cause − 99 to be displayed.   **count** means "the value stored in the memory area allocated to **count**."   <**what_zzz_points_to**> means "the value stored in the memory area pointed to by **zzz**."   How do we express<**what_zzz_points_to**> in C?   I briefly mentioned the notation that means "what **zzz** points to," or "the value stored where the pointer is pointing," or "the value that the pointer points to."   Unfortunately that notation uses a symbol that we have already used for two other purposes.   The symbol "*" has been used (1) for multiplication, for example,

```
number * count
```

and (2) in the declaration of a pointer, for example,

```
int * q;
```

I use the third notation **outside** of declarations:

```
                              *q

ADDRESS    IDENTIFIER      CONTENTS
------------------------------------

 1000      number               1
 1002      count              -99
 1004      resistance         1.2
 1008      choice             'y'
 1100      q                 1000
 1200      zzz               1002
 1300      r_ptr             1004
 1400      this_is_a_pointer 1008
```

Figure 5-20   Memory map for pointer assignments.

```
ADDRESS    IDENTIFIER      CONTENTS
------------------------------------
1000       number            1
1002       count             1 <==== NOTE
1004       resistance        1.2
1008       choice           'y'
1100       q               1000
1200       zzz             1002
1300       r_ptr           1004
1400       this_is_a_pointer 1008
```

Figure 5-21 Memory map.

to represent "what **q** points to." This obviously is not part of a product and is not in a declaration. *__*q__ means "the value that's stored in the variable that **q** points to," or "what **q** points to." Here's the output statement that causes "the value stored in the memory area pointed to by **zzz**" to be printed:

```
printf("%d", *zzz);
```

That is, legal C for **<what_zzz_points_to>** is just *__*zzz__. The **printf()** statement causes the value −99 to be displayed. Here's why; **zzz** points to **count** and **count** has the value −99, so the value of *__*zzz__ is −99. Used like this—outside of declarations—the "*" is called the "indirection operator."

Let's look at a few more applications of this strange notation.

```
count = *q;
```

q points to **number** and the value of number is 1. This statement, then, acts like "**count** gets 1." Literally, "**count** gets the value of what **q** points to" (see Fig. 5-21).

```
*zzz = -25;
```

zzz points to **count**, so this statement changes the value stored in **count** (see Fig. 5-22).

```
++(*zzz);
```

```
ADDRESS    IDENTIFIER      CONTENTS
------------------------------------
1000       number            1
1002       count           -25 <==== NOTE
1004       resistance        1.2
1008       choice           'y'
1100       q               1000
1200       zzz             1002
1300       r_ptr           1004
1400       this_is_a_pointer 1008
```

Figure 5-22 Memory map.

```
ADDRESS    IDENTIFIER      CONTENTS
-------------------------------------------
1000       number             1
1002       count            -24 <==== NOTE
1004       resistance       1.2
1008       choice           'y'
1100       q               1000
1200       zzz             1002
1300       r_ptr           1004
1400       this_is_a_pointer 1008
```

Figure 5-23 Memory map.

This is an increment of what **zzz** points to.   It is the same as if we had written

$$*zzz = *zzz + 1;$$

or

$$*zzz += 1;$$

The parentheses help make things clear.   The memory map after the increment is made is shown in Fig. 5-23.

I know that you are probably thinking that indirection is a strange way to manipulate the values of simple variables, especially when we can get at those variables directly.   But that is exactly the point.   We will use indirection for those situations where we **cannot** get to a simple variable directly.   And those occur often when we are passing values back and forth, to and from functions.

Back to Our Function

Now, we can go back to our discussion of **swap**().   Recall that we wanted a function that we could call like this:

```
swap( &a, &b );
```

so that the values stored in **a** and **b** would be interchanged.   We want to pass addresses to the function and we now know that addresses are stored in pointers, so the function declaration prototype might look like this:

```
void swap(float *, float *);
```

Note that we use the * by itself to designate a pointer parameter, just as we used [] by itself to designate an array parameter.   We use **void** because we are not going to use **return** in the function definition.   The prototype parameter list states that

```
void swap(float * first, float * second)
{
        float temp;

        temp = *first;
        *first = *second;
        *second = temp;
}
```

Figure 5-24 A pass-by-reference function.

```
#include <stdio.h>
main()
{
     /* stub program to test "swap" function */

     void swap(float *, float *);  /* declaration */

     float a = 12.0, b = -1e3;

     printf("\Before:  a = %7.1f and b = %7.1f", a, b);
     swap(&a, &b);              /* call */
     printf("\nAfter:  a = %7.1f and b = %7.1f", a, b);
}


void swap(float * first, float * second)  /* header */
{
     float temp;

     temp = *first;      /* 1 */
     *first = *second;   /* 2 */
     *second = temp;     /* 3 */
}
```

Figure 5-25 A SWAP program.

both actual parameters will be pointers to **floats**. Figure 5-24 shows the complete function definition.

The header shows two formal parameters, **first** and **second**; each is a pointer to a **float**. We'll explain the function itself with the program shown in Fig. 5-25. which produces this result:

```
Before: a =    12.0 and b = -1000.0
After:  a = -1000.0 and b =    12.0
```

After the declaration/initialization statements in **main**( ) are executed, suppose that memory looks like Fig. 5-26. Then **main**( ) calls the function **swap**( ). Now, memory might look like Fig. 5-27.

The address of "**a**" is now stored in **first**, and the address of "**b**" is stored in **second**. After the declarations and the statement **temp = *first**; we would see the memory map shown in Fig. 5-28. That is, the value stored in the variable pointed to by **first** is assigned to **temp**. And after executing ***first = *second**;,

ADDRESS	IDENTIFIER	CONTENTS
1000	a	12.0
1004	b	1E3
2000	first	1000
2100	second	1004

ADDRESS	IDENTIFIER	CONTENTS
1000	a	12.0
1004	b	1E3

Figure 5-26 Memory map.

Figure 5-27 Memory map.

```
ADDRESS    IDENTIFIER    CONTENTS
--------------------------------
1000       a             12.0
1004       b             1E3
2000       first         1000
2100       second        1004
2200       temp          12.0  <==== NOTE
```

Figure 5-28   Memory map.

```
ADDRESS    IDENTIFIER    CONTENTS
--------------------------------
1000       a             1E3  <==== NOTE
1004       b             1E3
2000       first         1000
2100       second        1004
2200       temp          12.0
```

Figure 5-29   Memory map.

```
ADDRESS    IDENTIFIER    CONTENTS
--------------------------------
1000       a             1E3
1004       b             12.0  <==== NOTE
2000       first         1000
2100       second        1004
2200       temp          12.0
```

Figure 5-30   Memory map.

```
ADDRESS    IDENTIFIER    CONTENTS
---------------------------------
1000       a             1E3
1004       b             12.0
```

Figure 5-31   Memory map.

memory would look like Fig. 5-29. Since **first** points to **a**, we have changed the value stored in **a**! After the third assignment, ***second = temp;**, is executed, memory would be as shown in Fig. 5-30. And, on returning to **main**(), memory would be as shown in Fig. 5-31 because, in **main** (), **first**, **second**, and **temp** do not exist. We have successfully changed the values of "**a**" and "**b**".

Here's a modification to our function to illustrate the values of **temp**, ***first**, and ***second** at each point in the function **swap**() (see Fig. 5-32).

The initial value of **temp** appears to have been 0.0 when I ran the program, but as I did not specifically initialize **temp** to that value, I cannot rely on finding 0.0 as the value every time I execute the program. It could be anything. "You can only trust variables you initialize yourself!"

I was curious as to the actual addresses that Turbo C used on my computer when I ran this program, so I added some statements to show the addresses of **a**, **b**, **temp**, **first**, and **second**. The results are shown in Fig. 5-33. The four-digit numbers that begin with "FF" are the base 16 (hexadecimal) values of the addresses. The addresses seem to have been picked at random. That's OK; we'll just let the C compiler worry about where to put things, and we'll simply use them, either by name or with the "address of" operator.

```
#include <stdio.h>
main()
{
        void swap(float *, float *);
        float a = 12.0, b = -1e3;

        printf("\nIn main(), before the call: a = %7.1f and b = %7.1f", a, b);
        swap(&a, &b);
        printf("\n\nIn main(), after the call:  a = %7.1f and b = %7.1f", a, b);
}


/* interchanges the values of two variables */
void swap(float * first, float * second)
{
        float temp;
        printf("\n\nIn the function swap()...");
        printf("\n\n     temp     *first     *second");
        printf("\n     ----------------------------");
        printf("\n%7.1f       %7.1f        %7.1f", temp, *first, *second);

        temp = *first;
        printf("\n%7.1f       %7.1f        %7.1f", temp, *first, *second);

        *first = *second;
        printf("\n%7.1f       %7.1f        %7.1f", temp, *first, *second);

        *second = temp;
        printf("\n%7.1f       %7.1f        %7.1f", temp, *first, *second);
}
```

Figure 5-32

This produces the following result:

```
In main(), before the call: a =    12.0 and b = -1000.0

In the function swap()...

temp      *first      *second
---------------------------
 0.0          12.0    -1000.0
12.0          12.0    -1000.0
12.0       -1000.0    -1000.0
12.0       -1000.0       12.0

In main(), after the call:  a = -1000.0 and b =    12.0
```

```
address of a is FFCE = 65486
address of b is FFD2 = 65490
a = 12.000000, b = -1000.000000

address of temp is FFC2 = 65474
address of A is FFCA = 65482
address of B is FFCC = 65484
a = -1000.000000, b = 12.000000        Figure 5-33   Actual addresses.
```

5-6 SOME FUNCTIONS FOR ELECTRICAL PROBLEMS

Let's go back to some of our earlier programs and rewrite them, using functions as appropriate.

Example One

The second program in Chapter 3 (Fig. 3-4) is a good one to "function-ize." It is shown again in Fig. 5-34. The multiline **switch** statement can be moved to a function that I'll call **power**(). That will make **main**() smaller. The resulting program is given in Fig. 5-35. The new function **power**() is declared **void** because it returns nothing. I decided to simply send the user's value to the function and let it do all the work, including displaying the result. A simple call from **main**() invokes the function. On returning to **main**(), we'll get a "Thank you!" displayed by **main**(). The function uses the one formal parameter in the definition code and needs no other local variables.

Example Two

The second program to convert (Fig. 3-10) is reproduced as Fig. 5-36. Here, we'll put all the calculations into a function, pass the values the user keys, and return the calculated resistance. The resulting program is shown in Fig. 5-37.

Example Three

Let's try to create a function in which we pass-by-reference. A fairly simple case can be worked out of Fig. 3-24 (reproduced as Fig. 5-38). Let's take all the calculations out of **main**() and put them into a new function, **color_vals**(). We'll pass the value of the user's input to **color_vals**(), and also pass the addresses of the three integers that are used to select colors out of the array **colors**[]. The resulting program is given in Fig. 5-39.

The function **color_vals**() has four formal parameters: one **float** and three pointers to **int**. We expect that the calling function will pass the value of a **float** and the addresses of three **int** variables. The function uses the value of the **float** to calculate three integer numbers. These are placed in memory at the addresses that were passed to the function.

The calculation of the third integer is performed directly on the variable that the third pointer points to. That is, if the call supplies the address of the **int**

```
#include <stdio.h>
main()
{
        int user_power;

        printf("\nThis program will tell you the prefix for any power");
        puts(" of ten you input.");
        printf("\nWhat is your power of 10 (e.g., -3)?  ");
        scanf("%d", &user_power);

        switch(user_power)
        {
        case -12:
                puts("\n-12 is the power for Pico.");
                break;
        case -9:
                puts("\n-9 is the power for Nano.");
                break;
        case -6:
                puts("\n-6 is the power for Micro.");
                break;
        case -3:
                puts("\n-3 is the power for Milli.");
                break;
        case 3:
                puts("\n3 is the power for Kilo.");
                break;
        case 6:
                puts("\n6 is the power for Mega.");
                break;
        case 9:
                puts("\n9 is the power for Giga.");
                break;
        case 12:
                puts("\n12 is the power for Tera.");
                break;
        default:
                printf("\nThere is no prefix for %d.\n", user_power);
        }

        puts("\nThank you!");
}
```

Figure 5-34

variable **zzz** as the last in the list, the **zzz** will be incremented by the statement

$$++(*pv\_3);$$

The calculation of the first integer is straightforward, but the calculation of the second depends on the value that was placed in memory for the first. That value (retrieved by ***pv_1**) is multiplied by 10.0 and then subtracted from the **r** value. The result is cast to an **int** and placed in memory where **pv_1** is pointing.

```
#include <stdio.h>
main()
{
    int user_power;

    void power(int);   /* declaration prototype */

    printf("\nThis program will tell you the prefix for any power");
    puts(" of ten you input.");
    printf("\nWhat is your power of 10 (e.g., -3)?  ");
    scanf("%d", &user_power);
    power(user_power);  /* call */
    puts("\nThank you!");
}


/* prints a prefix for the value passed to it */
void power(int user_power)
{
    switch(user_power)  /* using the dummy variable */
    {
    case -12:
        puts("\n-12 is the power for Pico.");
        break;
    case -9:
        puts("\n-9 is the power for Nano.");
        break;
    case -6:
        puts("\n-6 is the power for Micro.");
        break;
    case -3:
        puts("\n-3 is the power for Milli.");
        break;
    case 3:
        puts("\n3 is the power for Kilo.");
        break;
    case 6:
        puts("\n6 is the power for Mega.");
        break;
    case 9:
        puts("\n9 is the power for Giga.");
        break;
    case 12:
        puts("\n12 is the power for Tera.");
        break;

    default:
        printf("\nThere is no prefix for %d.\n", user_power);
    }
}
```

Figure 5-35

```
#define rho 10.37
#include <stdio.h>
main()
{
     float R, length_inch, length, diam, mils, A;

     printf("\nThis program calculates the resistance of a");
     printf(" copper wire.\n");
     printf("\nWhat is the length in inches?  ");
     scanf("%f", &length_inch);
     printf("What is the diameter in inches?  ");
     scanf("%f", &diam);
     length = length_inch / 12.0;
     mils = diam * 1000.0;
     A = mils * mils;
     R = rho * length / A;

     printf("The resistance is %.2f ohms.", R);
}
```

Figure 5-36

```
#define rho 10.37
#include <stdio.h>
main()
{
    float R, length_inch, diam, resist(float, float);

     printf("\nThis program calculates the resistance of a");
     printf(" copper wire.\n");

     printf("\nWhat is the length in inches?  ");
     scanf("%f", &length_inch);
     printf("What is the diameter in inches?  ");
     scanf("%f", &diam);

     R = resist(length_inch, diam);  /* the call */

     printf("The resistance is %.2f ohms.", R);
}

/* resist() is passed two values and returns one,
   the calculated resistance */
float resist(float length_inch, float diam)
{
     float length, mils, A;

     length = length_inch / 12.0;
     mils = diam * 1000.0;
     A = mils * mils;

     return (rho * length / A);  /* NOTE : rho is a constant!  */
}
```

Figure 5-37

Sec. 5-6   Some Functions for Electrical Problems

```
#include <stdio.h>
main()
{
      int val_1, val_2, val_3 = 0;
      float R;

      char colors[][7] =
      {
            "black",
            "brown",
            "red",
            "orange",
            "yellow",
            "green",
            "blue",
            "violet",
            "gray",
            "white"
      };

      printf("Enter a resistance value in ohms:  ");
      scanf("%f", &R);

      temp = R;

      while ( temp >= 100.0 )
      {
            temp = temp / 10.0;
            ++val_3;
      }
      /* temp is now < 100; a two-digit number */

      val_1 = (int) temp / 10.0; /* the "cast" */
      val_2 = (int) (temp - 10.0 * val_1); /* another one */

      printf("The color code is: %s - %s - %s.", colors[val_1],
            colors[val_2], colors[val_3]);
}
```

Figure 5-38

Think of this situation as two people trying to work a math problem over the telephone. Bob has the problem statement while Tim has the knowledge of how to solve it and the calculator. Bob calls Tim [just as **main**() calls **color_vals**()] and says "I want to calculate the three integer digits of a resistance value." Tim says "Give me the value of the resistance." Bob tells him, say, 42000 ohms. (We would know the answer immediately. Who says computers are smart?) Tim divides 42000.0 by 10.0, gets 4200.0, and says to Bob "Increment the third integer variable, please." Tim then divides again (result 420.0) and repeats his message to Bob. Finally, Tim divides again (to get 42.0) and repeats the message; the third integer variable has now been incremented three times. The interesting part is that Tim doesn't know—nor does he care—what name Bob is using for the third integer variable! Now, Tim takes the current value of the resistance (42.0), divides it by

```
#include <stdio.h>
main()
{
      int val_1, val_2, val_3 = 0;
      float R;

      /* the function declaration is next */
      void color_vals(float, int *, int *, int *);

      char colors[][7] =
      {
            "black",
            "brown",
            "red",
            "orange",
            "yellow",
            "green",
            "blue",
            "violet",
            "gray",
            "white"
      };

      printf("Enter a resistance value in ohms:   ");
      scanf("%f", &R);

      /* calling the function */
      color_vals(R, &val_1, &val_2, &val_3);

      printf("The color code is: %s - %s - %s.", colors[val_1],
      colors[val_2], colors[val_3]);
}


/*****************************************************************
      color_vals() accepts a resistance value "r" and the addresses
      of three integers, and calculates the values of those three
      integers.
      "pv_n" is a pointer variable ("n" is either 1, 2, or 3).
*****************************************************************/

void color_vals(float r, int * pv_1, int * pv_2, int * pv_3)
{
      while ( r >= 100.0 )
      {
            r = r / 10.0;
            ++(*pv_3);          /* increment the value of the
                                    variable that pv_3 points to
                              */
      }
            /* r is now < 100; a two-digit number */
```

Figure 5-39

```
        /* the variable that pv_1 points to gets the value
           from the right-hand side calculation. */


        *pv_1 = (int) (r / 10.0); /* the cast */

        /* the variable that pv_2 points to gets a value from
           the right-hand side calculation. */

        *pv_2 = (int) (r - 10.0 * (*pv_1)); /* another cast */
    }
```

Figure 5-39   (Continued)

10.0, truncates the result, and says "The value of the first integer variable is 4."
Finally, Tim asks "What's the value of the first integer variable?" Bob answers,
"4." So Tim takes the 4, multiplies it by 10.0 to get 40.0, and subtracts it from
42.0. Then he says, "The value of the second integer variable is 2. Bye!" and
hangs up. You see that Bob doesn't know what Tim is doing; he just passes
information to Bob and puts what he receives where he is told. Tim, on the other
hand, doesn't know what Bob is doing; he only knows that a certain calculation
must be done and he can do it. So he tells Bob what he wants and gives results
back to Bob. Neat!

The declaration in **main**( ) spells out that **color_vals**( ) returns no value, but
will be passed a **float**, and three pointers to **int**. The call in **main**( ),

$$color\_vals(R, \&val\_1, \&val\_2, \&val\_3);$$

sends the value of actual variable **R** and the addresses of actual variables **val_1**,
val_2, and **val_3** to **color_vals**( ).

Example Four

Our last example will involve a function that accepts input from the keyboard.
This particular function will be relatively simple, but the idea is useful because we
could write a function that would "bulletproof" each input, without cluttering
main( ) with the details. What's more, if the input function is general enough, we
might be able to use it in every program that requires input. That will save us a
lot of future coding.

We'll use Fig. 3-13 as the test bed (modified as in Fig. 5-40).

We'll take the first eight lines of code and place them in a function called
input( ). Some of the lines have **scanf**( ) in them; for example,

```
        scanf("%f", &diam);
```

Placing **scanf**( ) statements in a function is a bit different from using **scanf**( ) in
main( ), because **scanf**( ) itself uses the **address** of a variable as a parameter. So,
if we use a pointer that points to **diam**—call it **ptr_to_diam** just to make it as
obvious as possible—we can rewrite the example statement like this:

```
        scanf("%f", ptr_to_diam);
```

```
#define rho 10.37
#define alpha 0.00393
#include <stdio.h>

main()
{
        float R, length_inch, length, diam, mils, A, temp, R2;

        printf("\nThis program calculates the resistance of a");
        printf(" copper wire.\n");

        printf("\nWhat is the length in inches?  ");
        scanf("%f", &length_inch);

        printf("What is the diameter in inches?  ");
        scanf("%f", &diam);

        printf("What is the temperature in degrees C?  ");
        scanf("%f", &temp);

        length = length_inch / 12.0;
        mils = diam * 1000.0;
        A = mils * mils;
        R = rho * length / A;
        R2 = R * ( 1 + alpha * ( temp - 20) );

        printf("The resistance is %.2f ohms at %.1f degrees C.",
             R2, temp);
}
```

Figure 5-40

Of course, we must declare **ptr_to_diam** as a pointer to **float** because **diam** is a real number. This means that **diam** will no longer appear in the function. Instead, it will appear as a variable in **main()**. Here's the idea behind that: If **diam** is a variable in **main()**, we can use it in calculations that are performed in **main()** or we can pass its value (or its address) to another function and have the calculations performed there. We are writing a function that is supposed to accept a value for **diam** from the keyboard and then put that value into the appropriate place in memory. If the **scanf()** that gets the value for **diam** were in **main()**, we would use the conventional call:

```
scanf("%f", &diam);
```

This tells **scanf()** where the memory area of **diam** is located so that it can take the value input and store it there. However, we are doing a two-step process in which the call to the **scanf()** that actually gets the value is in a function. So **main()**—which calls the function we are writing—must pass the address of **diam** to that function. Consider the following lines from **main()**:

```
float diam;
void input(float *);   /* declaration */
input(&diam);        /* function call */
```

The declaration tells that **input()** returns nothing and accepts a pointer to **float** as a parameter. In other words, **main**() will pass the address of a float variable to **input**(). The function call shows that the address of **diam** is the address being passed. Now consider these lines from the definition of **input**().

```
void input(float * d)   /* definition */
printf("What is the diameter in inches?   ");
scanf("%f", d);
```

The header line shows that **input**() returns nothing and accepts the value of a pointer, **d**. That is, it accepts an address that it stores in the variable **d**. The **scanf**() statement shows how the pointer **d** is used. No **&** is needed in front of **d** because the value of **d** is already an address! When **input**() is executed, it prompts the user to enter a value for the diameter. It stores that value at the address that is the value of **d**. But if the call was

```
input(&diam);
```

as we said it was, then the value of **d** is the *address* of **diam** because that address is what **main**() passes to **input**()!

We have three variables that need values from the user, so our program becomes that shown in Fig. 5-41. The declaration

```
void input(float *, float *, float *);
```

says that **input**() returns nothing, but must be passed the addresses of three **float** variables.

The call

```
input ( &length_inch, &diam, &temp );
```

simply passes the addresses of **length_inch**, **diam**, and **temp**, respectively, to the function.

The function places those addresses in the three pointers, **l_i**, **d**, and **t**, respectively. In other words, **input**() stores the addresses as the values of the three variables **l_i**, **d**, and **t**. (There's no rule that says that pointer names MUST be long!) Each call to **scanf**(), typified by

```
scanf("%f", d);
```

will get a value from the keyboard, convert it to **float**, and place it in memory at the address contained in **d**. That address is the address of **diam**, so that **diam** gets the value entered and converted.

We can extend this idea by having the prompt string passed to the input function in the call. We'll rewrite **input**() so that it outputs a one-line string and accepts one float value. A string is an array of characters, and we already know how to pass arrays to functions. Our declaration would be

```
void inputf(char [], float *);
```

the call might be

```
inputf("What is the diameter in inches?", &diam);
```

```
#define rho 10.37
#define alpha 0.00393
#include <stdio.h>
main()
{
        float R, length_inch, length, diam, mils, A, temp, R2;

        void input(float *, float *, float *); /* the declaration */

        input(&length_inch, &diam, &temp);      /* the call  */

        length = length_inch / 12.0;
        mils = diam * 1000.0;
        A = mils * mils;

        R = rho * length / A;

        R2 = R * ( 1 + alpha * ( temp - 20) );

        printf("The resistance is %.2f ohms at %.1f degrees C.",
                R2, temp);
}

/* gets three values from the keyboard */
void input(float * l_i, float * d, float * t)
{
        printf("\nThis program calculates the resistance of a");
        printf(" copper wire.\n");

        printf("\nWhat is the length in inches?  ");
        scanf("%f", l_i);

        printf("What is the diameter in inches?  ");
        scanf("%f", d);

        printf("What is the temperature in degrees C?  ");
        scanf("%f", t);
}
```

Figure 5-41

and the corresponding header

```
        void inputf(char str[], float * ptr)
```

Our program becomes that shown in Fig. 5-42.

A Little "Bulletproofing"

Of course, **inputf**() is pretty simple, but we could, as suggested above, add some
bulletproofing to it.   This would make **inputf**() more complex but wouldn't change
main() at all.   We will get input from the user as a *string* rather than as a *float*
and convert it to a *float*.   This way, we can examine the input and discard it if we
don't like it.   We use the C library functions **gets**() (pronounced "*get ess*") and

```
#define rho 10.37
#define alpha 0.00393
#include <stdio.h>
main()
{
        float R, length_inch, length, diam, mils, A, temp, R2;

        void inputf(char [], float *);

        printf("\nThis program calculates the resistance of a");
        printf(" copper wire.\n");

        /* three separate calls to the function */
        inputf("\nWhat is the length in inches?  ", &length_inch);
        inputf("\nWhat is the diameter in inches?  ", &diam);
        inputf("\nWhat is the temperature in degrees C?  ", &temp);

        length = length_inch / 12.0;
        mils = diam * 1000.0;
        A = mils * mils;
        R = rho * length / A;
        R2 = R * ( 1 + alpha * ( temp - 20) );

        printf("The resistance is %.2f ohms at %.1f degrees C.", R2, temp);
}

/* accepts a string and returns a value */
void inputf(char str[], float * ptr)
{
        printf("%s", str);
        scanf("%f", ptr);
}
```

Figure 5-42

atof() (pronounced "*a to f*") to get the input string and convert it to a float.   **atof**() is declared in the file **math.h**, and has a header

```
                    float atof(char * ptr)
```

That is, **atof**() accepts a string and returns a float.   Here's how the new **inputf**() uses **atof**():

```
        char s[80];
        float x;
        ...
        gets(s);
        x = atof(s);
```

The converted value is placed in the variable *x*.   The string that **atof**() will accept may begin with any number of tabs or spaces and will ignore them.   It may contain an optional sign ($+$ or $-$) followed by a string of zero or more digits and an optional decimal point, followed by a string of zero or more digits, followed by zero or more tabs and/or spaces. So the following are inputs that **atof( )** can accept:

"   1"

"   1.   "

"   1.2345"

".12345"

atof( ) can also handle an input in scientific notation: zero or more tabs and/or spaces, followed by one or more digits, followed by an optional decimal point, followed by 'e' or 'E', followed by a signed integer, followed by zero or more tabs and/or spaces. For example,

"0.e-23"

"1E3"

When **atof( )** senses an illegal character in the string, it stops converting. If the illegal character is the first one in the string, it returns 0.0. Thus **inputf( )** becomes what is shown in Fig. 5-43.

The loop I've used is different from the ones I've used before. The

```
for (;;)
```

is a **for** statement that is completely empty (except for the semicolon delimiters)! This construction is a so-called "do forever" or "endless" loop. It is endless because the conditional statement is empty and is therefore never false! (This is one example of how **for** is more flexible than **while**.) How does one break out of

```
#include <math.h>  /* needed for "atof()" */

void inputf(char str[], float * ptr)
{
    char s[80];  /* a place to put the input string */

    for (;;)          /* endless loop */
    {
        printf("%s", str);
        gets(s);          /* get string from keyboard */
        *ptr = atof(s);   /* convert to float and store
                             in a variable in the
                             calling function
                          */
        if (*ptr != 0.0)
        {
            break;
        }
    }
}
```

Figure 5-43

an endless loop? By using **break** in an **if** statement. Specifically, I used

```
if (*ptr != 0.0)
{
        break;
}
```

This means that if the value that **ptr** points to is NOT 0.0, we should break out of the loop. That would bring us to the end of the **inputf()** function and return to **main()**. If ***ptr == 0.0**, that means that **atof()** was given an input string that had an illegal character in the first position, so the loop would be repeated. Unfortunately, **atof()** doesn't really bulletproof the input as much as we would like, so in the next chapter, we'll rewrite the **inputf()** function for better bulletproofing.

There's really no need to write an endless loop with a **break** in it. Figure 5-44 shows a new version of **inputf()** with an equivalent loop that may look a bit more familiar. I just wanted you to see what an endless loop looks like in C.

In Fig. 5-44, you see that we convert the user's input to a **float** value and store it in memory at the place pointed to by **ptr**. Then we check to see if the conversion was successful or not; that is, we test to see if **0.0** was written to the location pointed to by **ptr**. If it was unsuccessful, we enter the **while** loop to repeat the same prompt until the user successfully enters a string that does not begin with an illegal character.

The "evil" of compactness. Once a typical C programmer gets a few months of coding under his belt, he begins to use some of the features of C that make for more compact source code. However, more compact source code does not always translate to more compact object code, just to less typing for the programmer. I do NOT recommend that you look for ways to make your source code more compact! If you make a program as compact as you can and then put it away for a few days, you may find—when next you look at it—that you cannot figure out what you were trying to do! However, I will show you—in Fig. 5-45—the compact equivalent to the function in Fig. 5-44 so that you will understand what I am talking about. A seven-line function has been rewritten in three lines! Although that may appeal to you, let me repeat the caution: *Don't do it!* Such

```
void inputf(char str[], float * ptr)
{
        char s[80];

        printf("%s", str);
        gets(s);
        *ptr = atof(s);
        while ( *ptr == 0.0 )
        {
                printf("%s", str);
                gets(s);
                *ptr = atof(s);
        }
}
```

Figure 5-44

```
void inputf(char str[], float * ptr)
{
        char s[80];

        printf("%s", str);

        while ( (*ptr = atof(gets(s))) == 0.0 )
                printf("%s", str);
}
```

Figure 5-45

compactness makes programs difficult to read, and that makes them difficult to debug.   And, by now, you know how difficult that is!

If you compile the program and run it, you will find that **atof**() will convert a part of a string to a **float**.   For example, if the user inputs "12A34" or "12 34", **atof**() will convert "12" to a **float** and ignore the rest of the string!   You see, **atof**() converts "on the fly," so to speak: All legitimate characters are converted until an illegal one appears!   This is not what we want.   We wanted a function that would reject any string that contains one or more illegal characters and request that the user enter a new value.   We'll need to rewrite **inputf**() to do so, and we'll do it in the next chapter.

5-7 REVIEW

In this chapter you learned how to:

- Use **return**() appropriately in C functions
- Declare functions correctly
- Write your own functions
- Understand the differences between "pass by value" and "pass by reference"
- Understand the differences between a formal parameter and an actual parameter
- State the properties of local variables
- Explain how a function can change the values stored in an array that is an actual parameter in the call to that function
- Use the "address of" operator with function parameters
- Use pointer variables correctly
- Use the "indirection operator" with pointers
- Convert programs without functions into programs with appropriate functions
- Use **atof**() appropriately
- Use **gets**() appropriately

PROBLEMS AND QUESTIONS

1. Explain what the purpose of **return**() is.
2. Explain the differences between a *function header* and a *function declaration*.
3. State the properties of a *local variable*.

4. Where are *formal parameters* used? Where are *actual parameters* used?

5. Write a function called **clrscr( )** that clears the screen by sending 24 newlines to it. Write a program that calls the function.

6. Write a function that accepts an *int* value and returns its square. Do not use **scanf( )** or **printf( )** in the function. Write a program that tests the function. What is the maximum value that can be passed to your function and still have it return a valid result?

7. Redo Problem 6 so that the maximum value the function accepts for a valid return is 46340.

8. Write a function that accepts *float* values for voltage (in volts) and resistance (in kilohms), and returns the power dissipated (in watts). As usual, do not use **scanf( )** or **printf( )** in the function. Write a program that tests the function.

9. Write a function that accepts *float* values for power (in watts) and cost (in cents per KW-hour), and an *int* value for number_of_hours. The function should then display a table of time in hours and total costs in dollars from 1 to number_of_hours. It should also return the last total cost displayed. As usual, do not use **scanf( )** in the function. Write a program that tests the function.

10. Write a function that accepts an array of **floats** and returns the average. The function must also accept an *int* representing how many numbers are being passed in the array. As usual, do not use **scanf( )** or **printf( )** in the function. Write a program that tests the function.

11. Write a function that accepts the address of an *int* variable and returns the square of its value. Do not use **scanf( )** or **printf( )** in the function. Write a program that tests the function.

12. Write a function that accepts the address of an *int* variable and changes its value to the absolute value of the number that was stored there originally. *Hint:* Use pointers and do not use **return( )**. Do not use **scanf( )** or **printf( )** in the function. Write a program that tests the function.

13. Write a function that accepts the value of one *int* variable and the address of a second *int* variable, and causes the square of the value of the first variable to be stored as the value of the second variable. *Hint:* Use pointers and do not use **return( )**. Do not use **scanf( )** or **printf( )** in the function. Write a program that tests the function.

14. C has a function **sqrt( )** which accepts a *double* and returns a *double* that is the square root of the first value. Its header file is **math.h**. Use it to write a function that returns both roots of the quadratic equation, using pointers. Do not use **scanf( )** or **printf( )** in the function. Write a program that tests the function.

6

The Art of Programming

6-1 INTRODUCTION AND OBJECTIVES

Writing programs seems to be an art rather than a science. However, it is possible to use some "rules" that will help you determine how to write successful programs. These rules are guidelines developed by successful programmers. I will not go into the theory of the guidelines as I might do if you were a computer science major, but I will try to give you some insight into the "engineering" of a program.

Upon successful completion of this chapter, you will be able to:

- Rewrite a problem statement in a form suitable for translation to a program
- "Decompose" a problem into simpler problems
- Write each module in pseudocode
- Write the lowest-level problem statement as a C program

6-2 SOFTWARE ENGINEERING

Software engineering is a term used in computer science. It means that people can design software in much the same way as engineers design products. The usual engineering approach to product design starts with a statement of what the engineer is trying to accomplish. It might be something like this:

> "Given some fluid in a tank, the device will
> display the amount of fluid in gallons."

Or:

> "Given a unit of meat/fish/cheese/etc. from a supermarket
> delicatessen counter and the price per pound of that item,
> the device will calculate the cost of the item on the scale
> and print a package label."

INPUT(S) → DEVICE → OUTPUT(S)

Figure 6-1 An engineering design.

Figure 6-1 shows the general block diagram engineers use to describe the design situation.

The basic engineering premise is that if you know exactly what the device is supposed to do (i.e., the output) and exactly what it has to work with (i.e., the inputs), you can design it. Of course, the engineer must know the components in his field and their properties quite well, so that he can decide which will go into his design, in what manner.

In a programming sense, we might view Fig. 6-1 as a software design, where the processing statements of a program replace the device. Consider Fig. 6-2. This figure contains statements that look like C code but are not. They are called "pseudocode" ("*SOO-dough code*") and are really English language statements that look like computer language statements. Pseudocode is a useful bridge between the language you think in and the language the computer needs.

Remember that this is pseudocode, not C. We have shown the functions with no parameters of any kind, and they don't seem to return anything. Also, we have not declared them, and we have not shown any variables in **main**(). All

```
main()
{
        get_inputs();
        process_them();
        display_results();
}

get_inputs()
{
        ...
}

process_them()
{

        ...

}

display_results()
{
        ...
}
```

Figure 6-2 A software design.

of this will come later, as we develop the details. What's important is the idea that we can described almost every programming problem as having three main parts: getting input values, processing them, and displaying results. The next step will be to examine each part (or module) in some detail and determine what steps go in each. You may find that the examination shows that even more levels of detail are needed. So you continue to refine each level until the pseudocode statements are very close to being source code statements in the programming language of choice—in our case, C. This approach is known as "top-down" programming: Start with the most general "solution" of the problem and get more detailed at each level. The final level will be so detailed that it will almost write itself as a C program!

Strict top-down programming is not always possible or desirable. At some point you may not be able to refine the current step into one that's a bit more detailed, but would like to jump to the end—writing some code. Sometimes, this helps you see what the step above that must be. This approach is called "bottom-up" programming. Or you may have a function in your personal library that you could use in the current problem. So you might have to work from the bottom (i.e., your function) up.

Baseball Statistics

To illustrate top-down programming, let's design a program that will calculate some statistics for a baseball team. You probably know already that a player's **batting average** is calculated by dividing the number of hits he has made by the number of "at-bats." Our problem is to get the numbers on the uniforms of up to 25 players, the number of at-bats and hits for each, and calculate the batting average for each player and the team batting average (total hits divided by total at-bats). For example, a player with 575 at-bats and 184 hits is said to have a **.320** batting average. We can write a program to do this, using software design. Let's call the three functions **get_inputs**(), **calc_avgs**(), and **output**().

For **get_inputs**(), let's set up arrays for the uniform numbers, the at-bats, and the hits, and fill them with information provided by the user (see Fig. 6-3). The next level of refinement is to actually set up the arrays and to make the looping mechanism ("for each player") more definitive. There are two ways to control the loop: Ask how many players there are and use a counting loop, or use a "dummy" uniform number that causes the loop to terminate. I prefer the latter,

```
get_inputs()
{
        for each player
        {
                get number
                get at-bats
                get hits
        }
}
```

Figure 6-3 get_inputs(), level one.

```
get_inputs()
{
        int number[25], atbats[25], hits[25], i = 0;


        while (number[i] is not 0)
        {
                get number[i]
                get atbats[i]
                get hits[i]
                i++;

        }

}
```

Figure 6-4   get_inputs( ), level two.

```
get number[i]
while (number[i] is not 0)
{
        get atbats[i]
        get hits[i]
        i++;

}
```

Figure 6-5   Revised loop control for get_inputs( ).

because I hate to count things ahead of time.   Let's choose **0** as the dummy number, and assume that there are no more than 25 players on a team.   That brings us to level two (Fig. 6-4).

We're getting close even though Fig. 6-4 is not legal C.   Let's fix up the logic of the loop first.   We can't test **number[i]** until we have a value, so let's move **get number[i]** to before the loop, as shown in Fig. 6-5.   But that will work only for the first test.   We still need **get number[i]** inside the loop.   Look at Fig. 6-6.

That's better.   We'll get the first number (i.e., **i = 0**) and test it.   If it's not **0**, we go into the loop and get the **atbats** and **hits** *for the same value of i* (i.e., for the same player).   Then we'll increment *i*, get the number for the next player, test it, and so on.   **get_inputs( )** now looks like Fig. 6-7.

Our goal here is to pass whatever information we receive in **get_inputs( )** on to **main( )**.   This means that the arrays should actually be in **main( )**.   Let's refine **main( )** to show this (see Fig. 6-8).   **main( )** will pass the addresses of the three

```
get number[i]
while (number[i] is not 0)
{
        get atbats[i]
        get hits[i]
        i++;
        get number[i]
}
```

Figure 6-6   Correct loop control for get_inputs( ).

```
get_inputs()
{
        int number[25], atbats[25], hits[25], i = 0;

        ask for number
        get number[i]
        while (number[i] is not 0)
        {
                ask for atbats
                get atbats[i]
                ask for hits
                get hits[i]
                i++;

                ask for number
                get number[i]
        }

}
```

Figure 6-7   get_inputs( ), level three.

```
main()
{
        int atbats[25], hits[25], number[25];

        /* get_inputs fills atbats[], hits[], and number[] */
        get_inputs();

        process_them();
        display_results();
}
```

Figure 6-8   **main**(), level one.

```
main()
{
        int atbats[25], hits[25], number[25];

        /* get_inputs fills atbats[], hits[], and number[] */
        get_inputs(number, atbats, hits);

        process_them();
        display_results();
}
```

Figure 6-9   **main**(), level two.

arrays to **get_inputs**( ) with a call like that shown in Fig. 6-9.   And that means that we need to change **get_inputs**( ) so that there are places to put those addresses (see Fig 6-10).   Recall from earlier programs that we need formal parameters in **get_inputs**( ) that are declared as arrays with empty brackets.

Now, we'll replace each *get* with prompting and **scanf**( ), as shown in Fig. 6-11.   One last thing.   As we will be using loops in the other parts of the program, we will need to know how many players we are dealing with.   We can get that from **get_inputs**( ) by having it return the last value of the counter, **i**.   The C code for **get_inputs**( ) is shown in Fig. 6-12.

```
get_inputs(int nr[], int at[], int hs[])
{
        int i = 0;

        ask for number
        get nr[i]
        while (nr[i] is not 0)
        {
                ask for at bats
                get at[i]
                ask for hits
                get hs[i]
                i++;
                ask for number
                get nr[i]
        }
}
```

Figure 6-10   **get_inputs**(), level four.

```
get_inputs(int nr[], int at[], int hs[])
{
    int i = 0;

    printf("Enter uniform number (0 to end): ");
    scanf("%d", &nr[i]);

    while (nr[i] != 0)
    {
        printf("Enter number of at bats: ");
        scanf("%d", &at[i]);

        printf("Enter number of hits: ");
        scanf("%d", &hs[i]);
        i++;
        printf("Enter uniform number (0 to end): ");
        scanf("%d", &nr[i]);
    }
}
```

Figure 6-11 **get_inputs**(), level five.

```
/*  Gets the number of the uniform, number of at bats, and
    number of hits for each player.  A 0 for the uniform
    number terminates the input.  Returns the number of players. */

int get_inputs(int nr[], int at[], int hs[])
{
    int i = 0;

    printf("Enter uniform number (0 to end): ");
    scanf("%d", &nr[i]);

    while (nr[i] != 0)
    {
        printf("Enter number of at bats: ");
        scanf("%d", &at[i]);

        printf("Enter number of hits: ");
        scanf("%d", &hs[i]);

        i++;


        printf("Enter uniform number (0 to end): ");
        scanf("%d", &nr[i]);
    }
    return (i);
}
```

Figure 6-12 **get_inputs**(), level seven: C code.

```
calc_avgs()
{
     for each player
     {
          calculate his batting average
          add his at bats to tot_atbats
          add his hits to tot_hits
     }
     calculate team_avg
}
```

Figure 6-13   calc_avgs(), level one.

Now that we have all the information in the three arrays, let's write a function to do the calculations, **calc_avgs()**. A first try is shown in Fig. 6-13. That seemed pretty easy compared to **get_inputs()**, didn't it? It should; you've been doing calculations for many years now, so they should be more familiar than getting values from a user at a keyboard! When **main()** calls this function, it will pass along the addresses of the **atbats** and **hits** arrays, and the value of the number of players. The function will use an additional array to hold the calculated batting average for each player, and it will also accumulate the total at-bats and the total hits, so it can calculate the team batting average (see Fig. 6-14).

That looks pretty straightforward, but did you see the problem? We're trying to calculate a real number by dividing two **integers**. As I mentioned earlier, that will result in a .000 batting average for each player. We'll need to *cast* some of the values to fix this (see Fig. 6-15).

Notice that I used some C shorthand in the accumulator statements and I decided to return the team batting average to the calling program rather than use a pointer. After all, C does allow you to return one value; you might as well take advantage of this feature. Now, let's write this as legal C code, as shown in Fig. 6-16.

Notice the new local variables *Tabs* and *Thits*. Can you guess why I used them to accumulate total at-bats and total hits instead of using the variables that *ptabs* and *pthits* point to? The answer lies in the fact that an accumulated variable

```
calc_avgs()
{
     int atbats[25], hits[25], num /* is number of players */, i;
     int tot_atbats, tot_hits;
     float avg[25], team_avg;

     for (i = 0; i < num; ++i)
     {
          avg[i] = hits[i] / atbats[i];
          tot_atbats = tot_atbats + atbats[i];
          tot_hits = tot_hits + hits[i];
     }
     team_avg = tot_hits / tot_atbats;
}
```

Figure 6-14   calc_avgs(), level two.

```
calc_avgs()
{
    int atbats[25], hits[25], num /* is number of players */, i;
    int tot_atbats, tot_hits;
    float avg[25], team_avg;

    for (i = 0; i < num; ++i)
    {
        avg[i] = (float) hits[i] / atbats[i];
        tot_atbats += atbats[i];
        tot_hits += hits[i];
    }
    team_avg = (float) tot_hits / tot_atbats;
    return (team_avg);
}
```

Figure 6-15   calc_avgs( ), level three.

must be initialized to a 0 (or 0.0, if it's real) value in order that the accumulation be accurate.   I could have specified that we initialize the appropriate variables to zero back in **main**( ) but I was concerned that I might forget to do it there, so I did it right here in **calc_avgs**( ).

Are you ready to write the last function?   That should be pretty simple (except

```
float calc_avgs(int n, int at[], int h[], float av[], int * ptabs,
                int * pthits)

/* n       is the number of players
   at      is the atbat array
   h       is the hit array
   av      is the average array
   ptabs   is a pointer to total at bats
   pthits  is a pointer to total hits
*/

{
    int i, Tabs = 0, Thits = 0;
    float team_avg;

    for (i = 0; i < n; ++i)
    {
        av[i] = (float) h[i] / at[i];
        Tabs += ats[i];
        Thits += h[i];
    }

    *ptabs = Tabs;
    *pthits = Thits;

    team_avg = (float) Thits / Tabs;
    return (team_avg);
}
```

Figure 6-16   calc_avgs( ), level four: C code.

Player	at bats	hits	average
2	345	100	0.290
4	320	125	0.391
7	563	201	0.357
9	502	198	0.394
Team	1730	624	0.361

Figure 6-17 Program output.

```
output ()
{
      print heading for table of values
      for each player
      {
            printf number, at bats, hits, average
      }
      print "Team", total at bats, total hits, ge
}
```

Figure 6-18 output(), level one.

for getting the screen display to look pretty!). We'll set up a loop and display number, at-bats, hits and average for each player, and then the string "Team," total at-bats, total hits, and team average on the last line. Our output might look like that shown in Fig. 6-17. The first level for **output**() is shown in Fig. 6-18. The second level should be pretty easy to write (see Fig. 6-19). We'll need to have those arrays and values passed to **output**() (see Fig. 6-20), which returns nothing. I'll leave "prettifying" the output to you.

```
output ()
{
      printf("Player  at bats  hits  average");
      for (i = 0; i < n; ++i)
      {
            printf("%d  %d  %d  %f", num[i], abs[i], h[i], av[i]);
      }
      printf("Team  %d  %d  %f", tabs, thits, tavg);
}
```

Figure 6-19 output(), level two.

```
void output(int n, int num[], int abs[], int h[], float av[], int tabs,
            int thits, float tavg)
{
      int i;

      printf("Player  at bats  hits  average\n");
      for (i = 0; i < n; ++i)
      {
            printf("%d  %d  %d  %f\n", num[i], abs[i], h[i], av[i]);
      }
      printf("Team  %d  %d  %f\n", tabs, thits, tavg);
}
```

Figure 6-20 output(), level three: C code.

```
main()
{
        int atbats[25], hits[25], number[25];


        /* get_inputs fills atbats[],nd number[] */
        get_inputs(number, atbats, hits);


        calc_avgs();
        output();
}
```

Figure 6-21   main( ), level two, repeated.

Now is the time to work on **main( )**.   We need to be sure we have arrays and variables for everything, declarations for the three functions, and appropriate calls. In Fig. 6-9, we had a call similar to the one shown in Fig. 6-21.

I see that we need to revise almost everything.   **get_inputs**( ) looks OK (are the parameters in the right order?) except that we need to put the value it returns somewhere, and it needs a declaration (see Fig. 6-22).

calc_avgs( ) needs a little work.   We can get its declaration from its definition, giving

float calc_avgs(int, int [], int [], float [], int *, int *);

This tells us we need an array for the batting average, and some variables for total at-bats, total hits, and team average (see Fig. 6-23).   Finally, we write the declaration and call for **output**( ) as shown in Fig. 6-24.   The program consists of Figs. 6-24, 6-12, 6-16, and 6-20.

Solving Determinants

Determinants arise frequently in multiloop circuit problems, so let us use the top-down approach to write programs that solve the second- and third-order determinants.

The second-order determinant.   As you know, a second-order determinant arises from a pair of simultaneous equations, such as

$$a_1 \times x + b_1 \times y = c_1$$
$$a_2 \times x + b_2 \times y = c_2$$

```
main()
{
        int atbats[25], hits[25], number[25], num;
        int get_inputs(int [], int [], int []);


        /* get_inputs fills atbats[], hits[], and number[] */
        num = get_inputs(number, atbats, hits);


        calc_avgs();
        output();
}
```

Figure 6-22   main( ), level three.

```
main()
{
        int atbats[25], hits[25], number[25], num;
        int get_inputs(int [], int [], int []);

        float avg[25], team_avg;
        int tot_atbats, tot_hits;
        float calc_avgs(int, int [], int [], float [], int *, int *);

        /* get_inputs fills atbats[], hits[], and number[] */
        num = get_inputs(number, atbats, hits);



        /* calculate batting averages */
        team_avg = calc_avgs(num, atbats, hits, avg, &tot_atbats, &tot_hits);

        output();
}
```

Figure 6-23 main( ), level four.

Form the determinant, D, by taking the coefficients of the unknowns, x and y, like this:

$$\begin{vmatrix} a_1 & b_1 \\ a_2 & b_2 \end{vmatrix} = a_1 \times b_2 - a_2 \times b_1 = D$$

The expression on the right is the "cross" product of the terms. That is, the top-left-hand value times the bottom-right-hand value minus the bottom-left-hand value times the top-right-hand value.

```
main()
{
        int atbats[25], hits[25], number[25], num;
        int get_inputs(int [], int [], int []);

        float avg[25], team_avg;
        int tot_atbats, tot_hits;
        float calc_avgs(int, int [], int [], float [], int *, int *);

        void output(int, int [], int [], int [], float [], int, int, float);

        /* get_inputs fills atbats[], hits[], and number[] */
        num = get_inputs(number, atbats, hits);

        /* calculate batting averages */
        team_avg = calc_avgs(num, atbats, hits, avg, &tot_atbats, &tot_hits);

        /* print the results */
        output(num, number, atbats, hits, avg, tot_atbats, tot_hits, team_avg);
}
```

Figure 6-24 main( ), level five: C code.

The solution for the variable x requires that you substitute the c values for the a values, as in

$$\begin{vmatrix} c_1 & b_1 \\ c_2 & b_2 \end{vmatrix} = c_1 \times b_2 - c_2 \times b_1$$

while solving for y requires substituting c values for b values:

$$\begin{vmatrix} a_1 & c_1 \\ a_2 & c_2 \end{vmatrix} = a_1 \times c_2 - a_2 \times c_1$$

Now, solving for x and y, we have

$$x = (c_1 \times b_2 - c_2 \times b_1)/D \qquad \text{and} \qquad y = (a_1 \times c_2 - a_2 \times c_1)/D$$

All of this work was needed before we could even begin to write our computer solution. Notice that the result of this work is three equations in assignment statement form!

We are now ready to state the problem and begin to decompose it into smaller and smaller pieces. In this example I want to show you the "across the board" approach. Instead of refining a function down to the C code level before going on to the next, I will refining each function one step at a time. All will reach C code level at approximately the same time.

Given two equations in two unknowns, solve for the values of the two unknowns. Also given are the values of the coefficients of the unknowns and the constant term in each equation. The solution involves these steps:

1. Get all the known values.

2. Calculate the values of the unknowns.

3. Print the results.

```
main()
{
        get_inputs();
        process_them();
        display_results();
}


get_inputs()
{
        ...
}


process_them()
{

        ...
}


display_results()
{
        ...
}
```

Figure 6-25 The general solution.

```
get_inputs()

{

        get the values for a_1, b_1, and c_1
        get the values for a_2, b_2, and c_2

}
```

Figure 6-26 Getting the known values, level one.

```
process_them()

{

        given a_1, a_2, b_1, and b_2, calculate D
        given c_1 and c_2, calculate x
        given c_1 and c_2, calculate y

}
```

Figure 6-27 Processing the inputs, level one.

Those steps remind me of Fig. 6-2, repeated here for your convenience as Fig. 6-25.

The **inputs** are the values for a_1, a_2, b_1, b_2, c_1, and c_2. Figure 6-26 shows the next level.

Processing these values is pretty simple. First calculate the determinant, D, and then calculate the values for x and y. Figure 6-27 shows level one for **process_them**(). Showing the results, level one, is also pretty simple, as indicated in Fig. 6-28.

Time for level two, where we can get to a little more detail. For **get_inputs**(), write a preamble—something that tells what the program does—as a "suitable prompt." Figure 6-29 shows level two for **get_inputs**().

```
display_results()

{

        given x and y, display them appropriately

}
```

Figure 6-28 display_results, level one.

```
get_inputs()

{

        print_preamble
        ask for a_1
        get a_1
        ask for a_2
        get a_2
        ask for b_1
        get b_1
        ask for b_2
        get b_2
        ask for c_1
        get c_1
        ask for c_2
        get c_2

}
```

Figure 6-29 get_inputs, level two.

```
print_preamble()
{
        describe the problem being solved
}
```

Figure 6-30 print_preamble, level one.

```
print_preamble()
{
        printf("This program solves the two simultaneous equations:\n\n");
        printf("\ta1 * x + b1 * y = c1, and\n");
        printf("\ta2 * x + b2 * y = c2\n\n");
        printf("You will be asked to supply the values for the a's,\n");
        printf("the b's, and the c's.  I will calculate x and y for");
        printf(" you.\n\n");
}
```

Figure 6-31 print_preamble, level two.

Let's work on level three for **get_inputs()**. We'll make **print_preamble** a function and give it its own set of levels. All it has to do is display some text, so it should be really easy to analyze and code. The rest of **get_inputs()** for this problem looks suspiciously like the **get_inputs()** of the first example of this chapter! Figures 6-30 and 6-31 show levels one and two of **print_preamble()**, while Fig. 6-32 shows level three for **get_inputs()**. Notice in Fig. 6-32 how the details of **print_preamble()** are hidden from the **get_inputs()** function. All **get_inputs()** needs to do is simply call **print_preamble()**! Does **get_inputs()** pass anything to **print_preamble()**, or does **print_preamble()** return a value to **get_inputs()**? No, to both questions. So **print_preamble()** can be declared like this

```
void print_preamble(void);
```

Consider now **get_inputs()**. Will **main()** pass anything to it, and will it return

```
get_inputs()
{
        float a1, a2, b1, b2, c1, c2;

        print_preamble();

        printf("Enter the value of a1: ");
        scanf("%f", &a1);
        printf("Enter the value of a2: ");
        scanf("%f", &a2);
        printf("Enter the value of b1: ");
        scanf("%f", &b1);
        printf("Enter the value of b2: ");
        scanf("%f", &b2);
        printf("Enter the value of c1: ");
        scanf("%f", &c1);
        printf("Enter the value of c2: ");
        scanf("%f", &c2);
}
```

Figure 6-32 get_inputs, level three.

```
void get_inputs(float * pa1, float * pa2, float * pb1, float * pb2,
    float * pc1, float * pc2))
{
    void print_preamble(void);

    print_preamble();

    printf("Enter the value of a1: ");
    scanf("%f", pa1);
    printf("Enter the value of a2: ");
    scanf("%f", pa2);
    printf("Enter the value of b1: ");
    scanf("%f", pb1);
    printf("Enter the value of b2: ");
    scanf("%f", pb2);
    printf("Enter the value of c1: ");
    scanf("%f", pc1);
    printf("Enter the value of c2: ");
    scanf("%f", pc2);
}
```

Figure 6-33   get_inputs, level four.

anything to **main**()?   **get_inputs**() is responsible for accepting six values from the
user and passing them along to **main**(), so—as we saw in Fig. 6-12 for the first
example—**main**() will have to pass the **addresses** of those six variables to **get_in-
puts**().   Figure 6-33 shows level four for **get_inputs**().   Notice that I changed the
names of the parameters by adding a "p" in front of each.   This is to remind you
that each parameter is a pointer to a variable in the determinant, not the variable
itself.   This is further emphasized in each **scanf**(): There is no need for a **&** in
front of something that is already an address!   Figure 6-34 shows level three for
print_preamble().

At this point, let me remark that we seemed to have done a lot of work to
arrive at a handful of lines of C code.   But let me remind you that the steps we
took were small and easily understood, and they are the reasons why we got
errorless code.   You will usually be more successful using this process than by
taking an intuitive leap from problem statement to code.

Level two of **process_them** ( ) is shown in Fig. 6-35, an extension of level
one.

The calculations are straightforward, so we ask: "What passes between **proc-**

```
void print_preamble(void)
{
    printf("This program solves the two simultaneous equations:\n\n");
    printf("\ta1 * x + b1 * y = c1, and\n");
    printf("\ta2 * x + b2 * y = c2\n\n");
    printf("You will be asked to supply the values for the a's,\n");
    printf("the b's, and the c's.  I will calculate x and y for");
    printf(" you.\n\n");
}
```

Figure 6-34   print_preamble, level three.

```
process_them()
{
        calculate D  =  (a₁*b₂ - a₂*b₁
        calculate x  =  (c₁*b₂ - c₂*b₁) / D
        calculate y  =  (a₁*c₂ - a₂*c₁) / D
}
```

Figure 6-35 process_them, level two.

ess_them() and **main()**?" **main()** must pass the values for the *a*'s, *b*'s, and *c*'s to **process_them()** which must return a value for *x* and a value for *y*. So the header for **process_them()** will

```
void process_them(float a1, float a2, float b1, float b2,
                  float c1, float c2, float * px, float * py)
```

Notice that the **values** of the *a*'s, *b*'s, and *c*'s and the **addresses** of *x* and *y* are passed to **process_them()**. Figure 6-36 shows the function. Note that the first calculation uses the local variable, **D**. The last two put the values calculated directly into **main()**'s variables **x** and **y**. Recall that ***px** means "what **px** points to."

```
void process_them(float a1, float a2, float b1, float b2,
                  float c1, float c2, float * px, float * py)
{
        D   =  (a₁*b₂ - a₂*b₁);
        *px =  (c₁*b₂ - c₂*b₁) / D;
        *py =  (a₁*c₂ - a₂*c₁) / D;
}
```

Figure 6-36 process_them, level three.

Level two for **display_results()** is also an extension of its level one form (see Fig. 6-37). As you see, the level two version is quite simple. To make this into C code, we need ask whether **display_results()** gets anything from **main()** and whether it passes anything back to **main()**. It must get values for *x* and *y*, but as it merely displays the results, it need not pass anything back to **main()**. Level three is shown in Fig. 6-38. The entire program is shown in Fig. 6-39.

```
display_results()
{
    printf("\nx = %f and y = %f", x, y);
}
```

Figure 6-37 display_results(), level two.

```
void display_results(float x, float y)
{
        printf("\nx = %f and y = %f\n", x, y);
}
```

Figure 6-38 display_results(), level three.

```
#include <stdio.h>
main()
{
    void get_inputs(float *, float *, float *, float * ,
        float *, float *);
    void process_them(float, float, float, float, float, float,
        float *, float *);
    void display_results(float, float);
    float a1, a2, b1, b2, c1, c2, x, y;

    get_inputs(&a1, &a2, &b1, &b2, &c1, &c2);
    process_them(a1, a2, b1, b2, c1, c2, &x, &y);
    display_results(x, y);
}


void get_inputs(float * pa1, float * pa2, float * pb1, float * pb2,
        float * pc1, float * pc2)
{
    void print_preamble(void);

    print_preamble();

    printf("Enter the value of a1: ");
    scanf("%f", pa1);
    printf("Enter the value of a2: ");
    scanf("%f", pa2);
    printf("Enter the value of b1: ");
    scanf("%f", pb1);
    printf("Enter the value of b2: ");
    scanf("%f", pb2);
    printf("Enter the value of c1: ");
    scanf("%f", pc1);
    printf("Enter the value of c2: ");
    scanf("%f", pc2);
}


void print_preamble(void)
{
    printf("This program solves the two simultaneous equations:\n\n");
    printf("\ta1 * x + b1 * y = c1, and\n");
    printf("\ta2 * x + b2 * y = c2\n\n");
    printf("You will be asked to supply the values for the a's,\n");
    printf("the b's, and the c's.  I will calculate x and y for");
    printf(" you.\n\n");
}


void process_them(float a1, float a2, float b1, float b2,
        float c1, float c2, float * px, float * py)
{
```

Figure 6-39   The second-order determinant program.

(*Continued*)

```
        float D;

        D    =  (a₁*b₂ - a₂*b₁);
        *px  =  (c₁*b₂ - c₂*b₁) / D;
        *py  =  (a₁*c₂ - a₂*c₁) / D;
}


void display_results(float x, float y)
{
        printf("\nx = %f and y = %f\n", x, y);
}
```

Figure 6-39   *(Continued)*

The third-order determinant.   The approach for third-order determinants is exactly the same as for second-order determinants.   Note that I did not say "the *program* for third-order determinants is exactly the same as for second-order determinants."   The programs will differ significantly in their detail, but the approach will be the same.   In other words, the level one modules will be almost identical, the level two modules will be somewhat different, while subsequent levels will be significantly different as the differences between second- and third-order determinants emerges.   However, it is vital that you recognize that the same approach is used.

As you know, a third-order determinant arises from a set of three simultaneous equations, such as

$$a_1 \times x + b_1 \times y + c_1 \times z = d_1$$

$$a_2 \times x + b_2 \times y + c_2 \times z = d_2$$

$$a_3 \times x + b_3 \times y + c_3 \times z = d_3$$

Form the determinant, D, by taking the coefficients of the unknowns like this:

$$\begin{vmatrix} a_1 & b_1 & c_1 \\ a_2 & b_2 & c_2 \\ a_3 & b_3 & c_3 \end{vmatrix} = A + B + C - P - Q - R = D$$

where

$$A = a_1 \times b_2 \times c_3$$

$$B = b_1 \times c_2 \times a_3$$

$$C = c_1 \times a_2 \times b_3$$

$$P = c_1 \times b_2 \times a_3$$

$$Q = b_1 \times a_2 \times c_3$$

$$R = a_1 \times c_2 \times b_3$$

Each of these expressions is the "cross" product of terms.   See your electrical circuits book for details.

The solution for the variable x requires that you substitute the d values for the a values, as in

$$\begin{vmatrix} d_1 & b_1 & c_1 \\ d_2 & b_2 & c_2 \\ d_3 & b_3 & c_3 \end{vmatrix} = E$$

where

$$E = d_1 \times b_2 \times c_3 + b_1 \times c_2 \times d_3$$
$$+ c_1 \times d_2 \times b_3 - c_1 \times b_2 \times a_3$$
$$- b_1 \times a_2 \times c_3 - a_1 \times c_2 \times b_3$$

Solving for y requires substituting d values for b values:

$$\begin{vmatrix} a_1 & d_1 & c_1 \\ a_2 & d_2 & c_2 \\ a_3 & d_3 & c_3 \end{vmatrix} = F$$

where

$$F = a_1 \times d_2 \times c_3 + d_1 \times c_2 \times a_3$$
$$+ c_1 \times a_2 \times d_3 - c_1 \times b_2 \times a_3$$
$$- b_1 \times a_2 \times c_3 - a_1 \times c_2 \times b_3$$

Solving for y requires substituting d values for c values:

$$\begin{vmatrix} a_1 & b_1 & d_1 \\ a_2 & b_2 & d_2 \\ a_3 & b_3 & d_3 \end{vmatrix} = G$$

where

$$G = a_1 \times b_2 \times d_3 + b_1 \times d_2 \times a_3$$
$$+ d_1 \times a_2 \times b_3 - c_1 \times b_2 \times a_3$$
$$- b_1 \times a_2 \times c_3 - a_1 \times c_2 \times b_3$$

Now, solving for x, y, and z,

$$x = E/D \qquad y = F/D \qquad \text{and} \qquad z = G/D$$

Figure 6-40 once again shows the general solution and Fig. 6-41 shows the level one modules for the third-order determinant. From these you should be able to continue the work and eventually write the program for solving a third-order determinant.

A Useful Input Function

In the last example of Chapter 5, our function **inputf()** called the C library function **atof()**, which converts a string of legitimate characters into a float number. I

```
main()
{
    get_inputs();
    process_them();
    display_results();
}

get_inputs()
{
    ...
}

process_them()
{

    ...
}

display_results()
{
    ...
}
```

Figure 6-40 The general solution (again).

pointed out that **inputf**( ) as we wrote it is not ideal for the problem we were doing, but that we would rewrite it to warn the user when she keyed a string that could not be converted to a float value. We will use the same header:

```
void inputf(char str[], float * ptr)
```

As a reminder, here in Fig. 6-42 is a slightly modified version of our original definition of **inputf**( ).

```
get_inputs()
{
    get the values for a₁, b₁, c₁, and d₁
    get the values for a₂, b₂, c₂, and d₂
    get the values for a₃, b₃, c₃, and d₃
}

process_them()
{
    given the coefficients, calculate D
    given d₁, d₂ and d₃, calculate x
    given d₁, d₂ and d₃, calculate y
    given d₁, d₂ and d₃, calculate z
}

display_results()
{
    given x, y, and z, display them appropriately
}
```

Figure 6-41 The three level one modules.

The Art of Programming   Chap. 6

```
void inputf(char str[], float * ptr)
{
        char s[80];  /* a place to put the input string */

        for (;;)            /* endless loop */
        {
              printf("%s", str);
              gets(s);            /* get string from keyboard */
              *ptr = atof(s);   /* convert to float value   */
        }
}
```

Figure 6-42 The original inputf( ) function.

We have our choice of several approaches to the new **inputf**( ), but in keeping with our desire to build on what we already have, let's simply add steps to test what the user keys. In fact, let's write a function that accepts the string that the user keys, tests it, and returns a value, say 1 if it's a good value and 0 if it contains illegal characters. We'll call the function **isfloat**( ) and use the header

```
int isfloat(char * str)
```

How shall we use it in the new **inputf**( )? Here's the scheme.

> get a string
> test it
> if it's OK, convert it to a float and exit
> if it's not OK, get a new string and repeat

That seems pretty reasonable. We have a loop of sorts that is controlled by the return value from **isfloat**( ). Something like

```
while( string is not OK )
{
        get a string
        test it

}
```

The expression **string is not OK** will be implemented using **isfloat**( ) like this:

```
isfloat(s) != 1
```

Figure 6-43 shows the new version of **inputf**( ), level one. All of the testing is done

```
inputf()
{
        get a string
        while the string is not OK, i.e., it contains illegal characters
        {
              get a new string
        }
        convert the OK string to a float
}
```

Figure 6-43 Level one of the new inputf( ).

```
inputf()
{
        printf("%s", str);  /* the prompt */
        gets(s); /* get a string */

        while(isfloat(s) != 1)
        {
                printf("%s", str);
                gets(s)  /* get a new string */
        }
        *ptr = atof(s);
}
```

Figure 6-44 Level two of the new inputf( ).

in the **while(isfloat(s) != 1)** statement. If the loop is executed, it simply asks for a new string and returns control to the **while** statement. Eventually, the user will enter a legitimate string and then **inputf**( ) will convert it to a **float**, as it did in the original version. Level two of the new **inputf**( ) is shown in Fig. 6-44. We add the finishing touches to produce Fig. 6-45, the level three code for **inputf**( ).

Now to design **isfloat**( )! The header for **isfloat**( ) is

```
int isfloat(char * p)
```

The pointer points to a string of characters which we must test to see if it contains any illegal characters. But first, let's review what the legal characters are. In Chapter 5, I said that **atof**( ) will ignore spaces and tabs at the beginning of the string. However, any spaces or tabs between legal characters cause **atof**( ) to stop converting, so we will consider spaces and tabs to be illegal, no matter where they occur. **atof**( ) can accept digits, plus and minus signs, a decimal point, and the letters "E" and "e". Everything else is illegal. We will set up a test for the legal characters because there are fewer of them then there are illegal ones. The C library has a function that will help us: **isdigit**( ). It tests for the digits 0 through 9, and returns 0 if the character tested is NOT any of the following: 0, 1, 2, 3, 4,

```
void inputf(char str[], float * ptr)
{
    char s[80];  /* a place to put the input string  */
    int isfloat(char *);

    printf("%s", str);  /* the prompt */
    gets(s); /* get a string */


    while(isfloat(s) != 1)
    {
        printf("%s", str);
        gets(s)  /* get a new string */
    }
    *ptr = atof(s);
}
```

Figure 6-45 Level three of the new inputf.

5, 6, 7, 8, or 9. C has a bunch of *isxxx* tests, and they all have the same general header:

```
int isxxx(char)
```

Their definitions are in the file **ctype.h**.

The scheme for **isfloat( )** could be

>accept a string
>
>point to the first character (remember that a string is really just
>>an array of characters)
>
>test it; return 0 if is illegal
>
>if legal, test the next character and continue in this manner until
>>(1) either an illegal character appears or
>>
>>(2) the end of the string (i.e., the character '\0' appears

It should be clear that the "test it" statement includes some kind of looping, so let's refine that statement. Using our experience with **while**, we can foresee something like this:

>while the character is not '\0'
>>if the character is not legal, return 0
>>
>>otherwise, advance to the next character.
>
>return 1 because no characters were illegal.

The testing can be done one case at a time with **switch( )** or with continued **else-ifs**. Level one for **isfloat( )** is shown in Fig. 6-46. Advancing the pointer brings us to the next character.

We know that the header will be **int isfloat(char * pc)**. That is, **isfloat( )** accepts a pointer to a character and returns an integer value. A string is an array

```
isfloat()
{
      point to first char of string
      while char is not '\0' (the end-of-string marker)
      {
            if char is a digit, advance pointer
            else if char is "E" or "e", advance pointer
            else if char is decimal point, advance pointer
            else if char is plus or minus, advance pointer
            else return 0
      }
      return 1 /* if we get to the end of the string and all the
                  characters have been legal, the string will
                  convert to a float value  */

}
```

Figure 6-46   isfloat( ), level one.

```
int isfloat(char * pc)
{
        char * ptr;
        ptr = pc;    /* point to the first character of the array */

        while (*ptr != '\0')
        {
                if (isdigit(*ptr) != 0)
                        ++ptr;
                else if (*ptr == 'E')
                        ++ptr;
                else if (*ptr == 'e')
                        ++ptr;
                else if (*ptr == '.')
                        ++ptr;
                else if (*ptr == '+')
                        ++ptr;
                else if (*ptr == '-')
                        ++ptr;
                else
                        return (0); /* the string has an illegal character */
        }

        return (1);   /* the string was perfectly legal */
}
```

Figure 6-47 Level two for isfloat( ).

of characters, and the name of the array is a synonym for the address of the first element of the array. But the value of the first element of a string is, by definition, a character. Thus, when **inputf**( ) passes the name of the array where it stores the characters of the string, it is passing the address of the first character. It is good practice to use a local pointer variable (I used **ptr**) to move through the string. This keeps the address of the first character available, should it be needed. Here's the final level, in Fig. 6-47. Note that executing "return 0" will cause **isfloat**( ) to terminate immediately.

There are at least two other ways to write this. One uses a single compound **if** in which all of the conditions are "OR'd" together (using ||), and the other uses a **switch**( ) statement. You'll be asked to write both as homework. Don't forget to add

#include <ctype.h>

to the program!

The loop could just have easily been written with **for** as with **while**. The initialization *ptr = pc* could be done in the **for** loop, as well as advancing the pointer! However, this would leave the **if** statements with nothing to do! This is shown in Fig. 6-48. A line with just a semicolon on it is a special C statement called the "null statement." It doesn't look like it's very useful, does it? Don't those **if**s just beg to be rewritten? You'll get your chance in a homework assignment.

```
int isfloat(char * pc)
{
        char * ptr;

        for (ptr = pc; *ptr != '\0'; ++ptr)
        {
                if (isdigit(*ptr) != 0)
                        ;
                else if (*ptr == 'E')
                        ;
                else if (*ptr == 'e')
                        ;
                else if (*ptr == '.')
                        ;
                else if (*ptr == '+')
                        ;
                else if (*ptr == '-')
                        ;
                else
                        return (0); /* illegal character */
        }
        return (1);  /* the string was perfectly legal */
}
```

Figure 6-48   A variation of isfloat().

6-3 REVIEW

In this chapter you learned how to:

- Rewrite a problem statement in a form suitable for translation to a program
- "Decompose" a problem into simpler problems
- Write each module in pseudocode
- Write the lowest-level problem statement as a C program

PROBLEMS AND QUESTIONS

1. What does the term "software engineering" mean?
2. In order to design an engineering device or a program, you need to know what the _____ are and what the _____ are supposed to be.
3. Almost all programs consist of three major modules.   They are usually called
   _____ ,
   _____ and
   _____ .
4. Why is it necessary to pass addresses to a function?
5. Rewrite the **output()** function of Fig. 6-20 so that the table it prints is lined up nicely.
6. Develop the code for **get_inputs()** for a third-order determinant.   Show all the levels as you proceed, and include the development of any subfunctions you need.
7. Develop the code for **process_them()** for a third-order determinant.   Show all the levels as you proceed, and include the development of any subfunctions you need.

8. Develop the code for **display_results()** for a third-order determinant. Show all the levels as you proceed, and include the development of any subfunctions you need.

9. Rewrite level two of **isfloat()** using a single, compound **if** statement.

10. Rewrite the code of **isfloat()** as shown in Fig. 6-48 using a single, compound **if** statement.

11. Rewrite the entire program for the second-order determinant so that it appears to solve an electric circuit problem instead of a general second-order determinant. Write it for the case of two loop currents as the unknowns.

12. Rewrite the entire program for the third-order determinant so that it appears to solve an electric circuit problem instead of a general third-order determinant. Write it for the case of three branch currents as the unknowns.

13. Solve problems assigned from your electronics circuits textbook.

7

Analyzing DC Circuits

7-1 INTRODUCTION AND OBJECTIVES

In this chapter, you will explore programs for additional electric circuit applications. Specifically, you will examine and modify programs dealing with mesh and nodal analysis, superposition, Thévenin's and Norton's theorems, and maximum power transfer. You will be pleased to discover that you know enough about programming and the C language so that the bulk of your efforts will come when you write the equations that describe the problem.

Upon successful completion of this chapter, you will be able to:

- Write programs for branch current analysis
- Write programs for mesh current analysis
- Write programs for node voltage analysis
- Write programs for Thévenin and Norton equivalents
- Write programs that use superposition
- Write programs that investigate maximum power transfer
- Use external variables
- Use two-dimensional arrays of numbers
- Plot results on the screen

7-2 BRANCH CURRENT ANALYSIS

Your electric circuits textbook has the rules for solving circuits using the branch current method, but let me repeat them here:

1. Assign a current to each branch. The direction you choose doesn't matter, but be sure to put a head on one end of each arrow!
2. Mark the polarity of the voltage drop across each resistor.

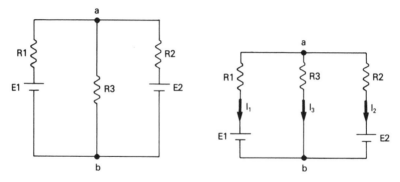

Figure 7-1

Figure 7-2

3. Apply Kirchhoff's voltage law (KVL) around each closed loop.
4. Apply Kirchhoff's current law (KCL) at the smallest number of nodes that includes all of the branch currents.
5. Solve the resulting simultaneous equations.

Let's look at a specific circuit, such as the one in Fig. 7-1. This circuit has three distinct branches: the left-hand one consisting of E1 and R1, the right-hand one consisting of E2 and R2, and the center one consisting of R3 alone. Suppose that we pick three currents: I1 in the left branch, I2 in the right branch, and I3 in the middle. Let's pick them pointing "down," as shown in Fig. 7-2. *Note:* If you are using Boylestad's *Introductory Circuit Analysis* as a circuits text, notice that my I1 and I3 are different from his. This will be a good test of whether you can really choose arbitrary directions for currents.

The voltage drops are shown in Fig. 7-3. Now, we apply KVL around the two loops. We'll start at the lower left-hand corner of the left-hand loop and go through E1, R1, and R3, in that order. When we come to an element, we will look at the sign we see first and use it. So the left-hand loop yields

$$- E1 - I1 \times R1 + I3 \times R3 = 0$$

Let's do the second loop—which contains E2, R2, and R3—by starting at the bottom of R3 and proceeding clockwise around it. This gives

$$- I3 \times R3 + I2 \times R2 + E2 = 0$$

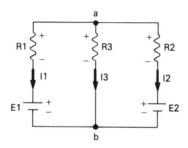

Figure 7-3

Analyzing DC Circuits   Chap. 7

This circuit has four nodes; two have only a resistor and a voltage source, and are trivial because they are involved with a single current each. The other two are involved with three currents, but they are the same three currents. So we need consider just one node, the one that I've marked "**a**" in all the figures. Applying KCL at node "**a**" gives

$$I1 + I2 + I3 = 0$$

This gives us three equations in three unknowns, and that should remind you of the determinant programs we wrote in Chapter 6. Let's rewrite the equations with the currents as the three unknowns. This gives

$$\begin{vmatrix} (-R1) \times I1 + (0) \times I2 + (R3) \times I3 \\ (0) \times I1 + (R2) \times I2 + (-R3) \times I3 \\ (1) \times I1 + (1) \times I2 + (1) \times I3 \end{vmatrix} \begin{matrix} = E1 \\ = -E2 \\ = 0 \end{matrix}$$

There's no need for us to write a new program; we can use the third-order determinant program you wrote for homework in Chapter 6. When it asks for **a1**, you can give it the value of **−R1**. When it asks for **a2**, use **0**. And use **1** when it asks for **a3**. Do you see how they correspond? If not, rewrite the **preamble**() and **get_inputs**() functions to ask for what is needed for this problem.

7-3 MESH ANALYSIS

Mesh analysis has two advantages over the branch current approach:

1. It has fewer unknowns and therefore fewer equations to solve.
2. It lends itself to a "format" approach in which you can arrive at the final equations more quickly.

The "format" method has some rules:

1. Assign a current to each closed loop, each in a *clockwise* direction.
2. In each loop, add up all the resistances that this loop's mesh currents passes through and make the sum the coefficient of that mesh current term.
3. Examine each resistance that has two mesh currents in it. The coefficient of the "other" mesh current is the negative of the resistance that is shared by two currents. This resistance is called the "mutual" or "shared" resistance.
4. The right-hand side is the algebraic sum of all voltage sources in the loop. A voltage source is algebraically *positive* if the mesh current enters it at the *minus* sign.
5. Solve the resulting simultaneous equations.

For example, let's do the same circuit using mesh currents. Figure 7-4 shows the circuit and the mesh currents. In the left-hand loop, **I1** passes through two resistances so there will be a term **(R1 + R3) × I1** in the first equation. **R3** has two currents in it, so there will be a term **(−R3) × I2** in the same equation. The

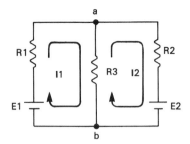

Figure 7-4

loop contains a single source, entered at the *minus*, so the right-hand side is **+E1**. Thus equation 1 is

$$(R1 + R3) \times I1 + (-R3) \times I2 = E1$$

In a similar way, the equation for the right-hand loop is

$$(-R3) \times I1 + (R2 + R3) \times I2 = -E2$$

The format approach will let us write a program to solve any circuit. Here's the scheme:

1. Find out how many loops there are—call it **numloops**—because that tells how many unknowns there will be and how many equations there will be. (Right now, we will be limited to either two or three loops, because we haven't written the program that can handle more than a 3 × 3 determinant.)

2. We'll make two programs out of this problem—one for two loops and one for three.

2a. (Two loops)
    get the sum of the resistances in loop 1—**r11**
    get the "mutual" resistance in loop 1—**r12**
    get the sum of the resistances in loop 2—**r22**
    get the mutual resistance of loop 2—**r21**
    get the right side for loop 1—**e1**
    get the right side for loop 2—**e2**
    use the second-order determinant program to solve

2b (Three loops)
    get the sum of the resistances in loop 1—**r11**
    get the resistance shared by loops 1 and 2—**r12**
    get the resistance shared by loops 1 and 3—**r13**
    get the sum of the resistances in loop 2—**r22**
    get the resistance shared by loops 2 and 1—**r21**
    get the resistance shared by loops 2 and 3—**r23**
    get the sum of the resistances in loop 3—**r33**
    get the resistance shared by loops 3 and 1—**r31**
    get the resistance shared by loops 3 and 2—**r32**
    get the right side for loop 1—**e1**

get the right side for loop 2—**e2**
get the right side for loop 3—**e3**
use the third-order determinant program to solve

Recall the second-order determinant program from Chapter 6, as shown in Fig. 7-5.

```
#include <stdio.h>
main()
{
    /* solves the equations
        a1 * x + b1 * y = c1
        a2 * x + b2 * y = c1
    */
    void get_inputs(float *, float *, float *, float *,
            float *, float *);

    void process_them(float, float, float, float, float, float,
            float *, float *);

    void display_results(float, float);

    float a1, a2, b1, b2, c1, c2, x, y;

    get_inputs(&a1, &a2, &b1, &b2, &c1, &c2);


    process_them(a1, a2, b1, b2, c1, c2, &x, &y);

    display_results(x, y);
}


void get_inputs(float * pa1, float * pa2, float * pb1, float * pb2,
        float * pc1, float * pc2)
{
    void print_preamble(void);

    print_preamble();

    printf("Enter the value of a1: ");
    scanf("%f", pa1);
    printf("Enter the value of a2: ");
    scanf("%f", pa2);
    printf("Enter the value of b1: ");
    scanf("%f", pb1);
    printf("Enter the value of b2: ");
    scanf("%f", pb2);
    printf("Enter the value of c1: ");
    scanf("%f", pc1);
    printf("Enter the value of c2: ");
    scanf("%f", pc2);
}
```

Figure 7-5   (*Continued*)

```
void print_preamble(void)
{
        printf("This program solves the two simultaneous equations:\n\n");
        printf("\ta1 * x + b1 * y = c1, and\n");
        printf("\ta2 * x + b2 * y = c2\n\n");
        printf("You will be asked to supply the values for the a's,\n");
        printf("the b's, and the c's.  I will calculate x and y for");
        printf(" you.\n\n");
}


void process_them(float a1, float a2, float b1, float b2,
                float c1, float c2, float * x, float * y)
{
        float D;

        D  =  (a1*b2 - a2*b1);
        *x =  (c1*b2 - c2*b1) / D;
        *y =  (a1*c2 - a2*c1) / D;
}


void display_results(float x, float y)
{
        printf("\nx = %f and y = %f\n", x, y);
}
```

Figure 7-5   (*Continued*)

It looks like it will take only minor changes to make this program solve two-loop mesh circuits! I used the Turbo C editor's "search and replace" command to replace all instances of **a1** with **r11**, **a2** with **r21**, **b1** with **r12**, **b2** with **r22**, **c1** with **e1**, and **c2** with **e2**. I also changed **x** to **i1** and **y** to **i2**. Use the "gnw" options of "search and replace" so that *display* isn't changed to *displai2*. The result is shown in Fig. 7-6.

```
#include <stdio.h>
main()
{
        /* solves the equations
                r11 * i1 + r12 * i2 = e1
                r21 * i1 + r22 * i2 = e2
        */
        void get_inputs(float *, float *, float *, float *,
                float *, float *);

        void process_them(float, float, float, float, float, float,
                float *, float *);

        void display_results(float, float);

        float r11, r21, r12, r22, e1, e2, i1, i2;
```

Figure 7-6

```
        get_inputs(&r11, &r21, &r12, &r22, &e1, &e2);

        process_them(r11, r21, r12, r22, e1, e2, &i1, &i2);

        display_results(i1, i2);
}


void get_inputs(float * pr11, float * pr21, float * pr12, float * pr22,
        float * pe1, float * pe2)
{
        void print_preamble(void);

        print_preamble();

        printf("Enter the value of r11: ");
        scanf("%f", pr11);
        printf("Enter the value of r21: ");
        scanf("%f", pr21);
        printf("Enter the value of r12: ");
        scanf("%f", pr12);
        printf("Enter the value of r22: ");
        scanf("%f", pr22);
        printf("Enter the value of e1: ");
        scanf("%f", pe1);
        printf("Enter the value of e2: ");
        scanf("%f", pe2);
}


void print_preamble(void)
{
        printf("This program solves the two simultaneous equations:\n\n");
        printf("\tr11 * i1 + r12 * i2 = e1, and\n");
        printf("\tr21 * i1 + r22 * i2 = e2\n\n");
        printf("You will be asked to supply the values for the r's\n");
        printf("and the e's.  I will calculate i1 and i2 for");
        printf(" you.\n\n");
}


void process_them(float r11, float r21, float r12, float r22,
            float e1, float e2, float * i1, float * i2)
{
        float D;

        D   =  (r11*r22 - r21*r12);
        *i1 =  (e1*r22 - e2*r12) / D;
        *i2 =  (r11*e2 - r21*e1) / D;
}


void display_results(float i1, float i2)
{
        printf("\ni1 = %f and i2 = %f\n", i1, i2);
}
```

Figure 7-6 (*Continued*)

The third-order determinant program can be manipulated in much the same way to give you a program that solves a three-loop mesh analysis problem. One of the things you probably didn't like about writing the third-order program in Chapter 6 was the number of lines of code in **get_inputs**( ), most of which were pretty repetitious. If you use an array for the resistances, you can get all nine values easily by using loops. Back in Chapter 3, I told you a little about the *two-dimensional* array, and we then used a two-dimensional array to define an array of strings. Since a string is itself an array of characters, I told you then that an array of strings was an "array of arrays of characters" or a "two-dimensional array of characters." I declared it like this:

```
char color[10][7];
```

This declaration means that **color** can hold 70 chars: 10 rows of 7 chars each. If I declare

```
float r[3][3];
```

that would mean that **r** can hold 9 floats in a table having 3 rows and 3 columns, as shown in Fig. 7-7.

However, in C, the first subscript is **0**, not **1**. Thus we have a choice to make. We can either renumber our table as shown in Fig. 7-8, or add an extra row and column, as in Fig. 7-9. Let's pick the one with the extra row and column

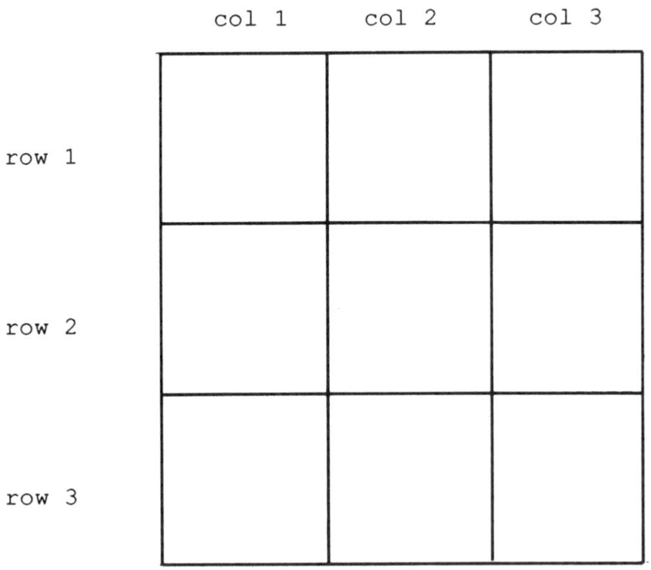

Figure 7-7

col 0   col 1   col 2

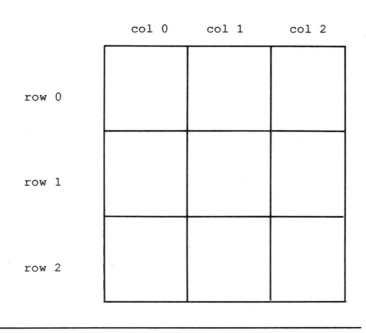

row 0

row 1

row 2

Figure 7-8

so that there will be a correspondence between the row and column number and the subscript on a resistor. To do so means that we must **ignore** row 0 and column 0. Thus we will pretend that the name of the element in the top left position is **r[1][1]**. (Yes, you do need both sets of brackets; you cannot write **r[1,1]**.) The element below it is **r[2][1]** and the one below it is **r[3][1]**. Here are the third-order equations:

```
r11 * i1 + r12 * i2 + r13 * i3 = e1
r21 * i1 + r22 * i2 + r23 * i3 = e2
r31 * i1 + r32 * i2 + r33 * i3 = e3
```

Figure 7-10 shows **get_inputs**() for the third-order determinant, if we don't use arrays. A dozen variables! We could simplify that by using a one-dimensional array for the **p_e's** and a two-dimensional array for the **p_r's**. When we use the array for **p_e**, we will need a loop that has an index that goes from 1 to 3 (there are three values of **p_e**). But the subscript of a C array starts at 0. This means that we must do one of two things:

1. Declare the array **float * p_e[3];** and use a loop index that goes from 0 to 2, or

2. Declare it **float * p_e[4];**, use an index that goes from 1 to 3, and ignore the element **p_e[0]**.

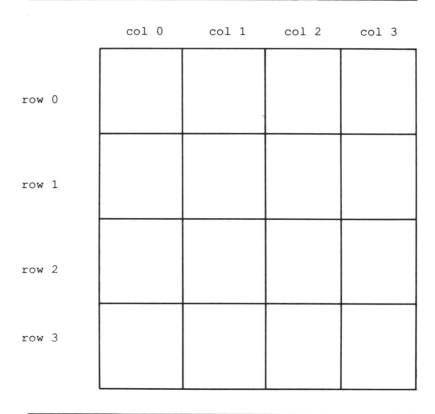

col 0   col 1   col 2   col 3

row 0

row 1

row 2

row 3

Figure 7-9

We'll choose the second case because it matches what we chose for the array of resistors. So we would have something like:

```
for (i = 1; i <= 3; ++i)
{
    printf("Enter the value of e%d: ", i);
    scanf("%f", p_e[i]);
}
```

to take care of the one-dimensional array.   This would print the line

```
Enter the value of e1:
```

and wait for the user to key in a value.

We could handle the two-dimensional array like this:

```
for (i = 1; i <= 3; ++i)
{
    printf("Enter the value of e1%d: ", i);
    scanf("%f", p_r[1][i]);
    printf("Enter the value of e2%d: ", i);
```

```
void get_inputs(float * p_r11, float * p_r21, float * p_r31,
        float * p_r12, float * p_r22, float * p_r32, float * p_r13,
        float * p_r23, float * p_r33, float * p_e1,  float * p_e2,
        float * p_e3)
{
        void print_preamble(void);
        print_preamble();
        printf("Enter the value of r11: ");
        scanf("%f", p_r11);
        printf("Enter the value of r21: ");
        scanf("%f", p_r21);
        printf("Enter the value of r31: ");
        scanf("%f", p_r31);
        printf("Enter the value of r12: ");
        scanf("%f", p_r12);
        printf("Enter the value of r22: ");
        scanf("%f", p_r22);
        printf("Enter the value of r32: ");
        scanf("%f", p_r32);
        printf("Enter the value of r13: ");
        scanf("%f", p_r13);
        printf("Enter the value of r23: ");
        scanf("%f", p_r23);
        printf("Enter the value of r33: ");
        scanf("%f", p_r33);
        printf("Enter the value of e1: ");
        scanf("%f", p_e1);
        printf("Enter the value of e2: ");
        scanf("%f", p_e2);
        printf("Enter the value of e3: ");
        scanf("%f", p_e3);
}
```

Figure 7-10 Third-order determinant's get_inputs( ) function.

```
        scanf("%f", p_r[2][i]);
        printf("Enter the value of e3%d: ", i);
        scanf("%f", p_r[3][i]);
    }
```

which uses the same simple loop we used for the one-dimensional array. But it somehow seems a little silly to write the same pair of lines three times. After all, they differ only in the use of the digits 1, 2, and 3. What we need is another loop.

```
    for (j = 1; j <= 3; ++j)
    {
        printf("Enter the value of e%d%d: ", j, i);
        scanf("%f", p_r[j][i]);
    }
```

Suppose that **i** has the value 1 when we start executing this loop. Then we would expect to see this output:

```
        Enter the value of e11: 7.2
        Enter the value of e21: -5
        Enter the value of e31: 0
```

Neat, isn't it? We're going to put the "j-loop" *inside* the "i-loop," like this:

```
for (i = 1; i <= 3; ++i)
{
        for (j = 1; j <= 3; ++j)
        {
                printf("Enter the value of e%d%d: ", j, i);
                scanf("%f", p_r[j][i]);
        }
}
```

This is called "nesting" of loops. A key thought to remember is that the **innermost** subscript changes most quickly. Thus our nested loops would accept values for resistances in this order:

$$11, 21, 31, 12, 22, 32, 13, 23, 33$$

Using nested loops makes an early level of **get_inputs**( ) look like Fig. 7-11. That's a function which is much easier to type than to read. Notice that I've declared both arrays as local variables. That is not going to be satisfactory because we want to pass the values entered by the user to variables declared in **main**( ). So we must ask the question about what **main**( ) passes to **get_inputs**( ) and what **get_inputs**( ) passes back to **main**( ). From before, we know that **main**( ) should pass the address of the first element of each array to **get_inputs**( ). You see, in C, arrays are stored in memory in a way so that a function can find each element of an array if it knows just two things: the data type of the array and the address of its first element. We know that the name of an array—say **e**—is the

```
void get_inputs()
{
        void print_preamble(void);
        int i, j;
        float r[4][4], e[4]; /* so we can use subscripts 1, 2, and 3 */

        print_preamble();

        for (i = 1; i <= 3; ++i)
        {
                for (j = 1; j <= 3; ++j)
                {
                        printf("Enter the value of r%d%d: ", j, i);
                        scanf("%f", &r[j][i]);
                }
        }

        for (i = 1; i <= 3; ++i)
        {
                printf("Enter the value of e%d: ", i);
                scanf("%f", &e[i]);
        }
}
```

Figure 7-11 Third-order determinant get_inputs( ) function with arrays.

```
void get_inputs(float r[][4], float e[])
{
        void print_preamble(void);
        int i, j;
        float r[4][4], e[4];
        print_preamble();

        for (i = 1; i <= 3; ++i)
        {
                for (j = 1; j <= 3; ++j)
                {
                        printf("Enter the value of r%d%d: ", j, i);
                        scanf("%f", &r[j][i]);
                }
        }

        for (i = 1; i <= 3; ++i)
        {
                printf("Enter the value of e%d: ", i);
                scanf("%f", &e[i]);
        }
}
```

Figure 7-12 Third-order determinant get_inputs( ) function with arrays.

address of its first element (i.e., **&e[0]**), so let's try a header that simply passes the name of each array, like this:

```
void get_inputs(float r[][4], float e[])
```

The brackets are needed. Without them, **get_inputs**( ) would expect a simple float variables called **r** and **e**. Also, C insists on knowing the size of the second (and higher, if there are any) dimension, so I included **[4]** for **r**. Figure 7-12 has the complete code for **get_inputs** with arrays. The call could be

```
get_inputs(r, e);
```

where **r** is the name of a two-dimensional array and **e** is the name of a simple array. The typing is much less repetitive now.

The other functions need some work, also. **display_results**( ) becomes the call shown in Fig. 7-13. You could include a loop that outputs each of the array elements, but since there are only three values, it probably isn't worth it.

process_them( ) gets a lot of retyping, but unfortunately, not much simplification. The use of the elements of the two-dimensional array doesn't fit any nice mathematical pattern that would permit us to use a loop or two. Figure 7-14 shows its final form. The header contains the names of the array parameters, just like **get_inputs**( ) does. But the calculations are just a brute-force mess! There are mathematical techniques for reducing sets of simultaneous equations in a simpler

```
void display_results(float i[])
{
        printf("\ni1 = %f\ni2 = %f\ni3 = %f\n", i[1], i[2], i[3]);
}
```

Figure 7-13

```
void process_them(float r[][4], float e[], float i[])
{
    float D, E, F, G;

    D = r[1][1] * r[2][2] * r[3][3] + r[1][2] * r[2][3] * r[3][1]
      + r[1][3] * r[2][1] * r[3][2] - r[1][3] * r[2][2] * r[3][1]
      - r[1][2] * r[2][1] * r[3][3] - r[1][1] * r[2][3] * r[3][2];

    E = e[1] * r[2][2] * r[3][3] + r[1][2] * r[2][3] * e[3]
      + r[1][3] * e[2] * r[3][2] - r[1][3] * r[2][2] * e[3]
      - r[1][2] * e[2] * r[3][3] - e[1] * r[2][3] * r[3][2];

    F = r[1][1] * e[2] * r[3][3] + e[1] * r[2][3] * r[3][1]
      + r[1][3] * r[2][1] * e[3] - r[1][3] * e[2] * r[3][1]
      - e[1] * r[2][1] * r[3][3] - r[1][1] * r[2][3] * e[3];

    G = r[1][1] * r[2][2] * e[3] + r[1][2] * e[2] * r[3][1]
      + e[1] * r[2][1] * r[3][2] - e[1] * r[2][2] * r[3][1]
      - r[1][2] * r[2][1] * e[3] - r[1][1] * e[2] * r[3][2];

    i[1]  =  E / D;
    i[2]  =  F / D;
    i[3]  =  G / D;
}
```

Figure 7-14

fashion than what we have done, but the theory for developing them is beyond the scope of this book. (I did put a C program for solving a set of up to 10 simultaneous equations into Appendix D, just in case you might ever need it.)

7-4 NODAL ANALYSIS

Nodal analysis is very much like mesh analysis, except that:

- The unknowns are voltages, not currents.
- The coefficient terms are conductances, not resistances.
- The constants are currents, not voltages.
- Kirchhoff's current law is applied, not the voltage law.

However, the net result is the same: A set of simultaneous equations that can be solved using the functions that we have already written. Well, that's not quite true. In electric circuits, element values are given for resistances in ohms, regardless of whether they are connected in series or parallel. So we must modify the functions so that they will accept resistance values and then use conductance values in the equations for nodal analysis. Consider the circuit of Fig. 7-15, with two current sources and three resistors.

Nodal analysis also has a "format" approach. The steps are:

1. Choose a reference node, and mark it as shown.

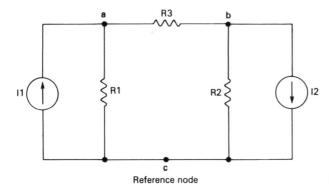

Figure 7-15

2. Label each additional node with a voltage name. There will be $N-1$ of these, where N is the total number of nodes.

3. At a given node, add the conductances attached to that node, and multiply by the node voltage.

4. Identify each conductance that is common ("mutual") to the given node and any other, and use the negative as the coefficient of the other node voltage.

5. The constant term on the right-hand side is the algebraic sum of the source currents. A source current is algebraically positive if it *enters* the node.

6. Repeat steps 4–6 for each of the $N-1$ nodes.

7. Solve the resulting simultaneous equations.

In Fig. 7-16, I have labeled the three nodes a, b, and c, and assigned **V1** to a, **V2** to b, and called c the reference node. Thus **V1** is really the voltage at a with respect to c.

At node a, there are two conductances, 1/R1 and 1/R3; the mutual term is 1/R3; and the constant is I1. So the first equation is

$$(1/R1 + 1/R3) \times V1 + (-1/R3) \times V2 = I1$$

At node b, there are two conductances, 1/R3 and 1/R2; the mutual term is 1/R3; and the constant is $-I2$ (why the *minus?*). The second equation is thus

$$(-1/R3) \times V1 + (1/R3 + 1/R2) \times V2 = -I2$$

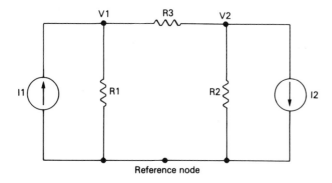

Figure 7-16

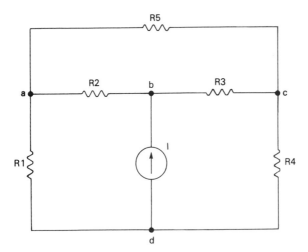

Figure 7-17

Because we're dealing with conductances and resistances, our program will have to do more for the user. That is, we would like to write the two equations as

$$\text{Ga} \times \text{V1} - \text{Gab} \times \text{V2} = \text{I1} \qquad \text{and} \qquad -\text{Gba} \times \text{V1} + \text{Gb} \times \text{V2} = -\text{I2}$$

Then we have our old friend

$$\text{a1} \times \text{x} + \text{b1} \times \text{y} = \text{c1}$$

$$\text{a2} \times \text{x} + \text{b2} \times \text{y} = \text{c2}$$

the second-order problem. It is clear that

$$\text{a1} = \text{Ga} = 1/\text{R1} + 1/\text{R3}$$

but the actual calculation isn't as simple as the case of series resistors. So when **get_inputs**() asks for resistor values, it must ask how many resistors are attached to the given node! For example, look at the "bridged" circuit of Fig. 7-17. Node *a* has three resistors, node *b* has two, and node *c* has three. Let's take our old second-order determinant program and modify it. Here it is, in Fig. 7-18. The

```
#include <stdio.h>
main()
{
        void get_inputs(float *, float *, float *, float *,
                float *, float *);

        void process_them(float, float, float, float, float, float,
                float *, float *);

        void display_results(float, float);

        float a1, a2, b1, b2, c1, c2, x, y;
```

Figure 7-18

```
        get_inputs(&a1, &a2, &b1, &b2, &c1, &c2);

        process_them(a1, a2, b1, b2, c1, c2, &x, &y);

        display_results(x, y);
}


void get_inputs(float * pa1, float * pa2, float * pb1, float * pb2,
        float * pc1, float * pc2)
{
        void print_preamble(void);

        print_preamble();

        printf("Enter the value of a1: ");
        scanf("%f", pa1);
        printf("Enter the value of a2: ");
        scanf("%f", pa2);
        printf("Enter the value of b1: ");
        scanf("%f", pb1);

        printf("Enter the value of b2: ");
        scanf("%f", pb2);
        printf("Enter the value of c1: ");
        scanf("%f", pc1);
        printf("Enter the value of c2: ");
        scanf("%f", pc2);
}

void print_preamble(void)
{
        printf("This program solves the two simultaneous equations:\n\n");
        printf("\ta1 * x + b1 * y = c1, and\n");
        printf("\ta2 * x + b2 * y = c2\n\n");
        printf("You will be asked to supply the values for the a's,\n");
        printf("the b's, and the c's.  I will calculate x and y for");
        printf(" you.\n\n");
}

void process_them(float a1, float a2, float b1, float b2,
            float c1, float c2, float * x, float * y)
{
        float D;

        D   =  (a1*b2 - a2*b1);
        *x  =  (c1*b2 - c2*b1) / D;
        *y  =  (a1*c2 - a2*c1) / D;
}


void display_results(float x, float y)
{
        printf("\nx = %f and y = %f\n", x, y);
}
```

Figure 7-18 (*Continued*)

```
void get_inputs()
{
        printf("\nHow many resistors are connected to the first node?: ");
        scanf("%d", &n);
        printf("\nAt the ?, enter a resistance value.\n");

        for (i=0; i<n; ++i)
        {
                printf("\n? ");
                scanf("%f", &r);
                g += g + 1/r;
        }

        a1 = g;

        printf("\nEnter the mutual resistance: ");
        scanf("%f", &r);
        b1 = -1/r;

        printf("\nHow many resistors are connected to the second node?: ");
        scanf("%d", &n);
        printf("\nAt the ?, enter a resistance value.\n");

        for (i=0; i<n; ++i)
        {
                printf("\n? ");
                scanf("%f", &r);
                g += g + 1/r;
        }

        b2 = g;

        printf("\nEnter the mutual resistance: ");
        scanf("%f", &r);
        a2 = -1/r;
}
```

Figure 7-19

only functions that need change are **get_inputs**() and **print_preamble**(). Figure 7-19 shows a simplified first try at a solution for **get_inputs**(). To complete the function, you'll need to write the appropriate header (*hint:* does it differ from the original header? In what way?), declare the local variables, and write the new **print_preamble**(). We'll save that as a homework problem.

The next thing to do would be to convert the third-order determinant program in a similar way. That will be another homework problem.

7-5 SUPERPOSITION

If you have written a program to solve for all the currents, voltages, and powers in a specific circuit, you have no need for superposition. As you have learned, superposition belongs in the same category as the circular mil: It was invented to

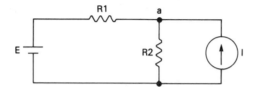

Figure 7-20 A circuit for superposition.

make calculations simpler—each source is considered separately, and then all the effects are algebraically added. However, doing superposition with a program can be quite interesting, and it will help you check your superposition homework.

Applying superposition to a circuit program is not difficult. Instead of simply solving simultaneous equations that involve all the sources, you calculate a solution for each source and then add the results. Suppose that you have a circuit with three voltage sources: E_1, E_2, and E_3. Write the equations to solve the problem as you normally would. Then write the program that solves them, but write it as a function that accepts values for the three voltage sources. Call the function three times, using 0.0 as the value for E_2 and E_3 the first call, 0.0 as the value for E_1 and E_3 the second call, and 0.0 as the value for E_1 and E_2 the third call! Then retrieve all the intermediate results and add them to get the final result.

If there are mixed sources, your approach might be a little different, as you may find that nodal analysis is preferred over mesh analysis. Consider the circuit of Fig. 7-20. We would like to calculate the current in the resistor R2 by super-position. If we were doing this by paper and pencil, we would write a single node equation at node *a:*

$$(1/R1 + 1/R2) \times Va + (-1/R1) E = I$$

This is a "one unknown" problem, so we must rewrite the equation into assignment statement form by clearing of fractions:

$$(R2 + R1) \times Va - R2 \times E = R1 \times R2 \times I$$

$$Va = (R1 \times R2 \times I + R2 \times E)/(R1 + R2)$$

$$= R2 \times (R1 \times I + E)/(R1 + R2)$$

But we were asked to solve for the current in R2; it is Va/R2 (heading away from node *a*), so

$$I2 = Va/R2 = (R1 \times I + E)/(R1 + R2)$$

Using superposition

$$I2' = (R1 \times I + 0.0)/(R1 + R2), \text{ and}$$

$$I2'' = (0.0 + E)/(R1 + R2)$$

This is actually too simple to bother writing a program for! Now that we have the superposition picture firmly in mind, let's look at a more involved circuit (see

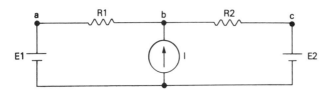

Figure 7-21

Fig. 7-21). We have four nodes, three sources, and two resistances. For each resistor, let us find the current in it, the voltage across it, and the power it dissipates.

Using nodal analysis, we see that there is only one unknown voltage, Vb. The unknown currents are I_{ba} (i.e., the current from b to a) and I_{bc}, (the current from b to c). They can be calculated from

$$Iba = (Vb - E1)/R1, \text{ and}$$

$$Ibc = (Vb - E2)/R2$$

Vb will be the solution of

$$(1/R1 + 1/R2) \times Vb + (-1/R1) \times E1 + (-1/R2) \times E2 = I$$

Clearing fractions yields

$$(R1 + R2) \times Vb - R2 \times E1 - R1 \times E2 = R1 \times R2 \times I$$

and

$$Vb = (R1 \times R2 \times I + R2 \times E1 + R1 \times E2)/(R1 + R2)$$

Using superposition, we obtain

$$Vb' = (R1 \times R2 \times I + 0 + 0)/(R1 + R2)$$

$$Vb'' = (0 + R2 \times E1 + 0)/(R1 + R2)$$

$$Vb''' = (0 + 0 + R1 \times E2)/(R1 + R2)$$

Since there are three calculations to do, let's write a program. The scheme will be the usual:

> print a preamble (we do this so often that I'm making it an official step)
> get the values
> process them
> display results

In more detail:

> print a description of the circuit
> get values for R1, R2, E1, E2, and I
> calculate Vb', Vb'', Vb'''; then calculate Vb, Iba, Ibc, V1, V2, P1, and

P2
display the results

I divided the calculations into two parts: the superposition voltages and all the rest. I did this because I want to do the superposition calculation by calling a function three times, like this:

E1 = 0, E2 = 0, I = its actual value; calculate Vb and call it Vb_1

E1 = its actual value, E2 = I = 0; calculate Vb and call it Vb_2

E1 = I = 0, E2 = its actual value; calculate Vb and call it Vb_3

If the Vb calculation is done by a function, the above can be handled simply, by using just three function calls, as I mentioned earlier. For example, suppose that header of the function is

```
float calc_Vb(float E1, float E2, float I)
```

Then the code section might be

```
vb_1 = calc_Vb(0.0, 0.0, I);
vb_2 = calc_Vb(E1, 0.0, 0.0);
vb_3 = calc_Vb(0.0, E2, 0.0);
```

calc_Vb() practically writes itself (see Fig. 7-22).

Ooops! We forgot to include a way to pass the resistance values to the function! Of course, we could just pass them as parameters, as we have done in the past, but since their values don't change during a run, let's make them "external." By declaring them *outside of* and *before* every function, we make the values of R1 and R2 accessible to *every function*, without the need to pass them as parameters. This means that our approach will be as in Fig. 7-23. External variables pose a problem. Since they are universally known to every function that follows, those functions had better use the external variable names **just** for the external variables. That is, the names are not hidden the way the names of local variables are.

I think that you can finish the details of this program without much difficulty. I hope you can see that we have done little that is new as far as programming is concerned. The same techniques that we used early on are still good, even in Chapter 7!

```
float calc_Vb(float E1, float E2, float I)
{
        return (R1 * R2 * I + R2 * E1 + R1 * E2)/(R1 + R2);
}
```

Figure 7-22

```
#include <stdio.h>
float R1, R2;      /* externals */
main()
{
       print_preamble();
       get_inputs();

       vb_1 = calc_Vb(0.0, 0.0, I);
       vb_2 = calc_Vb(E1, 0.0, 0.0);
       vb_3 = calc_Vb(0.0, E2, 0.0);

       vb = vb_1 + vb_2 + vb_3;

       iba = (vb - E1) / R1;
       ibc = (vb - E2) / R2

       P1 = iba * iba * R1;
       P2 = ibc * ibc * R2;

       display_results();
}
```

Figure 7-23

7-6 THÉVENIN'S AND NORTON'S THEOREMS

These theorems are much more useful to the practitioner of things electronic than is superposition! Many times, a device having two terminals is described by its Thévenin equivalent circuit, and knowing this makes things easier for the people who must connect "loads" to these two terminals. As you know the Thévenin equivalent circuit of a "two-terminal bilateral dc network" is a series circuit consisting of a voltage source and a resistor. Therefore, there are two calculations to be made: (1) the Thévenin voltage and (2) the Thévenin resistance. We will handle each circuit as a unique case (e.g., see Fig. 7-24).

Suppose that we want the Thévenin equivalent circuit with respect to terminals a and b. We find R_{Th} by replacing the voltage source with its own internal resistance and then reducing the resulting resistive circuit to a single resistance. The result is shown in Fig. 7-25. We see that Rint is in parallel with R3, and that combination

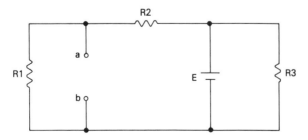

Figure 7-24

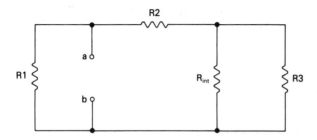

Figure 7-25

is in series with R2 across terminals *a* and *b*. R1 is also across *a* and *b* and that means that it is in parallel with the previous combination:

$$R23 = R2 + Rint \times R3/(Rint + R3)$$

$$R_{Th} = R1 \times R23/(R1 + R23)$$

The Thévenin voltage is calculated by one of the usual circuit techniques. We recognize that $E_{Th} = V_{ab}$ is the voltage across R1. We see from Fig. 7-24 that we can use a simple voltage divider to find the voltage across R1:

$$V1 = E \times R1/(R1 + R2)$$

Our program is then quite simple (see Fig. 7-26).

```
#include <stdio.h>
main()
{
        float R1, R2, R3, E, Rint, R23, Rth, Eth;
        void print_preamble(void);

        print_preamble();

        printf("What is the value of R1?  ");
        scanf("%f", &R1);
        printf("What is the value of R2?  ");
        scanf("%f", &R2);
        printf("What is the value of R3?  ");
        scanf("%f", &R3);
        printf("What is the value of the internal resistance of the source?  ");
        scanf("%f", &Rint);
        printf("What is the value of E?  ");
        scanf("%f", &E);

        R23 = R2 + (Rint * R3)/(Rint + R3);
        Rth = R1 * R23 / (R1 + R23);

        Eth = E * R1 / (R1 + R2);
```

Figure 7-26   (*Continued*)

```
printf("\nThe Thevenin equivalents for the circuit shown are:\n\n\n");
printf("     --- %.3f ohms ---o a\n", Rth);
printf("     |\n");
printf("     ---   %.3f volts\n", Eth);
printf("     =\n");
printf("     |\n");
printf("     ------------------o b\n");
}


void print_preamble(void)
{
    printf("This program calculates the Thevenin equivalent of\n\n\n");
    printf("     -----o-----R2----o-----\n");
    printf("     |    |         |    |\n");
    printf("     |    o  a      |    |\n");
    printf("     R1            E  =   R3\n");
    printf("     |    o  b      ---   |\n");
    printf("     |    |         |    |\n");
    printf("     ----------------------\n\n");
}
```

Figure 7-26 (*Continued*)

The Norton equivalent can be calculated directly from the Thévenin equivalent by changing the voltage source to a current source. Thus $R_N = R_{Th}$ and $I_N = E_{Th}/R_{Th}$. From a programming standpoint, you will generally benefit from writing only Thévenin equivalent programs and then apply the two equations for converting the Thévenin equivalent to a Norton equivalent. Complex circuits are "Théveninized" using general circuit analysis principles—usually mesh analysis—and not shortcuts such as voltage divider or current divider. Consider Fig. 7-27.

It looks like nodal analysis will give us E_{Th}. Node b is the reference; node a is the unknown V.

$$(1/R1 + 1/R2 + 1/R3 + 1/R4) \times V - (1/R1) \times E1 - (1/R3) \times (-E2) = -I$$

When the sources are replaced by their internal resistances (suppose that the sources

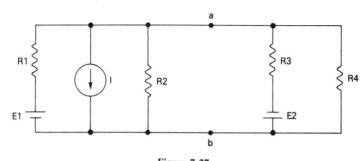

Figure 7-27

Analyzing DC Circuits   Chap. 7

```
#include <stdio.h>
main()
{
      void preamble(void);
      float R1, R2, R3, R4, Rth, E1, E2, I, Eth, In;

      preamble();

      printf("What is the value of R1?  ");
      scanf("%f", &R1);
      printf("What is the value of R2?  ");
      scanf("%f", &R2);
      printf("What is the value of R3?  ");
      scanf("%f", &R3);
      printf("What is the value of R4?  ");
      scanf("%f", &R4);
      printf("What is the value of E1?  ");
      scanf("%f", &E1);
      printf("What is the value of E2?  ");
      scanf("%f", &E2);
      printf("What is the value of I?  ");
      scanf("%f", &I);

      Rth = 1/(1/R1 + 1/R2 + 1/R3 + 1/R4);
      Eth = (I + E1/R1 + E2/R3) * Rth;
      In = Eth / Rth;

      printf("\nThe equivalents are:\n\n");
      printf("\tThevenin resistance: %.3f ohms\n", Rth);
      printf("\tThevenin voltage: %.3f volts\n", Eth);
      printf("\n");
      printf("\tNorton resistance: %.3f ohms\n",Rth);
      printf("\tNorton current: %.3f amps\n\n", In);
}


void preamble(void)
{

      printf("This program calculates the Thevenin and Norton");
      printf(" equivalents of\n\n\n");
      printf("                                a\n");
      printf("       ----------o---------o----o----o----------\n");
      printf("       |         |         |         |         |\n");
      printf("       R1        |         R2        R3        R4\n");
      printf("       |        V I        |         |         |\n");
      printf("      ---        |         |         =         |\n");
      printf("  E1   =         |         |    E2  ---        |\n");
      printf("       |         |         |         |         |\n");
      printf("       ----------o---------o----o----o----------\n");
      printf("                                b\n\n");
}
```

Figure 7-28

are ideal), you will see that the four resistors are simple in parallel across $a-b$. So

$$1/Rth = 1/R1 + 1/R2 + 1/R3 + 1/R4 = 1/Rn$$

and

$$In = Eth/Rn.$$

The program is given in Fig. 7-28.

7-7 MAXIMUM POWER TRANSFER

The maximum power transfer theorem states that the power transferred from source to load will be greatest when the load resistance is equal to the Thévenin equivalent resistance of the source. A computer program is a handy tool for examining the behavior of circuits transferring power because it is easy to set up a loop that causes the load resistance to vary over a specified range. And it is not necessary to calculate the Thévenin equivalents.

Consider the circuit in Fig. 7-29 as a candidate for a maximum power transfer program. If we know either the voltage (V_L) across the load (R_L), or the current (I_L) in it, we can easily calculate the power dissipated. As the circuit stands, it looks like nodal analysis is what we want. Figure 7-30 shows the circuit with the nodes indicated.

Node c is the common or reference node, and the voltages at a and b are the unknowns. Vb is also the voltage across the load, so let's set up to solve for it.

$$(1/R1 + 1/R2) \times Va + (-1/R1) E + (-1/R2) \times Vb = I$$

$$(1/R2 + 1/RL) \times Vb + (-1/R2) \times Va = 0$$

The program appears in Fig. 7-31.

You can see that for such a simple problem, I did not bother with functions and that I manipulated the original equations into assignment statement form before I wrote the program. There are a few interesting aspects to this program, so let's look at it again without comments but with line numbers, as shown in Fig. 7-32.

In line 4, I declared three "extra" variables. They are needed because we want to vary the load resistance over a given range. **RL0** is the initial or smallest value in the range, and **RLN** is the final or largest value. **RLd** is the step size; that is, the amount the user wants **RL** to change each time through the loop. Lines 16 through 21 show how the program gets these values from the user.

Lines 23 through 26 contain calculations that do not depend on the value of **RL**. That is, once the user has entered values for all the circuit elements, certain

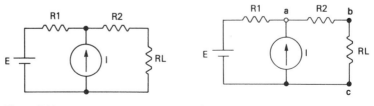

Figure 7-29   Figure 7-30

```
#include <stdio.h>
main()
{
     float R1, R2, RL, RL0, RLN, RLd, E, I, Vb, P;
     float g12, g2, g2L, g1, num;

     /* get the circuit component values */

     printf("Enter the value for R1: ");
     scanf("%f", &R1);
     printf("Enter the value for R2: ");
     scanf("%f", &R2);
     printf("Enter the value for E: ");
     scanf("%f", &E);
     printf("Enter the value for I: ");
     scanf("%f", &I);

     /* get the load resistance values for looping */

     printf("Enter the smallest value for RL: ");
     scanf("%f", &RL0);
     printf("Enter the largest value for RL: ");
     scanf("%f", &RLN);
     printf("Enter the amount that RL changes each step: ");
     scanf("%f", &RLd);

     /* these are quantities that do not change as RL changes,
        so they need be calculated only once */

     g1 = 1/R1;
     g2 = 1/R2;
     g12 = g1 + g2;
     num = g2 * (I + g1 * E);

     /* print heading for output table */

     printf("\n Load    Voltage    Power");

     /* run the loop and calculate and print results */

     for (RL = RL0; RL <= RLN; RL += RLd)
     {
          g2L = g2 + 1/RL;
          Vb = num / (g12 * g2L - g2 * g2);
          P = Vb * Vb /RL;
          printf("\n%6.3f    %6.3f    %6.3f", RL, Vb, P);
     }
}
```

Figure 7-31

```
1:    #include <stdio.h>
2:    main()
3:    {
4:         float R1, R2, RL, RL0, RLN, RLd, E, I, Vb, P;
5:         float g12, g2, g2L, g1, num;
6:
7:         printf("Enter the value for R1: ");
8:         scanf("%f", &R1);
9:         printf("Enter the value for R2: ");
10:        scanf("%f", &R2);
11:        printf("Enter the value for E: ");
12:        scanf("%f", &E);
13:        printf("Enter the value for I: ");
14:        scanf("%f", &I);
15:
16:        printf("Enter the smallest value for RL: ");
17:        scanf("%f", &RL0);
18:        printf("Enter the largest value for RL: ");
19:        scanf("%f", &RLN);
20:        printf("Enter the amount that RL changes each step: ");
21:        scanf("%f", &RLd);
22:
23:        g1 = 1/R1;
24:        g2 = 1/R2;
25:        g12 = g1 + g2;
26:        num = g2 * (I + g1 * E);
27:
28:        printf("\n Load     Voltage     Power");
29:
30:        for (RL = RL0; RL <= RLN; RL += RLd)
31:        {
32:             g2L = g2 + 1/RL;
33:             Vb = num / (g12 * g2L - g2 * g2);
34:             P = Vb * Vb /RL;
35:             printf("\n%6.3f    %6.3f    %6.3f", RL, Vb, P);
36:        }
37:    }
```

Figure 7-32

variables do not change. Thus, as an effort to increase the efficiency of the program, I have done certain calculations *before* starting the loop. Certainly, these statements could be placed inside the loop, but to do so means that the computer would calculate a value it already has, each time the loop is executed. Unnecessary and wasteful. Also outside the loop is line 28, a "title" for the chart that the program prints.

In the loop are the calculations for the load voltage and power, and a statement (#35) that prints the calculated values of load resistance, voltage, and power dissipated each time the loop is executed. Note that I have mixed statements previously separated into "process_them" and "display_results." This is OK for small programs.

Here (in Fig. 7-33) is a set of outputs. Note that the first run was a "coarse"

```
A>p708
Enter the value for R1: 20
Enter the value for R2: 5
Enter the value for E: 10
Enter the value for I: 5
Enter the smallest value for RL: 5
Enter the largest value for RL: 100
Enter the amount that RL changes each step: 5


   Load     Voltage    Power
   5.000     18.333     67.222
  10.000     31.429     98.775
  15.000     41.250    113.437
  20.000     48.889    119.506
  25.000     55.000    121.000  <--- near this value
  30.000     60.000    120.000
  35.000     64.167    117.639
  40.000     67.692    114.556
  45.000     70.714    111.122
  50.000     73.333    107.556
  55.000     75.625    103.984
  60.000     77.647    100.484
  65.000     79.444     97.099
  70.000     81.053     93.850
  75.000     82.500     90.750
  80.000     83.810     87.800
  85.000     85.000     85.000
  90.000     86.087     82.344
  95.000     87.083     79.826
 100.000     88.000     77.440


A>p708
Enter the value for R1: 20
Enter the value for R2: 5
Enter the value for E: 10
Enter the value for I: 5
Enter the smallest value for RL: 20
Enter the largest value for RL: 30
Enter the amount that RL changes each step: 1


   Load     Voltage    Power
  20.000     48.889    119.506
  21.000     50.217    120.085
  22.000     51.489    120.507
  23.000     52.708    120.790
  24.000     53.878    120.950
  25.000     55.000    121.000  <--- near this value
  26.000     56.078    120.953
  27.000     57.115    120.821
  28.000     58.113    120.612
  29.000     59.074    120.336
  30.000     60.000    120.000
```

Figure 7-33   (*Continued*)

```
A>p708
Enter the value for R1: 20
Enter the value for R2: 5
Enter the value for E: 10
Enter the value for I: 5
Enter the smallest value for RL: 24
Enter the largest value for RL: 26
Enter the amount that RL changes each step: .1
```

Load	Voltage	Power	
24.000	53.878	120.950	
24.100	53.992	120.959	
24.200	54.106	120.968	
24.300	54.219	120.976	
24.400	54.332	120.982	
24.500	54.444	120.988	
24.600	54.556	120.992	
24.700	54.668	120.996	
24.800	54.779	120.998	
24.900	54.890	121.000	|
25.000	55.000	121.000	| <-- any of these
25.100	55.110	121.000	|
25.200	55.219	120.998	
25.300	55.328	120.996	
25.400	55.437	120.992	
25.500	55.545	120.988	
25.600	55.652	120.983	
25.700	55.759	120.977	
25.800	55.866	120.970	
25.900	55.973	120.962	

Figure 7-33 (*Continued*)

one: A large range was used for **RL** and a large value for the step size. The first run shows the region where the power transferred is maximized. Run 2 shows that we have tried to pin down the actual value of **RL** for maximum power transfer more closely, and run 3 shows the results for a small range and a very small step in **RL**. You can see that the curve of power dissipated versus load resistance does not have a sharp point that can be easily identified as *the* maximum. However, from an engineering point of view, this broad area of maximum power transfer is preferable because the load resistance can be an ordinary resistor rather than an expensive precision resistor.

It is possible to plot these results on your screen. What you need to do is somehow convert the number of watts to a number of spaces. For example, the first run showed that the power varied from about 65 watts to about 125 watts, a difference of 60. The screen is 80 spaces wide, so if we say that the leftmost column represents 60 watts and each space represents 1 watt, the plot will fit on the screen. Each line will represent one step in the value **RL**, in this case, 5 ohms.

We must replace line 35 with something that will print the appropriate number of spaces and then an "o" or an "x". Consider this scheme:

for a given value of RL,
      calculate P and round it off
      print *P-61* spaces
      print an "o" and a newline

There are two new activities: rounding off, and printing a given number of spaces. The second is easier. To print *N* spaces, simply print one space *N* times!

```
for (i=0; i<P-61; ++i)
{
        printf(" ");
}
printf("o\n");
```

The code above prints *P-61* spaces, an "o", and goes to the next line.

Rounding is not difficult if you remember the rules. To round to the nearest unit, (i.e., 78.685 to 79), look at the digit to the right of the decimal point. If it is 5 or more, drop the digits to the right of the decimal point and add one to the units place. If it is 4 or less, just drop the digits to the right of the decimal point. In C, this is easily done like this:

```
(int) (P + 0.5)
```

If P is, say, 78.685, then P + 0.5 is 79.185 and **(int) 79.185** is 79. If P is 78.222, then P + 0.5 is 78.722 and **(int) 78.722** is 78. You will be asked to work out a more general scheme for homework.

It looks like line 35 should be replaced by the following code:

```
/* round-off P and subtract 61 */
for (i = 0; i < ( (int)(P + 0.5) - 61 ); ++i)
        printf(" ");
printf("o  %7.2f\n",P);
```

In the last line, I added code to print the actual value of P. Here's what a run looks like (Fig. 7-34). You could improve this by printing the value of RL as the first thing on each line, as shown in Fig. 7-35.

```
A>p708a
Enter the value for R1: 20
Enter the value for R2: 5
Enter the value for E: 10
Enter the value for I: 5
Enter the smallest value for RL: 5
```

Figure 7-34   (*Continued*)

```
Enter the largest value for RL: 100
Enter the amount that RL changes each step: 5

           o    67.22
                                              o    98.78
                                                       o    113.44
                                                              o    119.51
                                                              o    121.00
                                                              o    120.00
                                                            o    117.64
                                                          o    114.56
                                                       o    111.12
                                                     o    107.56
                                                   o    103.98
                                                 o    100.48
                                               o    97.10
                                             o    93.85
                                            o    90.75
                                          o    87.80
                                        o    85.00
                                      o    82.34
                                    o    79.83
                                  o    77.44
```

Figure 7-34   (*Continued*)

```
A>p708b
Enter the value for R1: 20
Enter the value for R2: 5
Enter the value for E: 10
Enter the value for I: 5
Enter the smallest value for RL: 5
Enter the largest value for RL: 100
Enter the amount that RL changes each step: 5

RL=   5:       o   67.22
RL=  10:                                        o  98.78
RL=  15:                                             o  113.44
RL=  20:                                                o  119.51
RL=  25:                                                o  121.00
RL=  30:                                                o  120.00
RL=  35:                                               o  117.64
RL=  40:                                             o  114.56
RL=  45:                                          o  111.12
RL=  50:                                        o  107.56
RL=  55:                                      o  103.98
RL=  60:                                    o  100.48
RL=  65:                                  o  97.10
RL=  70:                                o  93.85
RL=  75:                              o  90.75
RL=  80:                            o  87.80
RL=  85:                          o  85.00
RL=  90:                        o  82.34
RL=  95:                      o  79.83
RL= 100:                    o  77.44
```

Figure 7-35

7-8 REVIEW

In this chapter you learned how to:

- Write programs for branch current analysis
- Write programs for mesh current analysis
- Write programs for node voltage analysis
- Write programs for Thévenin and Norton equivalents
- Write programs that use superposition
- Write programs that investigate maximum power transfer
- Use external variables
- Use two-dimensional arrays of numbers
- Plot results on the screen

PROBLEMS AND QUESTIONS

1. Rewrite the second-order determinant program so that it shows the circuit of Fig. 7-1 and asks for the appropriate values.

2. Modify the third-order determinant program using the functions of Figs. 7-12, 7-13, and 7-14.

3. Modify the third-order determinant program so that it is suitable for solving nodal equations. *Hint:* See Fig. 7-19.

4. Complete the program of Fig. 7-23.

5. Rewrite the program of Problem 4 using no *external variables*.

6. Rewrite the program of Fig. 7-26 into a **main( )** plus four other functions, one of which is **print_preamble( )**.

7. Rewrite the program of Fig. 7-28 into a **main( )** plus four other functions, one of which is **preamble( )**.

8. Rewrite the program of Fig. 7-31 into a **main( )** plus four other functions.

9. Change the program of Problem 8 to include a function that plots the results. Should it be separate from the **calculations** function?

10. Complete the function of Fig. 7-35, and incorporate it into a second-order determinant program that solves any circuit with two nodes (plus the reference).

11. Write a function *float fround(float x, int n)* that accepts a float value x and rounds it off to the nth decimal place. For example, *fround(12.3456, 1)* would return **12.3**, while *fround(12.3456, 2)* would return **12.35**. *Hint:* In order to use an *int* cast, you will need to multiply the number by 10.0 one or more times before adding 0.5 and casting.

12. Write programs for problems assigned from your circuits textbook.

8

Transient Circuit Applications

8-1 INTRODUCTION AND OBJECTIVES

In this chapter you will write and examine programs that deal with electric fields, capacitors, *RC* circuits, magnetic fields, inductors, and *RL* circuits. Also, you will meet one or two new C library functions.

Upon successful completion of this chapter, you will be able to:

- Write programs for calculating currents and voltages in *RC* charging circuits
- Write programs for calculating currents and voltages in *RC* discharging circuits
- Write programs for calculating currents and voltages in *RL storage* circuits
- Write programs for calculating currents and voltages in *RL release* circuits
- Use the C library functions *exp( )* and *log( )*

8-2 CAPACITANCE-RELATED CALCULATIONS

In your circuits course, you learned several formulas that are needed for performing electric field calculations. They include the ones for calculating flux density and electric field strength. These formulas are very similar to the ones you've used for Ohm's law, power calculations, and so on, so that programming for these should present you with a very familiar situation.

This is also true for many of the formulas involving capacitance. There is a formula for capacitance that involves the *permitivity* of the material separating the capacitor's conducting surfaces, the area of the surfaces, and the distance between them. It should remind you of the formula for resistance, which included the *resistivity* of the wire, as well as its area and length. Programming a capacitance calculation should also be quite familiar.

What is not so familiar is the calculation for *RC* circuits. Unlike purely resistive circuits, those having both *R* and *C* in them change their voltages and currents over a period of time. In other words, *RC* circuits contain *transients*. To fully analyze a transient circuit requires more math than you are expected to have at this point. However, if the circuit can be reduced to a series circuit with one resistor and one capacitor (*hint:* apply Thévenin's theorem to the circuit connected across the capacitor), you can use the "standard" solutions to the two most common transient situations: charging and discharging.

You know that when a voltage is placed across a capacitor, it will retain that voltage for an indefinite period of time. We say that the capacitor is charged. If a resistor is placed across a charged capacitor, the capacitor will discharge and eventually have 0 volts cross its terminals.

Charging Calculations

Charging a capacitor usually involves a circuit having a voltage source, a resistor, and a capacitor in series (see Fig. 8-1). Call the voltage across the capacitor V_c, measured with respect to node c. If V_c is less than E, then when the switch that can connect points a and b together is closed, the capacitor will charge toward E volts. The time it takes to get there depends on the value of V_c before the switch was closed, E, R, and C. If V_c is greater than E, then when the switch is closed, the capacitor will discharge toward E volts. Usually, we consider charging circuits in which V_c is 0, and discharging circuits in which E is 0. This makes our analysis simpler.

The formula for the current in the charging circuit is

$$i_c = (E/R)e^{-t/RC}$$

This assumes that the capacitor was completely discharged at the instant of time that the switch was closed. You see two new factors in this equation: the e and the t. The e is the symbol for one of those ever-popular "universal constants" and has an approximate value of 2.718281828. You will find it on your calculator on a key marked e^x. The t stands for the time elapsed since the switch was closed.

C has a library function

```
double exp(double x)
```

which performs the e^x calculation, so the assignment statement form of the above is

```
    i = (E/R) * exp(-t/(R*C));
```

(*Note:* The parentheses around $R * C$ are absolutely necessary!) The voltage across the resistor is given by Ohm's law:

```
    v_r = i * R = E * exp(-t/(R*C));
```

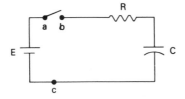

Figure 8-1

```
#include <stdio.h>
#include <math.h>          /* needed for exp() */
main()
{
     float e, r, c, t, i, T;

     printf("This program solves the RC charging circuit");
     printf(" for current.\n");
     printf("\nEnter the source voltage: ");
     scanf("%f", &e);
     printf("Enter the resistance value: ");
     scanf("%f", &r);
     printf("Enter the capacitance value: ");
     scanf("%f", &c);

     T = r * c;
     for (t=0.0; t <= 5*T; t += T/4)
     {
          i = e/r * exp(-t/T);
          printf("\n%f       %f", t, i);
     }
}
```

Figure 8-2

```
This program solves for the current in an RC charging circuit.

Enter the source voltage: 40
Enter the resistance value: 8000
Enter the capacitance value: 4e-6

                                                             0.005
          |----|----|----|----|----|----|----|----|----|----|----|
   0.0000 |                                                       +
   0.0080 |                                                  +
   0.0160 |                                             +
   0.0240 |                                        +
   0.0320 |                                   +
   0.0400 |                              +
   0.0480 |                           +
   0.0560 |                       +
   0.0640 |                    +
   0.0720 |                  +
   0.0800 |                +
   0.0880 |              +
   0.0960 |            +
   0.1040 |          +
   0.1120 |          +
   0.1200 |          +
   0.1280 |        +
   0.1360 |        +
   0.1440 |        +
   0.1520 |        +
   0.1600 |        +
   0.1680 |        +
```

Figure 8-3

and the voltage across the capacitor, by Kirchhoff's voltage law:

$$v_c = E - v_r = E * (1 - exp(-t/(R*C)));$$

The charge in the capacitor can be calculated from

$$q = C * v_c = C * E * (1 - exp(-t/(R*C)));$$

The declaration of *exp( )* is in *math.h*, and a simple program to calculate the current in a charging circuit is shown in Fig. 8-2.

The product $T = r * c$ is called the "time constant." My loop in Fig. 8-2 extends for five time constants and has steps of T/4, giving 20 steps in all. The 5*T is important because the current at that instant of time is less than 1% of the original. That is, the circuit has very nearly reached *steady state*.

Let's write a program that plots the current versus time, as we did in an earlier chapter. But let's write a "smarter" program—one that adjusts values so that the plot fits on the screen. To do this, we must know the maximum value of the variable we want to plot. We'll need a function that will pick out the maximum value from a group of values. Then we'll use that maximum to scale the plot. We would like a function that, when used in the program of Fig. 8-2, results in a graph like the one in Fig. 8-3. The number above the dashed line is the maximum value of the plotted variable. The numbers in a column at the left are values of time.

Figure 8-4 shows the program that produced the output in Fig. 8-3. Let's examine it in detail. The first four lines

```
#include <stdio.h>
#include <math.h>
#define SIZE 21
#define WIDTH 50
```

are for the preprocessor. *SIZE* tells the program how many values it is to calculate, while *WIDTH* is used in the scaling: we will consider that the horizontal space for plotting values is *WIDTH* columns wide.

The loop

```
for (t = 0.0, k = 0; k <= SIZE; ++k, t += T/4)
{
        i[k] = e/r * exp(-t/T);
}
```

calculates each value of the current and stores it in an element of an array, *i[k]*. Note the unusual *for* statement. I could have written it like this:

```
t = 0.0;
for (k = 0; k <= SIZE; ++k)
{
        i[k] = e/r * exp(-t/T);
        t += T/4;
}
```

```
#include <stdio.h>
#include <math.h>
#define SIZE 21
#define WIDTH 50
main()
{
      float e, r, c, t, T, imax;
      float i[SIZE];
      float max(float [], int n);
      int j, k;

      printf("This program solves for the current ");
      printf("in an RC charging circuit.\n");
      printf("\nEnter the source voltage: ");
      scanf("%f", &e);
      printf("Enter the resistance value: ");
      scanf("%f", &r);
      printf("Enter the capacitance value: ");
      scanf("%f", &c);

      T = r * c;

      for (t = 0.0, k = 0; k <= SIZE; ++k, t += T/4)
      {
            i[k] = e/r * exp(-t/T);
      }

      imax = max(i, SIZE);

      for (j = 0; j < 66; ++j)
      {
            printf(" ");
      }
      printf("%f\n", imax);

      printf("         |----|----|----|----|----|----|----");
      printf("|----|----|----|----|----|");

      for (k = 0, t = 0.0; k <= SIZE; ++k, t += T/4)
      {
            printf("\n%6.4f |", t);

            for (j = 0; j <= WIDTH * i[k]/imax; ++j)
            {
                  printf(" ");
            }
            printf("+");
      }
}

float max(float x[], int n)
{
      float xmax = -1e38;
      int i;
```

Figure 8-4

```
for (i = 0; i < n; ++i)
{
        if (x[i] > xmax)
        {
                xmax = x[i];
        }
}
return (xmax);
```

}

Figure 8-4 (*Continued*)

but the compact form is appealing because it puts all the 'bookkeeping'' action—
for *k* and *t*—between the parentheses. Note that in the compact form, there are
still only two semicolons. Any multiple statements between semicolons are separated by commas. Although it is not unusual to have comma-separated statements
in the first and third positions, it is quite unusual to have them in the middle
position.

The next set of statements shows the definition and the call for the function
max( ).

Definition:

```
float max(float x[], int n)
{
        float xmax = -1e38;
        int i;

        for (i = 0; i < n; ++i)
        {
                if (x[i] > xmax)
                {
                        xmax = x[i];
                }
        }
        return (xmax);
}
```

The call:

```
imax = max(i, SIZE);
```

max( ) returns a *float* and accepts the name of a *float* array and an *int*. The *int*
value tells *max( )* how many items will be compared. We initialize the function
with a very large negative number for *xmax* and replace it with any value that's
bigger (i.e., more positive). By the time we've gone completely through the loop,
the largest value in the array will be the value for *xmax*.

These statements

```
for (j = 0; j < 66; ++j)
{
        printf(" ");
}
printf("%f\n", imax);
```

print the maximum value near the right-hand edge of the screen.

The following statements refer back to the array of values for the current, $i[k]$, so that each value can be plotted.

```
for (k = 0, t = 0.0; k <= SIZE; ++k, t += T/4)
{
      printf("\n%6.4f |", t);

      for (j = 0; j <= WIDTH * i[k]/imax; ++j)
      {
            printf(" ");
      }
      printf("+");

}
```

Again, I used a "compact" *for* statement so that everything about k and t and how they change is between the parentheses at the top of the loop. The first *printf()* puts the value of t on the screen and follows it with the " | " character. Then a number of spaces are printed, followed by a " + ". The number of spaces is the scaled value of $i[k]$. $i[k]/imax$ "normalizes" $i[k]$ (i.e., the largest value of $i[k]/imax$ is 1.00). Then I multiplied by *WIDTH* to convert the normalized value of $i[k]$ to a reasonable number of spaces.

We could improve this program by writing the plotting stuff as a function. It would include the *max()* function, code for printing the axes, and code for labeling the top axis with several values. The header could be

```
void plot(float [], int)
```

It would also be useful if it could determine the relative sizes of the calculated values for t and $i[k]$ so that it could plot them in appropriate units. For example, if *imax* = 0.000856 ampere, it could plot current in hundreds of microamperes, or if T = 0.0234 second, it would plot time in milliseconds. Does that sound like it's going to be a homework assignment?

Discharging Calculations

Figure 8-5 shows the simplest possible circuit for capacitor discharge. Suppose that the capacitor has been charged to some voltage, V_0, and then the switch is closed. The resulting voltage (it's across both R and C) is given by

$$v = V_0 \times \exp(-t/T)$$

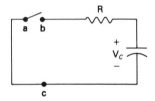

Figure 8-5

```c
#include <stdio.h>
#include <stdlib.h>
#include <math.h>
main()
{
    float e, r, c, t, T, vf, If;
    int choice;

    printf("This program solves the RC discharging ");
    printf("circuit for the time at which \na variable ");
    printf("reaches a given value.  The variables are:\n");
    printf("\t1.  capacitor voltage\n");
    printf("\t2.  resistor voltage\n");
    printf("\t3.  current\n");
    printf("Please choose 1, 2, or 3:  ");
    scanf("%d", &choice);
    printf("\nEnter the capacitor initial voltage: ");
    scanf("%f", &e);
    printf("Enter the resistance value: ");
    scanf("%f", &r);
    printf("Enter the capacitance value: ");
    scanf("%f", &c);

    T = r * c;

    if (choice == 1 || choice == 2)
    {
        printf("\nEnter the final voltage: ");
        scanf("%f", &vf);
        if (vf > e)
        {
            printf("\n\nERROR!!\n\n");
            exit(1);
        }
        t = -T * log(vf/e);
    }
    else if (choice == 3)
    {
        printf("\nEnter the final current: ");
        scanf("%f", &If);
        if (If > e/r)
        {
            printf("\n\nERROR!!\n\n");
            exit(1);
        }
        t = -T * log(If/e/r);
    }

    printf("\nThe time constant is %f seconds.\n", T);
    printf("\nThe time to reach the final value is %f seconds.", t);
}
```

Figure 8-6

while the current is simply v/R:

$$i = V_0/R \times \exp(-t/T)$$

where $T = R \times C$, as before. Clearly a program for these is quite straightforward.

Time Calculations

One of the interesting questions a person might ask, given an *RC* circuit, is: How long after the switch is closed will the voltage across the capacitor be *X* volts? To solve this, you need to know whether you have a charging circuit or a discharging circuit, and the values of the elements. The discharging equation for the voltage across the capacitor is

$$v = V_0 \times \exp(-t/T)$$

while the charging equation is

```
v = E * (1 - exp(-t/T));
```

where $T = R \times C$. Solving for *t* in the first gives

$$t = -T \times \ln(1 - v/V_0)$$

while solving for the second gives

$$t = -T \times \ln(v/E)$$

In both cases, you will need a function that can produce the natural logarithm (*ln*) of a number. The C library includes such a function; its header is

```
double log(double)
```

Let's investigate a program that calculates the time in a discharge circuit. It is shown in Fig. 8-6.

8-3 INDUCTANCE-RELATED CALCULATIONS

In a real sense, everything you learned about *RC* circuit and capacitor calculations can be applied directly to *RL* circuits and inductances. Where capacitance is a phenomenon of electric fields, inductance arises from magnetic fields. We have magnetic flux density, permeability, reluctance, magnetizing force, and Ampère's law giving rise to the same kinds of formulas you learned to program early in this book. Further, there's a formula for *self-inductance* that will remind you of those for resistance and capacitance. Also, there are transients in *RL* circuits.

Although it is not correct to say that an inductor *charges* and *discharges*, it does have the ability to store energy and later release it. During the storage activity in a series *RL* circuit, the current is given by

$$i = E/R \times (1 - e^{-t/T})$$

where $T = L/R$. Thus the voltage across the resistor will be

$$v_c = i \times R = E \times (1 - e^{-t/T})$$

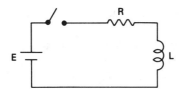

Figure 8-7

so that the voltage across the inductor will be

$$v_L = E - v_r = E \times e^{-t/T}$$

I think that you can see why I said that what you learned about *RC* circuits can be applied to *RL* circuits! A series circuit is shown in Fig. 8-7. When the switch connects *a* and *b*, the inductor receives energy from the voltage source. When the switch is thrown to connect **b** and **c**, the energy in the inductor's magnetic field is returned to the circuit. Incidentally, this is exactly the kind of circuit one uses to turn a motor on and off, but it has one "interesting" characteristic. Because you are trying to interrupt a current in an inductance, the circuit will *arc* across the switch contacts as they are opened. The inductor is trying mightily to maintain its current! A less spectacular circuit would use a two position "make-before-break" switch and a second resistor to insure that no attempt is made to interrupt the current.

The release phase depends on the value of current in the inductor just before the release phase begins—just as the discharge phase of the *RC* circuit depends on the voltage across the capacitor just as the discharge begins. Given the same *R* and *L*, the current is given by

$$i = E/R \times e^{-t/T}$$

where $T = L/R$. Thus the voltage across the resistor (and inductor) will be

$$v = i \times R = E \times e^{-t/T}$$

You will have no trouble writing programs for these circuits.

8-4 REVIEW

In this chapter you learned how to:

- Write programs for calculating currents and voltages in *RC* charging circuits
- Write programs for calculating currents and voltages in *RC* discharging circuits
- Write programs for calculating currents and voltages in *RL storage* circuits
- Write programs for calculating currents and voltages in *RL release* circuits
- Use the C library functions *exp( )* and *log( )*

PROBLEMS AND QUESTIONS

1. Write a program for calculating the capacitance of a parallel-plate capacitor in which the user is asked to enter the area in square meters and the distance between plates in

millimeters, and is also asked to choose from among a list of at least four different dielectric materials.

2. Write a program that lets the user select one unknown from the formula $C = Q/V$ and solves for it. The user is to be asked to supply values for the two knowns.

3. Modify the program in Fig. 8-4 so that *main( )* calls a function to do the plotting (as suggested in the text).

4. Write a function that accepts a float value and returns a string that includes the engineering version of that value. For example,

call	return
f(1200000.0)	1.2 M
f(32555.0)	32.555 K
f(128.4)	128.4
f(0.002345)	2.345 m
f(0.000333456)	333.456 u (*u* for *micro*)

5. Write a program that does calculations for an *RC* circuit that is discharging.

6. Write a program for calculating the inductance of a coil of wire—a so-called *air-core* coil—in which the user is asked to enter the area in square meters, the length of the wire in meters, and the number of turns.

7. Write a program that does calculations for an *RL* circuit that is storing energy in a coil.

8. Write a program that does calculations for an *RL* circuit that is releasing energy that was being stored in a coil.

9. Write programs for problems assigned from your electric circuits textbook.

9

C and Sinusoids

9-1 INTRODUCTION AND OBJECTIVES

In this chapter you will write and examine programs that deal with sinusoidal ac circuits. In previous chapters you met and wrote programs that dealt with dc circuits consisting of resistors and sources, and a few that included inductance or capacitance and their transient effects. The analysis of ac circuits requires that you use complex numbers in your algebraic calculations, as well as some trigonometry. However, as usual, the computer takes the "sting" out of the computations once you have learned to use C's trigonometric functions.

Upon successful completion of this chapter, you will be able to:

- Write programs for converting *period* to *frequency*, and vice versa
- Write programs for converting between *radian* and *degrees*
- Write programs for calculating *angular velocity* and *frequency*
- Write programs for calculating instantaneous values and phase angles
- Write programs for calculating impedance of *R, L,* and *C*
- Write programs for calculating average and rms values of specific waveforms
- Use the C library functions for trigonometry calculations

9-2 FUNDAMENTALS OF SINUSOIDS

An ac voltage source is quite different from a dc voltage source. The dc voltage is constant over all time, while the ac voltage varies between a maximum and a minimum value. Not only does it vary, but the variation is a particular type called a *sinusoid*. The most general sinusoids can be expressed as either

$$A \times \sin(\omega t + \theta)$$

or

$$A \times \cos(\omega t + \theta)$$

A is called the amplitude and is one-half of the maximum "swing" of the sinusoid. Both ω*t* and θ (this is called the *phase angle*) are angles measured in radians. As you may know, there are 2π radians in a circle. This relationship is the key to converting between radians and degrees because a circle also represents 360°. Thus 1 π radian = 180°.

Radians and Degrees

Here is a simple program that will convert radians to degrees or degrees to radians for you (see Fig. 9-1).

I've made use of several techniques that we discussed previously. By declaring

```
char units[2][8] = {"radians", "degrees"};
```

I can use the array *units* in the output statement

```
printf("\nThe converted angle is %f %s.\n", angout, units[i]);
```

It seems like there should be a more efficient way to do this: I used both a *char* variable **ang** and an *int* variable **i** to represent the answer to the question. Also, I did not bulletproof the input but assumed that an answer other than *y*

```
#include <stdio.h>
#define PI 3.14159
main()
{
        float angin, angout;
        int i;
        char ques;
        char units[2][8] = {"radians", "degrees"};

        printf("\nThis will convert a given angle from degrees ");
        printf("to radians, \nor from radians to degrees.\n\n");
        printf("Do you want RADIANS TO DEGREES (y or n)? ");
        scanf("%c", &ques);
        printf("\nEnter the angle: ");
        scanf("%f", &angin);

        if (ques == 'y')
        {
                angout = (180/PI) * angin;
                i = 1;
        }
        else
        {
                angout = (PI/180) * angin;
                i = 0;
        }
        printf("\nThe converted angle is %f %s.\n",
                angout, units[i]);
}
```

Figure 9-1

meant that the user wanted *DEGREES TO RADIANS*. Sounds like a homework assignment coming up!

Angular Velocity, Frequency, and Period

The ω in the expressions for *sin* and *cos* represents *angular velocity*, angular because sinusoidal motion is **circular** motion. We normally don't think about anything rotating when we see circuit problems, so engineers have related angular velocity to another quantity called **f**, the *frequency*, like this:

$$\omega = 2\pi f$$

That is, 1 radian/second is the same as 2π hertz (the unit of frequency). It should be easy to modify my *radian-degree* conversion program to make it a *angular velocity–frequency* conversion program. While you're at it, you may as well include the relation between the frequency and its reciprocal, **T**, the period. This, as you know, is the amount of time for whatever is rotating to complete a full circle, or *cycle*.

Instantaneous Values

The instantaneous value of a sinusoid depends on the answers to five questions:

1. Is it described by *sin* or *cos*?
2. What is the value of ω?
3. What is the value of *t*?
4. What is the value of θ?
5. What is the value of the amplitude?

Writing a C program to find the instantaneous value depends on your knowledge of C's trigonometric functions: *double cos(double)* and *double sin(double)*. For both functions, the argument **must** be in **radians**. These functions are declared in *math.h*. Once we make the calculation, we can plot it, as we did for transient voltages and currents. Figure 9-2 shows a program that does just that.

There are a couple of noteworthy lines in this program. First, note how I used the string function *strcmp()* to see what form the user entered:

```
#include <string.h>
char form[4];
if (strcmp("cos", form) == 0)
        ang += 90;
```

strcmp() returns **0** if the strings are identical. Also, I took advantage of the relationship between *sin* and *cos*: *cos* "leads" *sin* by 90°.

Plotting Two Sinusoids

The concept of the *relative phase angle* between two sinusoid is a puzzlement to many students. Seeing the two is a great help, but plotting two sinusoids at one time takes some planning. It is fairly easy to do in C but a little awkward.

```
#include <stdio.h>
#include <string.h>
#include <math.h>
#define PI 3.14159
main()
{
        char form[4];
        float ang, x, i;
        int j;

        printf("\nThis program plots one cycle of the sinusoid ");
        printf("that you define.\nThe amplitude is normalized to 1.0\n");
        printf("\nEnter the form (sin or cos): ");
        scanf("%s", form);
        printf("Enter the phase angle (in degrees): ");
        scanf("%f", &ang);

        if (strcmp("cos", form) == 0)
                ang += 90;

        for (i = 0; i < 2 * PI + 2 * PI / 50; i += 2 * PI / 50)
        {
                x = sin(i + PI * ang / 180);
                for (j = 0; j < 30 * x + 30; ++j)
                        printf(" ");
                printf("+ %f\n", x);
        }
}
```

Figure 9-2

Basically, you need to compute both values at each point of time and find out which is larger. Then you can plot the larger using our usual technique of spacing over a number of spaces (proportional to the size of the variable being plotted) and printing a mark. Then return the cursor all the way to the left and plot the smaller. This will insure that plotting one does not wipe out the mark for the other. Figure 9-3 shows a demonstration program that plots a *sin* and a *cos*, while Fig. 9-4 shows the output of that program. Note that the statement

```
printf("#\r");
```

means "print the # and then return the cursor to the left-hand edge of the screen on the same line." Compare "\r" with "\n", which brings the cursor to the left-hand edge of the screen on the *next* line.

Impedance Calculations

When an ac voltage is applied to a circuit element, an ac current results. The current's waveform will be a sinusoid having the same frequency as the source voltage sinusoid, but it may have a different amplitude and may be out of phase with the voltage (i.e., they may have different phase angles). The relationship between the current and the voltage is called the *impedance, Z*. *Z* is a complex number; that is, it has a real part and an imaginary part. It may also be represented

```c
#include <stdio.h>
#include <string.h>
#include <math.h>
#define PI 3.14159
main()
{
      float x, y, i;
      int j;

      printf("\nThis program plots one cycle of two sinusoids.\n ");
      printf("x is represented by +, y by #\n\n");

      printf("      -1                        0");
      printf("                              +1\n");

      printf("      |----|----|----|----|----|----|----");
      printf("|----|----|----|----|----|\n");

      for (i = 0; i < 2 * PI + 2 * PI / 50; i += 2 * PI / 50)
      {
            x = sin(i);
            y = cos(i);
            if (y < x)
            {
                  for (j = 0; j <= 30 * x + 35; ++j)
                  {
                        printf(" ");
                  }
                  printf("+\r");
                  for (j = 0; j <= 30 * y + 35; ++j)
                  {
                        printf(" ");
                  }
                  printf("#\n");
            }
            else
            {
                  for (j = 0; j <= 30 * y + 35; ++j)
                  {
                        printf(" ");
                  }
                  printf("#\r");
                  for (j = 0; j <= 30 * x + 35; ++j)
                  {
                        printf(" ");
                  }
                  printf("+\n");
            }
      }
}
```

Figure 9-3

A:>p903

This program plots one cycle of two sinusoids.
 x is represented by +, y by #

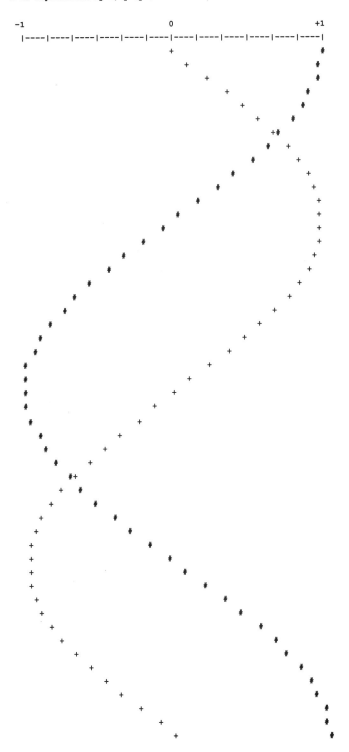

Figure 9-4

as a *vector*, having a magnitude and an angle. The magnitude, z, is simply the ratio of the magnitude of the voltage vector to the magnitude of the current vector, while the angle is the phase difference between the voltage and the current.

For a resistor, $z = R$ and the angle $= 0$.
For an inductor, $z = \omega L$, angle $= 90°$.
For a capacitor, $z = 1/(\omega C)$, angle $= -90°$.

Put in another way, the current and voltage of a resistor are in phase. For an inductor, the voltage leads the current by $90°$, while for a capacitor, the voltage lags the current (or the current leads the voltage) by $90°$.

If you calculate current using the amplitude (or "peak value") of the sine wave, you will get the corresponding current amplitude. If you use the rms or *effective* voltage value, you will get the rms value of the current.

Let's examine a program that lets the user pick an element and its value, and a frequency range, and produces a table of impedance values for that element. Figure 9-5 shows such a program. Here I used the *switch* operator in the middle of a loop. *switch* makes it easy to deal with upper/lowercase distinctions.

Average and RMS Values

A voltage described by

$$e = E_m \sin(\omega t + \theta)$$

has an infinite number of values, from $-E_m$ to $+E_m$. By measuring the heating effect of such a voltage and comparing it to the dc voltage that produces the same heating effect, engineers have produced a single number to describe that ac voltage—it is called the *effective* value. Mathematicians arrive at the same number by calculating the square **root** of the **mean** (or average) value of the **square** of a sine wave over a full cycle, and calling that the *rms* (i.e., root-mean-square) value.

For a sinusoid, the rms value, E, is equal to 0.707 times the peak value, E_m, measured over a full cycle. The *average* value of a sinusoid **over a full cycle** is 0.

Mathematically, rms and average values of waveforms are meaningful only if the waveforms are periodic (i.e., have a period and thus a frequency). Further, we can calculate the average and rms values of periodic waveforms that are made up of a series of constants over the period (e.g., see Fig. 9-6). We can get the average value and the rms value by considering the area under the curve. For example, the area under the curve in Fig. 9-6 is

$$6 \times 8 = 48, \text{ above the line} \tag{1}$$

$$2 \times 2 = -4, \text{ below the line} \tag{2}$$

or a net of $48 + (-4) = 44$. Dividing by the period, 10, gives 4.4 as the average value.

To find the rms, we need the average value of the square of the waveform. The individual areas would be

$$6^2 \times 8 = 36 \times 8 = 288 \tag{1}$$

$$2^2 \times 2 = 4 \times 2 = 8 \tag{2}$$

```
#include <stdio.h>
#define PI 3.14159
main()
{
        float imp, f, fi, ff, fs, val;
        char ele;

        printf("\nThis program will produce a table of impedance ");
        printf("values for an\nelement you specify.\n\n");

        printf("Do you want R, L, or C? (r, l, c): ");
        scanf("%c", &ele);
        printf("Enter its value in ohms, millihenries, or microfarads: ");
        scanf("%f", &val);
        printf("Enter lowest frequency, in Hz: ");
        scanf("%f", &fi);
        printf("Enter highest frequency, in Hz: ");
        scanf("%f", &ff);
        printf("Enter step size, in Hz: ");
        scanf("%f", &fs);

        printf("\n\n\t          frequency       impedance");
        printf("\n\t---------------------------------------");

        for (f = fi; f <= ff; f += fs)
        {
              switch(ele)
              {
                    case 'r':
                    case 'R':  imp = val;
                            break;
                    case 'l':
                    case 'L':  imp = 2 * PI * f * val / 1000;
                            break;
                    case 'c':
                    case 'C':  imp = 1000000 / (2 * PI * f * val);
                            break;
              }
              printf("\n\t\t%10.3f%14.3f", f, imp);
        }
}
```

Figure 9-5

or a net of 288 + 8 = 296. The mean value is 296/10 = 29.6, and the rms value
is the square root of that, 5.441.

You can see that the scheme for calculating this is

1. do the average value calculations

2. do the RMS calculations

3. report the results

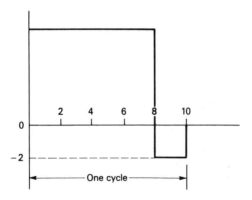

Figure 9-6

To do this properly, we must find out how many segments there are, the height of each, and the time duration of each. Figure 9-7 shows an interesting case. There are four segments, as follows:

Number	Height	Width
1	10	2
2	−4	4
3	4	2
4	−2	3

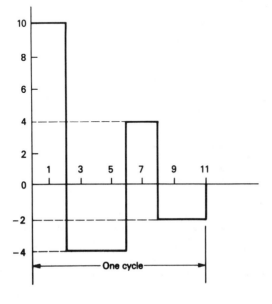

Figure 9-7

Let's extend the table to calculate the areas for average.

Number	Height	Width	Area
1	10	2	20
2	-4	4	-16
3	4	2	8
4	-2	3	-6

Total area: 6

Total time: 11

Average value: 0.5455

We can extend that further to calculate the areas for rms.

Number	Height	Width	Height^2	Area
1	10	2	100	200
2	-4	4	16	64
3	4	2	16	32
4	-2	3	4	12

Total area: 308

Total time: 11

Average of the square: 28.0

Square root of average: 5.292

Here's the refined scheme:

1. get the number of segments, *num*
2. for each segment,
2.1   get the height and duration
2.2   calculate the area for the average
2.3   square the height and calculate the rms area
3. sum the "average" area and the durations
4. calculate the average value
5. sum the rms area
6. calculate the rms value

Figure 9-8 shows a program that can handle as many as 10 segments. A program like this becomes more interesting if we can include triangular sections along with the rectangles. Let's divide the period into segments so that any triangular segments are right triangles. Then the area of a right-hand triangular

```
#include <stdio.h>
#include <math.h>
main()
{
      int num, i;
      float h[11], t[11], avg_area = 0, RMS_area = 0;
      float period = 0, avg, RMS;

      printf("\nThis program will calculate the average and RMS values ");
      printf("of any periodic\nrectanguar waveform having 10 or fewer ");
      printf("segments per period.\n\n");
      printf("Enter the number of segments in a period: ");
      scanf("%d", &num);

      for (i = 0; i < num; ++i)
      {
            printf("\nEnter the height of segment %d: ", i+1);
            scanf("%f", &h[i]);
            printf("Enter the duration of segment %d: ", i+1);
            scanf("%f", &t[i]);
            avg_area += h[i] * t[i];
            RMS_area += h[i] * h[i] * t[i];
            period += t[i];
      }

      avg = avg_area / period;
      RMS = sqrt(RMS_area / period);
      printf("\nThe average value is %f.\nThe RMS value is %f.\n",
            avg, RMS);


}
```

Figure 9-8

segment will be 0.5. × h[i] × t[i]. However, if you look at the graph of the square
of a triangular section, you will see a curved line! And there's no easy way for
us to calculate the area under a curve.

9-3 REVIEW

In this chapter you learned how to:

- Write programs for converting period to frequency, and vice versa
- Write programs for converting between *radian* and *degrees*
- Write programs for calculating angular velocity and frequency
- Write programs for calculating instantaneous values and phase angles
- Write programs for calculating impedance of R, L, and C
- Write programs for calculating average and rms values of specific waveforms
- Use the C library functions for trigonometric calculations

PROBLEMS AND QUESTIONS

1. Modify the program of Fig. 9-1 so that a single variable can be used to select both the mode of conversion and the proper output unit.

2. Modify your program from Problem 1 to bulletproof the input. That is, accept only *y* and *n* (or their uppercase relatives).

3. Modify the program of Problem 2 so that it will accept either *angular velocity*, *frequency*, or *period*, and calculate the other two.

4. Rewrite the program of Fig. 9-2 to bulletproof the input for *form*. Also, make the program more efficient by *#define*-ing several more constants. *Note:* You are permitted to "nest" definitions. For example, the following is perfectly legal:

```
#define PI 3.14159
#define TWOPI (2 * PI)
```

TWOPI will have the value 6.28318

5. In Fig. 9-2, why is 2 * PI + 2 * PI/50 the upper limit on **i**? What is the significance of each *30* in

```
for (j = 0; j < 30 * x + 30; ++j)
```

6. Modify the program in Fig. 9-3 to plot any two sinusoids of the form

$$\sin(\omega t + \theta_1) \quad \text{and} \quad \cos(\omega t + \theta_2)$$

Ask the user which form, and for the values of the angular velocity or frequency and the angles (θ_1, θ_2) in degrees.

7. In the program of Fig. 9-5, why do I have 1000 and 1000000 as "fudge factors" for two of the cases?

8. Modify the program of Fig. 9-5 to plot the impedance values. *Hint:* Calculate the maximum impedance of the run first and use it to scale your plot.

9. Modify the program of Fig. 9-8 to calculate the average value of a periodic waveform that has both rectangular and right-triangular segments.

10. Write programs for problems assigned from your ac circuits textbook.

10

Applying C to AC Circuits

10-1 INTRODUCTION AND OBJECTIVES

In this chapter you will write and examine programs that deal with ac circuit analysis, including calculation of power dissipation and power factor.

Upon successful completion of this chapter, you will be able to:

- Write programs that calculate power in ac circuits
- Convert complex numbers from polar to rectangular, and vice versa
- Add, subtract, multiply, and divide complex numbers in programs
- Write programs involving Ohm's law for ac circuits
- Write programs to solve simple series ac circuits
- Write programs to solve simple parallel ac circuits
- Write programs to solve ac circuits using mesh currents
- Write programs to solve ac circuits using node voltage

10-2 AVERAGE POWER AND POWER FACTOR

Because the current and voltage in an ac circuit change continuously, the power does, too. However, as we are usually concerned with the heating effect of a circuit, we need to look at the *average power* rather than the instantaneous power. A mathematical analysis of the average power equation tells us that it can be calculated from

$$P = VI \cos \theta$$

where V is the rms value of the voltage

I is the rms value of the current

θ is the difference in phase between the instantaneous current and voltage; in other words, it is the angle associated with the impedance of the circuit

The term $cos\theta$ is called the *power factor* of the circuit and is almost always a positive number. If the circuit is primarily inductive, the power factor is called a *lagging* power factor because the current will lag the voltage. If the circuit is primarily capacitive, the power factor will be *leading*.

Writing a program to solve for any of the four unknowns—*P, V, I,* or θ (or the power factor)—given the other three is easy except for solving for θ. On the one hand, both first and fourth quadrant angles (i.e., $-90 < \theta < +90$) have positive cosines, so the sign of the angle depends on whether the power factor is leading or lagging. The inverse cosine, *arccos*, is represented in C's math library by a function having this header:

```
double acos(double)
```

The argument must lie between 0 and π, and the result will be returned in, yes, radians!

10-3 COMPLEX NUMBERS

One of the things that make ac circuit analysis tedious is that the numbers used are complex. That is, each current, voltage, and impedance is represented by *two* numbers. The two numbers represent a point in a plane—either the *x-y* rectangular coordinates or the *r-θ* polar coordinates. What's worse, you cannot just say, "well, I'll learn one set of coordinates and forget the other" because ac circuit analysis frequently requires that you go back and forth between them. Don't despair, though. We're going to write programs to make your life easier. Let's begin by studying the conversions between forms.

Polar-to-Rectangular Conversion

The mathematics for polar to rectangular form is pretty simple. Given a radius *R* at an angle θ, the corresponding rectangular values are given by

$$x = R \cos \theta \quad \text{and} \quad y = R \sin \theta$$

Figure 10-1 shows a function (and a stub) that will do the polar-to-rectangular conversion. Nothing spectacular here; everything in this function has been done before. That should be a comforting fact.

There is something special you can do that will make life a little easier for yourself later in this chapter. Start Turbo C and enter the program of Fig. 10-1. Save it as *p10-1.c* by keying *Alt-F* and *W*. Then bring the cursor to the very top of the program at the left-hand margin and key *ctrl-KB*. Then bring the cursor down until it's on top of the *v* in *void* that marks the header (not the declaration!) of the function *p_to_r( )*. Key *ctrl-KY*, and all the characters from the beginning of the program to the cursor will disappear. You will be left with the definition of *p_to_r( )*. Key *Alt-F* and *W* and use the name *p_to_r.fun*. Exit Turbo C. You have created a file containing only the definition of the polar-to-rectangular function.

```
#include <stdio.h>
#include <math.h>
#define PI 3.14159
main()
{
     float r, ang, x, y;
     void p_to_r(float, float, float *, float *);

     printf("This program calls a function that converts from\n");
     printf("polar to rectangular.\n\n");
     printf("Enter the radius value: ");
     scanf("%f", &r);
     printf("Enter the angle (in degrees): ");
     scanf("%f", &ang);

     p_to_r(r, ang, &x, &y);

     printf("The rectangular coordinates are:\n\tx= %.3f\n\ty= %.3f",
          x, y);
}

void p_to_r(float R, float A, float * X, float * Y)
{
     *X = R * cos(PI * A / 180);
     *Y = R * sin(PI * A / 180);
}
```

Figure 10-1

Rectangular-to-Polar Conversion

It should be just as easy to write a rectangular-to-polar conversion function, based on the equations

$$r = \text{sqrt}(x^2 + y^2) \quad \text{and} \quad \theta = \tan^{-1}(y/x)$$

$sqrt()$ and $tan^{-1}()$ are new to us; they are declared in *math.h*, like this
and

```
double sqrt(double),
double atan(double),
```

where the argument of *atan()* is in radians (of course!) and must lie between $-\pi/2$ and $+\pi/2$. Figure 10-2 has the function (and stub) for this conversion, while Fig. 10-3 shows some typical results.

```
#include <stdio.h>
#include <math.h>
#define PI 3.14159
main()
{
     float x, y, r, ang;
     void r_to_p(float, float, float *, float *);
```

Figure 10-2

(Continued)

```
        printf("This program converts rectangular coordinates\n");
        printf("of a point in a plane to the equivalent polar ones.\n\n");
        printf("Enter the x value: ");
        scanf("%f", &x);
        printf("Enter the y value: ");
        scanf("%f", &y);

        r_to_p(x, y, &r, &ang);


        printf("The polar coordinates are\n\tradius = %.3f", r);
        printf("\n\tangle = %.3f", ang);
}


void r_to_p(float X, float Y, float * R, float * A)
{
        *R = sqrt(X*X + Y*Y);
        *A = 180/PI * atan(Y/X);
}
```

Figure 10-2 (*Continued*)

(1) The first run:

```
This program converts rectangular coordinates
of a point in a plane to the equivalent polar ones.

Enter the x value: 3
Enter the y value: 4

The polar coordinates are
     radius = 5.000
     angle = 53.130 degrees
```

(2) The second run:

```
This program converts rectangular coordinates
of a point in a plane to the equivalent polar ones.

Enter the x value: -6
Enter the y value: 3

The polar coordinates are
     radius = 6.708
     angle = -26.565 degrees   !!! SHOULD BE A 2ND QUADRANT ANGLE
```

(3) The third run:

```
This program converts rectangular coordinates
of a point in a plane to the equivalent polar ones.

Enter the x value: -6
Enter the y value: -7

The polar coordinates are
     radius = 9.220
     angle = 49.399 degrees    !!! SHOULD BE A 3RD QUADRANT ANGLE
```

Figure 10-3

Oh, oh! Looks like *atan()* can't tell what quadrant the point lies in! So we'll have to program to make up for that. Let's see. The quadrant depends on the signs of the *x* and *y* values; *atan()* seems to return a first or fourth quadrant value regardless! That makes sense because *y/x* will be positive for two positive AND for two negative values (signifying first and third quadrants, respectively), while it will be negative if the values have opposite signs (second or fourth quadrants). Here's a table that shows the last sentence:

x	y	Quadrant	Angle range
$+$	$+$	1	0 to 90
$-$	$+$	2	90 to 180
$-$	$-$	3	180 to 270
$+$	$-$	4	270 to 360 or -90 to 0

Let's extend the table to show what *atan()* returns so that we can for easily see what "fudge factor" we need.

x	y	Quadrant	Angle range	*atan ()* angle
$+$	$+$	1	0 to 90	0 to 90
$-$	$+$	2	90 to 180	-90 to 0
$-$	$-$	3	180 to 270	0 to 90
$+$	$-$	4	-90 to 0	-90 to 0

For both quadrants, the correct angle will be given by

$$\text{atan } (y/x) + 180$$

Figure 10-4 shows the revised function; Fig. 10-5 shows sample results.

There is one more problem. Since this program depends on the division of *y* by *x*, it had better see if the user entered 0 for *x*. Otherwise, the computer will become very unhappy at being asked to divide something by 0 and will quit running your program. Attempting to check for a 0 value for *x* gives rise to another problem: You cannot test a *float* for exact equality! The way out of this dilemma is to test *x* to ensure that it is not smaller than a very small number, say 1e-35:

```
if (fabs(x) < 1e-35)
{
        "the point is on the Y axis"
}
```

fabs() is another function declared in **math.h**. It returns the absolute value of a noninteger. Specifically, its declaration is

```
double fabs(double)
```

The final version of our program is in Fig. 10-6.

```
#include <stdio.h>
#include <math.h>
#define PI 3.14159
main()
{
        float x, y, r, ang;
        void r_to_p(float, float, float *, float *);

        printf("This program converts rectangular coordinates\n");
        printf("of a point in a plane to the equivalent polar ones.\n\n");
        printf("Enter the x value: ");
        scanf("%f", &x);
        printf("Enter the y value: ");
        scanf("%f", &y);


        r_to_p(x, y, &r, &ang);

        printf("The polar coordinates are\n\tradius = %.3f", r);
        printf("\n\tangle = %.3f", ang);
}

void r_to_p(float X, float Y, float * R, float * A)
{
        *R = sqrt(X*X + Y*Y);
        if (X > 0.0)
                *A = 180/PI * atan(Y/X);
        else
                *A = 180 + 180/PI * atan(Y/X);
}
```

Figure 10-4

Figure 10-7 shows a full range of sample runs. Load the program of Fig. 10-7 into the Turbo C editor, and remove everything except the code for the definition of $r\_to\_p()$. Save that definition in a file called $r\_to\_p.fun$. You now have two conversion functions that can be introduced into your ac circuit analysis programs.

Addition and Subtraction

Addition and subtraction of complex numbers is best done in rectangular form. If you are asked to add two complex numbers given in rectangular form, go ahead and add the two *reals* (i.e., the *x* values) and then add the two *imaginaries* (i.e., the two *y* values). For example,

$$(2 + j3) + (6 + j5) = (2 + 6) + j(3 + 5) = 8 + j8$$

If the numbers are supplied in polar form, convert to rectangular, add (or subtract), and then convert back to polar. A program to do this will use the two conversion functions we examined above.

```
A:>p10-3
This program converts rectangular coordinates
of a point in a plane to the equivalent polar ones.

Enter the x value: 3
Enter the y value: 4

The polar coordinates are
        radius = 5.000
        angle = 53.130 degrees

A:>p10-3
This program converts rectangular coordinates
of a point in a plane to the equivalent polar ones.

Enter the x value: -3
Enter the y value: 4


The polar coordinates are
        radius = 5.000
        angle = 126.870 degrees

A:>p10-3
This program converts rectangular coordinates
of a point in a plane to the equivalent polar ones.

Enter the x value: -3
Enter the y value: -4

The polar coordinates are
        radius = 5.000
        angle = 233.130 degrees

A:>p10-3
This program converts rectangular coordinates
of a point in a plane to the equivalent polar ones.

Enter the x value: 3
Enter the y value: -4

The polar coordinates are
        radius = 5.000
        angle = -53.130 degrees
```

Figure 10-5

```
#include <stdio.h>
#include <math.h>
#define PI 3.14159
main()
{
        float x, y, r, ang;
        void r_to_p(float, float, float *, float *);

        printf("This program converts rectangular coordinates\n");
        printf("of a point in a plane to the equivalent polar ones.\n\n");
        printf("Enter the x value: ");
        scanf("%f", &x);
        printf("Enter the y value: ");
        scanf("%f", &y);


        r_to_p(x, y, &r, &ang);

        printf("The polar coordinates are\n\tradius = %.3f", r);
        printf("\n\tangle = %.3f degrees", ang);
}


void r_to_p(float X, float Y, float * R, float * A)
{
        *R = sqrt(X*X + Y*Y);
        if (fabs(X) < 1e-35)            /* approx. 0 */
        {
                if (Y > 0.0)
                        *A = 90.0;
                else
                        *A = -90.0;
        }
        else if (X > 0.0)        /* first or fourth quadrant */
                *A = 180/PI * atan(Y/X);
        else                            /* second or third quadrant */
                *A = 180 + 180/PI * atan(Y/X);
}
```

Figure 10-6


```
A:>p10-6
This program converts rectangular coordinates
of a point in a plane to the equivalent polar ones.

Enter the x value: 3
Enter the y value: 4

The polar coordinates are
        radius = 5.000
        angle = 53.130 degrees


A:>p10-6
This program converts rectangular coordinates
of a point in a plane to the equivalent polar ones.
```
Figure 10-7

```
Enter the x value: -3
Enter the y value: 4

The polar coordinates are
        radius = 5.000
        angle = 126.870 degrees

A:>p10-6
This program converts rectangular coordinates
of a point in a plane to the equivalent polar ones.

Enter the x value: -3
Enter the y value: -4

The polar coordinates are
        radius = 5.000
        angle = 233.130 degrees

A:>p10-6
This program converts rectangular coordinates
of a point in a plane to the equivalent polar ones.

Enter the x value: 3
Enter the y value: -4

The polar coordinates are
        radius = 5.000
        angle = -53.130 degrees


A:>p10-6
This program converts rectangular coordinates
of a point in a plane to the equivalent polar ones.

Enter the x value: 0
Enter the y value: 4

The polar coordinates are
        radius = 4.000
        angle = 90.000 degrees

A:>p10-6
This program converts rectangular coordinates
of a point in a plane to the equivalent polar ones.

Enter the x value: 0
Enter the y value: -4

The polar coordinates are
        radius = 4.000
        angle = -90.000 degrees
```

Figure 10-7 (*Continued*)

Multiplication and Division

Multiplication and division of complex numbers can be done with either rectangular or polar form numbers. However, it is simpler in polar form. For example, to multiply 5 at an angle 30° by 3 at an angle 90°, just multiply the magnitudes and add the angles:

$$5 \times 3 \text{ at an angle } (30° + 90°) = 15 \text{ at an angle } 120°$$

If the values are given in rectangular form, convert to polar, multiply (or divide), and convert back. A program to do this will use the two conversion functions we examined above.

Ohm's Law for AC Circuits

The version of Ohm's law we use for dc resistive circuits is a special case of the more general Ohm's law for ac circuits, which is

$$V = IZ$$

where **V** is the *phasor* voltage
    I is the *phasor* current
    Z is the complex impedance

All three quantities, **V**, **I**, and **Z**, are complex numbers and can be represented in either polar or rectangular form. For example, suppose that you had a 120-ohm resistor (**Z** = 120 $\angle 0°$ with a current 10 $\angle 30°$ in it. The voltage across it would be

$$(120 \angle 0)\ (10 \angle 30) = 1200 \angle 30 \text{ volts}$$

As another example, calculate the impedance of a circuit that has a current of 20 $\angle -53.13$ in it and a voltage 100 $\angle 0$ across it. The impedance would be

$$(100 \angle 0)/(20 \angle -53.13) = 5.0 \angle 53.13 \text{ ohms}$$

(Remember that in division, you divide magnitudes and *subtract* angles.)

Series AC Circuits

Ac circuits may have sources, resistances, inductances, and capacitances in them, connected in any series–parallel configuration. We will first look at series circuits.

Before you can calculate anything in an ac circuit, you must know the frequency of the source. You need this to calculate the impedance of all the *L*s and *C*s. Consider the simple series circuit in Fig. 10-8. Suppose that

$$\mathbf{E} = 100 \angle 0$$

$$f = 1500 \text{ Hz}$$

$$R = 5 \text{ ohms}$$

$$L = 530 \text{ microhenries}$$

Suppose that we want to know the current in the circuit, the voltage across each

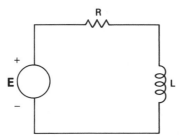

Figure 10-8

element, the power factor, and the average power dissipated. We must first calculate the impedances:

$$\mathbf{Z}_R = 5.0 \angle 0$$

$$\mathbf{Z}_L = 2\pi fL \angle 90 = 2(3.14159)\,(1500)\,(530 \times 10^{-6}) \angle 90$$

$$= 4.995 \angle 90 \text{ ohms}$$

The total impedance is $\mathbf{R}_R + \mathbf{Z}_L$, best handled in rectangular form. Then the current $\mathbf{I}$ is $\mathbf{E/Z}$, or $E/Z \angle \text{power factor angle}$.

This brief discussion leads immediately to the program in Fig. 10-9.

```
#include <stdio.h>
#include <math.h>
#define PI 3.14159
main()
{
        float e, a_e, f, r, l;
        float zr, a_r, zl, a_l, Z, A;
        float i, a_i, pf, p, vr, a_vr, vl, a_vl;
        void r_to_p(float, float, float *, float *);

        printf("This program solves the AC R-L series circuit.\n\n");
        printf("Enter the RMS value of the voltage: ");
        scanf("%f", &e);
        printf("...and its angle: ");
        scanf("%f", &a_e);
        printf("...and its frequency in Hz.: ");
        scanf("%f", &f);
        printf("Now enter the resistance in ohms: ");
        scanf("%f", &r);
        printf("...and the inductance in henries: ");
        scanf("%f", &l);

        zr = r;
        a_r = 0.0;
        zl = 2 * PI * f * l;
        a_l = 90.0;
```

Figure 10-9   (*Continued*)

Sec. 10-3   Complex Numbers

273

```
/* we know that R is pure real and XL is pure imaginary
   so that Z is a "nice" complex number
*/


r_to_p(zr, zl, &Z, &A);


i = e / Z;
a_i = -A;
printf("\n\nThe current is %.3f amps at an angle %.2f degrees.\n",
       i, a_i);

pf = cos(PI * a_i / 180);
p = e * i * pf;
printf("\nThe power is %.2f watts ", p);
printf("at a power factor of %.4f.\n", pf);

vr = i * r;
a_vr = a_i;
vl = i * zl;
a_vl = a_i + 90.0;
printf("\nThe voltage across the resistor is %.2f", vr);
printf(" at an angle %.2f degrees.\n", a_vr);
printf("\nThe voltage across the inductor is %.2f", vl);
printf(" at an angle %.2f degrees.\n", a_vl);
}


void r_to_p(float X, float Y, float * R, float * A)
{
    *R = sqrt(X*X + Y*Y);
    if (fabs(X) < 1e-35)
        if (Y > 0.0)
            *A = 90.0;
        else
            *A = -90.0;
    else if (X > 0.0)
        *A = 180/PI * atan(Y/X);
    else
        *A = 180 + 180/PI * atan(Y/X);
}
```

Figure 10-9 *(Continued)*

I should point out that I did not retype the code for the rectangular-to-polar function. While I was typing the program in the Turbo C editor, I stopped after typing the *#includes*, the *#define*, and the code in *main( )*, with the cursor in the left-hand margin after the closing brace of *main( )*. Then I keyed *ctrl-KR*. Turbo C asked me what file I wanted to read a block from, and I typed *r_to_p.fun*. Obediently, Turbo C went to my disk, found that file, and inserted into the edit buffer at the cursor! That beats retyping the entire function, doesn't it?

Adding a series capacitor makes the program a little more complicated because it has to calculate the capacitor impedance. This makes the total impedance calculation a little more complicated, and gives extra steps in other calculations. However, if you sort things out carefully, you come up with this scheme:

1. get the given values
2. calculate total impedance
3. calculate total current
4. calculate power factor and power
5. calculate voltage drops

The program that results is shown in Fig. 10-10.

```
#include <stdio.h>
#include <math.h>
#define PI 3.14159
main()
{
      float e, a_e, f, r, l, c;
      float xl, a_l, xc, a_c, x, a_x, Z, A;
      float i, a_i, pf, p, vr, a_vr, vl, a_vl, vc, a_vc;
      void r_to_p(float, float, float *, float *);

/* get the input values .... */

      printf("This program solves the AC R-L-C series circuit.\n\n");
      printf("Enter the RMS value of the voltage: ");
      scanf("%f", &e);
      printf("...and its angle: ");
      scanf("%f", &a_e);
      printf("...and its frequency in Hz.: ");
      scanf("%f", &f);
      printf("Now enter the resistance in ohms: ");
      scanf("%f", &r);
      printf("...and the inductance in henries: ");
      scanf("%f", &l);
      printf("...and the capacitance in farads: ");
      scanf("%f", &c);

/* calculate the inductive and capacitive reactances .... */

      xl  = 2 * PI * f * l;
      a_l = 90.0;
      xc  = 1 / (2 * PI * f * c);
      a_c = -90.0;

/* calculate total reactance ... */

      x = xl - xc;
      if (xl > xc)
            a_x = a_l;
```

Figure 10-10   (*Continued*)

```
                else
                        a_x = a_c;

/* convert the impedance to polar form ... */
        r_to_p(r, x, &Z, &A);
/* calculate the current, the power, and the voltages ... */
        i = e / Z;
        a_i = -A;
        printf("\n\nThe current is %.3f amps at an angle %.2f degrees.\n",
                i, a_i);

        pf = cos(PI * a_i / 180);
        p = e * i * pf;
        printf("\nThe power is %.2f watts ", p);
        printf("at a power factor of %.4f ", pf);

        if (xl > xc)
                printf("lagging.\n");
        else
                printf("leading.\n");

        vr   = i * r;
        a_vr = a_i;
        vl   = i * xl;
        a_vl = a_i + 90.0;
        vc   = i * xc;
        a_vc = a_i - 90.0;

        printf("\nThe voltage across the resistor is %.2f", vr);
        printf(" at an angle %.2f degrees.\n", a_vr);
        printf("\nThe voltage across the inductor is %.2f", vl);
        printf(" at an angle %.2f degrees.\n", a_vl);
        printf("\nThe voltage across the capacitor is %.2f", vc);
        printf(" at an angle %.2f degrees.\n", a_vc);
}


void r_to_p(float X, float Y, float * R, float * A)
{
        *R = sqrt(X*X + Y*Y);

        if (fabs(X) < 1e-35)
                if (Y > 0.0)
                        *A = 90.0;
                else
                        *A = -90.0;
          else if (X > 0.0)
                *A = 180/PI * atan(Y/X);
          else
                *A = 180 + 180/PI * atan(Y/X);
}
```

Figure 10-10 (*Continued*)

In a program that does not use many functions, *comments* are essential! Notice how breaking up the code with comments lets readers focus on a part of the program and also gives them a clue as to what is (supposed to be) happening in that section.

Incidentally, you may be wondering why I've written recent programs without functions after we spent so much effort learning about functions earlier. The answer is simple: We use functions when they justify themselves, such as when each represents a general tool such as the two conversion functions. Also, we use functions in large programs because a function is easier to debug than a large program. However, none of our recent programs have been large. Finally, converting these examples to programs with functions will be good practice for you.

Voltage Divider

The voltage-divider rule can be used with impedances. For example, using the circuit of Fig. 10-8, the voltage across the inductance can be found from

$$\mathbf{V}_L = \mathbf{E}\mathbf{Z}_L/(\mathbf{Z}_L + \mathbf{Z}_R) = \mathbf{E}\mathbf{Z}_L/\mathbf{Z}_T$$

where

$$\mathbf{Z}_L = X_L \angle 90$$

$$\mathbf{Z}_R = R \angle 0$$

and $\mathbf{Z}_T$ is the total impedance, calculated by vector addition. Separating two magnitude calculations and angle calculations, we have

$$V_L = EX_L/Z_T \quad \text{and} \quad \theta_L = \theta_E + \theta_L - \theta_T$$

As you can see, there will be a conversion involved. First, to calculate $\mathbf{Z}_T$, we will write $\mathbf{Z}_L$ and $\mathbf{Z}_R$ in rectangular form for the addition, and then convert the result to polar form for the division. The program to do this is given in Fig. 10-11. Of course, you can do this for series RC or RLC, with any number of elements.

Parallel AC Circuits

Consider the parallel RLC circuit of Fig. 10-12. To solve this for the driving-point characteristics, we can use *admittance, conductance,* and *susceptance.* For the resistor, $\mathbf{Y}_R = (1/R) \angle 0$. For the inductance, $\mathbf{Y}_L = (1/X_L) \angle -90$. And for the capacitance, $\mathbf{Y}_c = (1/X_c) \angle 90$. We will calculate the reactances from the usual formulas. Then the total admittance, $\mathbf{Y}_T$, is just the sum of the individual admittances. (Of course, you will have to write them in rectangular form if you want to add them up.) Then the total impedance, $\mathbf{Z}_T$, will be the reciprocal of the admittance. If the source is a current, $\mathbf{I}$, entering at the top left node, we can find each current and the voltage across the pair of nodes by the branch current method or by applying the current-divider rule. Figure 10-13 shows the branch current approach.

```
#include <stdio.h>
#include <math.h>
#define PI 3.14159
main()
{
     float e, a_e, f, r, l;
     float zr, a_r, zl, a_l, zt, a_t;
     float vr, a_vr, vl, a_vl;
     void r_to_p(float, float, float *, float *);

     printf("This program illustrates using voltage divider techniques ");
     printf("\nin the AC R-L series circuit.\n\n");
     printf("Enter the RMS value of the voltage: ");
     scanf("%f", &e);
     printf("...and its angle: ");
     scanf("%f", &a_e);
     printf("...and its frequency in Hz.: ");
     scanf("%f", &f);
     printf("\nNow enter the resistance in ohms: ");
     scanf("%f", &r);

     printf("...and the inductance in henries: ");
     scanf("%f", &l);

     zr   = r;
     a_r = 0.0;
     zl   = 2 * PI * f * l;
     a_l = 90.0;
     r_to_p(zr, zl, &zt, &a_t);
     vr   = e * zr / zt;             /* across the resistor  */
     a_vr = a_e + a_r - a_t;

     vl   = e * zl / zt;             /* across the inductance */
     a_vl = a_e + a_l - a_t;

     printf("\nThe voltage across the resistor is %.2f", vr);
     printf(" at an angle %.2f degrees.\n", a_vr);
     printf("\nThe voltage across the inductor is %.2f", vl);
     printf(" at an angle %.2f degrees.\n", a_vl);
}

void r_to_p(float X, float Y, float * R, float * A)
{
     *R = sqrt(X*X + Y*Y);
     if (fabs(X) < 1e-35)
          if (Y > 0.0)
               *A = 90.0;
          else
               *A = -90.0;
     else if (X > 0.0)
          *A = 180/PI * atan(Y/X);
     else
          *A = 180 + 180/PI * atan(Y/X);
}
```

Figure 10-11

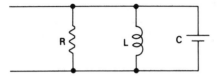

Figure 10-12

```
#include <stdio.h>
#include <math.h>
#define PI 3.14159
main()
{
      float e, a_e, f, r, l, c;
      float g, b_l, b_c, i_r, i_l;
      float i_c, I, A;
      void r_to_p(float, float, float *, float *);

      printf("This program solves the parallel R-L-C ");
      printf("circuit by the branch current method.\n\n");
      printf("Enter the source voltage magnitude: ");
      scanf("%f", &e);

      printf("...and the angle (in degrees): ");
      scanf("%f", &a_e);
      printf("...and the frequency (in Hz.): ");
      scanf("%f", &f);
      printf("\nEnter the resistance (in ohms): ");
      scanf("%f", &r);
      printf("Enter the inductance (in henries): ");
      scanf("%f", &l);
      printf("Enter the capacitance (in farads): ");
      scanf("%f", &c);

/*  calculate the individual admittances  */

      g   = 1/r;
      b_l = 1 / (2 * PI * f * l);
      b_c = 2 * PI * f * c;
      i_r = g * e;
      i_l = b_l * e;
      i_c = b_c * e;

      r_to_p(i_r, i_l - i_c, &I, &A);

      /* adjust the admittance angle to be the angle
         of the total current  */
      A = a_e - A;

      printf("\nThe currents are:\n\n");
      printf("type          magnitude        angle\n");
      printf("resistive     %8.3f        %8.3f\n", i_r, a_e);
```

Figure 10-13   (*Continued*)

```
        printf("inductive    %8.3f      %8.3f\n", i_l, a_e - 90.0);
        printf("capacitive   %8.3f      %8.3f\n", i_c, a_e + 90.0);
        printf("total        %8.3f      %8.3f\n\n\n", I, A);
    }


void r_to_p(float X, float Y, float * R, float * A)
{
        *R = sqrt(X*X + Y*Y);
        if (fabs(X) < 1e-35)
                if (Y > 0.0)
                        *A = 90.0;
                else
                        *A = -90.0;
        else if (X > 0.0)
                *A = 180/PI * atan(Y/X);
        else
                *A = 180 + 180/PI * atan(Y/X);

}
```

Figure 10-13 (*Continued*)

Current Divider

The current-divider rule for ac uses admittances. For example, suppose that you had a three-branch parallel circuit with the branches having the admittances of Y_1, Y_2, and Y_3, respectively. If the total current is I_T, the current in, say, branch 3 will be

$$I_3 = I_T Y_3 / Y_T$$

where Y_T is the sum of the three admittances.

AC Circuit Analysis

The two major methods of analyzing general ac circuits are *mesh* and *nodal*, just as they were for dc resistive circuits. However, as you know, the algebra for these will be much more complicated, and will require conversions.

Mesh Analysis

Figure 10-14 shows a two-loop ac circuit, written in general terms. Using the *format* approach, the describing equations are

$$I_1 (Z_1 + Z_2) - I_2 (Z_2) = E_1$$

$$-I_1 (Z_2) + I_2 (Z_2 + Z_3) = -E_2$$

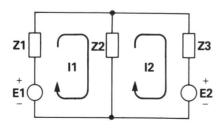

Figure 10-14

Applying C to AC Circuits   Chap. 10

Using determinants, the solutions are

$$I_1 = (E_1 (Z_2 + Z_3) - E_2 Z_2)/\Delta$$

$$I_2 = (E_1 Z_2 - E_2(Z_1 + Z_2))/\Delta$$

where

$$\Delta = (Z_1 + Z_2)(Z_2 + Z_3) - Z_2^2$$

Each impedance can be of the form $R + jX$, where X is $X_L - X_C$, so these are in rectangular form, suitable for adding together, as called for in the equations for the two Is and Δ. Thus, calculating $Z_{12} = Z_1 + Z_2$ and $Z_{23} = Z_2 + Z_3$ will be simple. However, we will have to convert them (and Z_2) to polar for the multiplication, and then convert the results to rectangular for the subtractions! Then these results will be converted back to polar for the final set of divisions. It's all in the program of Fig. 10-15, in which I've followed the practice of most circuits textbooks in having the user input ohmic values rather than farads and henries.

Now, **that** is impressive!! You could make each expression more complicated in the hope of making the program shorter, but that would make the program harder to debug. I deliberately chose lots of variables with seemingly obscure names to challenge you to discover what each represents. For example, *r12* is the combined resistance of loops 1 and 2, and *x12* is their combined reactance. They are rectangular form quantities. *z12* is the magnitude and *a_z12* the angle of the polar form of the combined impedance of loops 1 and 2.

Nodal Analysis

The principles of nodal analysis are the same ones you learned in dc circuits. As with the mesh approach to ac circuits, there is a lot of algebra and trigonometry.

```
#include <stdio.h>
#include <math.h>
#define PI 3.14159
main()
{
    float r[4], xl[4], xc[4];
    float e[3], a_e[3], i1, i2, a_i1, a_i2;
    float z[4], a_z[4];
    float r12, x12, z12, a_z12;
    float r23, x23, z23, a_z23;
    float r123, x123, z123, a_z123;
    float r22, x22, z22, a_z22;
    float r_det, x_det, det, a_det;
    float t1_i1, a_t1_i1, x1_i1, y1_i1;
    float t2_i1, a_t2_i1, x2_i1, y2_i1;
    float t1_i2, a_t1_i2, x1_i2, y1_i2;
    float t2_i2, a_t2_i2, x2_i2, y2_i2;
    float Ni1, Na_i1, Ni2, Na_i2;

    int j;
```

Figure 10-15   (*Continued*)

```
        void r_to_p(float, float, float *, float *);
        void p_to_r(float, float, float *, float *);

        printf("\nThis program solves the general-two loop ");
        printf("AC circuit problem.\n\n");

        for (j = 1; j < 4; ++j)
        {
              printf("Enter the resistance of R[%d]: ", j);
              scanf("%f", &r[j]);
              printf("Enter the reactance of L[%d]: ", j);
              scanf("%f", &xl[j]);
              printf("Enter the reactance of C[%d]: ", j);
              scanf("%f", &xc[j]);
        }

        for (j = 1; j < 3; ++j)
        {
              printf("\nEnter E[%d]: ", j);
              scanf("%f", &e[j]);
              printf("...and its angle: ");
              scanf("%f", &a_e[j]);
        }

/*  calculate the determinant */

        r12 = r[1] + r[2];
        x12 = xl[1] + xl[2] -xc[1] -xc[2];
        r_to_p(r12, x12, &z12, &a_z12);

        r23 = r[2] + r[3];
        x23 = xl[2] + xl[3] -xc[2] -xc[3];
        r_to_p(r23, x23, &z23, &a_z23);

        r_to_p(r[2], (xl[2]-xc[2]), &z[2], &a_z[2]);

        z22 = z[2] * z[2];
        a_z22 = 2 * a_z[2];
        p_to_r(z22, a_z22, &r22, &x22);

        z123 = z12 * z23;
        a_z123 = a_z12 + a_z23;
        p_to_r(z123, a_z123, &r123, &x123);

        r_det = r123 - r22;
        x_det = x123 - x22;
        r_to_p(r_det, x_det, &det, &a_det);

/*  calculate the two currents ...... */
/*  current I1 ...                    */

        t1_i1 = e[1] * z23;
        a_t1_i1 = a_e[1] + a_z23;
        p_to_r(t1_i1, a_t1_i1, &x1_i1, &y1_i1);
```

Figure 10-15 (*Continued*)

```
        t2_i1 = e[2] * z[2];
        a_t2_i1 = a_e[2] + a_z[2];
        p_to_r(t2_i1, a_t2_i1, &x2_i1, &y2_i1);


        r_to_p((x1_i1 - x2_i1), (y1_i1 - y2_i1), &Ni1, &Na_i1);
        i1 = Ni1 / det;
        a_i1 = Na_i1 - a_det;

/*  current I2 ... */

        t1_i2 = e[2] * z12;
        a_t1_i2 = a_e[2] + a_z12;
        p_to_r(t1_i2, a_t1_i2, &x1_i2, &y1_i2);

        t2_i2 = e[1] * z[2];
        a_t2_i2 = a_e[1] + a_z[2];
        p_to_r(t2_i2, a_t2_i2, &x2_i2, &y2_i2);

        r_to_p((-x1_i2 + x2_i2), (-y1_i2 + y2_i2), &Ni2, &Na_i2);
        i2 = Ni2 / det;
        a_i2 = Na_i2 - a_det;

/*  The answers are ..... !! */

        printf("\n\nThe currents are:\n\n");
        printf("I1: %6.3f at an angle %6.2f\n", i1, a_i1);
        printf("I2: %6.3f at an angle %6.2f\n", i2, a_i2);
}


void r_to_p(float X, float Y, float * R, float * A)
{
        *R = sqrt(X*X + Y*Y);
        if (fabs(X) < 1e-35)
                if (Y > 0.0)
                        *A = 90.0;
                else
                        *A = -90.0;
        else if (X > 0.0)
                *A = 180/PI * atan(Y/X);

        else
                *A = 180 + 180/PI * atan(Y/X);
}


void p_to_r(float R, float A, float * X, float * Y)
{
        *X = R * cos(PI * A / 180);
        *Y = R * sin(PI * A / 180);
}
```

Figure 10-15 (*Continued*)

to do. I tried to give you a good picture of the work in the program of Fig. 10-15. If I was successful, you should be able to combine your previous knowledge of nodal analysis with your new knowledge about ac calculations, and write a nodal analysis program without any prompting from me.

10-4 REVIEW

In this chapter you learned how to:

- Write programs that calculate power in ac circuits
- Convert complex number from polar to rectangular, and vice versa
- Add, subtract, multiply, and divide complex numbers in programs
- Write programs involving Ohm's law for ac circuits
- Write programs to solve simple series ac circuits
- Write programs to solve simple parallel ac circuits
- Write programs to solve ac circuits using mesh currents
- Write programs to solve ac circuits using node voltage

PROBLEMS AND QUESTIONS

1. Write a program that will accept three values for the power factor equation and solve for the fourth.
2. Write a program that will add or subtract two complex numbers given in either polar or rectangular form.
3. Write a program that will multiply or divide two complex numbers given in either polar or rectangular form.
4. Modify the program of Fig. 10-10 so that there can be as many as five series resistors, five series inductors, and five series capacitors in the circuit.
5. Modify the program of Fig. 10-11 so that it handles circuits having an R and an L, an R and a C, and an R, an L, and a C.
6. Modify the program of Fig. 10-13 so that it can also handle RL and RC parallel circuits.
7. Rewrite the program of Fig. 10-13 to use the current-divider rule instead of the branch current method.
8. Write a program to solve the more general two-loop mesh circuit shown in Fig. 10-16.
9. Write a program to perform nodal analysis on the circuit shown in Fig. 10-17.

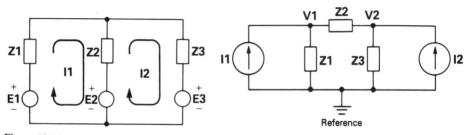

Figure 10-16   **Figure 10-17**

11

Resonant and Three-Phase Circuits

11-1 INTRODUCTION AND OBJECTIVES

In this chapter you will write and examine programs that deal with resonance in ac circuits, and with three-phase circuit analysis.

Upon successful completion of this chapter, you will be able to write programs to:

- Solve series resonant circuit problems
- Solve parallel resonant circuit problems
- Plot circuit values for resonant circuits
- Solve three phase wye–wye (Y–Y) circuits
- Solve three phase delta–delta (Δ–Δ)

11-2 RESONANCE

Resonant or *tuned* circuits are very important in electronic communications. They determine the frequency of operation of radio and television devices. In its simplest form, a resonant circuit includes capacitance, inductance, and resistance.

Series Resonance

The circuit of Fig. 11-1 shows the simplest possible series resonant circuit. R_{total} represents all the resistance in the circuit—the source resistance, the resistance of the coil, and so on. The impedance of the circuit is

$$Z = R + j(X_L - X_C)$$

Series resonance occurs when $X_C = X_L$. At that point, the circuit looks to be purely resistive:

$$Z = R$$

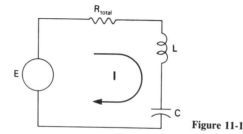

Figure 11-1

As you know from your circuits course, this occurs when $\omega^2 = 1/(LC)$. Or at a frequency given by

$$f_s = 1/(2\pi\text{sqrt}(LC)) \qquad \text{Hz.}$$

From that, it is a simple matter to write the other equations associated with series resonance:

$$Q_s = \omega L/R$$

$$V_{Ls} = V_{Cs} = Q_s E$$

$$\omega_2 = -R/(2L) + 0.5\text{sqrt}((R/L)^2 + 4/(LC))$$

$$\omega_1 = -R/(2L) - 0.5\text{sqrt}((R/L)^2 + 4/(LC))$$

$$\text{BW} = f_s/Q_s$$

$$f_1 = f_s - \text{BW}/2$$

$$f_2 = f_s + \text{BW}/2$$

$$P_{\text{max}} = I_s^2 R = E^2 R$$

$$P_{\text{HPF}} = 0.5 P_{\text{max}}$$

Now we can write a program to calculate all these values, given E, the applied voltage, R, L, and C. The result is in Fig. 11-2. Figure 11-3 shows several sample runs of the program in Fig. 11-2

Plotting Current

An engineer can get a much better feel of a tuned circuit by looking at a plot of current versus frequency near resonance. The "width" of the curve can tell much about Q and bandwidth. We can use the same plotting techniques that we used in previous programs, but first we must determine the starting and end points— and the step size—for the frequency. Let's start at $0.9f_s$ and end at $1.1f_s$, dividing that interval into, say, 200 steps. That is, the step size will be $BW/50$. The current comes from $\mathbf{E}/\mathbf{Z}$, where $Z = \text{sqrt}(R^2 + (X_L - X_C)^2)$. Of course, that means that the program will calculate a new value of $\mathbf{Z}$ at each value of $\mathbf{f}$. Hard for us, easy

```
#include <stdio.h>
#include <math.h>
#define PI 3.14159
main()
{
        float E, R, L, C;
        float f, omega, XL, XC, ZT, I, Q, VL, VC, VR;
        float PH, PM, f2, f1, BW;

        printf("\nThis program solves the series resonant ");
        printf("circuit of R, L, and C.\n\n");
        printf("Enter the source voltage, E: ");
        scanf("%f", &E);
        printf("Enter the total resistance in ohms: ");
        scanf("%f", &R);
        printf("...the inductance in henries: ");
        scanf("%f", &L);
        printf("...and the capacitance in farads: ");
        scanf("%f", &C);

        omega = 1 / sqrt(L * C);   /* angular frequency */
        f = omega / (2 * PI);      /* frequency */
        XL = XC = omega * L;       /* reactance */
        Q = XL / R;                /* Q */
        BW = f / Q;                /* bandwidth */
        f2 = f + BW/2;             /* upper half-power freq */
        f1 = f - BW/2;             /* lower half-power freq */
        ZT = R;                    /* total impedance */
        I = E / R;                 /* resonant current */
        PM = I * I * R;            /* resonant power */
        PH = PM / 2;
        VL = VC = I * XL;          /* reactive voltage */

        printf("\nAt resonance,\n");
        printf("\tthe angular velocity is %.2f rad/sec.\n", omega);
        printf("\tthe frequency is %.2f Hz.\n", f);
        printf("\tthe inductive reactance is %.2f ohms\n", XL);
        printf("\tthe capacitive reactance is %.2f ohms\n", XC );
        printf("\tthe inductive voltage is %.2f volts\n", VL);
        printf("\tthe capacitive voltage is %.2f volts\n", VC);
        printf("\tthe current is %.2f amps\n", I);
        printf("\tthe maximum power is %.2f watts\n", PM);
        printf("\tQ is %.2f\n", Q);
        printf("\tthe bandwidth is %.2f Hz\n", BW);
        printf("\tthe upper half-power point is %.2f Hz.\n", f2);
        printf("\tthe lower half-power point is %.2f Hz.\n", f1);
}
```

Figure 11-2

```
A>p11-2
This program solves the series resonant circuit of R, L, and C.

Enter the source voltage, E: 20
Enter the total resistance in ohms: 20
...the inductance in henries: 1e-3
...and the capacitance in farads: 1e-6

At resonance,
        the angular velocity is 31622.78 rad/sec.
        the frequency is 5032.93 Hz.
        the inductive reactance is 31.62 ohms
        the capacitive reactance is 31.62 ohms
        the inductive voltage is 31.62 volts
        the capacitive voltage is 31.62 volts
        the current is 1.00 amps
        the maximum power is 20.00 watts
        Q is 1.58
        the bandwidth is 3183.10 Hz
        the upper half-power point is 6624.48 Hz.
        the lower half-power point is 3441.37 Hz.


A>p11-2
This program solves the series resonant circuit of R, L, and C.

Enter the source voltage, E: 50
Enter the total resistance in ohms: 20
...the inductance in henries: 2e-3
...and the capacitance in farads: .01e-6

At resonance,
        the angular velocity is 223606.80 rad/sec.
        the frequency is 35588.16 Hz.
        the inductive reactance is 447.21 ohms
        the capacitive reactance is 447.21 ohms
        the inductive voltage is 1118.03 volts
        the capacitive voltage is 1118.03 volts
        the current is 2.50 amps
        the maximum power is 125.00 watts
        Q is 22.36
        the bandwidth is 1591.55 Hz
        the upper half-power point is 36383.93 Hz.
        the lower half-power point is 34792.38 Hz.
```

Figure 11-3

for a computer! The code might look like this (assuming that all variables have been declared properly):

```
for (f = fs - BW; f <= fs + BW; f += BW/200)
{
    omega = 2 * PI * f;
    XL = omega * L;
    XC = 1 / (omega * C);
    X = XL - XC;
    Z = sqrt (R * R + X * X);
    I = E / Z;
    IN = I / IMAX;
}
```

We have our choice: we can save each value of the normalized current, **IN**, in an array or we can ask the program to plot it as soon as we have calculated it. Since **IMAX** is always **E/R**, there's really no need to save all the values, so I've chosen to plot the values "on the fly," so to speak. All I have to do is add the following to the loop given above:

```
for (i = 0; i <= WIDTH * IN; ++i)
    printf(" ");
printf("o\n");
```

In fact, I can add *printf("%f",f);* just before the *i* loop and change the last line to *printf("o %f\n",IN);* so that the program will display values of the frequency and the normalized current. The program, a modification of the one in Fig. 11-2, appears in Fig. 11-4. You'll find the results of two runs, the first having a relatively high Q while the second has a relatively low Q, in Fig. 11-5.

Parallel Resonance

The circuit calculations for a parallel resonant circuit are a little more involved because of the resistance of the wire in the inductor. However, once we have written the program, the computer will take care of the added calculations.

Figure 11-6 shows the parallel resonant circuit under discussion. The parallel equivalent of the series R_L-L has a resistance, R_p, of Z^2/R_L, and an inductance, L_p, of Z^2/L. After many algebraic manipulations, the equation for the resonant frequency becomes

$$f_p = f_s \text{ sqrt } (1 - R_1^2 C/L)$$

where f_s is the resonant frequency of the equivalent series circuit

$$f_s = 1/(2\pi \text{ sqrt } (LC))$$

The Q of a parallel resonant circuit is

$$Q = R_e/X_{Lp}$$

where R_e is R_1 in parallel with R, and X_{Lp} is $(R_L^2 + X_L^2)/X_L$.

```
#include <stdio.h>
#include <math.h>
#define PI 3.14159
#define WIDTH 50
main()
{
     float E, R, L, C;
     float fs, omega, XL, XC, I, Q;
     float BW, f, Z, X, IN;
     int i;

     printf("\nThis program solves the series resonant ");
     printf("circuit of R, L, and C.\n\n");
     printf("Enter the source voltage, E: ");
     scanf("%f", &E);
     printf("Enter the total resistance in ohms: ");
     scanf("%f", &R);
     printf("...the inductance in henries: ");
     scanf("%f", &L);
     printf("...and the capacitance in farads: ");
     scanf("%f", &C);

     omega = 1 / sqrt(L * C);
     fs = omega / (2 * PI);
     XL = XC = omega * L;
     Q = XL / R;
     BW = fs / Q;

     printf("\nAt resonance,\n");
     printf("\tthe angular velocity is %.2f rad/sec.\n", omega);
     printf("\tthe frequency is %.2f Hz.\n", fs);
     printf("\tQ is %.2f\n", Q);
     printf("\tthe bandwidth is %.2f Hz\n", BW);

     printf("\n\nThe following is a plot of the normalized ");
     printf("current vs. frequency, \nin the ");
     printf("vicinity of resonance.\n\n");

     for (f = 0.9 * fs; f <= 1.1 * fs; f += fs / 200)
     {
          omega = 2 * PI * f;
          XL = omega * L;
          XC = 1 / (omega * C);
          X = XL - XC;
          Z = sqrt(R * R + X * X);
          I = E / Z;
          IN = I / (E / R);

          printf("%.0f", f);
          for (i = 0; i <= WIDTH * IN; ++i)
               printf(" ");
          printf("o %0.2f\n", IN);
     }
}
```

Figure 11-4

```
A>p11-4
```

This program solves the series resonant circuit of R, L, and C.

Enter the source voltage, E: <u>10</u>
Enter the total resistance in ohms: <u>2</u>
...the inductance in henries: <u>5e-3</u>
...and the capacitance in farads: <u>1e-7</u>

At resonance,
      the angular velocity is 44721.36 rad/sec.
      the frequency is 7117.63 Hz.
      Q is 111.80
      the bandwidth is 63.66 Hz

The following is a plot of the normalized current vs. frequency, in the vicinity of resonance.

```
6406     o 0.04
6441     o 0.04
6477     o 0.05
6513     o 0.05
6548     o 0.05
6584     o 0.06
6619      o 0.06
6655      o 0.07
6691      o 0.07
6726      o 0.08
6762       o 0.09
6797       o 0.10
6833        o 0.11
6869         o 0.12
6904          o 0.15
6940           o 0.17
6975            o 0.22
7011              o 0.28
7046                  o 0.41
7082                             o 0.67
7118                                          o 1.00
7153                             o 0.67
7189                  o 0.41
7224             o 0.29
7260            o 0.22
7296          o 0.18
7331          o 0.15
7367         o 0.13
7402        o 0.11
7438        o 0.10
7474       o 0.09
7509      o 0.08
7545      o 0.08
7580      o 0.07
```

Figure 11-5

(*Continued*)

```
7616     o 0.07
7651     o 0.06
7687   o 0.06
7723   o 0.05
7758   o 0.05
7794   o 0.05
```

A>p11-4

This program solves the series resonant circuit of R, L, and C.

Enter the source voltage, E: 2
Enter the total resistance in ohms: 10
...the inductance in henries: 1e-4
...and the capacitance in farads: 1e-8

At resonance,
      the angular velocity is 1000000.00 rad/sec.
      the frequency is 159155.08 Hz.
      Q is 10.00
      the bandwidth is 15915.51 Hz

The following is a plot of the normalized current vs. frequency, in the vicinity of resonance.

```
143240                       o 0.43
144035                       o 0.45
144831                        o 0.47
145627                        o 0.49
146423                         o 0.51
147218                         o 0.54
148014                          o 0.57
148810                           o 0.60
149606                            o 0.63
150402                            o 0.66
151197                             o 0.70
151993                              o 0.74
152789                               o 0.77
153585                                o 0.81
154381                                 o 0.85
155176                                  o 0.89
155972                                   o 0.93
156768                                   o 0.96
157564                                    o 0.98
158359                                    o 1.00
159155                                     o 1.00
159951                                     o 1.00
160747                                     o 0.98
161543                                    o 0.96
162338                                   o 0.93
163134                                  o 0.90
163930                                 o 0.86
```

Figure 11-5 (Continued)

```
164726                                    o 0.82
165521                                     o 0.79
166317                                    o 0.75
167113                                   o 0.72
167909                                  o 0.68
168705                                 o 0.65
169500                                o 0.62
170296                               o 0.59
171092                              o 0.57
171888                             o 0.54
172683                            o 0.52
173479                           o 0.50
174275                          o 0.48
```

Figure 11-5 (*Continued*)

The program for doing parallel resonant calculations is very similar to the one for series resonant calculations. I show it in Fig. 11-7.

Figure 11-8 shows a sample run for a circuit having a source resistance of 1 megohm, a 50-microhenry coil with 25 ohms of resistance, and a 200-picofarad capacitor.

One of the practical questions that arises in the design of parallel tuned circuits is: What size capacitor do I need to resonate at X Hz with a coil having L henries of inductance and R ohms of resistance? A program for this is the target of a homework problem.

Plotting current, voltage, impedance, or admittance follows the process we discussed above. Essentially, all you need is the equation for the quantity to be plotted, and you're in business!

Number of Digits in Answers

Notice that using a computer for circuit analysis means that you do not have to make approximations. However, this is *not necessarily* an advantage. Developing a feeling for the numbers is an important part of engineering. If you have an 18,163-ohm resistor in a circuit with an 8.92-V battery, and you measure 1.00 milliamperes of current, you should know *without a calculator or computer* that something is wrong. The resistance is approximately 18 kilohms and the voltage, about 9 V. The current should be in the neighborhood of (9 V)/(18 kilohms) = 0.5 mA. A calculator would say 0.4911083 microampere, but that much precision is unnecessary.

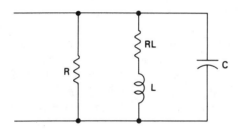

Figure 11-6

```
#include <stdio.h>
#include <math.h>
#define PI 3.14159
main()
{
    float R, L, RL, C;
    float o_s, fs, omega, XL, XC, Q;
    float XLp, Rp, BW, RE, fp;

    printf("\nThis program solves the parallel resonant ");
    printf("\ncircuit having R, L + RL, and C.\n\n");
    printf("Enter the resistance in ohms: ");
    scanf("%f", &R);
    printf("...the inductance in henries: ");
    scanf("%f", &L);
    printf("...and the resistance in ohms of the coil: ");
    scanf("%f", &RL);
    printf("...and finally, the capacitance in farads: ");
    scanf("%f", &C);

    o_s = 1 / sqrt(L * C);   /* omega for the series case */
    fs = o_s / (2 * PI);     /* series resonant frequency */
    fp = fs * sqrt(1 - RL * RL * C / L); /* parallel resonant frequency */
    omega = 2 * PI * fp;     /* parallel omega */
    XC = 1/(omega * C);      /* reactances */
    XL = omega * L;
    Rp = (RL * RL + XL * XL) / RL;   /* inductor equivalent resistance */
    XLp = (RL * RL + XL * XL) / XL;  /* inductor equivalent reactance  */
    RE = R * Rp / (R + Rp);          /* circuit equivalent resistance  */
    Q = RE / XLp;
    BW = fp / Q;

    printf("\nAt resonance,\n");
    printf("\tthe series res. freq. is %.2f kHz.\n", fs/1000);
    printf("\tthe parallel freq. is %.2f kHz.\n", fp/1000);
    printf("\tthe inductive reactance is %.2f ohms.\n", XL);
    printf("\tthe capacitive reactance is %.2f ohms.\n", XC );
    printf("\tthe par. ind. reactance is %.2f ohms.\n", XLp);
    printf("\tthe par. equiv. R is %.2f ohms.\n", Rp);
    printf("\tQ is %f\n", Q);
    printf("\tthe bandwidth is %.2f kHz\n", BW/1000);
}
```

Figure 11-7

A student who simply accepts a 6- or 8- or 10-digit answer given by a computer or a calculator is not showing that he or she understands what the circuit is doing. It is usually far better to have a 2- or 3- or 4-digit approximation that helps you understand what's happening. For example, in Fig. 11-8, the two frequencies were displayed as 1591.55 and 1589.56 KHz for the series and parallel resonant frequencies. Having two 6-digit answers may have kept you from seeing that the parallel frequency was only slightly smaller than the series one, indicating that the

```
A>p11-7

This program solves the parallel resonant
circuit having R, L + RL, and C.

Enter the resistance in ohms: 1e6
...the inductance in henries: 50e-6
...and the resistance in ohms of the coil: 25
...and finally, the capacitance in farads: 200e-12

At resonance,
        the series res. freq. is 1591.55 kHz.
        the parallel freq. is 1589.56k Hz.
        the inductive reactance is 499.37 ohms.
        the capacitive reactance is 500.63 ohms.
        the par. ind. reactance is 500.63 ohms.
        the par. equiv. R is 10000.00 ohms.
        Q is 19.777212
        the bandwidth is 80.37 kHz
```

Figure 11-8

coil's resistance did not have a big effect on the behavior of his circuit. That is corroborated by the Q value (about 20). Note that the computer reported Q as an **8-digit** number! Considering that each component value was specified as a 2- or 3-digit number, an 8-digit result is ludicrous. The computer is supposed to be used to eliminate the dogwork—the tedious repeated calculations. **Don't stop thinking!**

11-3 POWER CALCULATIONS IN THREE-PHASE AC CIRCUITS

Balanced-load three-phase circuits interest engineers who work with both power distribution and control systems. Let's write some simple programs to do power calculations for a variety of load configurations.

The Wye–Wye (Y– Y) Connection

Consider a three-phase Y-connected generator with a phase voltage, E_p, connected to a balanced, Y-connected load having $R + jX$ in each leg. Given values for R, X, and the generator phase voltage, you can calculate line voltage, load phase current, phase impedance, phase power, total power, reactive power, and apparent power. Figure 11-9 shows a program to do so. Figure 11-10 shows two sample runs.

The Delta–Delta (Δ–Δ) Connection

This is just as simple as the Y–Y connection and will be left as a homework problem.

The Delta–Wye Load

Suppose that the load consists of a delta-connected set of impedances having a per phase load of $R_d + jX_d$, superimposed on a wye-connected set having a per phase load of $R_y + jX_y$. I didn't use the word "superimposed" lightly; you analyze this

```
#include <stdio.h>
#include <math.h>
main()
{
    float Ep, R, X, El, P, PT, Q, QT;
    float Ip, ST, pf;

    printf("This program solves the Y-Y 3-phase\n");
    printf("balanced load circuit.\n\n");

    printf("Enter the generator phase voltage: ");
    scanf("%f", &Ep);
    printf("Now enter the resistive load per phase: ");
    scanf("%f", &R);
    printf("...and the reactive load per phase: ");
    scanf("%f", &X);
    printf("\nThank you.\n\n");

    El = sqrt(3.0) * Ep;            /* line voltage */
    Ip = Ep / sqrt(R * R + X * X);  /* phase current */
    P = Ip * Ip * R;                /* phase power */
    PT = 3 * P;                     /* total power */
    Q = Ip * Ip * X;               /* phase vars */
    QT = 3 * Q;                     /* total vars */
    ST = sqrt(PT * PT + QT * QT);   /* total apparent power */
    pf = PT / ST;                   /* power factor */

    printf("The line voltage is %.2f volts.\n", El);
    printf("The phase current is %.2f amps.\n", Ip);
    printf("The phase power is %.2f watts,\n", P);
    printf("   and the total power is %.2f watts.\n", PT);
    printf("The phase reactive power is %.2f vars,\n", Q);
    printf("   and the total reactive power is %.2f vars.\n", QT);
    printf("The apparent power is %.2f VA,\n", ST);
    printf("   and the power factor is %.4f watts.\n", pf);
}
```

Figure 11-9

```
A>p11-9
This program solves the Y-Y 3-phase
balanced load circuit.

Enter the generator phase voltage: 120
Now enter the resistive load per phase: 3
...and the reactive load per phase: 4

Thank you.

The line voltage is 207.85 volts.
The phase current is 24.00 amps.
```

Figure 11-10

```
The phase power is 1728.00 watts,
    and the total power is 5184.00 watts.
The phase reactive power is 2304.00 vars,
    and the total reactive power is 6912.00 vars.
The apparent power is 8640.00 VA,
    and the power factor is 0.6000 watts.


A>p11-9
This program solves the Y-Y 3-phase
balanced load circuit.


Enter the generator phase voltage: 110
Now enter the resistive load per phase: 100
...and the reactive load per phase: 40


Thank you.


The line voltage is 190.53 volts.
The phase current is 1.02 amps.
The phase power is 104.31 watts,
    and the total power is 312.93 watts.
The phase reactive power is 41.72 vars,
    and the total reactive power is 125.17 vars.
The apparent power is 337.04 VA,
    and the power factor is 0.9285 watts.
```

Figure 11-10   (*Continued*)

```c
#include <stdio.h>
#include <math.h>
main()
{
        float El, Rd, Xd, Ry, Xy;
        float Id, Iy, Pd, Py, PTd, PTy, PT;
        float Qd, Qy, QTd, QTy, QT;
        float STd, STy, ST, pf;

        printf("This program solves the DELTA-WYE 3-phase\n");
        printf("balanced load circuit.\n\n");

        printf("Enter the generator line voltage: ");
        scanf("%f", &El);
        printf("\nNow enter the resistive load per delta phase: ");
        scanf("%f", &Rd);
        printf("...and the reactive load per delta phase: ");
        scanf("%f", &Xd);
        printf("\nNow enter the resistive load per wye phase: ");
        scanf("%f", &Ry);
        printf("...and the reactive load per wye phase: ");
        scanf("%f", &Xy);
        printf("\nThank you.\n");
```

Figure 11-11   (*Continued*)

```
/* calculations for the delta-connected load */
Id = El / sqrt(Rd * Rd + Xd * Xd);
Pd = Id * Id * Rd;
PTd = 3 * Pd;
Qd = Id * Id * Xd;
QTd = 3 * Qd;
STd = sqrt(PTd * PTd + QTd * QTd);

/* calculations for the wye-connected load */
Iy = (El / sqrt(3.0)) / sqrt(Ry * Ry + Xy * Xy);
Py = Iy * Iy * Ry;
PTy = 3 * Py;
Qy = Iy * Iy * Xy;
QTy = 3 * Qy;
STy = sqrt(PTy * PTy + QTy * QTy);

PT = PTd + PTy;
QT = QTd + QTy;
ST = sqrt(PT * PT + QT * QT);
pf = PT / ST;

printf("\nFor the WYE...\n");
printf("\tThe phase power is %.2f watts,\n", Py);
printf("\t   and the total power is %.2f watts.\n", PTy);
printf("\tThe phase reactive power is %.2f vars,\n", Qy);
printf("\t   and the total reactive power is %.2f vars.\n", QTy);
printf("\tThe apparent power is %.2f VA.\n", STy);

printf("\nFor the DELTA...\n");
printf("\tThe phase power is %.2f watts,\n", Pd);
printf("\t   and the total power is %.2f watts.\n", PTd);
printf("\tThe phase reactive power is %.2f vars,\n", Qd);
printf("\t   and the total reactive power is %.2f vars.\n", QTd);
printf("\tThe apparent power is %.2f VA.\n", STd);
printf("\nThe total power is %.2f watts,\n", PT);
printf("   the total reactive power is %.2f vars,\n", QT);
printf("   the total apparent power is %.2f VA,\n", ST);
printf("   and the power factor is %.4f watts", pf);

if (QT < 0.0)
      printf(" leading.\n");
else
      printf(" lagging.\n");
}
```

Figure 11-11 (*Continued*)

load by analyzing the delta and wye parts separately, and then adding the phase powers. The program is merely a combination of Fig. 11-9 and the one you're going to write for homework. It appears in Fig. 11-11. And Fig. 11-12 shows a sample run. Please note that capacitive reactance must be entered as a negative value in the program.

```
A>p11-11
This program solves the DELTA-WYE 3-phase
balanced load circuit.

Enter the generator line voltage: 200

Now enter the resistive load per delta phase: 6
...and the reactive load per delta phase: -8

Now enter the resistive load per wye phase: 4
...and the reactive load per wye phase: 3

Thank you.

For the WYE...
        The phase power is 2133.33 watts,
          and the total power is 6400.00 watts.
        The phase reactive power is 1600.00 vars,
          and the total reactive power is 4800.00 vars.
        The apparent power is 8000.00 VA.

For the DELTA...
        The phase power is 2400.00 watts,
          and the total power is 7200.00 watts.
        The phase reactive power is -3200.00 vars,
          and the total reactive power is -9600.00 vars.
        The apparent power is 12000.00 VA.

The total power is 13600.00 watts,
   the total reactive power is -4800.00 vars,
   the total apparent power is 14422.21 VA,
   and the power factor is 0.9430 watts leading.
```

Figure 11-12

11-4 REVIEW

In this chapter you learned how to:

- Solve series resonant circuit problems
- Solve parallel resonant circuit problems
- Plot circuit values for resonant circuits
- Solve three-phase Y–Y circuits
- Solve three-phase Δ–Δ circuits

PROBLEMS AND QUESTIONS

1. For the circuit of Fig. 11-1, write a program that accepts the voltage, the resistance, the inductance, and the resonant frequency, and calculates the necessary capacitance, and the resulting power dissipation, Q, and BW.

2. Modify the program of Problem 1 to accept either L or C (and E, R, and f_s), and calculate the other, along with power, Q, and BW.

3. For the circuit of Fig. 11-6, write a program that accepts I, R, R_L, L, and f_p, and calculates the necessary C, and the resulting Q and BW.
4. Add the ability to plot the voltage versus frequency to the program of Problem 3.
5. Write the program to solve the $\Delta-\Delta$ balanced load problem.
6. Write a program that solves the unbalanced Y load problem.
7. Write a program that solves the unbalanced Δ load problem.
8. Write programs for problems assigned from your circuits textbook.

12

C and Electronics Circuits

12-1 INTRODUCTION AND OBJECTIVES

In this chapter you will write and examine programs that deal with nonlinear electronic circuits: circuits that include diodes, transistors, and operational amplifiers (*op amps*). Upon successful completion of this chapter, you will be able to:

- Write programs that read in values from a data file
- Write "trial and error" programs for nonlinear diode circuits
- Write programs to find the Q point of transistor circuits
- Write programs that calculate small-signal characteristics of transistor circuits
- Write programs that explore the characteristics of op amp circuits

12-2 DIODE CIRCUITS

If you have the characteristic $V-I$ curve for a particular diode, you can determine its operating point by drawing a load line on the graph. However, if the data points for a given diode can be entered into the computer, a program for finding the required "Q point" will give you more speed and flexibility.

This approach presents two problems, in as much as the data points for a diode curve will be 25 or more pairs of values. The first problem is that entering 50 or more numbers without error is probably too much to expect from a user. The second occurs when the operating point lies between data point values. We will solve the first by using a **data file** whose contents is read by the program. And we will solve the second by developing a method of **interpolation** on the computer.

Data in a File

Our data file is nothing more than a text file. That is, it's just like a C program except that it contains data values rather than C statements. To create it, just call the Turbo C editor for a file called DIODE-1.DTA, and type the following:

```
0 .1
0 .2
0 .3
0 .5
.5 .35
1 .45
2 .55
3 .6
4 .65
5 .675
6 .7
7 .72
8 .725
9 .74
10 .75
20 .8
30 .85
40 .9
60 .95
100 1
```

Each pair represents a current in milliamps and the corresponding voltage in volts for a fictitious diode. When all pairs have been entered, EXACTLY as shown, key *Alt-X* and save the file. Incidentally, there's nothing special about the name (*DIODE-1.DTA*) I chose. Any name will do, but don't forget to include a "dot" and one, two, or three letters or digits after it.

The next problem is that of getting the information from the data file into the program. It should be fairly obvious that the program needs to have two arrays–**Id[ ]** and **Vd[ ]**— to hold the values. There are 19 pairs in the file, so we could declare the arrays as

```
float Id[20], Vd[20];
```

However, in the program, I'm going to allow room for 30 values, just in case.

To read data from a file, C insists that we "open" the file, using the function *fopen (filename, mode);*. In our case, *filename* would be "**DIODE-1.DTA**," while *mode* would be "*r*" for *read* (the quotation marks are mandatory for both parameters). Specifically, our program will have a line like this:

```
fopen("DIODE-1.DTA", "r");
```

fopen( ) returns something called a "*file pointer*" or a "pointer to **FILE**." What that is, exactly, is immaterial. You need only learn the rules for using file pointers, and they are much simpler than the rules for using general pointers. Of course, a file pointer must have a name; for example, *infp* is a perfectly good name for a pointer that points to an "input file" (i.e., one that we're going to read data from). So there will be two lines in our program that deal with files:

```
FILE * infp;
infp = fopen("DIODE-1.DTA", "r");
```

(Incidentally, **FILE** is defined in *stdio.h*.) If the file cannot be opened (it's missing or somehow damaged), *fopen* returns something called *NULL* (also defined in *stdio.h*). Otherwise, it returns a value used by the program but NOT by the programmer. That's great! One less thing to worry about. However, we should test for successful opening by adding an **if** statement:

```
FILE * infp;
infp = fopen("DIODE-1.DTA", "r");
if (infp == NULL)
{
     printf("\n\nCOULD NOT OPEN DIODE-1.DAT\n\n");
     exit(1);
}
```

Most C programmers do the "attempt to open" and the test in one step, like this:

```
if ((infp = fopen("DIODE-1.DTA", "r")) == NULL)
{
     printf("\n\nCOULD NOT OPEN DIODE-1.DAT\n\n");
     exit(1);
}
```

If the *fopen()* does **not** return *NULL*, you can rest assured that the file was opened successfully, so we can proceed with reading it.

To read data from a file, we can use the "file version" of *scanf()*. It's called *fscanf()*, and is used like this:

```
fscanf(infp, "%f", &num);
```

The first argument is a file pointer that tells *fscanf* what file to read from, the second is the conversion specification, and the third, the address of the variable that will receive data. In our program, we have two numbers per line, separated by a space, so our *fscanf()* will be

```
fscanf(infp, "%f %f", &Id[i], &Vd[i]);
```

The "**%f %f**" is exactly what you must have. It represents a float number, a space, and a float number. Leaving out the space (or having more than one space) *could* lead to disaster.

Figure 12-1 shows a simple program that opens DIODE-1.DTA, reads its contents into a pair of arrays, and outputs the array values.

This program will work for any data file that has exactly 19 pairs of data values. To make it more general, let's require that the first value in the file be a

```
#include <stdio.h>
#include <stdlib.h>
main()
{
        float Id[31], Vd[31];
        int i;
        FILE * infp;

        if ((infp = fopen("DIODE-1.DTA", "r")) == NULL)
        {
                printf("\n\nCAN'T OPEN FILE\n\n");
                exit(1);
        }
        for (i = 1; i < 20; ++i)
                fscanf(infp, "%f %f", &Id[i], &Vd[i]);

        for (i = 1; i < 20; ++i)
                printf("%10.3f %10.3f\n", Id[i], Vd[i]);
}
```
Figure 12-1

single number—the answer to the question: How many pairs of data values are there in this file? Figure 12-2 shows the modified data file and program.

Interpolation

Our problem is this: Given a value of voltage—say Vx—that lies between $Vd[j]$ and $Vd[j + 1]$, find the corresponding value of Id. Figure 12-3 shows the "interpolation triangle." As with any linear interpolation scheme, I'm assuming that the diode curve is a straight line between data points. The equation of a straight line is $y = mx + b$, where m is its slope. For our curve, the slope is

$$m = (Id[j + 1] - Id[j])/(Vd[j + 1] - Vd[j])$$

Using similar triangles,

$$Ix - Id[j] = m (Vx - Vd[j])$$

or

$$Ix = Id[j] + m (Vx - Vd[j])$$

Figure 12-4 contains a simple program to interpolate the data in DIODE-1.DTA, given the value of the voltage, Vx.

    After reading the data file and asking for the unknown voltage, the program tests to insure that Vx is valid for the given curve. Then, it starts at $i = 1$, the first data point, and works its way up the curve until it reaches the first voltage that's larger than Vx. This establishes the top point on the triangle. Next, we decrement i to get to the lower point on the triangle. Now, $j == i$, and the interpolation formulas are valid. The rest simply uses those formulas.

    It seems sensible to rewrite the interpolation part as a function (we haven't done that for a while), partly because its use is uniquely identified, and partly

```
19
0 .1
0 .2
0 .3
.5 .35
1 .45
2 .55
3 .6
4 .65
5 .675
6 .7
7 .72
8 .725
9 .74
10 .75
20 .8
30 .85
40 .9
60 .95
100 1


#include <stdio.h>
#include <stdlib.h>
#define SIZE 31    /* maximum number of data pairs */
main()
{
     float Id[SIZE], Vd[SIZE];
     int i, num;
     FILE * infp;

     if ((infp = fopen("DIODE-1.DTA", "r")) == NULL)
     {
          printf("\n\nCAN'T OPEN FILE\n\n");
          exit(1);
     }

     /* how many data pairs in the file? */
     fscanf(infp, "%d", &num);

     if (num >= SIZE)
     {
          printf("\n\nTOO MUCH DATA\n\n");
          exit(2);
     }

     for (i = 1; i <= num; ++i)
          fscanf(infp, "%f %f", &Id[i], &Vd[i]);

     for (i = 1; i <= num; ++i)
          printf("%10.3f %10.3f\n", Id[i], Vd[i]);
}
```

Figure 12-2

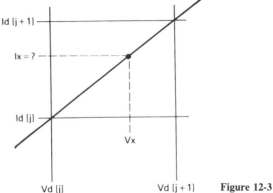

Figure 12-3

because the program is starting to get a little large. The header can be

```
float interpolate(float, int)
```

assuming that the arrays are **global**, and that the desired voltage and the size of the data file are passed as parameters. That will be OK for this example, but is not general enough to be truly useful. A more general function would have the value of Vx (or whatever the user-entered value is called), and the two arrays (and their sizes) passed as parameters. That would make a good homework problem, wouldn't it? Figure 12-5 shows our program with the interpolation program and global arrays.

Diode Operating Point

Now that we have the ability to read a data file and to interpolate between values, let's now write the program that finds the Q point of a diode circuit consisting of the diode whose characteristics are in DIODE-1.DTA, a resistor R, and a forward-biasing voltage source, E. This equation must be satisfied at the Q point:

$$E = V_d + I_d R$$

and the point (I_d, V_d) must lie on the diode characteristic curve. This implies a trial-and-error approach. That is, pick a value of V_d, calculate the value of I_d from

$$I_d = (E - V_d)/R$$

and check to see if (I_d, V_d) is on the diode curve. Here's some code:

```
for (v = Vd[1]; v <= Vd[num]; v += Vd[num]/1000.0)
{
        I = (E - Vd) / R;
        Id = interpolate(Vd);
        if (I == Id)
                break;
}
```

```
#include <stdio.h>
#include <stdlib.h>
#define SIZE 31
main()
{
     float Id[SIZE], Vd[SIZE], Vx, m, Ix;
     int i, num;
     FILE * infp;

     /* read the diode characteristic data */

     if ((infp = fopen("DIODE-1.DTA", "r")) == NULL)
     {
          printf("\n\nCAN'T OPEN FILE\n\n");
          exit(1);
     }

     fscanf(infp, "%d", &num);

     for (i = 1; i <= num; ++i)
          fscanf(infp, "%f %f", &Id[i], &Vd[i]);

     /* get the unknown voltage */

     printf("\nWhat is the value of Vx? ");
     scanf("%f", &Vx);

     /* make sure it's a legal value */

     if ( (Vx < Vd[1]) || (Vx > Vd[19]) )
     {
          printf("\n\nVoltage out of range\n\n");
          exit(2);
     }

     /* work up through the arrays until you pass Vd[j],
        the bottom of the interpolation triangle
     */

     for (i = 1; Vx > Vd[i]; ++i)
          ;  /* an empty loop!  all the work is
                done between the parentheses !!  */

     /* now, back off one to get to the correct Vd[i] */

     --i;

     /* calculate the slope and the current */

     m = (Id[i+1] - Id[i])/(Vd[i+1] - Vd[i]);
     Ix = Id[i] + m * (Vx - Vd[i]);

     printf("\nFor a voltage of %.3f volts, the current is %.3f\n",
          Vx, Ix);
}
```

Figure 12-4

```
#define SIZE 31
float Id[SIZE], Vd[SIZE];
#include <stdio.h>
#include <stdlib.h>
main()
{
      float Vx, Ix, interpolate(float, int);
      FILE * infp;
      int i, num;

      if ((infp = fopen("DIODE-1.DTA", "r")) == NULL)
      {
            printf("\n\nCAN'T OPEN FILE\n\n");
            exit(1);
      }

      fscanf(infp, "%d", &num);

      for (i = 1; i <= num; ++i)
            fscanf(infp, "%f %f", &Id[i], &Vd[i]);

      printf("\nWhat is the value of Vx? ");
      scanf("%f", &Vx);

      Ix = interpolate(Vx, num);

      printf("\nFor a voltage of %.3f volts, the current is %.3f\n",
            Vx, Ix);
}

float interpolate(float v, int n)
{
      float m;
      int i;

      if ( (v < Vd[1]) || (v > Vd[n]) )
      {
            printf("\n\nVoltage out of range\n\n");
            exit(2);
      }

      for (i = 1; v > Vd[i]; ++i)
            ;

      --i;

      m = (Id[i+1] - Id[i])/(Vd[i+1] - Vd[i]);
      return (Id[i] + m * (v - Vd[i]));
}
```

Figure 12-5

num, you'll remember, is the number of pairs of data values. Notice that we are taking tiny steps in the voltage. We would be bored silly if we were to do this by hand, but the computer is so fast, we'll never even know how many calculations it does!

But there's another problem, Both I and I_d are *floats*, so they will never be exactly equal. We'll have to decide on a reasonable amount for error–say, 1 percent of the present value perhaps?—and change the test to

```
if (fabs(I - Id) < 0.001 * I)
      break;
```

fabs() is the absolute value function for *floats*, and has the header

```
float fabs(float)
```

If *break* is executed, the computer will exit the *for* loop.

Figure 12-6 has the program, and Fig. 12-7, three sample runs.

Reading Any Data File

In all of our programs so far, only the file called "DIODE-1.DTA" was read. This is not practical because there are several different models for diodes and therefore several different data files—with different names. It would be much more useful if the user could tell the program what file to read. One way to accomplish this is to use the mechanism in C that lets the user specify the data file name as she invokes the program. For example, if the program were called DIODE.EXE and the data file, DATA.D1, the user could key

```
A>diode data.d1
```

DOS would accept *DATA.D1* as a "command line parameter" and pass it to the program as the value of a special C variable called *argv[1]*. The name means "(command line) argument variable number 1." There is a companion special C variable called *argc*, the "(command line) argument count" (i.e., the number of command line arguments). Using these requires a change in the way we have been writing *main()*:

```
main(int argc, char * argv[])
```

will be the new header for *main()*. The declaration *char * argv[]* means that *argv* is an array of pointers to *char* (i.e. *argv* is an array of strings).

```
#define SIZE 31
float Id[SIZE], Vd[SIZE];
#include <stdio.h>
#include <stdlib.h>
#include <math.h>
main()
{
      float interpolate(float, int);
      float v, E, I, R, Ix;
      FILE * infp;
      int i, num;
```

Figure 12-6   (*Continued*)

```
        if ((infp = fopen("DIODE-1.DTA", "r")) == NULL)
        {
              printf("\n\nCAN'T OPEN FILE\n\n");
              exit(1);
        }


        fscanf(infp, "%d", &num);

        for (i = 1; i <= num; ++i)
              fscanf(infp, "%f %f", &Id[i], &Vd[i]);

        printf("\nWhat is the value of the source voltage? ");
        scanf("%f", &E);

        printf("\nWhat is the value of the resistance? ");
        scanf("%f", &R);

        for (v = Vd[1]; v <= Vd[num]; v += Vd[num]/1000.0)
        {
              I = 1000.0 * (E - v) / R; /* in milliamps */
              Ix = interpolate(v, num);

              if (fabs(I - Ix) < 0.01 * I)
              {
                    printf("\nThe Q point is:");
                    printf("\n\tVd = %.3f", v);
                    printf("\n\tId = %.3f", Ix);
                    break;
              }
        }
}

float interpolate(float v, int n)
{
        float m;
        int i;

        if ( (v < Vd[1]) || (v > Vd[n]) )
        {
              printf("\n\nVoltage out of range\n\n");
              exit(2);
        }

        for (i = 1; v > Vd[i]; ++i)
              ;
        --i;

        m = (Id[i+1] - Id[i])/(Vd[i+1] - Vd[i]);
        return (Id[i] + m * (v - Vd[i]));
}
```

Figure 12-6 (*Continued*)

```
What is the value of the source voltage? 10
What is the value of the resistance? 2e3

The Q point is:
        Vd = 0.666
        Id = 4.640


A>p12-6


What is the value of the source voltage?   20
What is the value of the resistance? 4e3

The Q point is:
        Vd = 0.670
        Id = 4.800

A>p12-6


What is the value of the source voltage? 10
What is the value of the resistance? 4e3

The Q point is:
        Vd = 0.567
        Id = 2.340
```

Figure 12-7

Here's a little program that displays the command line arguments each time you run it. Figure 12-8 has the program, while Fig. 12-9 has some sample runs. Note that *argv[0]* is the name of the program, including the disk drive letter and any directories!

```
#include <stdio.h>
main(int argc, char * argv[])
{
      int i;

      printf("\n\nThere were %d command line arguments.\n\n", argc);
      printf("They were:\n");

      for (i = 0; i < argc; ++i)
            printf("\targv[%d] = %s\n", i, argv[i]);
}
```

Figure 12-8

Sec. 12-2   Diode Circuits   311

```
A>p12-8 this is fun
```

There were 4 command line arguments.

They were:

```
        argv[0] = A:\P12-8.EXE
        argv[1] = this
        argv[2] = is
        argv[3] = fun
```

```
A>p12-8 you can't trick me 23 -1.5
```

There were 7 command line arguments.

They were:

```
        argv[0] = A:\P12-8.EXE
        argv[1] = you
        argv[2] = can't
        argv[3] = trick
        argv[4] = me
        argv[5] = 23
        argv[6] = -1.5
```

Figure 12-9

```c
#include <stdio.h>
#include <stdlib.h>
#define SIZE 31
main(int argc, char * argv[])
{
     float Id[SIZE], Vd[SIZE];
     int i, num;
     FILE * infp;

     if ((infp = fopen(argv[1], "r")) == NULL)
     {
          printf("\n\nCAN'T OPEN FILE\n\n");
          exit(1);
     }

     fscanf(infp, "%d", &num);

     for (i = 1; i <= num; ++i)
          fscanf(infp, "%f %f", &Id[i], &Vd[i]);

     for (i = 1; i <= num; ++i)
          printf("%10.3f %10.3f\n", Id[i], Vd[i]);
}
```

Figure 12-10

C and Electronics Circuits   Chap. 12

```
A>p12-10 diode-1.dta
```

0.000	0.100
0.000	0.200
0.000	0.300
0.500	0.350
1.000	0.450
2.000	0.550
3.000	0.600
4.000	0.650
5.000	0.675
6.000	0.700
7.000	0.720
8.000	0.725
9.000	0.740
10.000	0.750
20.000	0.800
30.000	0.850
40.000	0.900
60.000	0.950
100.000	1.000

```
A>p12-10 diode-2.dta

CAN'T OPEN FILE

A>p12-10 diode-1

CAN'T OPEN FILE
```

Figure 12-11

Now we'll modify our diode program to use *argv[]* and *argc*. The result is in Fig. 12-10, with two sample runs in Fig. 12-11.

There's a more conventional approach, in which the program **asks** for the name of the data file, just like it asks for the value of the resistance or the source voltage. Figure 12-12 has the program, while Fig. 12-13 has some runs.

You see the new code in the program

```
char fname[13];

printf("What is the name of the data file? ");
scanf("%s", fname);

if ((infp = fopen(fname, "r")) == NULL)
```

```
#include <stdio.h>
#include <stdlib.h>
#define SIZE 31
main()              /* our old header */
{
     float Id[SIZE], Vd[SIZE];
     int i, num;
     FILE * infp;
     char fname[13];     /* a buffer to hold the file name */

     printf("What is the name of the data file? ");
     scanf("%s", fname);

     if ((infp = fopen(fname, "r")) == NULL)
     {
          printf("\n\nCAN'T OPEN FILE\n\n");
          exit(1);
     }

     fscanf(infp, "%d", &num);

     for (i = 1; i <= num; ++i)
          fscanf(infp, "%f %f", &Id[i], &Vd[i]);

     for (i = 1; i <= num; ++i)
          printf("%10.3f %10.3f\n", Id[i], Vd[i]);
}
```

Figure 12-12

```
A>p12-12

What is the name of the data file? diode-1.dta

     0.000        0.100
     0.000        0.200
     0.000        0.300
     0.500        0.350
     1.000        0.450
     2.000        0.550
     3.000        0.600
     4.000        0.650
     5.000        0.675
     6.000        0.700
     7.000        0.720
     8.000        0.725
     9.000        0.740
    10.000        0.750
```

Figure 12-13

```
        20.000        0.800
        30.000        0.850
        40.000        0.900
        60.000        0.950
       100.000        1.000

     A>p12-12

     What is the name of the data file? diode-1

     CAN'T OPEN FILE
```

Figure 12-13 (*Continued*)

fname is an array of *char*, and acts as if it were a *string variable*. We have used this approach before.

12-3 TRANSISTOR CIRCUITS

Transistors are both a little more complicated and also a little simpler than diodes. A transistor has more currents and voltages to calculate, but the dc model of a transistor does not require that we use data files because it is a linear model.

Biasing Circuits

Determining the Q point for a bipolar junction transistor (BJT) circuit is an appropriate chore for a computer because of the number of equations involved in the calculations and the number of different bias arrangements. Figure 12-14 shows the circuit diagram. The equations are right out of your electronics circuits book:

$$V_{TH} = V_{CC}R_2/(R_1 + R_2)$$

$$R_{TH} = R_1R_2/(R_1 + R_2)$$

$$I_B = (V_{TH} - 0.7)/(R_{TH} + (\beta + 1)R_E)$$

$$I_C = \beta I_B$$

$$I_E = (\beta + 1)I_B$$

$$V_E = I_E R_E$$

$$V_C = V_{CC} - I_C R_C$$

$$V_{CE} = V_C - V_E$$

Note that if R_2 is missing (i.e., an open circuit, or a value of 1e38), the circuit is the "emitter-stabilized" bias circuit, while if R_E is a short circuit (value = 0), the circuit is the "fixed-bias" one. With R_2 and R_E present, the circuit is the "voltage-divider" bias configuration.

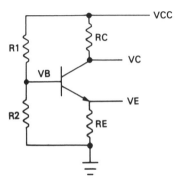

Figure 12-14 A BJT biasing circuit.

The program should make a few decisions for you. For one, if V_{TH} is less than 0.7 volt, then the transistor will be "cut off," so the program should set $I_B = 0$. Also, if the sum of the voltages across R_C and R_E is greater than V_{CC}, the circuit is "saturated" and

$$I_C = I_E = V_{CC}/(R_C + R_E)$$

There will be a large section for inputting all the values, a section for making calculations and decisions, and a section for printing the results. Figure 12-15 has the program; Fig. 12-16 has some sample runs.

```
#include <stdio.h>
#include <stdlib.h>
main()
{
        float R1, R2, RC, RE, VCC, beta;
        float VTH, RTH, IB, IC, IE;
        float VC, VE, VCE;

        printf("\nThis program solves the three BJT biasing");
        printf("\ncircuits.  Enter values as requested.");
        printf("\n\nFor emitter-stabilized bias, enter 1e38 for R2.");
        printf("\nFor fixed bias, enter 0 for RE.");

        printf("\n\nEnter the values for:");
        printf("\n\tR1: ");
        scanf("%f", &R1);
        printf("\tR2: ");
        scanf("%f", &R2);
        printf("\tRC: ");
        scanf("%f", &RC);
        printf("\tRE: ");
        scanf("%f", &RE);
        printf("\tVCC: ");
        scanf("%f", &VCC);
        printf("\tthe DC beta: ");
        scanf("%f", &beta);
```

Figure 12-15

```
VTH = R2 * VCC / (R1 + R2);
RTH = R1 * R2 / (R1 + R2);

if (VTH > 0.7)
      IB = (VTH - 0.7) / (RTH + (beta + 1.0) * RE);
else
{
      IB = 0.0;
      printf("\nThe transistor is cut off.\n\n");
      exit(1);
}

IC = beta * IB;
IE = IC + IB;

if (IC * RC + IE * RE > VCC)
{
      printf("\n\nSaturation!");
      IC = IE = VCC / (RC + RE);
}

VE = IE * RE;
VC = VCC - IC * RC;
VCE = VC - VE;

printf("\n\nThe Q point is at:");
printf("\n\tVCE = %7.3f volts", VCE);
printf("\n\tIC = %7.3f milliamps", 1000 * IC);
printf("\n\tand IB = %7.1f microamps", 1e6 * IB);
}
```

Figure 12-15 *(Continued)*

Small-Signal Analysis

In your electronics courses, you studied at least one small-signal model of the BJT. The following program is based on the "*h*-parameter" model of an emitter-stabilized circuit. This model includes many, many equations, but the computer won't mind—once we've written the program! They include:

$$R_p = R_L R_c / (R_L + R_c) \qquad (R_L \text{ is the load resistance})$$

$$FF1 = h_f / (1 + h_0 R_p)$$

$$R_z = h_i - h_r R_p(FF1)$$

$$R_b = R_1 R_2 / (R_1 + R_2)$$

$$R_i = R_z R_b / (R_z + R_b)$$

The value of R_t depends on h_0 and h_r. If they are both nonzero, then

$$R_t = 1/(h_0 - h_f h_r / (h_i + R_s)) \qquad (R_s \text{ is the resistance of the source})$$

Sec. 12-3   Transistor Circuits

```
A>p12-15

This program solves the three BJT biasing
circuits.  Enter values as requested.

For emitter-stabilized bias, enter 1e38 for R2.
For fixed bias, enter 0 for RE.

Enter the values for:
        R1: 18.6e3
        R2: 11.4e3
        RC: 1e3
        RE: 1e3
        VCC: 15
        the DC beta: 100

The Q point is at:
        VCE =    5.700 volts
        IC =    4.627 milliamps
        and IB =    46.3 microamps



A>p12-15

This program solves the three BJT biasing
circuits.  Enter values as requested.

For emitter-stabilized bias, enter 1e38 for R2.
For fixed bias, enter 0 for RE.

Enter the values for:
        R1: 68e3
        R2: 56e3
        RC: 3.9e3
        RE: 4.7e3
        VCC: 12
        the DC beta: 100

The Q point is at:
        VCE =    3.926 volts
        IC =    0.934 milliamps
        and IB =    9.3 microamps


A>p12-15

This program solves the three BJT biasing
circuits.  Enter values as requested.

For emitter-stabilized bias, enter 1e38 for R2.
For fixed bias, enter 0 for RE.
```

Figure 12-16

```
Enter the values for:
        R1: 18.6e3
        R2: 11.4e3
        RC: 1000
        RE: 1000
        VCC: 15
        the DC beta: 50

The Q point is at:
        VCE =    6.303 volts
        IC =    4.305 milliamps
        and IB =    86.1 microamps

A>p12-15

This program solves the three BJT biasing
circuits.  Enter values as requested.

For emitter-stabilized bias, enter 1e38 for R2.
For fixed bias, enter 0 for RE.

Enter the values for:
        R1: 18.6e3
        R2: 11.4e3
        RC: 1000
        RE: 1000
        VCC: 15
        the DC beta: 150

The Q point is at:
        VCE =    5.479 volts
        IC =    4.745 milliamps
        and IB =    31.6 microamps
```

Figure 12-16 (*Continued*)

Otherwise, $R_t = \infty$. Continuing, we obtain

$$R_o = R_t R_c/(R_t + R_c)$$

The current gain is

$$A_i = (R_i/R_z)(FF1)(R_p/R_L)$$

while the voltage gain is given by

$$A_v = -h_f R_c/(h_i + R_c(h_i h_0 - h_f h_r))$$

The transistor's **input** voltage is

$$V_i = R_i V_s/(R_i + R_s)$$

where V_s is the source voltage. The output voltage is then

$$V_o = A_v V_i$$

and the load voltage is

$$V_L = R_L V_o / (R_L + R_o)$$

The program that manipulates all of these equations is straightforward and appears in Fig. 12-17 (sample runs in Fig. 12-18). If you have the equations for any small-signal model, you can write the program.

```c
#include <stdio.h>
main()
{
        float R1, R2, Rc, hi, ho, hr, hf, Vs;
        float Rp, Rz, Rb, Ri, Rt, Ro, Rs, RL;
        float FF, Ai, Av, Vi, Vo, VL;

        printf("h-parameter transistor circuit analysis\n\n");
        printf("Please enter values for the following:\n");
        printf("\tR1: ");
        scanf("%f", &R1);
        printf("\tR2: ");
        scanf("%f", &R2);
        printf("\tRc: ");
        scanf("%f", &Rc);

        printf("\nPlease enter the values for the circuit elements.\n");
        printf("\tLoad R: ");
        scanf("%f", &RL);
        printf("\tSource R: ");
        scanf("%f", &Rs);
        printf("\tSource voltage: ");
        scanf("%f", &Vs);

        printf("\nPlease enter the values for the h-parameters.\n");
        printf("\thie: ");
        scanf("%f", &hi);
        printf("\thfe: ");
        scanf("%f", &hf);
        printf("\thoe: ");
        scanf("%f", &ho);
        printf("\thre: ");
        scanf("%f", &hr);

        Rp = Rc * RL / (Rc + RL);
        FF = hf / (1 + ho * Rp);
        Rz = hi - hr * Rp * FF;
        Rb = R1 * R2 / (R1 + R2);
        Ri = Rz * Rb / (Rz + Rb);

        if ( (ho != 0.0) && (hr != 0.0) )
                Rt = 1 / (ho - hf * hr / (hi + Rs));
```

Figure 12-17

```
                else
                        Rt = 1e38;   /* open circuit */

                Ro = Rt * Rc / (Rt + Rc);
                Ai = (Ri / Rz) * FF * Rp / RL;
                Av = - hf * Rc / (hi + Rc * (hi * ho - hr * hf));
                Vi = Ri * Vs / (Ri + Rs);
                Vo = Av * Vi;
                VL = Vo * RL / (RL + Ro);

                printf("\nThe results are:\n");
                printf("\tinput impedance = %7.2f Kohms\n", Ri/1000.0);
                printf("\toutput impedance = %7.2f Kohms\n", Ro/1000.0);
                printf("\tvoltage gain = %7.2f\n", Av);
                printf("\tcurrent gain = %7.2f\n", Ai);
                printf("\tno-load output voltage = %7.2f volts\n", Vo);
                printf("\tload voltage = %7.2f volts.\n\n", VL);
        }
```

Figure 12-17   (*Continued*)

```
A>p12-16

h-parameter transistor circuit analysis

Please enter values for the following:
        R1: 68e3
        R2: 56e3
        Rc: 3.9e3

Please enter the values for the circuit elements.
        Load R: 82e3
        Source R: 1000
        Source voltage: .01

Please enter the values for the h-parameters.
        hie: 2100
        hfe: 75
        hoe: 1e-6
        hre: 0

The results are:
        input impedance =    1.97 Kohms
        output impedance =    3.90 Kohms
        voltage gain = -138.74
        current gain =    3.18
        no-load output voltage =   -0.92 volts
        load voltage =   -0.88 volts.

A>p12-16

h-parameter transistor circuit analysis
```

Figure 12-18   (*Continued*)

```
Please enter values for the following:
        R1: 40000
        R2: 2000
        Rc: 3000

Please enter the values for the circuit elements.
        Load R: 1500
        Source R: 0
        Source voltage: .01

Please enter the values for the h-parameters.
        hie: 1500
        hfe: 100
        hoe: 0
        hre: 0


The results are:
        input impedance =    0.84 Kohms
        output impedance =    3.00 Kohms
        voltage gain = -200.00
        current gain =   37.30
        no-load output voltage =   -2.00 volts
        load voltage =    -0.67 volts.        Figure 12-18   (Continued)
```

12-4 OP AMP CALCULATIONS

With a computer, you can avoid having to make simplifying assumptions because the computer will do as much work as you ask it to do. Consider the op amp equivalent circuit in Fig. 12-19, and the equations that describe it. At the V_i node,

$$(V_i - V_1).R_1 + (V_i - V_o).R_f + V_i/R_i = 0$$

At the V_o node,

$$(V_o - V_i)/R_f + (V_o - (-A_vV_i))/R_o = 0$$

The notation gets awkward because of the reciprocal resistances, but if we make some substitutions:

$$G_1 = 1/R_1$$

$$G_f = 1/R_f$$

$$G_i = 1/R_i$$

$$G_{1fi} = G_1 + G_f + G_i$$

$$\text{FF} = -(R_o + R_f)/(A_vR_f - R_o)$$

we can write the voltage gain as

$$\text{VG} = V_o/V_1 = G_1/((\text{FF})(G_{1fi}) - G_f)$$

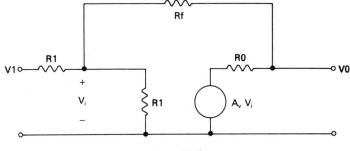

Figure 12-19

The approximate voltage gain for this circuit is simply R_f/R_1 if

$$A_v \gg 1$$

$$A_v R_1 \gg R_f$$

Figure 12-20 shows a program that varies A_v over a range of values and prints it and VG until VG is within 1 percent of R_f/R_1. You'll then be able to see the minimum value of A_v for which the approximation is true (Fig. 12-21). The minimum value of A_v (270, 380, 420) is considerably larger than 100, the usual value that we believe satisfies $A_v \gg 1$. Also, note the effect that the internal resistances have on the minimum value of A_v.

```
#include <stdio.h>
#include <math.h>
main()
{
        float Rf, R1, Ro, Ri, Av;
        float RR, VG=0.0, FF;
        float G1FI, G1, GF;
        char c;

        printf("Op Amp Calculations\n\n");
        printf("Please enter values in ohms for...\n");
        printf("\texternal input R: ");
        scanf("%f", &R1);
        printf("\texternal feedback R: ");
        scanf("%f", &Rf);
        printf("\tinternal input R: ");
        scanf("%f", &Ri);
        printf("\tinternal output R: ");
        scanf("%f", &Ro);

        RR = Rf/R1;

        printf("\nRf/R1 = %7.2f is the VG if ", RR);
        printf("\Av >> 1 and Av * R1 >> Rf\n");
```

Figure 12-20   (Continued)

```
printf("\nKey G and ENTER for a table of Av and VG values that\n");
printf("stops when VG is within 1 percent of Rf/R1.\n");
scanf("%d", &c);

printf("\n    Av           VG\n");

G1 = 1/R1;
GF = 1/Rf;
G1FI = G1 + GF + 1/Ri;

for (Av = 10 * RR; (Av < 1000 * RR) && (VG < .99 * RR); Av += 10 * RR)
{
     FF = (Ro + Rf)/(Ro - Av * Rf);
     VG = fabs(G1 / (FF * G1FI - GF));
     printf("%8.3f      %8.3f\n", Av, VG);
}
}
```

Figure 12-20   (*Continued*)

```
A>p12-20

Op Amp Calculations

Please enter values in ohms for...
        external input R: 100e3
        external feedback R: 100e3
        internal input R: 195e3
        internal output R: 8e3

Rf/R1 =    1.00 is the VG if Av >> 1 and Av * R1 >> Rf

Key G and ENTER for a table of Av and VG values that
stops when VG is within 1 percent of Rf/R1.
g

    Av             VG
    10.000        0.785
    20.000        0.880
    30.000        0.917
    40.000        0.936
    50.000        0.948
    60.000        0.957
    70.000        0.963
    80.000        0.967
    90.000        0.971
   100.000        0.974
   110.000        0.976
   120.000        0.978
   130.000        0.980
   140.000        0.981
   150.000        0.982
   160.000        0.983
```

Figure 12-21

```
        170.000          0.984
        180.000          0.985
        190.000          0.986
        200.000          0.987
        210.000          0.987
        220.000          0.988
        230.000          0.988
        240.000          0.989
        250.000          0.989
        260.000          0.990
        270.000          0.990


A>p12-20


Op Amp Calculations


Please enter values in ohms for...
        external input R: 100e3
        external feedback R: 100e3
        internal input R: 70e3
        internal output R: 10.5e3


Rf/R1 =    1.00 is the VG if Av >> 1 and Av * R1 >> Rf


Key G and ENTER for a table of Av and VG values that
stops when VG is within 1 percent of Rf/R1.
  g

        Av               VG
        10.000           0.723
        20.000           0.840
        30.000           0.888
        40.000           0.913
        50.000           0.929
        60.000           0.941
        70.000           0.949
        80.000           0.955
        90.000           0.960
       100.000           0.963
       110.000           0.967
       120.000           0.969
       130.000           0.972
       140.000           0.974
       150.000           0.975
       160.000           0.977
       170.000           0.978
       180.000           0.979
       190.000           0.980
       200.000           0.981
       210.000           0.982
       220.000           0.983
       230.000           0.984
       240.000           0.984
```

Figure 12-21   (*Continued*)

```
250.000        0.985
260.000        0.986
270.000        0.986
280.000        0.987
290.000        0.987
300.000        0.988
310.000        0.988
320.000        0.988
330.000        0.989
340.000        0.989
350.000        0.989
360.000        0.990
370.000        0.990
380.000        0.990


A>p12-20

Op Amp Calculations

Please enter values in ohms for...
        external input R: 100e3
        external feedback R: 200e3
        internal input R: 195e3
        internal output R: 8e3


Rf/R1 =    2.00 is the VG if Av >> 1 and Av * R1 >> Rf

Key G and ENTER for a table of Av and VG values that
stops when VG is within 1 percent of Rf/R1.
g

     Av              VG
     20.000         1.653
     40.000         1.810
     60.000         1.869
     80.000         1.900
    100.000         1.920
    120.000         1.933
    140.000         1.942
    160.000         1.949
    180.000         1.955
    200.000         1.959
    220.000         1.963
    240.000         1.966
    260.000         1.968
    280.000         1.971
    300.000         1.972
    320.000         1.974
    340.000         1.976
    360.000         1.977
    380.000         1.978
    400.000         1.979
    420.000         1.980
```

Figure 12-21 (*Continued*)

12-5 REVIEW

In this chapter you learned how to:

- Write programs that read in values from a data file
- Write "trial and error" programs for nonlinear diode circuits
- Write programs to find the Q point of transistor circuits
- Write programs that calculate small-signal characteristics of transistor circuits
- Write programs that explore the characteristics of op amp circuits

PROBLEMS AND QUESTIONS

1. Create another data file for a different diode, and find the Q point for that diode with $E = 12$ V and $R = 15$Kohms. Use the approach of Fig. 12-12.

2. Rewrite the program of Fig. 12-5 so that *interpolate( )* accepts not only the voltage value and the number of data points, but also the (starting addresses of the) two arrays.

3. Write a program to calculate the Q point of a JFET having a fixed bias. Do not use any approximations.

4. Repeat Problem 3 for a JFET with self-bias. Then, combine the two into a single program like the one in Fig. 12-15.

5. Rewrite the program of Fig. 12-17 using an alternative equivalent circuit for the transistor.

6. Write programs to solve electronics circuits, as assigned from your electronics textbook.

13

Frequency Response and Modulation

13-1 INTRODUCTION AND OBJECTIVES

In this chapter you will write and examine programs that deal with plotting variables on a logarithmic scale, such as is needed for frequency response analysis. Also, you will write and examine programs that calculate gains, impedances, and frequencies in the small-signal analysis of transistor circuits. And you will write and examine programs that perform calculations pertaining to amplitude and frequency modulation.

Upon successful completion of this chapter, you will be able to write programs that:

- Plot a variable against a logarithmic scale
- Calculate small-signal frequency response of a transistor amplifier
- Do calculations for AM and FM systems

13-2 FREQUENCY RESPONSE PLOTTING

Up until now, we have written programs that plot variables on linear scales. That is, 1 inch = x units of the variable. In electronics, many devices operate over a very wide range of frequencies. Important things happen both at very low frequencies and at the other end of the scale. Plotting the frequency response curve for such a device on a linear frequency scale would mean that either the low-end or high-end characteristics would not be plotted clearly. For that reason, frequency plots are almost always made with the **logarithm** of the frequency as the abscissa.

Obviously, logarithmic spacing along an axis is not linear. To determine the spacing, we use the program of Fig. 13-1, which looks at the difference between the logs of successive numbers. Figure 13-2 shows the output of the program. Figure 13-3 shows the program for plotting a logarithmic abscissa, and Fig. 13-4

```
#include <stdio.h>
#include <math.h>
main()
{
    int i, j;

    printf("\n\nNumber   Distance\n");
    for (j = 0; j < 9; ++j)
        printf("\n%2d    %8.0f", j+1, 10*(log(j+2)-log(j+1)));
}
```

Figure 13-1

```
A>p13-1
            Number    Distance

              1          7
              2          4
              3          3
              4          2
              5          2
              6          2
              7          1
              8          1
              9          1
```
Figure 13-2

```
#include <stdio.h>
#include <math.h>
main()
{
    /* prints a logarithmic vertical axis (abscissa) */

    int step[] = {7, 4, 3, 2, 2, 2, 1, 1, 1, 1};
    int label[] = {100, 200, 300, 400, 500, 600, 700, 800, 900};
    int i, j;

    for (j = 0; j < 9; ++j)
    {
        printf("\n%4d +", label[j]);
        for (i = 0; i < step[j]; ++i)
            printf("\n     | ");
    }
}
```

Figure 13-3

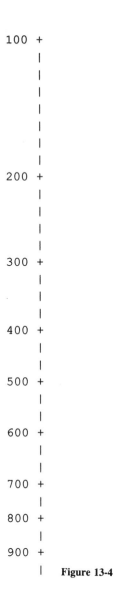

```
100 +
     |
     |
     |
     |
     |
     |
     |
200 +
     |
     |
     |
     |
300 +
     |
     |
     |
400 +
     |
     |
500 +
     |
     |
600 +
     |
     |
700 +
     |
800 +
     |
900 +
     |
```

Figure 13-4

shows that plot. The spacing of the numbers 100, 200, . . . is approximately logarithmic.

The program of Fig. 13-5 will plot the gain in decibels (dB) versus the log of the frequency in the simplified form known as a "Bode plot" for a device that is an unspecified kind of high-pass filter. You supply the number of "breakpoints" and the frequencies at which they occur, and the program will make the plot over the range 100 to 1000 Hz., that is, one *decade* of frequency (see Fig. 13-6). Plotting more than one decade is not just a simple extension of this program!

```
#include <stdio.h>
#include <math.h>
#include <process.h>
#define WIDTH 60
#define MARGIN 6
main()
{
    int numBP, i, j, pt, p[3], ff;
    int step[] = { 0, 7, 4, 3, 2, 2, 2, 1, 1, 1 };
    float f[3], dB[3], dBt;
    char dataline[WIDTH + 1], mark[] = "123";

    printf("BODE Plot of a High-pass Filter\n\n");
    printf("How many breakpoints (1, 2, or 3)? ");
    scanf("%d", &numBP);

    for (i = 0; i < numBP; ++i)
    {
        printf("Enter break frequency %d: ", i+1);
        scanf("%f", &f[i]);
        if ( (f[i] < 10) || (f[i] > 100) )
        {
            printf("OUT OF RANGE\n\n");
            exit(1);
        }
    }

    printf("\n\n");

    /* print the legend for the ordinate */

    for (i = 0; i < 19; ++i)
        printf(" ");
    for (i = 0; i <= 40; i += 5)
        printf("%-6d", i - 40);
    printf("db\n");

    /* print the vertical axis */

    for (i = 0; i < MARGIN; ++i)
        printf(" ");
    for (i = 0; i <= WIDTH + 1; ++i)
        printf("-");

    /*
        for each frequency in the range:
        print a piece of the abscissa,
        calculate a value, and plot it
    */
```

Figure 13-5

(Continued)

```
for (ff = 10, j = 0; ff <= 100; ff += 10, ++j)
{
    dBt = 0.0;

    for (i = 0; i < numBP; ++i)
    {
        dB[i] = -20 * log10(f[i]/ff);

        if (dB[i] > 0) dB[i] = 0;

        dBt += dB[i];
    }

    if (dBt > 0)  dBt = 0;

    for (i = 0; i < step[j]; ++i)
        printf("\n        |");

    printf("\n%5d +", ff);

/* fill in a line of data with blanks and marks */

    for (i = 0; i <= WIDTH; ++i)
        dataline[i] = ' ';

    for (i = 0; i < numBP; ++i)
    {
        p[i] = WIDTH - (int)fabs(dB[i]);
        if (p[i] > MARGIN)
            dataline[p[i]] = mark[i];
    }

    pt = WIDTH - (int)fabs(dBt);
    if (pt > MARGIN)
        dataline[pt] = 'x';

    for (i = 0; i <= WIDTH; ++i)
        printf("%c", dataline[i]);

} /* one frequency done! */
}
```

Figure 13-15 (*Continued*)

```
A>p13-3

BODE Plot of a High-pass Filter

How many breakpoints (1, 2, or 3)? 3
Enter break frequency 1: 20
Enter break frequency 2: 50
Enter break frequency 3: 80
```

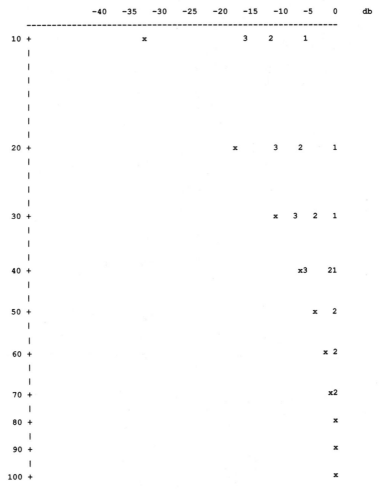

Figure 13-6

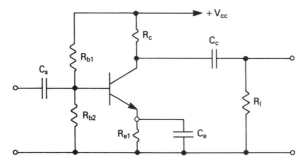

Figure 13-7

13-3 AN ANALYSIS OF AN AMPLIFIER CIRCUIT

Consider the BJT circuit of Fig. 13-7. The model I used is based on the following equations:

$$Z_i = 1/(G_{b1} + G_{b2} + 1/(h_{ie} + (1 + h_{fe}) R_{e1}))$$

$$Z_o = R_c$$

$$A_v = h_{fe}R_{lc}/(h_{ie} + (1 + h_{fe})R_{e1}))$$

$$h_{ib} = h_{ie}/(1 + h_{fe})$$

$$f_1 = 1/(2\pi C_e(h_{ib} + R_{e1}))$$

where

$$G_{b1} = 1/R_{b1}$$

$$G_{b2} = 1/R_{b2}$$

$$R_{1c} = R_1 \parallel R_c$$

The program is in Fig. 13-8, with a sample run in Fig. 13-9. As usual, once you have the set of equations in assignment statement form, the rest is easy!

```
#include <stdio.h>
#define PI 3.14159
main()
{
      float Rb1, Rb2, Rc, Re1, Rl;
      float Cs, Cc, Ce, hfe, hie;
      float Zi, Zo, Av, hib, f1, XCs, XCc;
      float h, Gb1, Gb2, Rcl, k;
```

Figure 13-8

```
printf("This program analyzes a BJT amplifier with\n");
printf("both voltage-divider and self-bias.\n\n");
printf("Please enter the values of the following:\n");
printf("\tRb1 (in kilohms): ");
scanf("%f", &Rb1);
printf("\tRb2 (in kilohms): ");
scanf("%f", &Rb2);
printf("\tRc (in kilohms): ");
scanf("%f", &Rc);
printf("\tRe1 (in kilohms): ");
scanf("%f", &Re1);
printf("\tRl (in kilohms): ");
scanf("%f", &Rl);
printf("\tCs (in microfarads): ");
scanf("%f", &Cs);
printf("\tCc (in microfarads): ");
scanf("%f", &Cc);
printf("\tCe (in microfarads): ");
scanf("%f", &Ce);
printf("\thie (in kilohms): ");
scanf("%f", &hie);
printf("\thfe: ");
scanf("%f", &hfe);

/* begin calculating */

h = hie + (1 + hfe) * Re1;
Zo = Rc;
Gb1 = 1/Rb1;
Gb2 = 1/Rb2;
Zi = 1 / (Gb1 + Gb2 + 1/h);
Rcl = Rc * Rl / (Rc + Rl);
Av = hfe * Rcl / h;
hib = hie / (1 + hfe);
k = 2 * PI;
f1 = 1000 / (k * Ce * (hib + Re1));
XCs = 1e6 / (k * f1 * Cs);
XCc = 1e6 / (k * f1 * Cc);

printf("\n\nThe voltage gain is %.1f", Av);
printf("\nThe lower cutoff frequency is %.1f Hz", f1);
printf("\nThe input Z is %.0f ohms", 1000 * Zi);
printf("\nThe output Z is %.0f ohms", 1000 * Zo);
printf("\nThe ratio XCs:Zi is %.2f", XCs/(1000 * Zi));
printf("\nThe ratio XCc:Rl is %.2f", XCc/(1000 * Rl));
}
```

Figure 13-8   (*Continued*)

```
A>p13-8
```

This program analyzes a BJT amplifier with
both voltage-divider and self-bias.
Please enter the values of the following:
        Rb1 (in kilohms): 68
        Rb2 (in kilohms): 56
        Rc (in kilohms): 3.9
        Re1 (in kilohms): .5
        Rl (in kilohms): 100
        Cs (in microfarads): 1
        Cc (in microfarads): .1
        Ce (in microfarads): 1
        hie (in kilohms): 2.1
        hfe: 75

The voltage gain is 7.0
The lower cutoff frequency is 301.6 Hz
The input Z is 17391 ohms
The output Z is 3900 ohms
The ratio XCs:Zi is 0.03
The ratio XCc:Rl is 0.05

Figure 13-9

13-4 MODULATION

Modulation is a vital concept in communications circuits and systems, and is thus a good candidate for programming. We will look at some programs for both AM (amplitude modulation) and FM (frequency modulation).

Amplitude Modulation

As you know, the principle of AM is that an audio information signal varies the amplitude of an RF (radio frequency) signal or carrier. This is needed because the audio signal occurs at too low a frequency for effective propagation of the information contained in it.

One of the most basic formulas for wave propagation is

$$f\lambda = c$$

That is, the frequency of a wave times its wavelength is a constant—the speed of light, 2.9979×10^8 meters/sec. The formula is of the same form as many that we discussed in the earliest chapters—Ohm's law, for one—so you will have no problem writing programs to solve either of its forms.

Somewhat newer are the formulas for percent modulation, m. Call the width of the modulated carrier *min* at its narrowest part, and *max* at the widest part. Then

$$m = 100(\text{max} - \text{min})/(\text{max} + \text{min})$$

Another way of calculating m is from the peak values of the amplitudes of the two waveforms:

$$m = 100(Ec_{max}/Em_{max})$$

where Ec_{max} is the peak amplitude of the carrier and Em_{max} is the peak amplitude of the audio signal. Further, if the frequency of the carrier is f_c, the spectrum of the modulator's output will include two additional frequencies, $f_c + f_a$ and $f_c - f_a$, where f_a is the frequency of the modulating waveform. These two frequencies are called **sidetones**. When the modulation is 0%, there are no sidetones, and all of the power generated by the modulator will go into the carrier. When the modulation is 100%, each sidetone will have an amplitude equal to one-half the amplitude of the carrier. Thus each sidetone will carry 25% of the power carried by the carrier, and the modulator will be generating half again as much power output.

All of these relationships can be combined into a single program, as shown in Fig. 13-10. Figure 13-11 shows the output that results from several runs.

Frequency Modulation

FM modulators also output sidetones, but the relationship between the sidetone frequency and the carrier frequency is more complicated because the modulation actually makes small changes in the carrier frequency. The *modulation index*, M, is given by $M = \Delta F/f_a$, where ΔF is the deviation of the carrier frequency from its unmodulated value, and F_a is the frequency of the modulating waveform. ΔF depends on the amplitude of the modulating signal.

A single modulating waveform will produce a band of sidetones (i.e., a **sideband**) at each of the frequencies $F + f_a$, $F \pm 2f_a$, $F \pm 3f_a$, $F \pm 4f_a$, and so on, where F is the unmodulated carrier frequency. The amplitude at each sideband frequency can be calculated by using a mathematical technique called Bessel functions. Usually, tables of Bessel functions are given in handbooks, so you can look up values and solve the problem manually. However, Bessel functions can be described mathematically as infinite series, so we can write a program to do the *entire* calculation. Specifically,

$$J_n(m) = x^n/(2^n n!)(1 - x^2/(2^2 \cdot 1!(n + 1))$$

$$+ x^4/(2^4 \cdot 2!(n + 1)(n + 2)) - x^6/(2^6 \cdot 3!(n + 1)(n + 2)(n + 3))$$

$$+ \cdots)$$

The number of terms needed depends on how quickly the series converges. You will see in the program of Fig. 13-14 that I had to use seven terms to get good agreement with handbook values! The relative amplitude of the waveform at the frequency of the unmodulated carrier is given by $J_0(m)$, that of the first harmonic by $J_1(m)$, that of the second harmonic by $J_2(m)$, and so on.

```
#include <stdio.h>
#include <stdlib.h>
main()
{
    float max, min, Ecm, Emm, m, Pc;
    int ans;
    printf("This program performs some calculations\n");
    printf("for amplitude modulated circuits.\n\n");
    printf("Do you know\n");
    printf("\t(1) the max and min of the modulated wave,\n");
    printf("or\t(2) the peaks of carrier and modulation?  ");
    printf("\n\nEnter 1 or 2:  ");
    scanf("%d", &ans);

    if ((ans != 1) && (ans != 2))
        exit(1);

    if (ans == 1)
    {
        printf("\nEnter the max value: ");
        scanf("%f", &max);
        printf("and the min value: ");
        scanf("%f", &min);
        m = (max - min)/(max + min);
    }
    else
    {
        printf("\nEnter the peak value of the carrier: ");
        scanf("%f", &Ecm);
        printf("and the peak value of the modulation: ");
        scanf("%f", &Emm);
        m = Emm/Ecm;
    }

    printf("Enter the power of the carrier: ");
    scanf("%f", &Pc);

    printf("\nThe modulation index is %f", m);
    printf("\nThe sideband power is %f watts.\n\n",
        Pc * m * m / 4);
}
```

Figure 13-10

Recursive functions.   The expression for the Bessel function requires that we calculate the **factorial** of a number.   We can do that easily in C because we remember certain facts about factorials:

$$0! = 1$$

$$1! = 1$$

$$2! = 2 \times 1$$

$$3! = 3 \times 2 \times 1 = 3 \times 2!$$

$$4! = 4 \times 3 \times 2 \times 1 = 4 \times 3!$$

```
A>p13-9

This program performs some calculations
for amplitude modulated circuits.

Do you know
     (1) the max and min of the modulated wave,
or   (2) the peaks of carrier and modulation?

Enter 1 or 2: 1

Enter the max value: 100
and the min value: 20
Enter the power of the carrier: 10

The modulation index is 0.666667
The sideband power is 1.111111 watts.

A>p13-9

This program performs some calculations
for amplitude modulated circuits.

Do you know
     (1) the max and min of the modulated wave,
or   (2) the peaks of carrier and modulation?

Enter 1 or 2: 1

Enter the max value: 100
and the min value: 10
Enter the power of the carrier: 10

The modulation index is 0.818182
The sideband power is 1.673554 watts.

A>p13-9

This program performs some calculations
for amplitude modulated circuits.

Do you know
     (1) the max and min of the modulated wave,
or   (2) the peaks of carrier and modulation?

Enter 1 or 2: 2

Enter the peak value of the carrier: 25
and the peak value of the modulation: 20
Enter the power of the carrier: 10

The modulation index is 0.800000
The sideband power is 1.600000 watts.
```

Figure 13-11

Sec. 13-4   Modulation

```
#include <stdio.h>
main()
{
    /* a stub for testing recursion */

    long fac(long);

    printf("0! = %ld\n", fac(0));
    printf("1! = %ld\n", fac(1));
    printf("3! = %ld\n", fac(3));
    printf("7! = %ld\n", fac(7));
}

long fac(long n)
{
    if (n <= 1)
        return (1);
    else
        return (n * fac(n -1));
}
```

Figure 13-12

The second form in the last two examples shows that you can calculate the factorial of an integer if you know it and the factorial of the next smaller integer. This approach is called **recursion** and C is one of the languages that permits it. That is, in C, a function can call itself to do a calculation. Figure 13-12 shows a program that calculates and prints the factorials calculated in the function *fac()*; Fig. 13-13 shows some results. Note that *fac()* returns a **long**. That's because *8!* is greater than the largest *int* value. Also note that I made the parameter a **long**, too. I did that because it is used in the calculation and I wanted to be sure that I multiplied **long**s by **long**s.

More on Bessel Functions

Figure 13-14 shows the function for calculating the value of the Bessel function, and Fig. 13-15 shows some results. You can either trust me or look up the values in a handbook.

```
A:>fac
0! = 1.000000
1! = 1.000000
3! = 6.000000
7! = 5040.000000
```
Figure 13-13

```
#include <stdio.h>
#include <math.h>
main()
{
     float Bessel(int, float);

     printf("\nJ0(.25) = %.3f\n", Bessel(0, .25));
     printf("\nJ0(2.0) = %.3f\n", Bessel(0, 2.0));
     printf("\nJ0(5.0) = %.3f\n", Bessel(0, 5.0));
     printf("\nJ1(2.0) = %.3f\n", Bessel(1, 2.0));
     printf("\nJ1(5.0) = %.3f\n", Bessel(1, 5.0));
     printf("\nJ2(2.0) = %.3f\n", Bessel(2, 2.0));
     printf("\nJ2(5.0) = %.3f\n", Bessel(2, 5.0));
}

float Bessel(int n, float x)
{
     float a, b, c, d ,e, f, g, h, y;
     long fac(long);

     y = x/2;

     a = pow(y, n)/fac(n);
     b = pow(y,2)/(n+1);
     c = pow(y,4)/(2*(n+1)*(n+2));
     d = pow(y,6)/(fac(3)*(n+1)*(n+2)*(n+3));
     e = pow(y,8)/(fac(4)*(n+1)*(n+2)*(n+3)*(n+4));
     f = pow(y,10)/(fac(5)*(n+1)*(n+2)*(n+3)*(n+4)*(n+5));
     g =
pow(y,12)/(fac(6)*(n+1)*(n+2)*(n+3)*(n+4)*(n+5)*(n+6));
     h =
pow(y,14)/(fac(7)*(n+1)*(n+2)*(n+3)*(n+4)*(n+5)*(n+6)*(n+7)-
);
     return (a * ( 1 - b + c - d + e - f + g - h));
}
```

Figure 13-14

```
A:>bessel

J0(.25) = 0.984
J0(2.0) = 0.224
J0(5.0) = -0.179
J1(2.0) = 0.577
J1(5.0) = -0.328
J2(2.0) = 0.353
J2(5.0) = 0.046
```
Figure 13-15

```
#include <stdio.h>
#include <math.h>

main()
{
    float Fa, DF, F, m, f, A;
    float Bessel(int, float);
    int n;

    printf("This program performs some calculations\n");
    printf("on frequency modulated circuits.\n\n");
    printf("Enter values for the following:\n");
    printf("\tcarrier frequency: ");
    scanf("%f", &F);
    printf("\tmodulation frequency: ");
    scanf("%f", &Fa);
    printf("\tthe deviation: ");
    scanf("%f", &DF);

    m = DF / Fa;
    printf("\nThe modulation index is %f", m);

    printf("\n\nThe frequency spectrum and amplitudes are:\n");

    A = Bessel(0, m);
    printf("\n%10.0f\t [carrier] %10f", F, A);

    for (f = F + Fa, n = 1; A > 0.01; f += Fa, ++n)
    {
        A = Bessel(n, m);
        printf("\n%10.0f and %10.0f  %10f",
            f, 2 * F - f, A);
    }
}
```

Figure 13-16

Now that we have a function to calculate the Bessel function, we can jump right into the main function, as shown in Fig. 13-16, with some results of running the entire program shown in Fig. 13-17.   The section of code

```
A = Bessel(0, m);
printf("\n%10.0f\t [carrier] %10f", F, A);

for (f = F + Fa, n = 1; A > 0.01; f += Fa, ++n)
{
    A = Bessel(n, m);
    printf("\n%10.0f and %10.0f  %10f",
        f, 2 * F - f, A);
}
```

```
A:>p13-11

This program performs some calculations
on frequency modulated circuits.

Enter values for the following:
        carrier frequency: 10e6
        modulation frequency: 10e3
        the deviation: 20e3


The modulation index is 2.000000

The frequency spectrum and amplitudes are:

     10000000        [carrier]    0.223891
     10010000 and     9990000     0.576725
     10020000 and     9980000     0.352834
     10030000 and     9970000     0.128943
     10040000 and     9960000     0.033996
     10050000 and     9950000     0.007040


A:>p13-11

This program performs some calculations
on frequency modulated circuits.

Enter values for the following:
        carrier frequency: 10e6
        modulation frequency: 20e3
        the deviation: 10e3


The modulation index is 0.500000

The frequency spectrum and amplitudes are:

     10000000        [carrier]    0.938470
     10020000 and     9980000     0.242268
     10040000 and     9960000     0.030604
     10060000 and     9940000     0.002564
```

Figure 13-17

requires some study. First, I calculated the Bessel function for the unmodulated
carrier. Then I started a loop to cover the side frequencies. Since the side
frequencies are symmetrical around the unmodulated carrier frequency, I started
the loop at **F + Fa**, the first side frequency above the carrier. However, in the
printf(), I printed both that value and the first one below the carrier, **2*F − f**.
Note that the loop tests the value of the last Bessel function we calculated. This
is a good example of something you can do in no other language: Initialize two
variables and adjust them after each loop execution, but test a third variable to
determine whether the loop will be executed again, and do it all in a single statement. Look again at Fig. 13-17 and see the results.

A:>p13-18

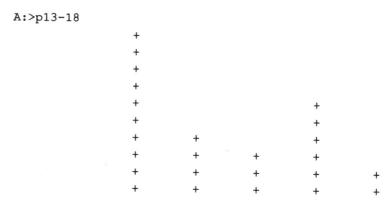

Figure 13-18

Plotting a Bar Graph

As usual, we would like a plot of these amplitudes rather than a table. Let's make it a bar graph, such as the one in Fig. 13-18. This kind of plotting is a bit more difficult because we want to plot it "right-side up." Let's examine the **bar_graph**() function in Fig. 13-19.

```
#define MAXROW 10
#define MAXCOL 6
#include <stdio.h>
main()
{
     /* a stub for testing */

     float J[5] = { 11.2, 4.6, 3., 7., 2.};
     void bar_graph(float [], int);

     bar_graph(J, 5);
}

void bar_graph(float J[], int n)
/* n is the number of values in the array */
{
     int top, row, col, i;
     char dataline[MAXROW][MAXCOL];
     float Jmax, max(float []), scale;

     /* blank out the grid */
     for (row = 0; row < MAXROW; ++row)
     {
          for (col = 0; col < MAXCOL; ++col)
               dataline[row][col] = ' ';
     }

     /* find maximum J for "scaling" */
```

Figure 13-19

```
        Jmax = max(J);
        scale = MAXROW / Jmax;

        /* now put a mark in the grid at the position
           that corresponds to the largest value */
        for (i = 0; i < n; ++i)
        {
                top = scale * (J[i] + 0.5); /* rounding */
                col = i + 1;
                for (row = 0; row < top; ++row)
                        dataline[row][col] = '+';
        }

        for (row = scale * (Jmax + 0.5) - 1; row >= 0; --row)
        {
                for (col = 0; col < MAXCOL; ++col)
                        printf("\t%c", dataline[row][col]);
                printf("\n");
        }
}


float max(float ar[])
{
        float max = -1e6;
        int i;

        for (i = 0; i < 6; ++i)
             if (ar[i] > max)
                     max = ar[i];

        return (max);
}
```

Figure 13-19 (*Continued*)

Let's examine the code in detail.

```
        void bar_graph(float J[], int n)
        /* n is the number of values in the array */
```

bar_graph() accepts two parameters: the name of an array and an integer telling
the number of elements in the array.

```
        /* blank out the grid */
        for (row = 0; row < MAXROW; ++row)
        {
                for (col = 0; col < MAXCOL; ++col)
                        dataline[row][col] = ' ';
        }
```

We'll define a grid consisting of *MAXROW* rows and *MAXCOL* columns, just as
if we had a piece of graph paper ruled off into *MAXROW* rows and *MAXCOL*

columns. Into each "square" we will put a blank character, so that we start with a piece of clean graph paper.

```
/* find maximum J for "scaling" */
Jmax = max(J);
scale = MAXROW / Jmax;
```

There is no reason to believe that the maximum value in the array will be the same value (or smaller) than the maximum number of rows on our graph paper, so we will scale the array values to make them fit. **scale** is the factor for each value in the array.

```
for (i = 0; i < n; ++i)
{
        top = scale * (J[i] + 0.5); /* rounding */
        col = i + 1;
        for (row = 0; row < top; ++row)
                dataline[row][col] = '+';
}
```

Each of the values in the array will be plotted in a different column, so we set up a loop that visits each column, one at a time. (What happens if **n** is greater than *MAXCOL*? Is there a way to make sure that this does not happen?) **top** is the scaled value of the array for the column under scrutiny, so the inside loop then fills one column of the grid with '+' marks from the bottom row to the row that corresponds to **top**.

```
for (row = scale * (Jmax + 0.5) - 1; row >= 0; --row)
{
        for (col = 0; col < MAXCOL; ++col)
                printf("\t%c", dataline[row][col]);
        printf("\n");
}
```

These lines plot the values in the grid, starting at the highest row. This is what gives us the "right-side-up" plot.

The next step would be to combine the last FM program with the plotting program so that the program could display the spectrum of frequencies and their amplitudes not only in a table, but also as a bar graph.

13-5 REVIEW

In this chapter you learned how to:

- Plot a variable against a log scale
- Calculate small-signal frequency response of a transistor amplifier
- Do calculations for AM and FM systems

PROBLEMS AND QUESTIONS

1. Write a program to solve the following problem. An AM transmitter at X KHz is Y miles from a receiver. What is the wavelength of the carrier? What is the period of the carrier, in microseconds? How far will a wave travel in one period? How long does a wave take to get from transmitter to receiver?

2. Write a program to solve the following problem. The average amplitude of an unmodulated carrier is 10 units. When modulated by a certain tone, the peaks have an amplitude of X units and the valleys, Y units. What is the percent modulation?

3. Write a program to solve the following problem. An AM transmitter has an unmodulated output power of X watts. What is the average power output when the modulation is Y percent?

4. Combine the last FM program with the bar graph plotting program.

5. Write programs to solve problems assigned from your communications electronics textbook.

14

Digital Systems

14-1 INTRODUCTION AND OBJECTIVES

In this chapter you will write and examine programs that deal with digital systems and number systems.

Upon successful completion of this chapter, you will be able to write programs to:

- Convert between base 2 and base 10
- Convert among base 2, base 16, and base 8
- Convert between base 10 and base 16
- Calculate digital codes
- Calculate truth tables for logic circuits

14-2 NUMBER SYSTEMS

Earlier in this book, we glossed over octal (i.e., base 8) and hexadecimal (i.e., base 16) numbers. And I told you that all values stored in memory locations in computers were stored as binary (i.e., base 2 numbers). I gave you some practice in converting binary numbers to their decimal (i.e. base 10) equivalents, but we didn't do anything with octal or "hex" numbers. It is now time to look at the relationships among all of the number systems that we use in conjunction with computers and digital systems.

Digital Systems and Binary Numbers

You know that the simplest digital system—a switch—is a "two-state" device. That is, it is either in the *ON* state or in the *OFF* state. In simpler terms, it is either *ON* or *OFF*. If we represent one of the states with a short vertical line and the other state with a circle, we will be on our way toward developing a symbolic representation for logic circuits. Look at the on/off switch on the PC in your lab. Is it marked 1/0 rather than ON/OFF? The "1" is the short vertical line I just mentioned, while the "0" is the circle. Even though they are symbolic representations of ON and OFF, we treat "1" and "0" as if they were the digits "one" and "zero"—after all, they do look like those digits, don't they?

"1" and "0" are the entire set of values of the binary number system. Therefore, any digital system made up of a string of ON–OFF devices can be represented by a string of "1"s and "0"s. Four of these "bits" (a contraction of "*binary* digi*ts*") is often called a "nibble" (some spell it "nYbble"), while a group of eight is frequently called a "byte" (NO one spells it "bIte"). The nibble *0100*, for example, is a binary or base 2 number, just as *184* is a decimal or base 10 number.

Binary-to-decimal conversions. It is easy to convert from binary to decimal because binary, like decimal, is a positional number system. That is, the least significant digit or bit (LSD or LSB)—the one farthest to the right of any integer—has a "weight" of $base^0$; the base for binary is, of course, 2, so the weight is 2^0, or 1. The next one, moving toward the most significant digit or bit (MSD or MSB), has a weight of 2^1, or 2; the next, 2^2 (4); and so on. If we want to input a string of 1s and 0s at the keyboard and evaluate it, we repeat these steps, starting with **i = 0:**

```
sum = sum + bit_value[i] * 2i;
++i;
```

You see that I envision the bits as being the values of the elements of an array. That's a necessity because *scanf()* has no conversion character that will accept a binary number entered at the keyboard. We will ask the user of our program to enter a binary number, but our program will grab the string of bits and place them, one at a time, into an array of *characters*. Then we will use some arithmetic to convert each character—'1' or '0'—to the corresponding digit—1 or 0. Here's a scheme for this idea:

1. Get the string of bits. We'll set up an array that can hold as many as 32 characters, just in case the user wants to enter a value that's as large an integer as we can handle on a PC. (Did you remember that a **long int** is stored in four bytes?)

2. Determine the number of characters entered. Call it **n.** Since the LSB has a weight of 2^0, the MSB will have a weight of 2^{n-1}.

3. The value of an element will be either '1' or '0' as a character, or 49 or 48 as a decimal integer. ("49" is the ASCII code for '1'; "48", the ASCII code for '0'.) You see that '1' is numerically (i.e., its ASCII code is) **1** higher than '0', so an easy way to convert a character to its numerical equivalent is to subtract '0' from it. Thus *bit*[*j*] − '*0*' will have the value **1** if *bit*[*j*] is '1', and **0**, if *bit*[*j*] is '0'. However, as the user entered the 1's and 0's, they went into the array **backwards**, that is, the MSB was entered first, but went into *bit*[0]. For example, suppose the user entered the number 1011. The MSB has a weight of 2^3 but it is stored in *bit*[0]. Similarly, the LSB has a weight

of 2^0 but is stored in *bit*[3]. Se we'll have to run our loop "backward" with respect to the bit positions.

4. Run a loop, starting at the MSB (i.e., $j = 0$) and heading toward $j = n - 1$. Calculate

$$\text{sum } += \text{ (bit[j]} - '0') * 2^{n-1-j}$$

The explanation of the exponent **n − 1 − j** is best demonstrated in the following table, for the number **1011** ($n = 4$):

bit value	subscript (j)	position (n - 1 - j)	
1	0	3	MSB
0	1	2	
1	2	1	
1	3	0	LSB

5. After converting the LSB, output the result.

Figure 14-1 shows the program, and Fig. 14-2 shows some results. Did you notice my attempt to trick the program by inputting leading 0s? It didn't work, did it?

Decimal-to-binary conversions. Logically, now, we need a program that will accept a decimal number and convert it to binary. Probably the most obvious way is to subtract 2^n from the number, reduce the value of **n**, and repeat until **n = 0**. Of course, we need to know what the first value of **n** is, and that won't

```c
#include <stdio.h>
#include <string.h>
#include <math.h>
main()
{
    char bit[33];
    int j, n;
    long unsigned sum = 0;

    printf("\nThis program will convert a binary number ");
    printf("of up to 32 bits\nto its decimal equivalent.\n");
    printf("\n    Enter a binary number:   ");
    scanf("%s", bit);

    n = strlen(bit);

    for (j = 0; j < n; ++j)
    {
        sum += (long unsigned) ((bit[j] - '0') *
            pow(2.0, (double)(n-1-j)));
    }

    printf("\n\t%s is %lu in base 10\n\n", bit, sum);
}
```

Figure 14-1

```
A:>p14-1

This program will convert a binary number of up to 32 bits
to its decimal equivalent.

   Enter a binary number:  111111111111

   111111111111 is 4095 in base 10


A:>p14-1

This program will convert a binary number of up to 32 bits
to its decimal equivalent.

   Enter a binary number:  100010

   100010 is 34 in base 10


A:>p14-1

This program will convert a binary number of up to 32 bits
to its decimal equivalent.

   Enter a binary number:  00000111

   00000111 is 7 in base 10
```

Figure 14-2

be too difficult to determine if we make it dependent on the kind of computer we
have. For instance, the largest integer number on a PC is an **unsigned long int**,
and its maximum value is 4,294,967,295, or $2^{32} - 1$. This is pretty straightforward,
so it will be a homework problem for you. A slicker way of getting the answer
is a method called "double dabble." It requires repeated division by 2 and obtains
bit values beginning with the least significant. Here's a sample—converting 43 to
binary—in Fig. 14-3. We divide 43 by 2, giving 21 with a remainder of 1. Then
we divide 21 by 2, resulting in 10 with a remainder of 1. Ten divided by 2 yields

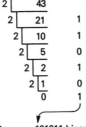

Answer: 101011 binary   **Figure 14-3**

5 with remainder 0. Five divided by 2 gives 2, remainder 1. Two divided by 2 is 1, remainder 0. One divided by 2 is zero—the stopping point—remainder 1. Arranging the remainders in *reverse order* gives the binary result *101011*.

Here's the scheme:

Until the result is 0,

1. Divide "number" by 2, saving the result and the remainder.
2. Give "number" the value of result.

How can we display the string of remainder bits? Oh, I gave it away! *"String* of remainder bits," eh? Suppose that we set up an array of characters. Then we keep track of which of **n** divisions we are presently doing and store the remainder in the proper element of the array. Here's a refinement of the scheme:

1. Set up **binary[33]** = "**00000000000000000000000000000000**".
2. Get the number.
3. Set n = 0.
4. Divide number by 2; save the result and remainder. If remainder is 1, store '1' in **binary[32 − n]**.
5. If *result* == *0*, stop. Otherwise, increment n and divide result by 2. Save the result and remainder. Repeat step 5.

Ready for the program? It appears in Fig. 14-4.

```c
#include <stdio.h>
main()
{

    /* program accepts any decimal number up to
       4,294,967,295 and converts it to binary. */

    unsigned long num, res;
    int rem, n = 0, i;
    char binary[33] = "00000000000000000000000000000000";

    printf("Enter a positive integer: ");
    scanf("%lu", &num);
    /* keep the original value */
    res = num;

    while (res != 0)
    {
        rem = res % 2;      /* must do this division first */
        res = res / 2;
        if (rem == 1)
        {
            binary[32-n] = '1';
        }
    ++n;
    }
```

Figure 14-4

```
Enter a positive integer: 25
25 decimal is 0000000000000000000000000000011001

A>p14-4

Enter a positive integer: 12345
12345 decimal is 0000000000000000000011000000111001        Figure 14-5
```

The program is just as described above. The only interesting aspect is the comment on the "remainder" division statement. Why must "remainder" division come first?

Figure 14-5 shows some sample results. That's OK, but those leading 0s seem unnecessary, don't you think? There's a neat way to eliminate them, but it makes the output section a little more complicated. Start after the string has been formed. Then, look at *binary[0]* and if it's a '0', go to the next element. That is, test *binary[i]*:

```
if (binary[i] == 0)
{
        ++i;
}
```

Well, that's not quite right: We need a loop. We could use a *while* loop, but this is a chance to show off a bit with a *for* loop or two. Take a look at this:

```
for (i = 0; binary[i] == '0'; ++i)
{
        ;
}
```

What's that? A loop with nothing in it? Right! The lonely semicolon is a special C statement which is completely empty, which gives rise to its name—the "null" statement. We use it here because all of the work has been done in the *for* loop header! It's usual to drop the braces around a null statement and to add a comment so that the programmer's eye is not fooled into thinking that it is something different from what it is. So we write

```
for (i = 0; binary[i] == '0'; ++i)
        /* NULL */ ;
```

From the present value of i to the end will contain a string of bit characters beginning with a '1'. Since we are printing only a part (i.e., the rest) of the string, we'll have to do it a character at a time. The new program is shown in Fig. 14-6.

The last *for* statement has an empty "initialize" statement, so this loop will begin with whatever value i has when this *for* starts executing. That will be the value of i that corresponds to the first element of *binary[]* that has a '1' in it. Perfect! Sample output appears in Fig. 14-7.

Decimal to octal and hexadecimal, and vice versa. Converting from decimal to octal takes the same approach as the double dabble method for con-

```
#include <stdio.h>
main()
{
    /* program accepts any decimal number up to
       4,294,967,295 and converts it to binary. */

    unsigned long num, res;
    int rem, n = 0, i;
    char binary[33] = "00000000000000000000000000000000";

    printf("Enter a positive integer: ");
    scanf("%lu", &num);

    res = num;
    while (res != 0)
    {
        rem = res % 2;
        res = res / 2;
        if (rem == 1)
        {
            binary[32-n] = '1';
        }
    ++n;
    }

    printf("%lu decimal is ", num);
    for (i = 0; binary[i] == '0'; ++i)
        /* NULL */ ;

    for ( ; i < 33; ++i)
    {
        printf("%c", binary[i]);
    }
    printf(" binary.\n");
}
```

Figure 14-6

verting decimal to binary, except that we divide by 8 instead of 2. Figure 14-8 shows the calculation for converting 12345 decimal to 30071 octal. Note that we need to store characters other than just '0' and '1' in the array of characters that contains the result. The program is shown in Fig. 14-9.

A>p14-6

Enter a positive integer: 25
25 decimal is 11001

A>p14-6

Enter a positive integer: 12345
12345 decimal is 11000000111001

Figure 14-7

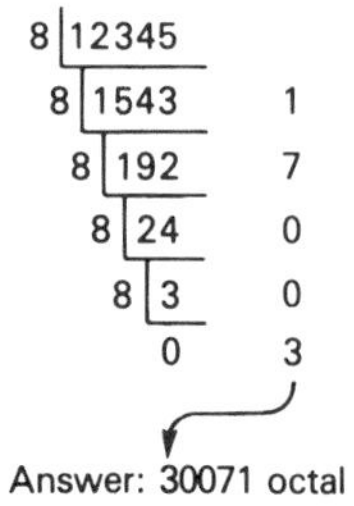

Answer: 30071 octal

Figure 14-8

```c
#include <stdio.h>
main()
{
        /* program accepts any decimal number up to
           4,294,967,295 and converts it to octal. */

        unsigned long num, res;
        int rem, n = 0, i;
        char octal[12] = "00000000000";

        printf("Enter a positive integer: ");
        scanf("%lu", &num);

        res = num;
        while (res != 0)
        {
                rem = res % 8;
                res = res / 8;
                switch (rem)
                {
                        case 0:
                                octal[11-n] = '0';
                                break;
                        case 1:
                                octal[11-n] = '1';
                                break;

                        case 2:
                                octal[11-n] = '2';
                                break;
                        case 3:
                                octal[11-n] = '3';
                                break;
                        case 4:
                                octal[11-n] = '4';
                                break;
                        case 5:
                                octal[11-n] = '5';
                                break;
                        case 6:
                                octal[11-n] = '6';
                                break;
                        case 7:
                                octal[11-n] = '7';
                                break;
                }
        ++n;
        }

        printf("%lu decimal is ", num);
        for (i = 0; octal[i] == '0'; ++i)
                ;
        for ( ; i < 12; ++i)
        {
                printf("%c", octal[i]);
        }
        printf(" octal.\n");

}
```

Figure 14-9

```
16 | 22222
    16 | 1388    14 ─────► E
       16 | 86    12 ─────► C
          16 | 5    6
               0    5
```

Answer: 56CE hexadecimal   **Figure 14-10**

```c
#include <stdio.h>
#include <stdlib.h>
#include <string.h>
#include <math.h>
#define BASE 8
main()
{
      char octal[15];
      int j, n;
      long unsigned sum = 0, weight = 1;

      printf("\nThis program will convert an octal number ");
      printf("of up to 11 octal digits\nto its decimal equivalent.\n");
      printf("\n   Enter an octal number:  ");
      scanf("%s", octal);

      /* The largest octal number that fits into
         32 bits is 37 777 777 777, so when the user
         enters an 11 digit octal number, we must test
         the first digit to be sure that it isn't
         bigger than 3.
      */

      n = strlen(octal);

      if ( ((octal[0] > '3') && (n == 11))
         || (n > 11) )
      {
           printf("\n\nNumber is too large.\n");
           exit(1);
      }

      /* everything's OK - start converting */

      for (j = n - 1 ; j >= 0; --j)
      {
           sum += (long unsigned) (octal[j] - '0') * weight;
           weight *= BASE;
      }

      printf("\n\t%s octal is %lu decimal.\n\n", octal, sum);
}
```

Figure 14-11

Converting from decimal to hexadecimal also uses the same approach, but the fact that the last six "digits" in hex are "A", "B", "C", "D", "E", and "F" makes things a bit more cumbersome. Figure 14-10 shows the conversion of 22222 decimal into 56CE hex. Note that when I did the division, two of the remainders— 14 and 12—were larger than 10. I recognized these as the hex digits **E** and **C**, respectively. When you write this program, you will need to add a test for each remainder to determine what to store in the array of characters that holds the result.

Converting from octal to decimal uses the same technique that we used for the binary to decimal conversion. The program is given in Fig. 14-11. Figure 14-12 shows some sample runs.

```
A>p14-11

This program will convert an octal number of up to 11 octal digits
to its decimal equivalent.

    Enter an octal number: 277
        277 octal is 191 decimal.

A>p14-11

This program will convert an octal number of up to 11 octal digits
to its decimal equivalent.

    Enter an octal number: 377
        377 octal is 255 decimal.

A>p14-11

This program will convert an octal number of up to 11 octal digits
to its decimal equivalent.

    Enter an octal number: 37777777777
        37777777777 octal is 4294967295 decimal.

A>p14-11

This program will convert an octal number of up to 11 octal digits
to its decimal equivalent.

    Enter an octal number: 40000000000

Number is too large.

A>p14-11

This program will convert an octal number of up to 11 octal digits
to its decimal equivalent.

    Enter an octal number: 123456789876

Number is too large.
```

Figure 14-12

Figure 14-11 can be used as a model for converting from hexadecimal to decimal. That will be an assignment.

Binary to octal and hexadecimal, and vice versa. Converting from binary to octal or hexadecimal is very simple to do with pencil and paper because of the mathematical relationship between binary (base 2) and octal (base $8 = 2^3$) and between binary (base 2) and hexadecimal (base $16 = 2^4$). You were taught to do the conversion by grouping. For example, the binary number **10011** is rewritten as **010 011**, and then each group is converted to an octal digit (2 and 3, in this case). Hex is handled similarly, with groups of four bits instead of three bits.

Writing a conversion program can be made simple by using the **DRTW** ("don't reinvent the wheel") approach. That is, we have a program that converts binary to decimal, one that converts decimal to octal and one that converts decimal to hexadecimal. Also, we have one that converts hex to decimal, one that converts octal to decimal, and one that converts decimal to binary. So *no new programs are needed*. Just put them together as desired. For example, Fig. 14-13 shows the binary-to-decimal-to-octal program. Some results are shown in Fig. 14-14.

```
#include <stdio.h>
#include <string.h>
#include <math.h>
main()
{
     char bit[33];
     char octal[12] = "00000000000";

     int i, j, n, rem;
     long unsigned sum = 0, weight = 1, res;

     printf("\nThis program will convert a binary number ");
     printf("of up to 32 bits\nto its octal equivalent.\n");
     printf("\n   Enter a binary number:  ");
     scanf("%s", bit);

     n = strlen(bit);

     for (j = n - 1 ; j >= 0; --j)
     {
          sum += (long unsigned) (bit[j] - '0') * weight;
          weight *= 2;
     }

     /* now convert from decimal to octal */

     n = 0;
     res = sum;
     while (res != 0)
     {
          rem = res % 8;
          res = res / 8;
```

Figure 14-13

```
        switch (rem)
        {
                case 0:
                        octal[11-n] = '0';
                        break;
                case 1:
                        octal[11-n] = '1';
                        break;
                case 2:
                        octal[11-n] = '2';
                        break;
                case 3:
                        octal[11-n] = '3';
                        break;
                case 4:
                        octal[11-n] = '4';
                        break;
                case 5:
                        octal[11-n] = '5';
                        break;
                case 6:
                        octal[11-n] = '6';
                        break;
                case 7:
                        octal[11-n] = '7';
                        break;
        }
        ++n;
}

printf("\n\t%s binary is ", bit);
for (i = 0; octal[i] == '0'; ++i)
        /* NULL */ ;

for ( ; i < 12; ++i)
{
        printf("%c", octal[i]);
}
printf(" octal.\n");
}
```

Figure 14-13 (*Continued*)

```
        A>p14-13

        This program will convert a binary number of up to 32 bits
        to its octal equivalent.

           Enter a binary number: 111000101010
              111000101010 binary is 7052 octal.

        A>p14-13

        This program will convert a binary number of up to 32 bits
        to its octal equivalent.
```

Figure 14-14   (*Continued*)

```
Enter a binary number: 1011
    1011 binary is 13 octal.


A>p14-13

This program will convert a binary number of up to 32 bits
to its octal equivalent.

Enter a binary number: 11111111111111111111111111111111
    11111111111111111111111111111111 binary is 37777777777 octal.
```

Figure 14-14 *(Continued)*

14-3 DIGITAL SYSTEMS AND CODES

In addition to the strictly numeric representations, digital systems can represent numbers using a binary code that is not strictly numerical. For example, the Gray code is frequently used in representing angular position data because consecutive

```c
/* This program accepts a binary number of a given
   length, and determines its Gray code equivalent.
*/
#include <stdio.h>
#include <stdlib.h>
main()
{
    char bin[17], gray[17] = "0000000000000000";
    int i, n;

    printf("How many bits in your number (no more than 16)? ");
    scanf("%d", &n);

    if (n > 16)
    {
        printf("\n\nToo many!\n");
        exit(1);
    }

    printf("Enter your binary number: ");
    scanf("%s", bin);

    /* the binary to Gray conversion */

    gray[0] = bin[0];  /* the MSBs */
    for (i = 0; i < n-1; ++i)
    {
        if (bin[i] == bin[i + 1])
            gray[i+1] = '0';
        else
            gray[i+1] = '1';
    }
    gray[i+1] = '\0';

    printf("\nBinary %s is \nGray    %s\n", bin, gray);
}
```

Figure 14-15

```
A>p14-15

How many bits in your number (no more than 16)? 4
Enter your binary number: 1000

Binary 1000 is
Gray    1100

A>p14-15

How many bits in your number (no more than 16)? 8
Enter your binary number: 00001111

Binary 00001111 is
Gray    00001000

A>p14-15

How many bits in your number (no more than 16)? 8
Enter your binary number: 11110000

Binary 11110000 is
Gray    10001000

A>p14-15

How many bits in your number (no more than 16)? 12
Enter your binary number: 101010101010

Binary 101010101010 is
Gray    111111111111
```

Figure 14-16

Gray code patterns differ in only one bit position. This eases the problem of constructing "angle-to-bit pattern" encoders. The scheme for converting a binary value into its equivalent Gray code looks like this:

1. The MSB of the binary is the MSB of the Gray.
2. Compare bit n with bit $n-1$. If they are the same, put a **0** as Gray bit $n-1$. Otherwise, put a **1** there.
3. Decrement n and repeat step 2, until $n == 1$

Figure 14-15 shows the program, while Fig. 14-16 shows some results.

14-4 DIGITAL SYSTEMS AND TRUTH TABLES

The behavior of a digital system made up only of gates can be described in terms of a truth table derived from a Boolean statement. The truth table can later be used as the input to a device that creates a read-only memory (ROM) chip or a programmed array logic (PAL) chip or the like.

We will set up a program that prints a truth table for the Boolean statement in the program. The program is a little like the ones we did for general dc circuits,

```
/* This program prints the truth table
   for one Boolean statement
*/

#include <stdio.h>
main()
{
     int X, A, B, C;

     printf("\nTruth Table for X = ABC\n\n");
     printf(" ABC    X\n ---------\n");

     for (A = 0; A <= 1; ++A)
     {
       for (B = 0; B <= 1; ++B)
       {
         for (C = 0; C <= 1; ++C)
         {
             X = A && B && C;
             printf("  %d%d%d    %d\n", A, B, C, X);
         }
       }
     }
}
```

Figure 14-17

in that each Boolean statement will require a different program. C has AND (**&&**), OR (**||**), and NOT (**!**), so it will be easy to write the program (see Fig. 14-17). The result of running this program is shown in Fig. 14-18.

In Fig. 14-19, I've used a different Boolean statement. The result of running this program is shown in Fig. 14-20. Notice how the NOT overbars were inserted in the program.

It certainly would be nice to be able to generalize this enough so that the user could input data representative of any Boolean statement that is a function

```
A>p14-17


Truth Table for X = ABC


        ABC    X

        ---------

        000    0

        001    0

        010    0

        011    0

        100    0

        101    0

        110    0

        111    1
```

Figure 14-18

```
/* This program prints the truth table
   for one Boolean statement
*/

#include <stdio.h>
main()
{
    int X, A, B, C;

    printf("\n                          _");
    printf("\nTruth Table for X = ABC + AB + BC\n\n");
    printf(" ABC   X\n ---------\n");

    for (A = 0; A <= 1; ++A)
    {
       for (B = 0; B <= 1; ++B)
       {
          for (C = 0; C <= 1; ++C)
          {
             X = (A && B && C) || (A && !B) || (B && !C);
             printf(" %d%d%d   %d\n", A, B, C, X);
          }
       }
    }
}
```

Figure 14-19

of, say, three variables. One possible data representation is a term-by-term numerical one. For example, a term like **ABC** would have the weight $4 + 2 + 1$
$= 7$, while the term **A !B C** would weight $4 + 0 + 1 = 5$. A term such as **B !C**
in a three-variable statement is the simplification of **A B !C + !A B !C** and would
carry *two* weights: $4 + 2 + 0 = 6$ and $0 + 2 + 0 = 2$. Thus a Boolean statement
like

$$x = \overline{A}BC + \overline{ABC} + A\overline{BC} \qquad \text{(weights: 3, 1, 4)}$$

```
A>p14-19

                       _   _
Truth Table for X = ABC + AB + BC

    ABC   X
    ---------
    000   0
    001   0
    010   1
    011   0
    100   1
    101   1
    110   1
    111   1
```

Figure 14-20

would have the following truth table:

A B C	Output	Weight
0 0 0	0	0
0 0 1	1	1
0 1 0	0	2
0 1 1	1	3
1 0 0	1	4
1 0 1	0	5
1 1 0	0	6
1 1 1	0	7

We would want the user to input that there are three terms, having the weights 3, 1, and 4 (the order does not matter). Then, as we go down the table, the output

```
/* This program accepts the numerical codes for
   the terms of a Boolean statement and prints
   the corresponding truth table.
*/

#include <stdio.h>
#include <stdlib.h>
main()
{
        int i, n, m, terms[8] = {0,0,0,0,0,0,0,0};
        char bin[4];

        printf("\nThis program will print a truth table for a\n");
        printf("Boolean statement of three variables.  Prepare the\n");
        printf("statement by writing the complete minterm for each\n");
        printf("term, and calculate the weight of each.  For\n");
        printf("example, the term ABC has a weight of 7 - 4 for\n");
        printf("the A, 2 for the B, and 1 for the C.\n\n");
        printf("How many terms? ");
        scanf("%d", &n);

        for (i = 0; i < n; ++i)
        {
            printf("\nEnter the weight of term %d: ", i+1);
            scanf("%d", &m);
            terms[m] = 1;
        }

        printf("\n\n ABC  X\n-------\n");

        for (i = 0; i < 8; ++i)
        {
            itoa(i, bin, 2);
            printf(" %3s  %d\n",bin, terms[i]);
        }
}
```

Figure 14-21

column will have a 1 wherever the weight is 1, or 3 or 4, and a 0 everywhere else. The program that does the trick is shown in Fig. 14-21.

The program has a neat C feature; it uses the function **itoa(i, bin, 2)**, declared in **stdlib.h**. The function converts an *int* value to a string (the "a" stands for *ASCII*). The argument of **itoa( )**, in order, are (1) the *int* value to be converted, (2) the name of the *char* array that will hold the string, and (3) the number base for the first parameter. Our call converts the binary number **i** and places the string in **bin[ ]**. A couple of sample runs are shown in Fig. 14-22.

You can see that **itoa( )** does not do exactly what we want, so let's think about a modification that will give us our conventional truth table. The problems occur when **i** is less than 4, because the numbers 0, 1, 2, and 3 can be represented by 1, 1, 2, and 2 bits, respectively. How can we stick leading '0's (note that I said **'0'** and not just **0**) on those strings? We'll take a "brute force" approach to this and check the length of **bin[ ]** after the call to **itoa( )**. If the length of **bin[ ]** is 1, we'll print two '0's and then the value of **bin[ ]**. If the length of **bin[ ]** is 2, we'll print just one '0' and then the value of **bin[ ]**. Figure 14-23 shows the modified program, and Fig. 14-24, one sample run.

```
A>p14-21

This program will print a truth table for a
Boolean statement of three variables.  Prepare the
statement by writing the complete minterm for each
term, and calculate the weight of each.  For
example, the term ABC has a weight of 7 - 4 for
the A, 2 for the B, and 1 for the C.

How many terms? 2
Enter the weight of term 1: 3
Enter the weight of term 2: 5

  ABC  X
  -------
    0  0
    1  0
   10  0
   11  1
  100  0
  101  1
  110  0
  111  0

A>p14-21

This program will print a truth table for a
Boolean statement of three variables.  Prepare the
statement by writing the complete minterm for each
term, and calculate the weight of each.  For
```

Figure 14-22

(*Continued*)

example, the term ABC has a weight of 7 - 4 for
the A, 2 for the B, and 1 for the C.

```
How many terms? 5
Enter the weight of term 1: 3
Enter the weight of term 2: 7
Enter the weight of term 3: 4
Enter the weight of term 4: 0
Enter the weight of term 5: 5

  ABC  X
  -------
    0  1
    1  0
   10  0
   11  1
  100  1
  101  1
  110  0
  111  1
```

Figure 14-22 (*Continued*)

```c
/* This program accepts the numerical codes for
   the terms of a Boolean statement and prints
   the corresponding truth table.
*/

#include <stdio.h>
#include <stdlib.h>
main()
{
    int i, n, m, terms[8] = {0,0,0,0,0,0,0,0};
    char bin[4];

    printf("\nThis program will print a truth table for a\n");
    printf("Boolean statement of three variables.  Prepare the\n");
    printf("statement by writing the complete minterm for each\n");
    printf("term, and calculate the weight of each.  For\n");
    printf("example, the term ABC has a weight of 7 - 4 for\n");
    printf("the A, 2 for the B, and 1 for the C.\n\n");

    printf("How many terms? ");
    scanf("%d", &n);

    for (i = 0; i < n; ++i)
    {
        printf("\nEnter the weight of term %d: ", i+1);
        scanf("%d", &m);
        terms[m] = 1;
    }
```

Figure 14-23

```
        printf("\n\n ABC  X\n-------\n");

        for (i = 0; i < 8; ++i)
        {
             itoa(i, bin, 2);

     /* print the appropriate 3-digit value of ABC */
             if (strlen(bin) == 1)
             {
                  printf(" 00%s", bin);
             }
             else if (strlen(bin) == 2)
             {
                  printf(" 0%s", bin);
             }
             else
             {
                  printf(" %3s", bin);
             }

     /* print the 0 or 1 in the output column */
             printf("  %d\n", terms[i]);
        }
    }
```

Figure 14-23 *(Continued)*

A>p14-23

This program will print a truth table for a
Boolean statement of three variables. Prepare the
statement by writing the complete minterm for each
term, and calculate the weight of each. For
example, the term ABC has a weight of 7 - 4 for
the A, 2 for the B, and 1 for the C.

How many terms? 3
Enter the weight of term 1: 3
Enter the weight of term 2: 4
Enter the weight of term 3: 7

```
 ABC  X
 -------
 000  0
 001  0
 010  0
 011  1
 100  1
 101  0
 110  0
 111  1
```

Figure 14-24

Sec. 14-4   Digital Systems and Truth Tables

14-5 REVIEW

In this chapter you learned how to write programs to:

- convert between base 2 and base 10
- convert among base 2, base 8, base 10, and base 16
- calculate digital codes
- calculate truth tables for logic circuits

PROBLEMS AND QUESTIONS

1. Write a program to convert any decimal number from 0 to 4,292,967,295 to its binary equivalent, using the "repeated division by 2^n" method mentioned early in this chapter.

2. Simplify the program of Fig. 14-9 by using the fact that the ASCII code for a digit is equal to the digit's numerical value plus the ASCII code for the character '0', that is,

$$n = n + '0';$$

3. Write a program to convert any decimal number from 0 to 4,292,967,295 to its hexadecimal equivalent, using the method analogous to double dabble.

4. Write a program to convert any hexadecimal number from 0 to FFFFFFFF to its decimal equivalent.

5. Write a program to convert from binary to hexadecimal by combining the binary-to-decimal program with the decimal-to-hex program.

6. Write a program that will convert from any one of decimal, octal, or hexadecimal to any one of decimal, octal, or hexadecimal. Use functions and let the user choose the desired conversion.

7. Rewrite the program of Problem 6 to include binary as one of the number systems.

8. The scheme for converting from Gray to binary is this:

  a. start with the MSB of both Gray and binary patterns (i.e., $gray_n$ and bin_n).

  b. if $gray_i == 0$, $bin_i = 0$; decrement i, and repeat step b

  c. if $gray_i == 1$, $bin_i = 1$

  d. decrement i and repeat the following until $i == 0$

  e. if $gray_i == 0$, $bin_i = bin_{i+1}$
   otherwise if $bin_{i+1} == 1$, $bin_i = 0$
   otherwise if $bin_{i+1} == 0$, $bin_i = 1$

  Write the program. Limit the user's input to four-bit Gray patterns.

9. Rewrite the program of Fig. 14-23 so that it handles Boolean statements of four variables.

Appendix A

The ASCII Table

Character	Decimal	Octal	Hexadecimal
NUL	0	0	0
SOH	1	1	1
STX	2	2	2
ETX	3	3	3
EOT	4	4	4
ENQ	5	5	5
ACK	6	6	6
BEL	7	7	7
BS	8	10	8
HT	9	11	9
LF	10	12	A
VT	11	13	B
FF	12	14	C
CR	13	15	D
SO	14	16	E
SI	15	17	F
DLE	16	20	10
DC1	17	21	11
DC2	18	22	12
DC3	19	23	13
DC3	20	24	14
NAK	21	25	15
SYN	22	26	16
ETB	23	27	17
CAN	24	30	18
EM	25	31	19
SUB	26	32	1A
ESC	27	33	1B
FS	28	34	1C
GS	29	35	1D

(*Continued*)

Character	Decimal	Octal	Hexadecimal
RS	30	36	1E
US	31	37	1F
	32	40	20
!	33	41	21
"	34	42	22
#	35	43	23
$	36	44	24
%	37	45	25
&	38	46	26
'	39	47	27
(	40	50	28
)	41	51	29
*	42	52	2A
+	43	53	2B
,	44	54	2C
−	45	55	2D
.	46	56	2E
/	47	57	2F
0	48	60	30
1	49	61	31
2	50	62	32
3	51	63	33
4	52	64	34
5	53	65	35
6	54	66	36
7	55	67	37
8	56	70	38
9	57	71	39
:	58	72	3A
;	59	73	3B
<	60	74	3C
=	61	75	3D
>	62	76	3E
?	63	77	3F
@	64	100	40
A	65	101	41
B	66	102	42
C	67	103	43
D	68	104	44
E	69	105	45
F	70	106	46
G	71	107	47
H	72	110	48
I	73	111	49
J	74	112	4A
K	75	113	4B
L	76	114	4C
M	77	115	4D
N	78	116	4E

Character	Decimal	Octal	Hexadecimal
O	79	117	4F
P	80	120	50
Q	81	121	51
R	82	122	52
S	83	123	53
T	84	124	54
U	85	125	55
V	86	126	56
W	87	127	57
X	88	130	58
Y	89	131	59
Z	90	132	5A
[	91	133	5B
\	92	134	5C
]	93	135	5D
^	94	136	5E
_	95	137	5F
`	96	140	60
a	97	141	61
b	98	142	62
c	99	143	63
d	100	144	64
e	101	145	65
f	102	146	66
g	103	147	67
h	104	150	68
i	105	151	69
j	106	152	6A
k	107	153	6B
l	108	154	6C
m	109	155	6D
n	110	156	6E
o	111	157	6F
p	112	160	70
q	113	161	71
r	114	162	72
s	115	163	73
t	116	164	74
u	117	165	75
v	118	166	76
w	119	167	77
x	120	170	78
y	121	171	79
z	122	172	7A
{	123	173	7B
|	124	174	7C
}	125	175	7D
~	126	176	7E
DEL	127	177	7F

Appendix B

Some Computer-Related Items

1. Getting things to the printer rather than the screen. Your instructor will undoubtedly want you to hand in some of your programs and their results. However, all of the sample programs in this book use only the screen for display, and that will not be satisfactory unless your instructor asks you to hand in your disk.

In any case, you will want to know how to get your program printed—we call that a *listing*—and how to get results printed. Neither is difficult to do.

Suppose you have a program called PROG1.C, and you want to list it and print results on paper. First, make sure that your disk has both *PROG1.C* and *PROG1.EXE* on it (use DIR A: to see the names of files on the disk in drive A). Then go to a computer with a printer. (I mention that because in my college's lab, we have one printer per three computers.) Turn the machine on and when you see the DOS prompt (*C>*), place your disk in drive A. Key *A:<cr>*. Get the printer ready and key the following:

TYPE PROG1.C^P<cr>

The *^P* connects the printer in parallel with the screen. From now on, anything that goes to the screen also goes to the printer. To return to *screen only* mode, key *^P* again. *^P* is called a "toggle": The first time you key it, it turns something on; the next time you key it, it turns it off; and so on. When the listing is done, key *^P*.

When you are ready to get results to paper, ready the printer, and key

PROG1^P<cr>

DOS will load PROG1.EXE and execute it, and will also print on both screen and printer. Don't forget to turn the printer toggle off before you leave.

2. TCC command line compiler. You can compile your C programs in the traditional way if you like, by using TCC, the Turbo C command line compiler.

It is a bit more difficult to use than the Integrated Environment (for one thing, you must use an editor program), but it does allow you to do some things that you cannot do easily in the IE.

Assuming that someone has properly set up the configuration file and sub-directories for TCC, all you do to compile PROG1.C is

1. Get a DOS prompt.
2. Key *tcc PROG1*<cr>.

The power of TCC lies in its options. For example, a command line like this:

```
tcc -a -f -C -O -Z -emyexe old1.c old2.c next.c
```

will compile the three *.c* files into MYEXE.EXE with "word alignment," "floating-point emulation," "nested comments," "jump optimization," and "register optimization" options selected! Of course, you have to be a pretty fair C programmer AND know a lot about computers to make good use of these options.

Appendix C

The Turbo C Environment and Editor

When you key *tc<cr>* at a DOS prompt, DOS loads the Turbo C Environment into your computer's memory, executes the TC.EXE program, and displays a "window" on your screen. The word *File* will be highlighted; that means that it is ready to receive commands that have to do with files. If you key <cr> (the *Enter* key), you will see a list of the commands displayed in a "pop-up" window, like this:

```
Load        F3
Pick    Alt-F3
New
Save        F2
Write to
Directory
Change dir
OS shell
Quit    Alt-X
```

You invoke a command by typing its initial letter. Four of the commands—LOAD, PICK, SAVE, and QUIT—can be invoked in two ways. The other way for LOAD, for example, is to key function key *F3*. These four commands are special in that you do not have to see this menu to invoke them; you can invoke any one from anywhere in the Turbo C Environment by keying the alternative invocation. For example, to QUIT, you may either go to this menu (by keying *Alt-F*) and they key **Q**, or you can just key *Alt-X*.

LOAD. When you invoke Load, Turbo C pops up another window like this:

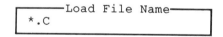

```
┌─────Load File Name─────┐
│ *.C                    │
└────────────────────────┘
```

At this point, you may either type the name of the program you want to edit, or key <cr>. If you key <cr>, Turbo C shows you a list of all the files whose names end in *.C*. Use the *arrow keys* to highlight one of them, and then key <cr>. This loads that file into the Turbo C editor.

PICK. We won't use this feature.

SAVE. Invoking this gives you the opportunity to save the contents of the editor in a file with either the name it already has or a new name. When it has stored the editor contents, it returns to the editing of the same file. If you have changed the name of the saved file with the SAVE command, the editor will now be editing the new file.

NEW. If you select this, Turbo C will load a new file called NONAME.C into the editor. This isn't very useful, because you certainly do not want a file called NONAME.C!

WRITE TO. Same as SAVE.

DIRECTORY. This shows you all the files in your current directory.

CHANGE DIR. You won't need this if you follow the scheme I have suggested.

OS SHELL. If your floppy disk is too full to hold the file you are trying to save, key *Alt-F* and select **OS Shell**. Turbo C gives you an **A>** prompt. Delete all **.OBJ** files (*DEL *.OBJ*<cr>). Then type *EXIT*<cr>. This returns you to the Integrated Development Environment so that you can now save that file.

QUIT. Exits from the Turbo C Environment.

You can bypass the File menu if you know the name of the file you want to edit. Just type *tc filename* at the DOS prompt instead of just *tc*. This will load the Turbo C Environment, and then load that file into the editor, leaving you ready to edit.

"Editing" in computing means "creating a new file or changing an existing file." The Turbo C editor is a competent one for doing both.

To create a new file, just start typing. Everything you type will appear on the screen. When you get near the right-hand margin, key <cr>.

If you make a mistake, use the *backspace* key (usually, the GRAY left arrow key that is not located near any other arrow keys). For example, the keyboard I am using right now has three left arrow keys and two of them are gray. But one of them is all by itself, just above the large *Enter* key, while the others have other arrow keys near them. The lone one is the *backspace* key.

If you like, you can ignore your mistakes as you type, and wait until you are finished before correcting them. Just use the arrow keys to move the cursor until it is under the incorrect letter. Key *Del*. The incorrect letter is removed and everything to the right of the cursor moves one column to the left to fill in the space. Key the correct letter. It is inserted at the cursor and everything to the right moves over one column to make room for it.

You can delete an entire line easily. Place the cursor anywhere on that line and key *ctrl-Y*.

You can delete a word easily. Place the cursor on the first letter of the word and key *ctrl-T*.

To return to the main menu, key *F10*. Your cursor will disappear but the word *Edit* will be highlighted.

At times when you are typing, it will seem that new keystrokes are not causing the others on the same line to be moved to the right. Look at the first line under *Edit*. Is the word *Insert* displayed? No? Key the *Insert* or *Ins* key. Is *Insert* there now? Good. Check that space every once in a while to make sure that you have not turned *Insert* off by accident.

When you are finished editing, key *Alt-X*.

The Turbo C editor has a nifty command just for C programs. It "auto-magically" checks for matching pairs of delimiters: { }, < >, ( ), [ ], /* */, " ", and ' '! Place the cursor on the left-hand one and key *^Q^[*. If there is a "mate," the cursor will jump to it. If there's no mate, the cursor will stay on the original delimiter. *^Q^[* works a little differently for < >, " ", ' ', and /* */. If you put the cursor on the left-hand one of these and key *^Q^[*, the cursor will jump to the next right-hand one of these, regardless of whether you have violated any C rules or not. It does the job well for { }, ( ), and [ ], and they are the most frequently abused delimiters.

There are many more editor commands, but you really do not need any of them. They are listed and explained in the Turbo C Reference Manuals.

When you are ready for Turbo C to compile your program, just tap the *F9* function key.

When you are ready to have your program execute (i.e., ready for a "run"), key *^F9*. Turbo C will compile, link, and execute your program, and then pop back into the editor window. To see the results of running, you must key *Alt-F5*.

Appendix D

A General Simultaneous Equation Solver

```c
#include <stdio.h>
#include <math.h>
main()
{
      float sum, ratio[10], k[10][10], s[10], x[10], rmax, c, r, xmult;
      int n, i, j, l[10], m, lk;

      printf("\nhow many?  ");
      scanf("%d", &n);

      for (i=1; i <= n; ++i)
      {

            for (j=1; j <= n; ++j)
            {
                  printf("A(%d,%d): ", i, j);
                  scanf("%f", &k[i][j]);
            }

            printf("RHS %d = ", i);
            scanf("%f", &ratio[i]);
            printf("\n");

      }

      for (i=1; i <= n; ++i)
      {
            l[i] = i;
            s[i] = 0.0;

            for (j=1; j <= n; ++j)
            {
                  c = fabs(k[i][j]);
                  if (c > s[i])
                        s[i] = c;
            }

      }

      for (m=1; m<=n-1; ++m)
      {
            rmax = 0;
```

```
        for (i=m; i <= n; ++i)
        {
                r = fabs((k[l[i]][m])/s[l[i]]);
                if (r <= rmax) continue;
                j=i;
                rmax = r;
        }

        lk = l[j];
        l[j] = l[m];
        l[m] = lk;

        for (i=m+1; i <= n; ++i)
        {
                xmult = (k[l[i]][m]) / k[lk][m];
                k[l[i]][m] = xmult;

                for (j=m+1; j <= n; ++j)
                        k[l[i]][j] -= xmult * k[lk][j];
        }

}

for (j=1; j<=n-1; ++j)

        for (i=j+1; i<=n; ++i)
                ratio[l[i]] -= k[l[i]][j] * ratio[l[j]];

x[n] = ratio[l[n]]/k[l[n]][n];

for (i=1; i<=n-1; ++i)
{
        sum = ratio[l[n-i]];
        for (j=n-i+1; j<=n; ++j)
                sum -= k[l[n-i]][j] * x[j];
        x[n-i] = sum / k[l[n-i]][n-i];
}

printf("\n\nX values are ......\n");

for (i=1; i<=n; ++i)
        printf("\nX(%d) = %f", i, x[i]);
}
```

Index

Nodal analysis, 269
Norton's theorem, 277
Null statement, 253, 402
Numbers:
  random, 123
Number systems:
  hexadecimal, 397
  octal, 397

O

Op-amp calculations, 371
Operating system, 9
Operators:
  AND and OR, 61
  arithmetic, 33, 37, 38
  assignment, 35
  relational, 47

P

Parameter:
  actual, 188, 195, 204
  array, 211
  declaring, 187
  formal, 190, 197, 198, 203
  formal and pointer, 206
  of function, 20
Parentheses:
  brackets and braces, 104
Passing an entire array, 200
Passing by reference, 204
Passing by value, 195
Period:
  of AC signal, 302
Plotting results, 285, 292, 302, 335
  bar graph, 393
  logarithmic scale, 377
Pointer:
  declaration, 206
  definition, 206
Pointer variables, 206
Pointing a pointer at a variable, 207
Post-increment, 51
Precision:
  of real values, 176
Pre-increment, 51
Preprocessor, 41

Printf( ), 35
Printing, 12
Program, 6
  bootstrap, 10
  control, 1
  examining a, 18
  first C, 4
  microwave oven, 2
  naming rules, 13
  translation, 13
Programming, 4
  the art of, 230
  and computers, 1
  control, 2
  cycle, 13
  errors, 23
  language, 3
  top-down, 232
Prototype, 20
  declaration, 183, 188, 201
  definition, 195
Pseudo-code, 231
Puts( ), 20, 21, 22, 90

R

Radians and degrees, 301
Random number:
  seed, 125
Random numbers, 123
Recursive functions, 387
Repetition, 45
Resonant circuits, 334
Return:
  data type, 187
Return( ), 188
Returned value:
  from scanf( ), 95
Returning:
  a value from a function, 188
Returning values, 193
RMS values, 306
Rounding off, 286

S

Sin( ), 302
Software engineering, 230

113   0
64 ⌐1
49
32 ⌐1
17
16 ⌐1
1
0
0
0
1 ⌐1

```
0 1 1 1 0 0 0 1
1 1 1 1 1 1 1 1
─────────────
0 1 1 0 0 0 1
```

```
4
4
2
```

```
{
{
{
```

```
0 1 1 1 0 0 0 1
1 1 1 1 1 1 1 1
─────────────
0 1
```

$$2 \times 2 \times 2 \times 2 \times 2 = 2^5 = 32$$
$$16 \times 2 = 32$$

$$2 \times 2 \times 2 \times 2 = 2^4 = 16$$
$$4 \times 2 \times 2$$
$$8 \times 2$$
$$16$$

```
 16
 16
────
 32
```

1 = yes   1 = true
0 = no   0 = false

1 = on   30 = ? in binary
0 = off

30
16 | 1   30 = 11110
14
8 | 1   16
6   8
4 | 1   4
2   2
2 | 1   0
0   30
1 | 0
              10
              10
              10
              3 0

              2
              4
              28
              16
              30

$$
\begin{array}{c}
1\ 0\ 0\ 1\ 1\ 1 \\
0\ 1\ 1\ 0\ 1\ 0 \\
\hline
0\ 0\ 0\ 0\ 1\ 0
\end{array}
$$

$$\begin{array}{r} 000 \\ 000 \\ \hline 000 \end{array}$$

$$\begin{array}{r} 101 \\ 010 \\ \hline 000 \end{array}$$

$$\begin{array}{r} 111 \\ 101 \\ \hline 101 \end{array}$$

$$\begin{array}{r} 1001 \\ 1111 \\ \hline 1001 \end{array} \qquad \begin{array}{r} 1111 \\ 0110 \\ \hline 0110 \end{array}$$

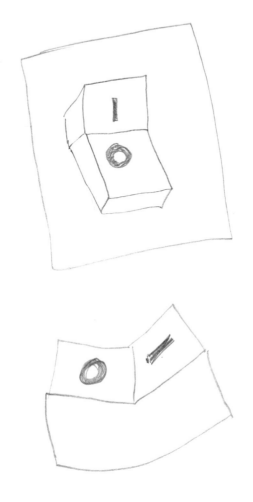

open